Criminal Justice
in Canada
a reader

Second Edition

Criminal Justice
in Canada

Second Edition

a reader

Julian V. Roberts, University of Ottawa

Michelle G. Grossman, M.A., M.S.W.

THOMSON

NELSON

Australia   Canada   Mexico   Singapore   Spain   United Kingdom   United States

THOMSON

NELSON

Criminal Justice in Canada: A Reader
Second Edition

by Julian V. Roberts and
Michelle G. Grossman

Editorial Director and Publisher:
Evelyn Veitch

Executive Editor:
Joanna Cotton

Marketing Manager:
Lenore Taylor

Senior Developmental Editor:
Edward Ikeda

Production Editors:
Tammy Scherer
Julie van Veen

Senior Production Coordinator:
Hedy Sellers

Copy Editor:
Karen Rolfe

Proofreader:
Margaret McClintock

Creative Director:
Angela Cluer

Interior Design:
Sonya V. Thursby, Opus House
Incorporated

Design Modifications:
Gabriel Sierra

Cover Design:
Ken Phipps

Compositor:
Carol Magee

Printer:
Transcontinental

National Library of Canada Cataloguing in Publication Data

Criminal justice in Canada : a reader / [edited by] Julian V. Roberts, Michelle G. Grossman. — 2nd ed.

Includes bibliographical references.
ISBN 0-17-622480-7

1. Criminal justice, Administration of—Canada. I. Roberts, Julian V. II. Grossman, Michelle G.

HV9960.C2C75 2003
364.971   C2003-901747-8

PREFACE

Julian V. Roberts, Ph.D., and Michelle Grossman, M.A., M.S.W.

A decade ago, teachers in the field of criminology and criminal justice who sought a text for their students had few Canadian works from which to choose. That has now changed; several excellent books are now available. Finding a collection of readings, however, remains a challenge. Although several good readers exist, they deal with crime rather than criminal justice or a specific topic, such as crime control policy. Instructors looking for a more general collection of primarily introductory readings have been forced to cobble together a collection of readings that are then made available to students through commercial or university print shops. All the while, instructors must keep a wary eye on Canada's restrictive and extremely complex copyright legislation. Identifying the holder of copyright is often a time-consuming task since academic authors rarely hold copyright over their own work.

The second edition of this text simplifies this task. This book is aimed at any course with a focus, primary or secondary, on the justice system. The volume was conceived to accompany criminal justice texts. We have generally used the most recent material available as of 2002 except for timeless pieces such as the reading by Palys and Divorski on sentencing disparity. We attempt to provide a diversity of views: some articles take a critical approach to criminal justice; others report findings from a more "mainstream" perspective. Almost all readings have been commissioned especially for this edition. This edition includes a section comprising the writings of people working in, or who have passed through, the criminal justice process. The reasoning behind these pieces is that there is no substitute for practical experience.

We have attempted to address two concerns: discrimination and variability of treatment. Whatever the merits of our criminal justice system (relative to other jurisdictions), certain elements of the population receive disproportionate attention from the police and, thereafter, inequitable treatment at the hands of other criminal justice professionals. This fundamental lack of equity is the single most important issue to bring to the attention of students of criminal justice. As for variability, it is important to note that the justice system accords criminal justice professionals a high degree of discretion, which inevitably results, rightly or wrongly, in variable treatment.

ACKNOWLEDGEMENTS

We thank, first and foremost, the authors whose work is represented here, and the copyright holders for their permission to reprint material. We would also like to acknowledge the important contributions of Joanna Cotton and Edward Ikeda from Nelson. We are also grateful to the following individuals for reviewing the first edition and making suggestions for improvement: Jacqueline Faubert, Simon Fraser University; Jon Frauley, Queen's University; Gregory P. Brown, Nipissing University; Anne-Marie Singh, University of Guelph; Winston Barnwell, Saint Mary's University; and Kim Varma, Brock University.

Julian V. Roberts and Michelle G. Grossman
Ottawa, December 15, 2002

A Note from the Publisher

Thank you for selecting *Criminal Justice in Canada*, eds. Julian V. Roberts and Michelle G. Grossman. The editors and publisher have devoted considerable time to the careful development of this book. We appreciate your recognition of this effort and accomplishment.

We want to hear what you think about *Criminal Justice in Canada*. Please visit our Web site at www.nelson.com. Your comments, suggestions, and criticisms will be valuable to us as we prepare new editions and other books.

CONTENTS

ABOUT THE AUTHORS

Julian V. Roberts holds a Ph.D. from the University of Toronto, and is currently a Professor in the Department of Criminology at the University of Ottawa. Since 1993 he has served as the editor of the Canadian Journal of Criminology and Criminal Justice. His most recent book is "Penal Populism and Public Opinion" (with M. Hough, L. Stalans and D. Indermaur) for Oxford University Press. He is currently working on a book on conditional sentencing to be published by Cambridge University Press in 2004.

Michelle G. Grossman has graduate degrees in Criminology and Social Work from the University of Toronto. In addition she has worked in a clinical capacity at Toronto Child Abuse Centre. Most recently she has worked in a policy/research capacity for the Government of Canada, at the Department of Justice and Solicitor General, with a particular focus on the issue of victims. She has published a number of articles in the area of sexual aggression.

Criminal Justice
in Canada

Second Edition

a reader

PART ONE
Introductory Readings

CHAPTER 1
Criminal Justice in Canada: An Introduction

Julian V. Roberts, University of Ottawa

This introductory chapter provides context for the rest of the volume. The chapter begins by noting two conflicting models of criminal justice in Canada and then reviews some findings from research on public opinion about crime and criminal justice. Many Canadians believe they know how the criminal justice system works (as well as how it should work), but as we shall see, there is sometimes a considerable gap between public knowledge and the actual functioning of the system. The chapter concludes by noting some of the current priorities for criminal justice in Canada.

Criminal justice in Canada—as elsewhere—involves a complex system of checks and balances, with responsibility for a criminal case divided among many different decision-makers. To further complicate matters, some of these decision-makers are guided by somewhat different mandates. Judges are guided by the principle of proportionality when they impose a sentence. This means that they attempt to ensure that the severity of the sentence imposed reflects the seriousness of the crime committed (and the offender's level of culpability). Parole boards, on the other hand, have a different mandate. They are more concerned with the possibility of risk to the community when they decide whether an inmate should be allowed out of prison to spend the remainder of his or her sentence in the community, under supervision.

The criminal justice system is complex because it must respond to a wide diversity of human behaviour. If crime were to comprise only a limited number of proscribed acts, the system could develop a far more focused (and predictable) response. But the variability in criminal conduct is immense, and the system needs to vary its response accordingly. The criminal justice system must be able to respond to cases of premeditated murder, minor acts of vandalism committed by bored teenagers, and all forms of criminality between these two extremes.

Finally, the system attempts to consider a number of interests, including those of the victim, the accused, and the community, which may conflict. For example, the victim of a crime may want the system to impose a more severe penalty, or, alternatively, the victim (particularly if it is a case of domestic assault) may not wish any penalty to be imposed. The system must somehow take these competing interests into account. Small wonder, then, that the system is poorly understood by members of the public and many politicians.

The criminal justice system is the subject of both intense media coverage and great public interest. Crime and criminal justice stories—especially the most publicized cases—fascinate the public: over 100 million people in North America watched television the year when the verdict in the O.J. Simpson trial was announced. (In fact, the Simpson trial received more coverage than any other news story that year.) Canada also has stories that attract a similar amount of attention. When Robert Latimer was convicted of the murder of his severely disabled daughter, the case became the source of heated discussion across the nation. Few Canadians were unaware of the verdict and subsequent sentence.

MODELS OF CRIMINAL JUSTICE

Two competing perspectives underlie our criminal justice system. These are known as the crime control model and the due process model. As its name implies, the crime control model stresses the importance of controlling crime and favours providing criminal justice professionals such as the police with considerable powers with which to respond to crime. On the other hand, the due process model prefers to place limits on the powers of the criminal justice system. For almost every important issue in criminal justice, one can find crime control as well as due process ways of responding.

For example, when it comes to police powers, crime control advocates argue that the police should have wide powers to gather evidence and to question and interrogate suspects and accused persons. Due process advocates, on the other hand, prefer to limit the powers of the police, to ensure that individual rights are not compromised, and to prevent innocent people from being stopped and detained by the police. The conduct of criminal trials also provides many examples of the conflict between due process and crime control models of criminal justice. During a criminal trial, an accused person is not obliged to take the stand and testify in his or her own defence. The onus is on the state, through the Crown, to establish the guilt of the accused beyond a reasonable doubt without any help from the testimony of the accused. The due process model defends this procedural rule by arguing that the accused should not have to cooperate with the state's case. In contrast, crime control proponents argue that the accused *should* have to testify because this is the only way to get to the truth, which will acquit the innocent and convict the guilty.

A criminal justice system founded exclusively on one perspective or the other would be problematic. Pursuing crime control to the exclusion of due process would inevitably result in an increase in the number of persons wrongfully convicted because due process procedural safeguards provide the innocent with a strong defence against a false accusation. However, a system that stresses due process considerations to the extreme would result in a higher number of wrongful acquittals; guilty people would evade punishment because the police would be hampered in their search for incriminating evidence. For this reason, the Canadian justice system has elements of both perspectives. But even a balanced approach can result in miscarriages of justice. As we shall see in Chapter 19, wrongful convictions can—and do—occur, resulting in the imprisonment of innocent people.

The ultimate arbiter of conflicts that arise between the two models of criminal justice is the Supreme Court of Canada, the decisions of which are binding upon Parliament and all courts in Canada. The Supreme Court frequently hears arguments regarding the constitutionality of specific pieces of criminal justice legislation and decides whether a particular law is consistent with the rights guaranteed by the *Canadian Charter of Rights and Freedoms*. A law that goes too far in the direction of controlling crime may violate one of the provisions of the *Charter of Rights and Freedoms*.

PUBLIC OPINION AND CRIMINAL JUSTICE IN CANADA

People in Canada (as elsewhere) tend to be quite critical of the criminal justice system. They view it as being overly lenient and biased more to the interests of the offender than of the victim. However, this perception is not always consistent with reality.

The public has a great deal of confidence in the police and far less confidence in other criminal justice professionals. For example, a survey conducted in 2002 found that over two-thirds of respondents rated the police as doing an "excellent" or "good" job, whereas only half expressed the same level of support for judges (Roberts, 2002). Table 1.1 summarizes findings from this survey of public ratings of four criminal justice professions.

The performance ratings show that Canadians have a more positive than negative view of their criminal justice professionals. Although Canadians can be critical of elements of the criminal justice system, they have quite positive opinions of the professions involved; the percentage of respondents rating the professions as poor or very poor is low. These ratings suggest that Canadians distinguish between the practice of the system (or what they perceive the practice to be) and the integrity of the professionals charged with administering the criminal justice system. Although respondents were not asked about parole authorities, parole boards typically generate the lowest levels of public

Table 1.1 *Public Evaluations of Criminal Justice Professions in Canada*

	Excellent or Good	Average	Poor or Very Poor
Police	67%	25%	7%
Defence Counsel	56%	36%	6%
Prosecutors	53%	40%	5%
Judges	50%	31%	17%

Source: Roberts (2002)

confidence. One earlier survey found that only 4 percent of respondents expressed a lot of confidence in parole authorities.

PUBLIC KNOWLEDGE OF CRIMINAL JUSTICE ISSUES

The following findings emerge from a review of public opinion polls in Canada containing questions on public knowledge of criminal justice issues. (For the sake of brevity, full bibliographic citations for works cited in this section of the chapter are omitted here but can be found in Roberts (1995) or Roberts and Stalans (1997)). Before dealing with public perceptions of the criminal justice system, however, it is worth noting one of the most important public misperceptions that affects attitudes toward the justice system.

Perceptions of Crime Trends

A general finding from public opinion surveys in several nations is that the public always think that crime rates are rising, whether crime is up, down, or stable. When representative samples of the public are asked whether the crime rate has increased, decreased, or stayed the same, the typical result is that most people respond that crime has increased (e.g., Environics, 1998). Public perception of crime trends is generally unrelated to actual trends.

The statistical reality reflected in both police statistics and victimization surveys tends not to reach the public. The resulting misperception has important consequences for public attitudes to the criminal justice system since most people tend to subscribe to the crime control perspective. According to this perspective, if crime rates are steadily increasing, the system has failed in its principal function. This misperception of crime trends, then, is probably responsible for much of the public criticism of the criminal justice system.

Sentencing

The question asked most often in opinion polls over the years concerns the courts and, specifically, the severity of sentences imposed. The percentage of Canadians who feel that sentences are too lenient has been high for more than 20 years. In 1970, approximately two-thirds of Canadians endorsed the view that sentences were not harsh enough. In 1992, the proportion expressing this view was 85 percent. A poll in 2000 found that 68 percent of Canadians felt that the justice system was "too soft" toward people convicted of crimes (Sanders and Roberts, 2000). However, this perception is often founded upon inaccurate knowledge of the actual level of penalties.

People tend to underestimate the severity of sentencing practices; approximately 90 percent of offenders convicted of robbery are sent to prison. However, fully three-quarters of respondents estimated the incarceration rate for this crime to be under 60 percent (Canadian Sentencing Commission, 1987). Similar results emerged for other offences. Thus, the perception of leniency in sentencing at the trial court level is based upon a misperception of the actual severity of sentences imposed.

Crime Control through Harsher Sentencing

Many people mistakenly believe that increasing the severity of penalties will have an appreciable impact on crime rates. The reality is that such a small percentage of offenders are actually sentenced that the ability of the sentencing process to reduce crime is very restricted. This point has been made repeatedly in the sentencing literature. Writing about the United Kingdom, Ashworth (2000) notes that judges deal with no more than about 3 percent of the offences actually committed. He concludes: "If criminal justice policy expects sentencing to perform a major preventive function, they are looking in the wrong direction" (Ashworth, 2000:25). Statistics Canada reports similar trends in this country: a sentence is imposed in fewer than 5 percent of crimes committed.

Sentences are imposed in such a small percentage of cases due to "case attrition" in the criminal justice process. Only some crimes are reported to the police and, of these, only some are deemed by the police to be "founded." Of the "founded" incidents, some do not result in the laying of a criminal charge. Of the charges actually brought to court, some are dropped or stayed, and the remainder do not all end in the conviction of an accused. If such a small percentage of crimes results in the imposition of a penalty, the length of sentence will have little impact on the overall volume of crime. Clearly, then, the sentencing system is severely limited in its ability to affect the crime rate.

Use of Incarceration as a Sanction

If one compares Canada with other jurisdictions, the perception of leniency seems inaccurate. Although international sentencing comparisons are always difficult because of the differences between criminal justice systems in terms of offence definitions and early release provisions, it is clear that incarceration rates in Canada are high relative to those in most other countries.

Commissions of inquiry as well as the federal government have long acknowledged that Canada relies too heavily on the use of imprisonment as a sanction. Members of the public are often unaware of this reality. In 1999, a poll asked Canadians whether the incarceration rate in this country was higher, lower, or the same as that in most other western countries. The answer, that the incarceration rate is higher here, was identified by only 15 percent of the sample. Most respondents believed that the incarceration rate was lower here (Roberts, Nuffield and Hann, 2000).

Corrections

Prison Conditions

There is a clear gap between public perception and the reality of prison life. Many Canadians feel that an inmate's life is an easy one and are not aware of the privations and difficulties suffered by incarcerated offenders. Most people are also unaware of the high rates of homicide, suicide, and assault in correctional institutions. One Gallup survey conducted in 1991 found that half the respondents felt that conditions in penal institutions were "too liberal," although fewer than 5 percent reported any firsthand experience in a correctional institution.

Many members of the public believe that if prison conditions were much harsher, prisoners would be less likely to reoffend and risk reincarceration. This is a myth too; research has shown that making prisons more austere and taking away various privileges may make prison life more unpleasant, but it does not prevent reoffending. Preventing reoffending involves ensuring that ex-offenders get jobs and have a stake in the community.

Early Release from Prison

The correctional issue that generates most public criticism concerns early release from prison. According to a 1988 survey, more than three-quarters of the respondents said that they had not much or no faith in the Canadian system of granting parole (Gallup, 1988). Most Canadians believe that too many inmates get released from prison too early. This view is based to a large degree upon misperceptions of the functioning of the parole system.

Parole Grant Rates

There are two principal public misperceptions with respect to this early release: that full parole grant rates have been increasing and that parole rates are more than 50 percent. One survey found that half the respondents overestimated the federal parole rate. Both these misperceptions feed the widespread opinion that the parole system is lenient. It is surprising that so many people have such a definite opinion on this issue without having any idea how many violent offenders are in fact released, or even what the release rate is for inmates serving sentences for violent crimes.

Success and Failure Rates of Offenders Released on Parole

The gap between public perception and reality is probably greater for this issue than for any other criminal justice topic. The cause of widespread public concern about prisoners released on parole is probably the intense media coverage of the small number of cases in which a parolee is charged with a serious offence. Single incidents such as these have an important impact on public knowledge of parole and, subsequently, public attitudes to release programs such as parole.

The public tend to believe that a significant percentage of parolees commit further offences. Most people overestimate the failure rate of offenders on parole, which tends to be quite low. Public misperceptions regarding parole recidivism may also fuel public opposition toward the early release of inmates serving terms of imprisonment for violent crimes.

Costs of Incarceration Versus Supervision in the Community

When the Gallup organization asked people to estimate the cost of keeping an offender in a federal penitentiary, fewer than 20 percent of respondents were able to accurately estimate the cost. Just as people underestimate the cost of incarceration, they also overestimate the cost of supervising an offender in the community. If the public knew how much money the system could save by punishing offenders in the community rather than in prison, they would probably be more supportive of community-based sentences and parole.

SUMMARY

Most people have a great deal of interest in criminal justice issues. However, this does not mean that they are necessarily well informed about the system. It would be naïve to expect the public to have accurate views of all aspects of crime and justice. While there are areas in which public awareness has increased, there remain important issues for which further public education is imperative. Crime is a serious problem in Canadian society, one that provokes a great deal of concern and debate over the nature of appropriate crime control policies. But when evaluating these policies in terms of public support, we should bear in mind what people actually know about crime and criminal justice. It is only when the public have a realistic understanding of crime and justice that an informed debate over crime control policies can take place.

CURRENT PRIORITIES FOR THE CANADIAN CRIMINAL JUSTICE SYSTEM

Aboriginal Justice

One priority concerns the treatment of Aboriginal offenders, who have long been overrepresented in correctional statistics in several provinces. For example, although Aboriginal Canadians represent only about 2 percent of the general population, in 2000–01 they accounted for 17 percent of admissions to federal penitentiaries (sentences of two years or longer) and 19 per-cent of provincial sentences (under two years). In some provinces (such as Saskatchewan), the problem of overrepresentation is far worse: Aboriginals accounted for approximately three-quarters of admissions to provincial prisons in 2000–01 (Hendrick and Farmer, 2002). Accordingly, there has been a concerted attempt to reduce the number of Aboriginal persons entering cus-tody (see Chapter 22).

A number of solutions have been proposed, including the creation of a separate Aboriginal justice system. In 1996, Parliament implemented a number of sentencing reforms, one of which was directed at the problem of high rates of Aboriginal admissions to prison. A provision in the *Criminal Code* urges judges to consider all possible alternatives to prison and diversion pro-grams, particularly when sentencing Aboriginal offenders. In addition, in some parts of the country sentencing circles are conducted with Aboriginal offenders. However, as of 2002, these solutions have not reduced the rate of Aboriginal admissions to custody. Chapter 22 explores the problem further.

Aboriginal peoples are not the only minority group disproportionately represented in criminal justice statistics. The 1995 report of the Commission on Racism in Ontario showed that black suspects were more likely to be denied bail than whites with similar profiles. More recently, in 2002, allega-tions were made that police officers in Toronto use racial profiling. The treat-ment of minorities by the criminal justice system is likely to remain a priority.

Youth Justice

In April 2003, the *Youth Criminal Justice Act* became law, replacing the *Young Offenders Act (YOA)*, which had been in force since 1984. Over the 1990s, no legislation had come under as much public criticism as the *YOA*. Central to the criticism had been the allegation that as a result of the *YOA* youth court judges imposed very lenient sentences, and this itself became a cause of youth crime. The *YCJA* attempts to address this criticism as well as a number of other issues relating to youth justice in Canada (see Chapter 9).

Conditional Sentencing

The conditional sentence of imprisonment was created in 1996 to reduce the number of admissions to custody (see Chapter 5). To many people, the con-ditional sentence is a paradox: an offender is sentenced to a term of custody but is allowed to spend it at home. The disposition was created to reduce the number of admissions to custody. Analyses have demonstrated that the con-ditional sentence has had an important impact on admissions to prison, which have declined significantly since 1996 (Roberts and Gabor, 2003). At the same time, the sentence has been imposed for some serious crimes, leading to calls for amendments to the provision.

MEDIATION AND OTHER ALTERNATIVES TO CRIMINAL JUSTICE PROCESSING

The traditional response to a crime has been the invocation of the criminal process. The system attempts to locate the alleged offender who may then become an accused and face a criminal proceeding. If found guilty to a specified legal standard (beyond a reasonable doubt), he or she will be sentenced. However, this is not necessarily the best way to resolve the problem; victims are not always satisfied by the criminal justice response, and offenders are sometimes stigmatized by the conviction in a way that increases, rather than decreases, the likelihood of further offending.

Third-party mediation is an alternative way of addressing the problem. This can take many forms, but it usually involves a face-to-face meeting between the victim and the suspect or accused in the presence of a third party. An agreement may arise out of this meeting that will result in some tangible benefit for the victim (perhaps restitution or reparation). Mediation can also be advantageous for the offender who, as a result of this meeting and the expression of remorse, may end up with a less severe penalty or even no penalty at all if the victim is satisfied with the outcome. Society benefits by saving the expense of a criminal trial as well as the costs of incarcerating the offender. Mediation does not work in all cases, and there are some dangers in giving the victim more influence over the disposition of a case, but in many instances, mediation is a more positive response to criminal conduct than the conventional criminal process (see Chapter 25).

Mediation is a part of a broader response to crime, called restorative justice, that is beginning to attract a great deal of attention internationally. Unlike the conventional criminal justice system, restorative justice attempts to build something positive following the commission of the crime. Restorative justice advocates claim that it can do more for victims and offenders, in contrast to the criminal justice system, which tends to ignore the former and simply punish the latter. This alternate form of justice is explored further in Chapter 24.

DRUG OFFENDERS

Offenders with substance abuse problems represent a unique challenge to the criminal justice system. If the system's response to these offenders is the same as its response to offenders without addictions, drug offenders are likely to return to crime, either as a means of supporting their drug habits, or through associating with others with drug problems. One solution involves the creation of Drug Treatment Courts, which now exist across the United States. These courts attempt to respond to drug offenders with punishment and treatment. Offenders who are processed through Drug Treatment Court follow a strict regime of treatment accompanied by urinalysis to ensure that they are refraining from further illegal drug use. Unlike a conventional criminal court, in Drug Treatment Court, offenders are encouraged and praised for taking steps to solve their drug dependency problems. Drug Treatment courts exist in Vancouver and Toronto, and there are plans for others elsewhere across Canada.

ROLE OF THE VICTIM

Criminal justice systems in western nations are paying increasing attention to the needs of victims, and Canada is no exception. Although the criminal process remains a dispute between two parties, the accused and the state, the victim cannot be ignored. Victims need information about the case, assistance to pursue their interests, and compensation for their losses. In this country, the criminal justice system has introduced a number of reforms at the provincial and federal levels to help victims. Part Three of this volume contains three readings addressing victims in the justice system.

PLAN OF THIS READER

This second edition provides, in a single volume, a diverse collection of contemporary readings in criminal justice. The goal of the book is to supplement textbooks in criminal justice by providing focused readings on selected critical issues. In particular, the reader is designed to complement *Canadian Criminal Justice: A Primer* by Curt Griffiths and Alison Hatch Cunningham (2003). Almost all the chapters have been written for this volume and accordingly reflect the latest (as of 2002) research findings and trends. Chapter 2 of this reader provides an overview of recent criminal justice trends. It is followed by a number of readings on the three principal components of the criminal justice system. Part Three explores the role of the victim. In Part Four, criminal justice professionals provide a look at the system through their own experiences. The volume concludes with chapters addressing some of the most important criminal justice issues being discussed today.

FURTHER READINGS

Griffiths, C. and Hatch Cunningham, A. 2003. *Canadian Criminal Justice: A Primer*. Toronto: Nelson.

Griffiths, C. and Verdun-Jones, S. 1994. *Canadian Criminal Justice*, 2nd ed. Toronto: Harcourt Brace.

Paciocco, D. 2000. *Getting away with Murder: The Canadian Criminal Justice System*. Toronto: Irwin Law.

Roach, K. 2001. *Criminal Law*, 2nd ed. Toronto: Irwin Law.

Further Readings on Public Opinion and Criminal Justice

Roberts, J. V. 1995. *Public Knowledge of Crime and Criminal Justice*. Ottawa: Department of Justice Canada. (Available on the Department of Justice Web site: http://canada.justice.gc.ca).

Roberts, J.V. and Stalans, L. 1997. *Public Opinion, Crime and Criminal Justice*. Boulder, Col.: Westview Press.

REFERENCES

Ashworth, A. 2000. *Sentencing and Criminal Justice*, 3rd ed. London: Butterworths.

Canadian Sentencing Commission. 1987. *Sentencing Reform: A Canadian Approach*. Ottawa: Supply and Services Canada.

Environics Canada. 1998. *Focus on Crime and Justice*. Toronto: Environics Canada Limited.

Gallup Canada (1988) Attitudes to Parole. Survey conducted for Canadian Criminal Justice Association. Ottawa: COCA.

Griffiths, C. and Hatch Cunningham, A. 2003. *Canadian Criminal Justice: A Primer*. Toronto: Nelson.

Hendrick, D. and Farmer, L. 2002. Adult correctional services in Canada, 2000/01. *Juristat*, Volume 22, Number 10.

Roberts, J.V. 2002. *Public Evaluations of Criminal Justice Professionals in Canada*. Ottawa: Department of Justice Canada.

Roberts, J.V. and Gabor, T. 2003 (in press). *The Impact of Conditional Sentencing: Decarceration and Widening of the Net*. Canadian Criminal Law Review.

Roberts, J.V., Nuffield, J. and Hann, R. 2000. "Parole and the Public: Attitudinal and Behavioural Responses." *Empirical and Applied Criminal Justice Research*, 1: 1–29.

Sanders, T. and Roberts, J.V. 2000. Public attitudes toward conditional sentencing: Results of a national survey. *Canadian Journal of Behavioral Science*, 32: 199–207.

CHAPTER 2
Trends in Criminal Justice in Canada

This chapter by Cynthia Benjamin provides some statistical context for the remainder of the book. Before considering the specific issues addressed in subsequent chapters, it is important to have some sense of the overall trends of criminal justice in Canada. Benjamin sets out a number of basic questions pertaining to the justice system, then answers these questions, drawing upon the most recent data available.

The Criminal Justice System in Canada: Essential Facts 2002
Cynthia J. Benjamin, Senior Evaluation Analyst, National Crime Prevention Centre

CRIMINAL JUSTICE SYSTEM FLOWS AND COSTS

The Institutions and Systems That Comprise the Criminal Justice System

When people talk about the criminal justice system (CJS), usually they mean the three interdependent institutions of police, courts, and corrections (Figure 2.1). The flow of individuals and cases through the CJS is dynamic, as a result of choices made by individuals involved (i.e., victims, police, Crown attorneys, defence lawyers, judges and juries, and corrections and parole personnel) at various stages of the process (Cunningham and Griffiths, 1997). A number of decisions will then determine whether the case proceeds through the criminal justice system. For example, the police will dismiss a certain percentage of crime reports as "unfounded." This means that, in the opinion of the police officer at least, no crime was committed or attempted. The cases that remain will be investigated further as the police attempt to lay a criminal charge against a suspect.

How much does it cost to run the criminal justice system?

In 2000/01, the CJS cost federal, provincial, and territorial governments over $11 billion annually. Taking into account the effects of inflation, this is a 3 percent increase over the previous year and a 10 percent increase since 1996/97. This works out to $362 per year for every person in Canada and represents 3 cents of every dollar of government spending. However, in comparison to other government spending priorities, this amount is relatively small. In 2000/01 governments spent proportionately more of every dollar on social services (30 cents or $133.3 billion), health care (16 cents or $69.4 billion), education (14 cents or $61.7 billion), and debt charges (13 cents or $57.9 billion) (Taylor-Butts, 2002).

Which justice sector is the most expensive?

Two components of the CJS receive the lion's share of funding—policing (61 percent or $6.8 billion) and adult corrections (22 percent or $2.5 billion) (see Figure 2.2). The justice system divided the rest of the budget among courts (9 percent or $1.0 billion), legal aid (5 percent or $512 million), and criminal prosecution expenses (3 percent or $335 million; see Taylor-Butts, 2002).

POLICING

After controlling for inflation, spending on policing rose 4 percent between 1996/97 and 2000/01. Policing the country now costs more than $6.8 billion annually ($221 per Canadian). However, in constant dollars, the annual figure is 4 percent lower than policing outlays in 1990/91. Municipal police services accounted for 57 percent of the total policing budget ($3.9 billion), followed by provincial and territorial police services (23 percent or $1.6 billion) and federal/national policing activities (19 percent or $1.3 billion) (Taylor-Butts, 2002).

Over the next five years, however, spending on policing will probably escalate in response to the events of September 11, 2001, and the subsequent emphasis on national security. In October 2001, the federal government initiated a $280 million Anti-Terrorism Plan, allocating $64 million to the Royal Canadian Mounted Police (RCMP) and the Department of the Solicitor General of Canada to develop new security technologies; enhance forensic, analysis, and intelligence systems and supports; improve coordination among criminal justice agencies; and hire more security personnel. In December 2001, the federal government announced a five-year, $7.7 billion budget for initiatives targeted at improving the security and safety of Canadians,

Figure 2.1 *Flow through the Canadian Criminal Justice System*

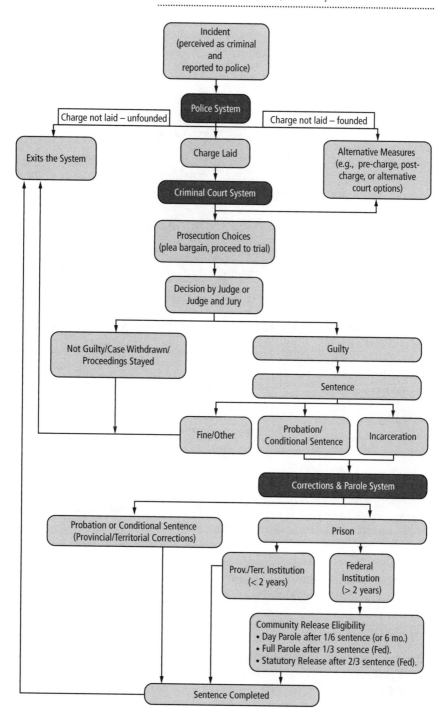

Figure 2.2 *Criminal Justice System Costs by Sector, 2000/01 ($ million, % total spending)*

Total annual spending = **$11.1 billion**

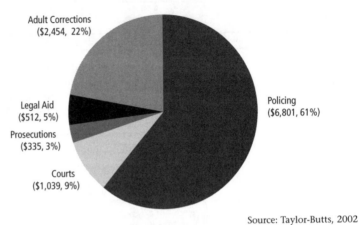

Adult Corrections
($2,454, 22%)

Legal Aid
($512, 5%)

Prosecutions
($335, 3%)

Courts
($1,039, 9%)

Policing
($6,801, 61%)

Source: Taylor-Butts, 2002

Figure 2.2a *Estimate Expenditures by Governments on the Criminal Justice System, 2000/01*

Criminal Justice Component	Total ($ millions)	% of Total Expenditures
Policing	$6,801	61%
Courts	$1,039	9%
Prosecutions	$335	3%
Legal Aid	$512	5%
Adult Corrections	$2,454	22%
Total	**$11,141**	**100%**

including a $1.6 billion boost to strengthen intelligence-gathering and policing (Taylor-Butts, 2002).

COURTS

The court system cost $1 billion in 2000/01 ($34 per person in Canada). This is a 4 percent increase in spending since 1998/99 (inflation-adjusted figures). Since they oversee the majority of cases in the criminal justice system, provincial and territorial courts received most of these funds (91 percent). Seven of 13 provincial or territorial jurisdictions increased their budgets in 2001, a reflection of the growing complexity of cases (Taylor-Butts, 2002). As in other areas of the justice system, salaries and employee benefits consumed the majority of the funds ($829 million or 80 percent). The remaining 20 percent of court system costs included other operating expenses such as law libraries, witness costs, travel, transcripts, office supplies, communications, and Section 96[i] judges' allowances and annuities (Snowball, 2002a).

LEGAL AID

The purpose of legal aid is to ensure that all Canadians have access to justice through the court system, regardless of income level. Legal aid is provincially administered and eligibility depends on the nature of the case (usually the offender must be charged with a serious criminal offence that could result in imprisonment) and on the client's financial circumstances. In 2000/01, there were 839,000 applications for legal aid assistance nationally, of which 518,000 were approved (Statistics Canada, 2002b). Following many years of decline, legal aid expenditures stabilized after 1998/99. Between 1999/00 and 2000/01, legal aid costs grew 2 percent (after inflation), to $512 million or $17 per Canadian (Taylor-Butts, 2002). Governments contribute 87 percent of the total revenues; the remainder comes from client contributions and cost recoveries (3 percent), legal profession contributions (1 percent), and other sources (9 percent) (Statistics Canada, 2002b).

CRIMINAL PROSECUTIONS

Following four years of stability, criminal prosecution spending rose 15 percent in 2000/01 (to $335 million or $11 per capita). Here too, salaries and benefits comprised 80 percent of the overall expenditures (Snowball, 2002b). Per capita costs vary greatly across the provinces and territories due to the different charge approval processes, crime rates, case workloads, geography, and population distribution of each jurisdiction. In addition, a small number of unusually expensive criminal proceedings will influence annual budget totals (Snowball, 2002b).

ADULT CORRECTIONS

The annual operating costs for the adult corrections system remained stable in 2000/01, at $2.5 billion ($80 per person in Canada). After inflation, this represents a mere 1 percent increase over the previous year, but a 17 percent jump since 1996/97 (Hendrick and Farmer, 2002). Custodial services accounted for 74 percent of the budget (down from 77 percent in 1996/97), followed by federal headquarters and National Parole Board costs (10 percent), provincial supervision costs (7 percent), federal supervision costs (6 percent), and provincial headquarters and parole boards costs (2 percent) (Hendrick and Farmer, 2002).

Fifty-two percent of the cost ($1.3 billion) was spent in the federal system, 3 percent less than the preceding year (in constant dollars). In contrast, provincial expenditures grew 6 percent over the previous year, to $1.2 billion (Taylor-Butts, 2002). In the federal system, the average daily cost per inmate has risen significantly (by 43 percent) since 1995/96 to $189.21 ($69,062 per inmate per year). On the provincial side, in 2000/01 the average daily cost per inmate was $137.44 ($50,166 annually), escalating 13 percent since 1995/96.

There are substantial gender differences in the costs of incarceration as well; in 2000/01, it cost on average $66,381 to house a male inmate. The cost per female inmate was $110,473 annually (CSC, 2002) due to the small number of women per institution. Federal corrections are more expensive per inmate than provincial facilities due to the higher security requirements and the obligation to provide more programming to long-term inmates (Hendrick and Farmer, 2002). For example, prisoners serving a life-sentence account for fully 18 percent of the federal prison population. In contrast to the expense of incarceration, the cost of supervising an offender on parole is approximately $16,800 annually (CSC, 2002).

HOW MANY PEOPLE WORK IN THE JUSTICE SYSTEM?

The criminal justice system had approximately 127,000 people[ii] working in policing, courts, criminal prosecutions, and legal aid and in corrections and parole services in 2000/01 (Taylor-Butts, 2002). This figure is up 5 percent over the preceding year, following a decline in the number of personnel through the early- to mid-1990s (Taylor-Butts, 2002). These figures do not include many thousands of people who work in the criminal justice system as unpaid volunteers or affiliated nongovernmental agencies' personnel.

Policing

As of June 15, 2001, there were 57,107 police officers (up from 55,954 in 2000) and 19,992 civilians employed in public policing services (see Figure 2.3) (Filyer, 2002). This works out to a rate of 184 police officers per 100,000 population in 2001. This figure is lower than the comparable rate of 247 in the United States (1998 figure) and 240 in England and Wales (2001 figure). Although the number of women officers multiplied over the past 30 years, they remain in the minority. In the 1960s and 1970s, only 1 percent of officers were women; by 2001, they comprised 14.5 percent of sworn personnel (8,291 officers) (Filyer, 2002).

Courts

The court system employed 11,901 people in 2000/01, a decrease of 3 percent since 1996/97 (Figure 2.3). Of these, 2,011 were judges (17 percent) and 9,890 were court staff (83 percent). National data on the gender of judges are not available; however, for the seven jurisdictions[iii] that record this information,

Figure 2.3 *Employees of the Justice System, Selected Sectors, 1996/97 and 2000/01*

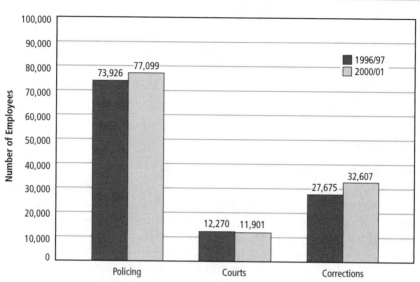

Source: Filyer (2002) and Taylor-Butts (2002).

men outnumbered women on the bench 4 to 1, but in contrast, men accounted for only 22 percent of the court staff (Snowball, 2002a).

Criminal prosecutions experienced a 15 percent increase in personnel between 1998/99 and 2000/01, bringing the total to 3,609 (Taylor-Butts, 2002). In 2000/01, 60 percent of employees were staff lawyers, another 5 percent provided prosecutorial support (e.g., students, paralegals), and approximately one-third of prosecutorial staff were lawyers hired on an *ad hoc* or *per diem* basis to act as Crown representatives. Almost half (43 percent) of all lawyers (staff and contract) were women, up from 38 percent in 1998/99 (Snowball, 2002b).

Legal aid is administered in different ways depending on the province or territory. Some provinces (Newfoundland and Labrador, Prince Edward Island, Nova Scotia, and Saskatchewan) primarily employ full-time staff lawyers to handle legal aid cases. New Brunswick, Ontario, and Alberta primarily cover these cases by Judicare (legal services are contracted out to private lawyers). The remaining jurisdictions (Quebec, Manitoba, British Columbia, and the three territories) use a mixed system of private and staff lawyers. The different delivery methods and fluctuations in case workloads impact the precise number of personnel working in this sector at any given time. As of March 31, 2001, there were 50,920 practising private lawyers, 24 percent (11,389) of whom provided legal aid. There were 1,029 staff lawyers in legal aid departments, and 84 percent provided direct legal services (Statistics Canada, 2002b).

Adult Corrections

In 2000/01, adult corrections employed 32,607 staff at provincial, territorial, and federal levels (Figure 2.3). This is up 8 percent since 1999/00 and 18 percent higher than in 1996/97 (Taylor-Butts, 2002). The provincial system employs 51 percent of all staff. The administration of custodial services accounted for 8 of 10 workers in both the federal and provincial systems. The proportion of federal employees jumped 44 percent since 1995/96, while the number of provincial employees declined 5 percent since the same period (Hendrick and Farmer, 2002).

POLICING

What is the structure of policing in Canada?

Federal, provincial, and municipal governments (with special policing agreements with First Nations governments in some Aboriginal communities) share the responsibility of providing policing services. The Royal Canadian Mounted Police falls under the federal government's jurisdiction and is primarily responsible for enforcing federal statutes nationally. However, the RCMP also delivers municipal, provincial, and territorial policing services on a contract basis across the country. In addition, the RCMP is responsible for maintaining the national information system called the Canadian Police Information Centre (CPIC), forensic laboratories, the Canadian Police College, and coordinating police officer participation in UN peacekeeping missions (Dunphy and Shankarraman, 2000).

Each province and territory administers its own provincial/territorial and municipal policing needs, including budget, training, and infrastructure. In general, provincial police enforce *Criminal Code* and related statutes, as well as provincial statutes in all areas of the province not covered by municipal police services, and laws on all major highways connecting the province. Only Newfoundland, Quebec, and Ontario have provincial police services: the Royal Newfoundland Constabulary, Sûreté du Québec, and the Ontario Provincial Police, respectively.

Municipal police services enforce *Criminal Code* and related statutes, provincial statutes, and municipal bylaws within the boundaries of a municipality (i.e., city, town) or several adjoining municipalities. In 2001, there were 595 municipal police services (201 of which were RCMP contracts and 75 of which were OPP contracts). Municipal police services employed two-thirds of all officers in Canada. Only Newfoundland, Yukon, the Northwest Territories, and Nunavut do not have municipal police services. The RCMP provides municipal services for the three territories; in Newfoundland, the Constabulary oversees the three largest municipalities, contracting the remaining part of the province to the RCMP (Filyer, 2002).

Have police officers' workloads increased?

The main determinant of police officers' workloads is the number of incidents reported to police departments, to which they have to respond, write reports, and possibly pursue from an initial investigation through to a court appearance. In 2001, there were 2,530,178 "actual" incidents (includes all *Criminal Code* and other federal statute offences such as drugs, but excludes traffic offences). This number represents 42 incidents per officer, down from its peak of 51 incidents per officer in 1991 (Filyer, 2002). However, the ratio of residents per officer continues to increase: in 1980, there was one officer for every 492 residents, by 2001, this figure had risen to 544. Expressed on a per capita basis, nationally there are 184 police officers per 100,000 population. The three territories had the largest officer per capita representation at 323, 372, and 405 for Nunavut, Northwest Territories, and Yukon, respectively. The rates in the North have always been higher given the issue of geography, terrain, and sparse population. The lowest rates were in Newfoundland and Labrador and Prince Edward Island (144 and 147, respectively) (Statistics Canada, 2002a).

COURTS

What is the structure of Canada's court system?

The Canadian court system is the shared responsibility of federal, provincial, and territorial governments. Figure 2.4 depicts the court structure in Canada. There are four levels of court. The first level, the provincial and territorial courts, falls exclusively under the jurisdiction of each province or territory. Provincial and Territorial Superior Courts and Appeal Courts are administered by the province or territory; however, judges are appointed by the federal government. The highest courts in Canada are the federal courts, which include the Supreme Court of Canada, the Tax Court of Canada, and the Federal Court of Canada. These courts have a national scope and are administered by the federal government.

How many cases went to adult criminal court this year?

The adult criminal courts of eight provinces and territories[iv] processed 375,466 cases in 2000/01, the majority of which terminated in provincial, territorial or Superior Court. There were 78,146 cases where the most serious offence (MSO)[v] was for a violent crime, 90,449 where it was for a property crime, and 112,668 cases where the MSO was for some other *Criminal Code* infraction. These three offence types comprised 75 percent of the total offences heard in court (Thomas, 2002).

In rank order, the five offences or offence categories that accounted for most of the cases heard in adult criminal court were common assault, impaired

Figure 2.4 *Court Structure in Canada*

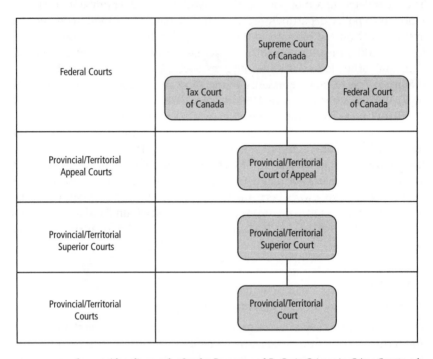

Source: After diagram by Sandra Besserer and R. Craig Grimes in *Crime Counts*, eds.
Leslie W. Kennedy and Vincent F. Sacco, 1996, as cited in Snowball (2002a):6.

driving, administration of justice (e.g., failure to appear in court, failure to comply with a probation order), theft, and major assault (Thomas, 2002).

What proportion of criminal charges resulted in convictions?

The majority of cases heard in adult court resulted in a conviction. In 2000/01, 61 percent of cases (226,979 cases) resulted in a conviction and 2 percent resulted in an acquittal (Thomas, 2002). Most of these convictions are a result of the accused's pleading guilty, often after his or her lawyer has engaged in plea discussions with the Crown (see Chapter 4). Altogether, one-third of cases had the charges withdrawn or stayed, meaning that all criminal proceedings against the accused were stopped. The conviction rate in adult court was highest for *Criminal Code* traffic offences (e.g., impaired driving), with 76 percent of cases resulting in a conviction. Violent and property offence cases resulted in a conviction 54 percent and 63 percent of the time, respectively (Thomas, 2002).

Which sanctions were imposed most often?

In 2000/01, the most severe sanctions[vi] handed down in adult court were nearly evenly distributed between custodial sentences (35 percent), fines (30 percent) and probation (29 percent). Thus approximately one-third of all offenders sentenced in Canada's courts receive a term of imprisonment. Prison or probation were the most frequent sanctions imposed for violent or property crime cases, while *Criminal Code* traffic and "other" federal offence cases were more likely to receive a fine as the most severe sanction (Thomas, 2002). The use of custody has been relatively stable over the past few years and has led to calls for the government to introduce new ways of lowering the number of offenders who are punished by being sent to prison.

Do the courts hear and resolve cases swiftly?

Although the total number of cases heard in adult court has declined in recent years, the amount of time to complete a case has escalated. In 2000/01, the median[vii] processing time for cases from first to last appearance in court was 87 days, up from 84 days in 1998/99 and 80 days in 1996/97 (Thomas, 2002). The number of times the accused must appear in court has a dramatic impact on the length of time it takes to resolve a case. In 2000/01, the average (mean) number of court appearances per case was five, which is an increase over previous years. (Thomas, 2002). One reason the number of appearances is higher today is that there are now more charges per case. The more charges to hear, the more time it takes to resolve each case.

CORRECTIONS

What is the distribution of correctional facilities by security level?

In 2000/01, there were 210 correctional facilities across Canada. Of these, 140 were provincial or territorial facilities (115 secure institutions and 25 open institutions such as halfway houses) with a capacity of 20,240 spaces. Another 53 were federal prisons (with a capacity of 13,696 spaces), and 17 were federal community correctional centres (CCCs), with 526 spaces (Hendrick and Farmer, 2002). Federal institutions provided 39 percent of the total institutional capacity, an increase of 10 percent since 1995/96 (Hendrick and Farmer, 2002).

The Correctional Service of Canada operates facilities with several different levels of security. In 2000/01, it supervised 8 maximum, 20 medium, 17 minimum, and 8 multi-level security facilities nationally. Five of these institutions are specifically designated for women, including a "healing lodge" in the prairie region (CSC, 2002). In addition to these government-run institutions, the Correctional Service of Canada has contracts with a number of nonprofit, community-based agencies to operate 175 residential facilities for federal offenders (CSC, 2002). Commonly referred to as "halfway houses," these facilities provide accommodation, counselling, and some programming to offenders making their transition back into society.

Provincial correctional authorities supervise[viii] probation and conditional sentences, custodial remands (e.g., person held for trial because he or she poses a risk to him- or herself or may not appear for trial), temporary detentions (e.g., immigration proceedings, parole suspension), and custodial sentences of less than two years. They also oversee the release of offenders into the community from provincial and territorial institutions. Federal corrections supervises custodial sentences of two years or longer and the graduated release of these offenders into the community via the National Parole Board (NPB).

The National Parole Board has the authority to grant, deny, terminate, or revoke community release orders (e.g., day and full parole and statutory release), detain certain offenders, and grant temporary absences for all federal offenders and for all provincial and territorial offenders except those housed in British Columbia, Ontario, and Quebec (these provinces operate their own parole boards). However, the Correctional Service of Canada (CSC) is responsible for the supervision of all offenders granted parole in Canada, including in these three provinces (Hendrick and Farmer, 2002).

What is Canada's incarceration rate? How many offenders are in custody?

One measure of the incarceration rate is the average number of adult inmates (i.e., those sentenced to prison, held in remand, or held in temporary detention) per 100,000 adult population. The incarceration rate in Canada for 2000/01 was 133 inmates per 100,000 adult population, the lowest incarceration rate in over a decade. The incarceration rate for offenders sentenced to provincial corrections is lower than the rate for federal corrections, as these offenders have convictions for less serious crimes and frequently serve their sentences in the community.

There are two measures commonly used to track the flow of individuals in the corrections system: admissions and average daily counts. Admissions data are collected when an offender enters an institution or community supervision program. This number does not include individual offenders (a single person could be readmitted into custody several times in one year, or could transfer from prison to community supervision), but provides insight into the corrections system workload in general. The second measure provides the average number of offenders (in prison, in remand, on probation, etc.) on any given day.

There were 344,493 admissions to adult corrections in 2000/01. On the provincial side, there were 80,928 sentenced admissions, 118,566 admissions to remand, 24,901 to temporary detention, and 101,768 admissions to community supervision (i.e., probation, provincial parole, and conditional sentences). On the federal side, there were 7,723 admissions into custody and 7,723 community releases (Hendrick and Farmer, 2002).

In 2000/01, the average daily count of adults under some form of corrections supervision was 151,500. Nearly 120,000 (79 percent) were under community supervision. On any given day in 2000/01, one offender in five was in custody. There were 12,732 federally and 10,953 provincially sentenced inmates, 7,428 persons held in remand, and an additional 434 in temporary detention (Hendrick and Farmer, 2002).

Over the past 10 years, there has been little fluctuation in custody counts and federal releases; however, the use of remand is climbing (from 4,713 counts in 1990/91 to 7,428 in 2000/01). The most dramatic movement in the past decade is the growth in the number of people on "community supervision," from a low of 84,635 offenders in 1990/91 to a high of 115,730 in 1997/98, to 111,885 offenders in 2000/01 (Hendrick and Farmer, 2002). This increase reflects in part a judicial move toward less punitive sentencing options.

What percentage of parolees successfully completed their release programs?

Federal offenders may be released into the community via escorted or unescorted temporary absences, parole, or statutory release. Temporary absences are when minimum- or medium-risk prisoners are permitted to leave an institution for a brief period for medical, administrative, program-related, or humanitarian reasons (e.g., parental responsibilities, death of a relative, community service, etc.). In 2000/01, 10,214 prisoners completed 34,491 escorted temporary absences (ETAs), and 4,046 prisoners completed 7,233 unescorted temporary absences (UTAs). Almost all (99 percent) of these temporary releases were completed successfully (CSC, 2002).

Federal offenders are eligible for conditional release (i.e., parole) after serving a portion of their sentence in prison. Generally, suitable offenders are eligible for day parole six months before they become eligible for full parole, or after one-sixth of their sentence, whichever is sooner. With day parole, offenders leave the prison during the day (usually for work or school) and return to the prison or community-based residential facility overnight. Most offenders can apply for full parole after serving one-third of their sentence in custody. This allows offenders to live and work independently in a community, giving them an opportunity to demonstrate that they can resume a "normal" life on the outside. The NPB releases parolees into the community under the supervision of a parole officer, and the offender must abide by a specific set of conditions (e.g., must work or attend school, abstain from alcohol, not associate with certain individuals, etc.) or risk having his or her parole revoked, resulting in a return to prison.

The *Corrections and Conditional Release Act* (*CCRA*) stipulates that once offenders complete two-thirds of their sentence they must be released to serve the remainder of their sentence under supervision in the community (called

"Statutory Release"), unless they waive this right or the NPB determines that they pose a serious threat to the public, in which case the individual prisoner may be detained until the end of his or her sentence.

In 2000/01, the majority of parolees successfully completed their terms in the community. For those who returned to prison, most had their parole revoked for breach of conditions (i.e., breaking one of the conditions of their release). Releases on day parole had the highest success rates (83 percent successfully completed). Of those on full parole, 74 percent successfully completed their term, 16 percent returned to prison for breach of conditions, and 10 percent committed a new offence (primarily nonviolent[ix]). Prisoners released on statutory release had lower success rates with only 59 percent successful.

DISCUSSION QUESTIONS

1. *How does this overview of the criminal justice system differ from your perceptions? Specifically, which finding did you find most interesting?*
2. *Do you think the way in which different provinces and territories administer their legal aid plans (ie., private, public, mixed) has an impact on access to the criminal justice system? Do you think that it would be a good idea to create a national legal aid program?*
3. *Given that the majority of cases heard in court are not for a violent offence, and in light of the escalating costs associated with incarceration, why do you think the most serious sanction continues to be a custodial sentence? What alternatives to incarceration can a judge impose? When do you think these alternatives might represent a more appropriate option?*

FURTHER READINGS

Bélanger, B. 2001. Sentencing in adult criminal courts, 1999/00. *Juristat*, 21 (10). Canadian Centre for Justice Statistics, Statistics Canada. Ottawa: Minister Responsible for Statistics Canada.

Pereira, J. and C. Grimes. 2001. Case processing in criminal courts, 1999/00. *Juristat*, 22 (1). Canadian Centre for Justice Statistics, Statistics Canada. Ottawa: Minister Responsible for Statistics Canada.

Savoie, J. 2002. Crime statistics in Canada, 2001. *Juristat*, 22 (6). Canadian Centre for Justice Statistics, Statistics Canada. Ottawa: Minister Responsible for Statistics Canada.

REFERENCES

Correctional Services Canada (CSC). 2002. *Basic Facts About Federal Corrections, 2001*. Ottawa: Public Works and Government Services Canada (http://www.csc-scc.gc.ca/text/faits/facts07_e.shtml). Retrieved April 22, 2003.

Cunningham, Alison Hatch and Curt T. Griffiths. 1997. *Canadian Criminal Justice: A Primer.* Toronto: Harcourt Canada.

Dunphy, Robert and Gayati Shankarraman. 2000. *Police Resources in Canada, 2000.* Canadian Centre for Justice Statistics, Statistics Canada Catalogue 85-225-XIE. Ottawa: Minister Responsible for Statistics Canada.

Filyer, Rebecca E. 2002. *Police Resources in Canada, 2001.* Canadian Centre for Justice Statistics, Statistics Canada Catalogue 85-225-XIE. Ottawa: Minister Responsible for Statistics Canada.

Hendrick, Dianne and Lee Farmer. 2002. Adult correctional services in Canada, 2000/01. *Juristat*, 22 (10). Canadian Centre for Justice Statistics, Statistics Canada. Ottawa: Minister Responsible for Statistics Canada.

Snowball, Katie. 2002a. *Courts Personnel and Expenditures, 2000/01.* Canadian Centre for Justice Statistics, Statistics Canada Catalogue 85-403-XIE. Ottawa: Minister Responsible for Statistics Canada..

Snowball, Katie. 2002b. *Criminal Prosecutions Personnel and Expenditures, 2000/01.* Canadian Centre for Justice Statistics, Statistics Canada Catalogue 85-402-XIE. Ottawa: Minister Responsible for Statistics Canada.

Statistics Canada, Canadian Centre for Justice Statistics. 2001. *Adult Correctional Services in Canada, 1999–2000.* Canadian Centre for Justice Statistics, Statistics Canada Catalogue 85-211-XIE. Ottawa: Minister Responsible for Statistics Canada.

Statistics Canada, Canadian Centre for Justice Statistics. 2002a. *Graphical Overview of the Criminal Justice Indicators, 2000–2001.* Canadian Centre for Justice Statistics, Statistics Canada Catalogue 85-207-XIE. Ottawa: Minister Responsible for Statistics Canada.

Statistics Canada, Canadian Centre for Justice Statistics. 2002b. *Legal Aid in Canada: Resource and Caseload Statistics, 2000/01.* Canadian Centre for Justice Statistics, Statistics Canada Catalogue 85F0015XIE. Ottawa: Minister Responsible for Statistics Canada.

Taylor-Butts, Andrea. 2002. Justice spending in Canada, 2000/01. *Juristat*, 22 (11). Canadian Centre for Justice Statistics, Statistics Canada. Ottawa: Minister Responsible for Statistics Canada.

Thomas, Mikhail. 2002. Adult criminal court statistics, 2000/01. *Juristat*, 22 (2). Canadian Centre for Justice Statistics, Statistics Canada. Ottawa: Minister Responsible for Statistics Canada.

ENDNOTES

[i] Section 96 of the *Constitution Act, 1867*, gives the federal government the authority to appoint judges to provincial and territorial Appeal and Superior Courts. This figure includes Section 96 judges and related costs.

[ii] All staffing figures cited, except those for legal aid, use full-time equivalents. Legal aid uses the actual number of employees on staff as of March

31 each year. All personnel figures are as of March 31 of each year, except for policing, which are as of June 15 (Taylor-Butts, 2002: 17).

iii Newfoundland and Labrador, Prince Edward Island, Alberta, Yukon, Northwest Territories, Nunavut, and all the federal courts.

iv The CCJS collects adult court data from Newfoundland and Labrador, Prince Edward Island, Nova Scotia, Quebec (except 140 municipal courts), Ontario, Saskatchewan, Alberta, and Yukon, which make up 80 percent of the national adult criminal court caseload.

v All discussions of "cases" by the CCJS refer to the "most severe offence" (MSO) when discussing cases with multiple charges. The ranking from most to least severe is based on the average length of prison for each offence. The higher one is considered the MSO (Thomas, 2002: 2).

vi Like the MSO above, the Most Serious Sentence (MSS) is ranked from the most to least restrictive sanction (e.g., prison versus community service).

vii The median is the mid-point of a group of values when they are listed from smallest to largest.

viii Interjurisdictional agreements—sometimes provincial offenders serve in federal facilities and vice versa.

ix Of the 10% revoked for an offence (175 cases), 86% (150 cases) were non-violent offences and 14% (25 cases) were violent offences. Of the total Federal full parole releases (1,796 cases), 9% (150 cases) were revoked for non-violent offences and 1% (25 cases) were revoked for violent offences.

Appendix A: The Internet as a Source of Information about Criminal Justice

This appendix contains two parts: the first presents a backgrounder for those readers with little experience researching on the Net; the second provides an annotated bibliography of useful Web sites that cover a broad range of criminal justice topics in Canada, the United States, and elsewhere.

PART 1: WELCOME TO THE INTERNET

A productive Web-searching session begins by preparing a detailed list of key words or phrases describing the research topic; the more specific the key words, the more specific the results returned to you. As well, read the information that each search engine gives regarding how to use the basic and advanced features to conduct and refine a search. For instance, if you want general facts on family violence in Canada, you may begin with key words such as "child abuse," "wife battering," "spousal assault," "sibling violence," "domestic disputes," "intimate homicides," "victimization–spousal," "family violence," "sentencing and assault," or "incarceration for assault" depending on which aspect you wish to explore. However, if you want only *research studies on sentencing options for spousal assault in Canada*, you must refine your search to something like: "research + spousal + assault + sentencing + Canada," to capture your exact research parameters.

The main advantage of online research is its speed. Information from news sources, nongovernmental agencies, community groups, libraries throughout the world, specialized academic journals, governments, research institutions, "think tanks," universities, special interest groups, conference proceedings, and personal Web pages are just a few "mouse clicks" away. Another bonus is that much of the information online is very recent. This is sometimes an advantage over journals and books, which take much longer to produce. Web-based searching is also convenient. Access to the Internet is widely available in North America and is possible even in remote regions of the world: at schools, colleges and universities, home, work, public libraries, and in Internet cafés.

However, for all of its ease and convenience, there are limitations to the Internet as a research tool. First, although organizations are increasingly getting online, many still do not have a Web site. Those institutions that are online often only display a fraction of the data they have in-house. For instance, the Canadian Centre for Justice Statistics (CCJS) provides only highlights of its *Juristat* publication online (although many universities and colleges have special agreements with Statistics Canada to allow access to entire publications). Likewise, some journals, such as the *Canadian Journal of Criminology and Criminal Justice,* put only abstracts of their articles online. Second, the quality of information found on the Internet varies tremendously: *caveat emptor!*

PART 2: THE INTERNET AND CRIMINAL JUSTICE RESEARCH

The Internet can help you find statistics, opinions, theories, results of research experiments, and expert opinions and may inspire you to explore in new directions. As you navigate the Net, keep a personal list of sites you find useful for future reference (known as "bookmarks" in computer lingo). Listed below are summaries of criminal justice–related Web sites in Canada, the United States, and overseas. However, this list is not exhaustive, and sites can change frequently. To get you started, the list is broadly organized by topic with an emphasis on Canadian criminal justice information.

When researching a topic, start broadly, and focus your search from there. For instance, if you want to know about "violence against minorities," note the key criminal justice sites listed below, but also search minority rights organizations, relevant government departments (such as the Human Rights Commission and Department of Justice), agencies and nongovernmental groups that work with visible minorities, related online chat or discussion groups, or organizations dedicated to the investigation of social justice issues.

Criminal Justice Links on the Web

Official Criminal Justice System Sites
Department of Justice Canada
http://canada.justice.gc.ca

This Web site provides an overview of the federal Department of Justice as well as news and views on current laws and regulations, ministers' speeches, and government crime initiatives (e.g., crime prevention, youth justice policies). It also provides links to courts and other government departments.

Related Sites
Law Commission of Canada: www.lcc.gc.ca
Canadian Legal Information Institute: www.canlii.org
World Legal Information Institute: www.worldlii.org
Australian Institute of Criminology: www.aic.gov.au

United States Department of Justice
www.usdoj.gov

Information on what's new and hot in U.S. justice, associated organizations, current issues of public interest, press releases, and a listing of fugitives and missing children.

British Home Office
www.homeoffice.gov.uk

The Home Office is the government department responsible for internal affairs and crime control and prevention in England and Wales. This site contains information on crime prevention, links to departments involved in criminal justice, press releases, publications, and miscellaneous research materials.

Department of the Solicitor General of Canada
www.sgc.gc.ca

The federal Department of the Solicitor General is responsible for providing leadership in the areas of public order and community safety. Information is presented on Aboriginal policing, corrections and parole, national security issues, public safety portal (www.safecanada.ca, a link to information on public safety and security in Canada), and law enforcement.

Related Sites:
Correctional Service Canada (CSC): www.csc-scc.gc.ca
Royal Canadian Mounted Police (RCMP): www.rcmp-grc.gc.ca
Criminal Intelligence Service Canada: www.cisc.gc.ca
Canadian Security Intelligence Service: www.csis-scrs.gc.ca
· Public Safety Web Site: www.safecanada.ca

Crime-Prevention Sites

National Crime Prevention Centre (NCPC)
www.prevention.gc.ca

The National Crime Prevention Strategy aims to reduce crime and victimization in Canada by tackling crime before it starts. The NCPC is the funding branch of the Strategy and solicits proposals for innovative, community-based crime-prevention initiatives that address the root causes of crime and victimization. These projects focus on the factors that put individuals at risk (like family violence, school problems, and drug abuse) and those that build resiliency in individuals and communities (like parenting skills and job creation programs). The Web site provides bilingual access to information about crime prevention projects and best practices from Canada and around the world.

Related Sites:
International Center for the Prevention of Crime (ICPC):
   www.crime-prevention-intl.org
National Crime Prevention Council (United States): www.ncpc.org
Canadian Council on Social Development: www.ccsd.ca
United Nations Office on Drugs and Crime:
   www.unodc.org/odccp/index.html

Criminal Justice Research and Statistics Sites

Access to Justice Network (ACJNET)
www.acjnet.org

This Web site provides the public with legal information and educational resources gathered nationally. Details are available on legal statutes and specific cases and on key individuals and organizations involved in the criminal justice field.

Related Sites:
Canadian Criminal Justice Association: www.ccja-acjp.ca
Network for Research on Crime and Justice: http://qsilver.queensu.ca/rcjnet
Lloyd Duhaime's Canadian Criminal Law Information (free plain-language
   articles on Canadian criminal law): www.duhaime.org
Canadian Criminal Justice Resource Page:
   http://members.tripod.com/BlueThingy/index.html

United Nations Interregional Crime and Justice Research Institute
www.unicri.it/index.htm

The objective of this UN institute is to promote, conduct, coordinate, and support action-oriented research and training on social problems involving juvenile delinquency and adult criminality and to develop strategies, policies, models, and systems for the prevention and control of these behaviours and activities on a global scale. This institute is part of the United Nations Crime Prevention and Criminal Justice Programme Network, which collaborates with other international agencies, such as INTERPOL, on criminal justice issues.

International Centre for Criminal Law Reform and Criminal Justice Policy
www.icclr.law.ubc.ca

The mandate of this organization is to improve the quality of justice through reform of criminal law policy and practice. It focuses on the use of democratic principles in the rule of law and respect for human rights. This site provides advice, information, research, and proposals for policy development and legislation, as well as technical assistance to governments and other agencies. Reports are available on international concerns such as Aboriginal justice, human rights in China, domestic violence, economic and organized crime, the environment, international criminal courts, and peacekeeping.

Canadian Centre for Justice Statistics (CCJS)
www.statcan.ca

The CCJS is a division of Statistics Canada devoted to the accumulation and analysis of national statistics and information related to crime and victimization. The CCJS maintains data on crime, homicide, police, adult and juvenile court, legal aid, corrections, and more. It is responsible for the generation and maintenance of numerous databases including the Revised Uniform Crime Reports (microdata on characteristics of criminal incidents). The CCJS also publishes the journal *Juristat* and an annual *Graphical Overview of the Criminal Justice Indicators*.

Related Sites:

Statistics Canada: www.statcan.ca

Australian Bureau of Statistics (go to "Themes" and choose "Crime and Justice"): www.abs.gov.au

Justice Research and Statistics Association (United States): www.jrsainfo.org

Bureau of Justice Assistance Evaluation Web site:
www.bja.evaluationwebsite.org

National Criminal Justice Reference Service (NCJRS)
www.ncjrs.org

The NCJRS Web site displays a wide range of abstracts on American criminal justice policies, proposals, and practices on a variety of topics, including capital punishment, probation and parole, HIV in prisons, juvenile/young offenders, alternatives to incarceration, prison riots, violent offenders, and terrorism.

Cecil Greek's Criminal Justice Links (Florida State University)
www.criminology.fsu.edu/cjlinks

This is an enormous site dedicated to criminal justice–related links on such topics as federal agencies, searchable law databases, forensics, restorative justice programs and research, criminal justice and criminology schools, and online criminal justice discussion groups. This is a great place to start exploring criminal justice topics. The site is user-friendly and an excellent starting point for your Web search.

Victim- and Offender-Related Sites

Canadian Association of Elizabeth Fry Societies (CAEFS)
www.web.apc.org/~kpate/caefs_e.htm

The John Howard Society of Canada (JHS)
www.johnhoward.ca

The CAEFS and the JHS are advocates for prisoners' rights. These Web sites offer information about their programs, services, guides, advice on dealing with the criminal justice system, current issues facing prisoners, and miscellaneous facts on prisons and prisoners (e.g., demographics, profiles, history of women's prisons).

> **Related Sites:**
> Family and Corrections Network (United States):
> www.fcnetwork.org/main.html
> Death Penalty Information Center (United States):
> www.deathpenaltyinfo.org
> *Journal of Prisoners on Prisons* (experiences and opinions of the criminal justice system by present and former prisoners of Canadian, U.S., and international prisons): www.jpp.org
> *Prison Legal News* (United States): www.prisonlegalnews.org
> International Circle of Penal Abolitionists (ICOPA):
> www.interlog.com/~ritten/icop/icopaix3.htm

London Family Court Clinic
www.lfcc.on.ca

The London Family Court Clinic is a nonprofit mental health agency located in London, Ontario, that advocates for the special needs of children and youth involved in the criminal justice system whether as young offenders, as victims of crime or abuse, or as the central players in custody disputes. This site offers online information and access to the clinic, including counselling services, research services, and publications. It is an excellent starting point for current information on youth- and child-related criminal justice issues.

National Crime Victims Research and Treatment Center (Medical University of South Carolina, Department of Psychiatry and Behavioral Sciences)
www.musc.edu/cvc

This Web site is committed to disseminating information related to victims and victimization based on medical models.

> **Related Sites:**
> National Victim Center: www.nvc.org
> Victim Assistance Online: www.vaonline.org
> International Victimology: www.victimology.nl

"Crime Control" Professionals

National Criminal Justice Association (NCJA)
www.ncja.org

Primarily interested in working with criminal justice professionals, the NCJA is a special interest group focusing on crime control and public safety issues including fraud, terrorism, victim assistance, and emergency preparedness. It has some good Web site links.

The Police Officer's Internet Directory
www.officer.com

Another special interest group site, the Police Officer's Internet Directory is the largest online resource by and for law enforcement personnel. It has links to U.S. and international policing organizations and criminal justice resources related to policing issues and debates.

United States Federal Bureau of Investigation (FBI)
www.fbi.gov

One of the Net's most popular criminal justice–related Web sites, the FBI online provides information on major investigations, their most wanted, uniform crime reports (statistics), terrorism, and congressional (government) affairs.

PART TWO
Police, Courts, and Corrections

CHAPTER 3
Community Policing

INTRODUCTION

Community policing represents one of the most important developments in contemporary policing. This approach to policing has re-emerged in recent years in response to a degree of disenchantment with the traditional approach to policing. At the heart of the community policing movement is an attempt to produce a closer connection between the police and the communities they serve. As well, community policing reflects a broader approach toward responding to crime. In the past, the emphasis of traditional policing was on individual offenders, and the response of the police stressed "solving crimes," which meant apprehending and charging suspects. That has changed with the advent of community policing. However, the so-called community policing revolution has not occurred overnight, and elements of the old-style policing still remain. In this reading, Barry Leighton, one of Canada's experts in the field of policing, explores the nature and function of community policing in Canada.

Community Policing in Canada: Something Old Is New Again
Barry N. Leighton, Carleton University

While community policing may appear in a variety of forms, its core ingredients are fairly basic. Yet it is often seen as something completely new, a fresh paradigm for policing and a panacea for solving crime and disorder in our communities. However, we can also interpret community policing as being rather like the traditional marriage garb of our grandmothers: "Something old, something new, something borrowed, and something blue." In the quest for a better understanding of this phenomenon, this chapter addresses the following questions: What is a useful definition of community policing? What theories support this approach? What is its current state in Canada? What is the empirical evidence that community policing is more effective than other approaches to policing? What are some of the unresolved issues in the field? Can we make an overall assessment of community policing? What is the future of community policing?

DEFINITION AND CORE STRATEGIES

What is "community policing?" While often also labelled "community-oriented policing," "community-based policing," and "problem-oriented policing," any one label seldom communicates its uniqueness. One way of looking at the concept is as a group of police behaviours that bear a family resemblance to each other, but where no single behaviour is a defining feature. Community policing is truly in the eye of the beholder, and whatever people mean by this concept, it is now the predominant approach to policing in western industrialized countries.

Community policing has been defined as "a philosophical, organizational, and operational approach to urban policing which emphasizes a police–community partnership to solve local crime and disorder problems" (Leighton, 1991). The two core strategies of community policing are *problem-solving* and *community partnerships*.

Problem Solving

Problem-solving means addressing local crime and disorder problems that are defined in terms of patterns between similar incidents (Goldstein, 1979; Murphy, 1991). Rather than responding to each call from the public as a separate case, appropriate crime reduction and prevention steps are taken to solve common, underlying causes. These steps may involve "target hardening" (e.g., installing better locks and lighting) and other prevention tactics prescribed by the *environmental design approach*, whose main strategy is to reduce opportunities for crime. Reducing crime opportunities may include arranging for more intensive policing around crime places at higher risk of hosting criminal events. These places are sometimes called crime "hot spots," such as "hot places" at "hot times." In general, police have a lead role in reducing opportunities for crime.

By contrast, longer-term steps are designed to reduce the motivations of offenders or potential offenders (especially young males) for committing crime. These solutions may involve crime prevention through social development activities that are undertaken in partnership with other community and government agencies. Other steps may be directed toward victims and vulnerable groups having a high statistical risk of becoming victims (especially women, children, and elderly people), such as encouraging them to reduce their exposure to high-risk circumstances. Where the appropriate solution involves addressing the underlying social causes of crime, the police contribute in a supportive way to the partnership. The police role is a secondary one where they alert their partners to the need for another type of response that is generally from outside the criminal justice system.

Community Partnership

The second core strategy of community policing is a *community partnership* between the police and the community they serve. This partnership usually takes the form of public participation and consultation. These activities provide the focal point for identifying local crime and disorder problems, setting priorities for the problems, and developing solutions. Problems are viewed as shared problems with shared solutions, which are provided by the police and other criminal justice agencies acting in partnership with social service agencies and other resources in the community. Local crime and disorder problems are viewed as being the joint responsibility of the community (as the police "client") together with the police (as the local agency delivering public safety solutions and services). This partnership in identifying and ameliorating local crime and disorder problems makes them "co-producers" of order and civility (Wilson and Kelling, 1982; Murphy and Muir, 1984) and "co-reproducers of order" (Ericson, 1982). Allied against crime, the police and their community form a "broad blue line" against crime.

While problem-solving and community partnership are conceptually joined as "Siamese twins," we may still find one twin surviving without the other. That is, police may undertake problem-solving on their own without community involvement. This is known simply as "problem-oriented policing," as championed by Herman Goldstein (Goldstein, 1979). On the other hand, community participation may exist without problem-solving, an approach known as "community relations." But both strategies are necessary in order to foster authentic community policing.

These two strategies have a number of organizational prerequisites, involving organizational arrangements, human resources, and financial resources (Leighton, 1991). In particular, decentralized police management and resource deployment empowers police officers to work with their community to use whatever tactics are appropriate to the neighbourhood and its crime problems. More recent renditions of these new management approaches found elsewhere in the public and private sectors include continuous quality improvement, customer orientation, client satisfaction, shared decision-making, workplace democracy, empowerment of the front line, decentralization, openness, inclusiveness, greater accountability, and so forth. However, it is debatable whether private sector business school approaches can be adapted to public sector service delivery without profit as the bottom line.

The two strategies may also be contrasted with a whole group of tactics with which the community policing approach is often associated. Where appropriate for a particular crime problem in a particular community, these tactics may include the use of police mini-stations or storefronts; neighbourhood patrol by car, foot, bicycle, or even by boat or horseback; officers dedicated to beats or zones; differential response; interagency partnerships; and consultative committees. Not all are appropriate for solving crime and disorder in all communities; for example, foot patrol may not be very effective in low-density, spread-out suburbs. Since the objective of these tactics is to facilitate greater police–citizen contact in order to fulfill the core strategy of a police–community partnership, the right tactics must be chosen for particular crime problems and they must be appropriate for the community's circumstances.

Returning to the definition of community policing, we find two key terms that should be explored further. First, widespread confusion over the meaning of "community" can render the notion of "community policing" meaningless. This is because most traditional interpretations of "community" rely on geographical space, such as neighbourhoods. But, in a highly mobile society that is increasingly more connected electronically than it is geographically, this is an outmoded notion. Many people only sleep in the suburbs while working and playing elsewhere. The consequence of adopting this traditional concept is to transform community policing into a fictional and romantic depiction of old-fashioned communities when there was very little crime and communities largely policed themselves.

By contrast, more modern notions of community are based on the concept of "social networks." This allows us to embrace both local and non-local types of communities (Leighton, 1988). The latter encompasses professional, business, and recreational communities. We can then apply "community as network" to a whole range of different community types other than neighbourhoods, including the electronic "global village." "Community as social network" also allows us to address different types of non-local crime problems such as organized crime and terrorism.

Community partnerships, as the second part of our definition of community policing, also invite closer scrutiny. While this concept opens up a number of complex questions, Mintzberg (1996) has developed a useful typology about the different roles we play in civil society that we can also apply to policing. First, Canadians are "citizens" who are entitled to a certain minimum level of police services (such as that established by a national standard of some sort). Then we can be "clients" who, because of recognized special needs (those at high risk of victimization under certain circumstances, such as women, children, and elderly people), are provided with additional policing services. Others can also be "customers" who decide to purchase additional services from the public police or, more commonly, from private police. Finally, we are all "subjects" with duties and responsibilities. For policing, this means taking reasonable measures, within the limits of the law, to protect ourselves, our families, and our communities. These responsibilities range from locking our doors at night to assisting the police and volunteering in other ways through our various communities.

MODELS OF POLICING AND AN ANALOGY BETWEEN POLICING AND HEALTH CARE

Having refined our definition further, we can also understand it better by contrasting community policing with other policing approaches. In much the same way as we often define what a Canadian is by contrasting ourselves with Americans, we may contrast community policing with ways in which it differs from the professional, bureaucratic, or traditional model of policing. Under the traditional model, crime is the exclusive "property" of the police, who use a technology-driven, rapid response strategy combined with random motorized patrol, in an attempt to deter potential criminal events (Kelling and Moore, 1988). Usually associated with the crime control approach under which the police "own" crime problems and exercise a monopoly on the response to them, the professional police are seen as forming a "thin blue line" against crime. However, with crime as their exclusive professional domain, they unfortunately may also form a thin blue line against the community. In contrast, community policing forms a "broad blue line" or coalition against local crime and disorder problems because the police–community partnership unleashes new or underutilized community resources (Leighton, 1991).

One way of contrasting the practical implications of the community policing model with those of the traditional model is by considering a health care analogy. Traditional policing corresponds to a police force that works like a hospital operating exclusively as an emergency ward. Most of the time the staff would be just waiting for a 911 call so an ambulance could make a rapid response to a life-threatening incident, even though these are relatively few in number compared with most hospital visits. Doctors would randomly cruise the streets in ambulances as a deterrent for accident-prone, high-risk people who are driving unsafely or under the influence of alcohol or illegal drugs. On very rare occasions, perhaps when cruising accident "hot spots," they might come across an accident in progress and be readily available for assistance. Consequently, most patients would arrive only by an emergency-response ambulance, regular wards would be used only for follow-up care, and addressing the underlying causes of health problems through prevention would be an unthinkable idea.

Community policing paints quite a different image by being closer to preventive medicine, with an ambulance making an emergency response in only a small proportion of calls for health care. The focus of treatment and response, or the "unit of analysis," is the individual rather then the event or incident. This holistic approach to health care would include the promotion and maintenance of good health through exercise and a balanced diet in much the same way as building a healthy community means a safer community with a lower chance of having crime and disorder problems. As a result, the police business costs less, is more affordable for communities, and is less of a burden on society in the long run. In short, community policing is sustainable policing.

Community Policing in Theory

While a comprehensive theory of community policing has yet to be developed, the "broken windows" argument advanced by Wilson and Kelling (1982) has gained much popular support and academic credibility (Kelling and Coles, 1996; Sparrow, Moore, and Kennedy, 1990). This view follows the "self-fulfilling prophecy" notion, developed years ago by sociologist W.I. Thomas, that if a situation is defined as being real, then it will be real in its consequences.

The broken windows theory proposes that when potential offenders perceive neighbourhood decay and deterioration in terms of some physical signs of crime (such as broken windows, derelict cars, or graffiti), they will likely conclude that the neighbourhood has few defences against crime and is ripe for the picking. However, when the visible signs of crime and urban decay are removed, neighbourhoods are more likely to be perceived as being low in crime because they are well defended, resulting in an actual reduction in crime. That is, when changes in perceptions and attitudes are fulfilled in reality, then crime is actually reduced, and streets and homes are safer.

But the idea that a neighbourhood defined as being in decay will inevitably lead, in a domino effect, to disorder and then to crime has been challenged (Greene and Mastrofski, 1988). Critics argue that it "explains too much" and might better serve as simply an explanation for neighbourhood disorder and order maintenance rather than overextending itself to cover crime as well. On the other hand, compelling research (Skogan and Hartnett, 1997) demonstrates an empirical link between disorder and crime, thereby providing strong support for this theory.

It is clear that the role of police under a police–community partnership, as proposed by the vision of community policing, requires further development in theory. A comprehensive theory of community policing that encompasses the underlying causes of crime, whether offender motivations or the foundations of these motivations in structured inequalities, has yet to emerge. Such a theory should also address the nature of the police response to crime. A good theory would explain why community policing emerged and whose interests it serves (Reiner, 1992), address broader perspectives such as an analysis of risk (Ericson and Haggerty, 1997), locate the police role in the context of social control, incorporate policing into a model of the state, and answer questions about the role of community in policing.

Community Policing in Practice

Despite much rhetoric in the media, the reality of community policing in the closing decades of the twentieth century did not live up to its own advertising.

In the beginning of the modern era of community policing, it was introduced as an add-on program, a side box on the organization chart along with public relations, victim services, and crime prevention units. The impact of this approach was to marginalize it and render it ineffective. For example, many of the first police mini-stations or storefront offices did not take calls for service from the public, thereby serving only as stationary "grin and wave squads" or public relations outposts that handed out crime prevention brochures. It is not surprising, therefore, that community policing was mistakenly identified with specific, highly visible but marginalized activities.

After a decade of experimenting with add-on programs, the distinction between strategies and tactics, mentioned above, was increasingly recognized. It was also demonstrated that the appropriateness of specific police tactics and other police services depends on the particular needs of the neighbourhood, on the local crime and disorder problem being addressed, and on the solutions jointly developed by the police and the community. Consequently, there is no standard recipe, template, or model that can be adapted from some other police service to fit each community and its crime and disorder problems. The appeal of community policing is its flexibility to deliver its two core strategies through a variety of tactics that differ from community to community and from problem to problem. Hence, community policing in practice is like designer jeans where no one size fits all. Instead, "designer policing" tailors its tactics and services to the local community.

The current state of community policing in Canada reflects the rhetoric and official positions of the majority of Canadian police chiefs and police boards. Second, it has been officially endorsed by the Solicitor General of Canada as the preferred approach to modern urban policing (Normandeau and Leighton, 1990). Third, many provincial governments have made it official policy. Indeed, the *Ontario Police Services Act* may still be the only enabling legislation in North America that provides for community policing principles in its preamble statement. Fourth, Canada's national police service, the Royal Canadian Mounted Police, along with provincial and municipal services, has formally adopted community policing.

Anecdotal evidence shows that the core strategy of problem-solving is alive and well, with Canadian police officers often winning top awards at conferences, even if sometimes disconnected from its twin core strategy of partnerships. The latter strategy is also commonly applied through the widespread use of community consultative committees. Some of these successes have been published through police- or government-sponsored reports. Good examples include reports on community policing in Edmonton (Koller, 1990) and in Montreal (Laudrum, 1998). However, there are still very few independently conducted research studies (Leighton, 1994), and the lack of empirical research in Canada is lamentable.

DOES COMMUNITY POLICING WORK?

Whether or not community policing is effective in reducing and preventing crime is a key concern about the current practice of community policing in Canada and elsewhere (Rosenbaum, 1994). Some claim that there is very little proof that community policing works or, if there is, community policing just makes people "feel good" by simply changing peoples' attitudes and levels of fear of being personally victimized. If it has an impact only on the perception of the crime problem rather than on solving the problem itself, then perhaps it belongs in the realm of "postmodern policing."

In the absence of a critical mass of rigorous empirical research on community policing in Canada, we can first look elsewhere for support. One well-known experiment is the City of New York in the 1990s where William Bratton, the commissioner of the New York Police Department (NYPD), claimed that the reduction in official crime was due to the effectiveness of community policing. Bratton had just taken over the NYPD after significantly reducing crime on the New York subway by applying the broken windows principle of cleaning up the signs of crime, especially graffiti. Beginning in 1993, crime statistics were produced daily and compared in weekly NYPD meetings (called "compstats") as feedback to police on their problem-solving and policing tactics (Silverman, 1999). However, critics have suggested that the emphasis on comparing statistics merely encourages precinct commanders to reduce crime rates at any cost. Hence the celebrated "compstat factor" may reflect as much the manipulation of crime and clearance rates as it does the success of problem-solving and other tactics that represent community policing's first core strategy. As well, there is little evidence of strengthened police–community relations.

To complicate the issue further, official rates for serious and violent crime declined for five years in a row across the United States, not just in New York City. In the end, it is difficult to untangle all the factors that contribute to a decline in crime. More affluent economic conditions and an aging society have as much to do with official crime levels as law enforcement and tougher laws do. The jury is still out on how much the decline in crime can be attributed to improved community policing of the broken windows variety and how much can be attributed to broad societal trends.

Meanwhile, in Canada, only three major evaluations of community-based policing programs provide the necessary empirical evidence. One described the history and development of the Metro Toronto Police mini-stations and found them to be well received by local residents (Murphy and de Verteuil, 1986; Murphy, 1988). Another study evaluated Victoria community police stations (Walker and Walker, 1989), finding that the majority of respondents were aware that a community station existed and that a significant proportion had also contacted one.

Perhaps one of the most rigorous evaluations of a community policing program conducted anywhere (Hornick et al., 1991) is of the Edmonton Police Service's Neighbourhood Foot Patrol Project, where 21 constables worked on foot based in mini-stations strategically located in selected neighbourhoods. The study reported that the project (1) significantly reduced the number of repeat calls for service in the beat neighbourhoods with foot patrol, (2) improved user satisfaction with police services, (3) improved constables' job satisfaction, and (4) increased constables' knowledge of the neighbourhoods and their problems. This pilot project led to the department-wide implementation of community policing.

This brief review of community policing in Canada suggests that (1) it is well beyond the stage of experimentation and demonstration, and (2) it is reflected in the daily operations of policing. On the other hand, we still find many police services where (1) it remains marooned as an add-on program of highly visible tactics, (2) the two core strategies are disconnected, (3) the tailoring of a specific package of tactics to specific community needs is not yet widespread, and (4) there is limited support for the approach at the working level.

While the evidence is still sketchy, we might still interpret it as suggesting that community policing has become "routinized." However, this does not necessarily mean it has been formally implemented in a systematic way on a department-wide basis. Instead, it is hypothesized here that community policing is now reflected in the everyday, routine policing operations and activities of most police departments in Canada.

One of the challenges in determining whether community policing works is identifying the appropriate criteria and indicators for success in terms of its effectiveness. Traditional performance indicators, such as crime rates, clearance rates, and response times, were developed for proving the effectiveness of the traditional policing model but are inappropriate for testing the effectiveness of community policing. Some of the indicators used in the Edmonton evaluation include: a reduction in the fear of being personally victimized, an increase in the level of police officer job satisfaction, a reduction in repeat calls for service from the same address based on a clear link with problem-solving exercises, and community satisfaction with police services in response to particular crime and disorder problems they have identified.

Research studies should build up from the street level of policing zones or beats by evaluating the effectiveness of particular community policing tactics to solve particular crime and disorder problems in particular neighbourhoods under specified conditions. In this way, a "logic model" can be constructed that establishes the causal linkages between the core community policing strategies and their intended outcomes on community safety. Such a logic model would enable the "performance story" of community policing to be better communicated, not just to the community and politicians but also to the police managers and police officers involved. This would then facilitate "evidence-based policing" (Sherman, 1998), such as the use of research and evaluation results by police managers (Schneider et al., 2000).

THE FUTURE OF COMMUNITY POLICING

What are the prospects for community policing surviving well into the twenty-first century? In the wake of the terrorist incidents on September 11, 2001, policing might have retrenched into the traditional model by concentrating permanently on combatting terrorism and other "hard crimes" such as organized crime. However, police agencies appear to have learned from their counterproductive, hard responses to the "Battle for Seattle" anti-WTO demonstrations in November 1999, the violent protests against the Summit of the Americas in Quebec City in April 2001, and the G20 Summit protests in Ottawa in November 2001. Subsequent police responses to generally nonviolent political protests have softened, as occurred during the G8 Summit meeting near Calgary in June 2002 and in Ottawa, where community policing tactics were used, such as the use of cycling gear rather than the confrontational combat outfit usually worn by police tactical squads. So rather than being eclipsed by the hard-policing, post–9-11 response to terrorism, policing responses now reflect the routinizing of community policing.

CONCLUSIONS

Is community policing just "something old, something new, something borrowed, and something blue?" For our assessment of whether it is "something old," we can look to the past and discover that problem-solving is not a new idea. Smart supervisors have always encouraged police officers to solve the underlying causes of similar crimes reoccurring in the same place. Enhancing community partnerships may also be an old idea. Smart police chiefs have always built strong ties with their communities because they could never keep the peace on their own. And smart police officers have always found that good working relationships with community members are a sound source of information and intelligence. The difference between traditional policing and recent developments is that community partnerships are now more formal and are often required by police management or by local government. An argument can be made, then, that community policing is essentially just something old that has now received a respectable name and academic blessing.

Is there "something new" about this old idea of community policing? There are good reasons why policing as it was done in the past is not completely suitable for modern society and its crime problems. First, communities are not what they used to be, and local geographical communities, while still alive, are anachronistic. The notion of community has kept pace with these changes through the broader concept of social networks. We now see society as having been transformed into a network of networks, a networked nation of mass communications and mass travel that is connected globally in a global electronic village, complete with global economics, global culture, and transnational organized crime and terrorism. With this radically changed environment for policing, both new and old approaches to crime and disorder problems are required. Community policing can also be applied to organized crime networks where police join forces in operations through a nationally and internationally networked police community. Consequently, we need both community policing and traditional policing in a balanced approach of complementary strategies.

Does community policing have "something borrowed?" Perhaps it is just a style of policing that was always done in rural areas and has simply been transplanted into urban policing. While there is some justification for this view, modern rural life has also been transformed by mass society. Further, the rural lifestyle is characterized as much by the oppressiveness of small town society and gossip as it is by its idyllic environment. Moreover, much of rural policing has been drawn into urban policing. So what is borrowed in community policing are the principles that may or may not have characterized small town and rural policing in the past.

Finally, what is "something blue" about community policing? Simply put, this is the colour of the uniform for the "broad blue line" of policing in partnership with the communities it serves. We can contrast this blue model with the brown model that represents the brown uniform of the paramilitary, command-and-control model of professional policing (Guth, 1987).

We might therefore conclude our assessment by declaring that community policing is indeed "something (relatively) old, something (slightly) new, something (much) borrowed, and something (symbolically) blue." While it may very well be the re-emergence, renewal, or revitalization of the original idea of urban public policing developed over 170 years ago in England by Sir Robert Peel, it is now a coherent approach that is adapted to the conditions of contemporary society, robustly supported by two core strategies, sustained by academic theory and critique, subjected to empirical research, endorsed by governments and police governing authorities, and applauded by the media and the public. Moreover, it has survived the test of police response to terrorism in a post–9-11 world.

DISCUSSION QUESTIONS

1. *How would you characterize the nature of the police presence in your community? Does it correspond to the community policing model outlined by Leighton, or has it changed as a result of the terrorist acts of September 11, 2001, to a more severe response to crime and disorder problems?*
2. *Building partnerships with communities is clearly at the heart of community policing. Do you think that closer relationships between the police and the*

communities they serve is a healthy thing, or is it something about which we should be suspicious?

3. *As noted earlier, recent public opinion polls show that Canadians have more confidence in the police than in any other branch of the criminal justice system. Do you think this high degree of confidence reflects the community policing movement or is it a product of the mass media, such as the "Mountie mystique"?*

FURTHER READINGS

Hornick, Joseph P., Barbara A. Burrows, Donna M. Phillips, and Barry Leighton. 1991. An impact evaluation of the Edmonton neighbourhood foot patrol program. *Canadian Journal of Program Evaluation* 6(1): 47–70.

Kelling, George, and Catherine Coles. 1996. *Fixing Broken Windows*. New York: Free Press.

Silverman, Eli B. 1999. *NYPD Battles Crime*. Boston: Northeastern University Press.

REFERENCES

Ericson, Richard. 1982. *Reproducing Order: A Study of Police Patrol Work*. Toronto: University of Toronto Press.

Ericson, Richard, and Kevin Haggerty. 1997. *Policing the Risk Society*. Toronto: University of Toronto Press.

Goldstein, Herman. 1979. Improving policing: A problem-oriented approach. *Crime and Delinquency* 25: 236–258.

Greene, Jack R., and Stephen D. Mastrofski, eds. 1988. *Community Policing: Rhetoric or Reality*. New York: Praeger.

Guth, DeLloyd J. 1987. The common law powers of police: The Anglo-Canadian tradition. Paper presented at the Canadian Law in History Conference, Carleton University, Ottawa, 8–10 June.

Hornick, Joseph P., Barbara A. Burrows, Donna M. Phillips, and Barry Leighton. 1991. An impact evaluation of the Edmonton neighbourhood foot patrol program. *Canadian Journal of Program Evaluation* 6(1): 47–70.

Kelling, George, and Catherine Coles. 1996. *Fixing Broken Windows*. New York: Free Press.

Kelling, George L., and Mark H. Moore. 1988. From political to reform to community: The evolving strategy of police. In J.R. Green and S.D. Mastrofski (Eds.), *Community Policing: Rhetoric or Reality*, (pp. 3–25). New York: Praeger.

Koller, Katherine. 1990. *Working the Beat: The Edmonton Neighborhood Foot Patrol*. Edmonton: Edmonton Police Service.

Laudrum, Kim. 1998. Measuring the results of community policing. *Canadian Police Chief Magazine*, July, 10–20.

Leighton, Barry. 1994. Community policing in Canada: An overview of experience and evaluations. In Dennis P. Rosenbaum (Ed.), *The Challenge of Community Policing: Testing the Promises*. Thousand Oaks, CA: Sage Publications.

———. 1991. Visions of community policing: Rhetoric and reality in Canada. *Canadian Journal of Criminology* 33(3–4): 485–522.

———. 1988. The concept of community in criminology: Toward a social network approach. *Journal of Research in Crime and Delinquency* 25(4): 351–374.

Mintzberg, Henry. 1996. Managing government, governing management. *Harvard Business Review* May–June, 75–83.

Murphy, Chris. 1991. *Problem-Oriented Policing*. Federal-Ontario Community Policing Report Series. Ottawa: Ministry of the Solicitor General of Canada.

———. 1988. Community problems, problem communities and community policing in Toronto. *Journal of Research in Crime and Delinquency* 25: 392–410.

Murphy, Christopher, and Jacques de Verteuil. 1986. *Metropolitan Toronto Community Policing Survey*. Ottawa: Ministry of the Solicitor General of Canada.

Murphy, Chris, and Graham Muir. 1984. *Community-based Policing: A Review of the Critical Issues*. Ottawa: Ministry of the Solicitor General of Canada.

Normandeau, André, and Barry Leighton. 1990. *The Future of Policing in Canada*. Ottawa: Solicitor General Canada.

Reiner, Robert. 1992. *The Politics of the Police*. Toronto: University of Toronto Press.

Rosenbaum, R. (ed.) 1994. *The Challenge of Community Policing: Testing the Promises*. Thousand Oaks, CA: Sage Publications.

Schneider, Frank W., Paul Pilon, Barry Horrobin, and Michael Sideris. 2000. Contributions of Evaluation Research to the Development of Community Policing in a Canadian City. *Canadian Journal of Program Evaluation* 15(1): 101–129.

Sherman, Lawrence W. 1998. Evidence-based policing. In *Ideas in American Policing*. Washington, DC: Police Foundation

Silverman, Eli B. 1999. *NYPD Battles Crime*. Boston: Northeastern University Press.

Skogan, Wesley, and Susan Hartnett. 1997. *Community Policing Chicago Style*. New York: Oxford University Press.

Sparrow, Malcolm, Mark Moore, and David Kennedy. 1990. *Beyond 911: A New Era for Policing*. New York: Basic Books.

Walker, Christopher R., and S. Gail Walker. 1989. *The Victoria Community Police Stations: An Exercise in Innovation*. Ottawa: Canadian Police College.

Wilson, James Q., and George Kelling. 1982. Broken windows. *Atlantic Monthly*, March, 29–38.

CHAPTER 4
Plea Bargaining

INTRODUCTION

Judges are frequently criticized for imposing lenient sentences, particularly for crimes of violence (although the news media do not always give the full story). Another important source of public dissatisfaction concerns the practice known as "plea bargaining." Many people were outraged when Karla Homolka was sentenced to only 12 years in prison for her role in the Bernardo murders. That sentence, which was universally denounced as too lenient, came about as a result of a plea bargain. The public was also outraged a few years earlier when a contract killer, who had been responsible for over 20 murders, pleaded guilty to manslaughter and became eligible for parole after having served seven years. This sentence was also the result of negotiations over his plea. In return for pleading guilty to the lesser charge of manslaughter, the offender provided authorities with a great deal of information about organized crime in Montreal.

Representative public polls have shown that people have a very negative perception of plea bargaining (Cohen and Doob, 1989). As with sentencing, however, our perceptions of this phenomenon may well be at odds with reality. We should not let examples of plea bargaining that led to unpalatable consequences determine our reaction to all instances in which discussions take place between the Crown and the counsel for the accused. As the following reading makes clear, plea bargaining consists of more than a simple exchange in which the offender receives a lenient sentence for having agreed to plead guilty. The public has the perception that plea bargaining always works to the offender's advantage at a cost to the state or the victim. However, systematic research into plea bargaining suggests that this perception is not necessarily accurate.

Plea Bargaining

Curt Griffiths and *Simon Verdun-Jones,* Simon Fraser University

Plea bargaining has, for some time, been one of the most controversial, and perhaps least understood, aspects of the Canadian criminal justice system. At first, the idea of accused persons bargaining for lenience behind closed doors is singularly unattractive. However, the reality of the situation is much more complex than this popular image would lead one to believe.

The Law Reform Commission of Canada (1975:45) once defined a plea bargain (also called "plea negotiation") as "any agreement by the accused to plead guilty in return for the promise of some benefit." Subsequently, the Commission (1989:3–4) indicated that it preferred the term "plea agreement," which it defined as "an agreement by the accused to plead guilty in return for the prosecutor's agreeing to take or refrain from taking a particular course of action." However, the term "plea bargain" is generally used in a much broader sense by those involved in criminal justice research. As Verdun-Jones and Hatch (1985:1) note, plea bargaining is really a compendious term used to describe a wide diversity of behaviours that occur among actors in the court system. The police, the Crown, and defence counsel may engage in behaviours ranging from simple discussions through negotiations to agreements. Clearly, discussions and negotiations may not ultimately lead to any form of agreement between the parties; however, these behaviours have generally been considered by researchers as falling within the concept of plea bargaining (Cousineau and Verdun-Jones, 1979).

Some researchers have questioned whether the terms plea negotiations and plea bargains are appropriate given the so-called realities of the criminal justice process. For example, Ericson and Baranek (1982) question whether the word "negotiate" is meaningful in light of the stark imbalance of power between the police and the Crown on the one hand and the defendant on the other. Furthermore, they argue that it is more realistic to view the accused's decisions within the criminal justice system as being "coerced" or "manipulated" and that, therefore, any accommodation with the Crown will scarcely be perceived by the accused as being a genuine "bargain."

Furthermore, even where an agreement is actually reached, it is perhaps a little misleading to refer to it as a "plea bargain" because, as we shall see, neither the Crown nor the defendant has any guarantee that such an agreement will ultimately be carried into effect by the sentencing judge, who is not bound by anything that has been agreed to by the parties concerned. In any event, we shall use the term plea bargaining in the following discussion because of its widespread use in the criminal justice research literature (just keep in mind that the term covers a broad range of potential interactions that may occur between the Crown and the defence in Canada).

If plea bargaining is concerned with reaching an agreement to secure a concession from the Crown in return for the accused pleading guilty, what concessions may the defence seek from Crown counsel? Broadly speaking, these benefits may be considered to fall into three overlapping categories: (1) promises relating to the charges to be laid; (2) promises relating to the ultimate sentence to be meted out by the court; and (3) promises relating to the facts that the Crown is willing to bring to the attention of court (assuming that the trial judge's knowledge of such facts will have a significant impact on the sentencing decision). Verdun-Jones and Hatch (1985:3) suggested the Crown might promise the following list of potential benefits.

Charge bargaining:

(a) reduction of the charge to a lesser or included offence;
(b) withdrawal or stay of other charges or the promise not to proceed on other possible charges; and
(c) promise not to charge friends or family of the defendant.

Sentence bargaining:

(a) promise to proceed summarily rather than by way of indictment;
(b) promise that the Crown will make a particular recommendation in relation to sentence;
(c) promise not to oppose defence counsel's sentence recommendation;
(d) promise not to appeal against sentence imposed at trial;
(e) promise not to apply for a more severe penalty (under section 665 of the *Code*);
(f) promise not to apply for a period of preventive detention under section 753 of the *Code*;
(g) promise to make a representation as to the place of imprisonment, type of treatment, etc.; and
(h) promise to arrange sentencing before a particular judge.

Fact bargaining:

(a) promise not to "volunteer" information detrimental to the accused (for example, not adducing evidence as to the defendant's previous convictions under section 255 of the *Code*); and
(b) promise not to mention a circumstance of the offence that may be interpreted by the judge as an aggravating factor (and, therefore, deserving a greater degree of severity of punishment).

The Official Response to Plea Bargaining

While it has probably been practiced for many years, plea bargaining was traditionally frowned upon, and most individuals involved in the criminal justice system would not openly admit that it took place (Cousineau and Verdun-Jones, 1979). Until relatively recently, plea bargaining was held in such low regard that the Law Reform Commission of Canada (1975:14) contended that it was "something for which a decent criminal justice system has no place." However, such attitudes now appear to be undergoing a significant degree of change. Only a decade after its extremely negative comment on the practice, the Law Reform Commission (1984) referred to plea bargaining, in one of its working papers, almost as a routine part of the court process and, by 1989, the Commission (1989:8) contended that "plea negotiation is not an inherently shameful practice" and recommended that the practice become more open and accountable.

A similar evolution of thought is apparent on the part of the judiciary, which was very critical of the practice until fairly recently (Cousineau and Verdun-Jones, 1979). In a case decided in 1979, a justice of the Supreme Court of Canada mentioned, without any apparent disapproval (and, indeed, almost as an afterthought) that the guilty plea had been obtained as a result of a plea bargain. Even professional bodies, such as the Canadian Bar Association, appear to have sanctioned certain forms of plea bargaining. The *Code of Professional Conduct* of the Canadian Bar Association (1988) recognizes the legitimacy of a defence lawyer's entering into a "tentative" plea agreement with the Crown and sets out ethical guidelines for the regulation of such conduct (Verdun-Jones and Hatch, 1985:22–23).

While they have not openly endorsed the practice of plea bargaining, Canadian courts have nevertheless subtly condoned and even encouraged the practice by establishing an atmosphere that permits it to flourish unchecked (Verdun-Jones and Hatch, 1985:29). In most cases, Canadian courts do not actively investigate the circumstances surrounding the entry of a guilty plea before they accept it. If the accused is represented by defence counsel, the trial judge will normally refrain from conducting a meticulous inquiry into the circumstances surrounding a guilty plea (Cousineau and Verdun-Jones, 1979; Watson, 1991:174). In these circumstances, it is unlikely that there will be any investigation into the nature of the inducements offered to an accused person to plead guilty or any inquiry into whether the accused really understands the full implications of any plea bargain into which he or she may have entered. Indeed, it may well be argued that the lack of a requirement under Canadian law that a judge ferret out the critical factors that may have led to the defendant's decision to plead guilty has effectively created an environment in which it is possible for Crown and defence counsel to enter into plea bargains behind the inscrutable veil of secrecy.

The courts may also give some tacit encouragement to the practice of plea bargaining as a consequence of the widespread belief that accused persons entering guilty pleas may legitimately expect to receive a more lenient sentence than if their guilt had been determined by a trial (Fitzgerald, 1990; Watson,

1991:198–200). This form of "sentence discounting" has been referred to as "tacit plea bargaining." A more lenient sentence may be justified on the basis that the guilty plea indicates remorse, that the community is spared the cost of a trial, that the victim does not have to undergo the trauma of testifying, or that the accused has cooperated with the police. These justifications are necessary in order to avoid the impression that accused persons may be penalized for exercising their right to a trial. In one case, for example, the judge stated:

> It is a fundamental concept of our system of justice that a person accused of crime is entitled to demand that the Crown prove his guilt by a fair and impartial trial. There is nothing that the court should ever do to whittle down or undercut that fundamental principle. At the same time, it would be unrealistic not to recognize that if everyone demanded a full and complete trial, our system of justice would come to an abrupt halt. It is for that reason that those who are guilty, and wish to so plead, should be given special consideration when they appear before the court.

By encouraging guilty pleas in this manner, the courts appear to be facilitating the practice of plea bargaining. However, there is, to date, little evidence to establish that those who plead guilty do, in fact, receive more lenient sentences than those who go to trial. Solomon's analysis of data taken from a study of the fictionally titled "Robert County," Ontario, did not reveal any evidence to support the notion that there was a penalty imposed for pleading not guilty. Solomon (1983:39) notes that in only one of the seven cases in which there was a conviction after a fully contested trial did the offender receive a more severe punishment than that received by those who had pleaded guilty to the same offences. However, Solomon (1983:39) rightly notes that these data are "too scanty to be conclusive."

Nevertheless, most of the defence lawyers in Robert County did genuinely believe that there was a discount for pleading guilty (Solomon, 1983:41), and this belief may well have exerted a strong influence over their clients' decision as to whether or not to plead guilty. Certainly, lawyers interviewed by Ericson and Baranek (1982) noted that the promise of a more lenient sentence can be extremely persuasive in convincing a reluctant client to plead guilty.

The courts have also facilitated plea bargaining practices by encouraging the submission of sentence recommendations by the Crown and defence (Verdun-Jones and Hatch, 1985:34). There is evidence that some Canadian courts are prepared to encourage joint sentence recommendations by the Crown and defence. Since many Canadian courts appear to permit, and frequently accept, such sentencing recommendations, they encourage plea bargaining by giving Crown counsel a valuable commodity to bargain with: in other words, a favourable sentence recommendation may be exchanged for a guilty plea.

However, the courts have consistently emphasized that they have absolute discretion in sentencing matters, and no particular recommendation, even one made as part of a plea bargain, is binding on the sentencing judge. Nevertheless, as Ruby (1987:74) points out, such sentencing recommendations are "customarily given considerable weight," and the Quebec Court of Appeal has stated that, while judges are in no way bound by a joint recommendation of Crown and defence counsel as to sentence, they "usually pay a good deal of attention to a common recommendation by experienced and competent counsel."

EMPIRICAL RESEARCH INTO PLEA BARGAINING IN CANADA

The empirical research conducted in Canada suggests that plea bargaining does occur at least in certain jurisdictions in this country. However, a number of these studies are affected by major methodological problems (Cousineau and Verdun-Jones, 1979). More recently, a group of researchers at the University of Toronto's Centre of Criminology conducted a major study of discretionary decision-making in the criminal justice process in the course of which a wealth of data based on a variety of research methods, including direct observation of the plea bargaining process, was uncovered. One hundred and one accused persons were tracked through the criminal justice system from arrest to sentence. The data from this study have been reported in several sources, the most comprehensive of which is a book by Ericson and Baranek (1982). A number of different research techniques were employed in the collection of the data. Verbatim transcripts were kept of interviews with the accused and interviews with lawyers; recordings were also made of conversations in the Crown attorney's office. Researchers also observed the court appearances of the defendants in the sample. This study represents the first time researchers have actually been able to document the dynamics involved in the process of plea bargaining.

Ericson and Baranek (1982:117) employ the term "plea discussions" rather than "plea bargaining" because the former expression makes it clear that discussions may be entered into without an agreement ever being reached. They concluded (1982:121) that "plea discussions were a widespread and integral part of the order out of court." In this respect, they found (1982:117–18) that of the lawyers for 80 accused persons who were interviewed, lawyers for as many as 57 accused said that they had entered into plea discussions. Furthermore, they found (1982:121) that participation in plea discussions was not confined to Crown and defence counsel; indeed, the police were frequently involved at various stages in the plea discussion process.

Ericson and Baranek suggest that the existence of multiple charges appears to constitute a major element in the circumstances that lead to plea discussions taking place. Of the 23 accused whose lawyers did *not* engage in such discussions, 17 had only one charge laid against them (as compared with only 9 of the 57 accused whose lawyers were involved in plea discussions). The authors suggest that this underlines the importance of multiple charging as a vital component of the plea discussion process in Canada; without the existence of multiple charges, the defence could not negotiate for the withdrawal of some charge(s) in return for the entry of a guilty plea to others. Lawyers who engaged in discussions with the Crown said that withdrawal of charges was the major topic of conversation (Ericson and Baranek, 1982:119).

Given that there was widespread involvement in plea discussions, what was the outcome of such involvement? The striking finding made by Ericson and Baranek (1982:143) was that, although many of the lawyers engaged in plea discussions, only about a quarter of them stated that they had reached an agreement that could be considered a bargain. For this group of lawyers, the most frequently mentioned bargain was one that included a sentence concession. Of the remaining lawyers who entered plea discussions, 12% stated that they had not reached an agreement, while lawyers for the remaining 88% claimed that the agreement reached brought no real advantage for the accused. More than half of the lawyers (representing 23 accused) who thought that an agreement had brought no tangible benefit stated that the charges withdrawn or reduced in their cases did not represent a concession because such charges were merely the result of overcharging by the police in the first place (Ericson and Baranek, 1982:145).

Solomon (1983) also analyzed the data gathered from the study conducted by the Centre of Criminology at the University of Toronto. He contends that the data suggest that plea bargaining occurred more frequently in the provincial courts of Robert County than might have been expected from a reading of the Canadian literature on the topic. However, as is the case with Ericson and Baranek, he contends that plea bargaining "did not result in important concessions for the accused." In the Provincial Court, almost 80% of the criminal cases that were not withdrawn by the Crown terminated with guilty pleas, and 60% of these cases involved plea discussions. It appears that the discussions between defence counsel and the Crown and/or police usually focused on the charges to which the accused would plead guilty rather than on the sentence (although there was some discussion of the approach that the Crown would adopt at the sentencing stage).

Plea agreements resulted in the dropping of charges (which were often not justified in the first place) and at least a tacit agreement about the Crown's recommendation as to sentence. However, Solomon (1983:37) points out that there was no clear relationship between the charges to which the accused ultimately pleaded guilty and the sentence handed down by the court. Furthermore, the sentencing recommendations made by the Crown had no direct impact upon the sentence actually handed down by the court. In these circumstances, an accused person who entered into a plea arrangement with the Crown had no guarantee that his or her guilty plea would make any difference whatsoever to the ultimate outcome of the case.

DISCUSSION QUESTIONS

1. *The large volume of criminal cases being processed by the system and the high percentage (approximately 90 percent) of accuseds who plead guilty means that abolishing plea bargaining would swamp the courts with additional trials. Abolition of this practice is therefore unlikely. Even if it were possible, however, would it necessarily be a good thing?*
2. *One criticism of plea bargaining is that it is invisible. Discussions between the Crown and the defence take place in corridors, in offices, and not in open court. One possible reform is to have all discussions regarding plea bargaining take place in open court, in front of a judge. Would this be an improvement? What problems might arise if this approach to plea negotiations were adopted?*
3. *Victims are sometimes shocked to learn that the Crown has accepted a plea to a lesser, included offence rather than proceed to trial on a more serious charge, with the accused pleading not guilty. Victims are seldom consulted or kept apprised of developments in negotiations with the accused. Should individual victims have a greater say in plea negotiations? Should they be given the power to overrule any plea arrangement?*

FURTHER READINGS

Ericson, R., and P. Baranek. 1982. *The Ordering of Justice: A Study of Accused Persons as Dependants in the Criminal Process.* Toronto: University of Toronto Press.

Law Reform Commission of Canada. 1989. *Plea Discussions and Agreements.* Working Paper No. 60. Ottawa: Law Reform Commission of Canada.

Verdun-Jones, S., and A. Hatch. 1985. *Plea Bargaining and Sentencing Guidelines.* Ottawa: Department of Justice Canada.

REFERENCES

Canadian Bar Association. 1988. *Code of Professional Conduct.* Ottawa: Canadian Bar Association.

Cohen, S., and A. Doob. 1989. Public attitudes towards plea bargaining. *Criminal Law Quarterly* 32:85–109.

Cousineau, D., and S. Verdun-Jones. 1979. Evaluating research into plea bargaining in Canada and the United States: Pitfalls facing the policymakers. *Canadian Journal of Criminology* 21:293–309.

Ericson, R., and P. Baranek. 1982. *The Ordering of Justice: A Study of Accused Persons as Dependants in the Criminal Process.* Toronto: University of Toronto Press.

Fitzgerald, O. 1990. *The Guilty Plea and Summary Justice.* Toronto: Carswell.

Law Reform Commission of Canada. 1975. *Criminal Procedure: Control of the Process.* Working Paper No. 15. Ottawa: Information Canada.

————. 1984. *Disclosure by the Prosecution.* Report No. 22. Ottawa: Ministry of Supply and Services.

————. 1989. *Plea Discussions and Agreements.* Working Paper No. 60. Ottawa: Law Reform Commission of Canada.

Ruby, C. 1987. *Sentencing,* 3d ed. Toronto: Butterworths.

Solomon, P. 1983. *Criminal Justice Policy, From Research to Reform.* Toronto: Butterworths.

Verdun-Jones, S., and A. Hatch. 1985. *Plea Bargaining and Sentencing Guidelines.* Ottawa: Department of Justice Canada.

Watson, J. 1991. Guilty pleas. *Criminal Law Quarterly* 33:163–203.

CHAPTER 5
Custody in the Community

INTRODUCTION

Canada has traditionally had a high rate of incarceration relative to other western nations. Although we have known about the problem for many years, little headway has been made in reducing the number of offenders who are sent to prison. In 1996, Parliament took several steps toward addressing the issue. Judges were directed, by means of new provisions in the *Criminal Code*, to use alternative sanctions to imprisonment, wherever possible and appropriate. In addition, Parliament approved the creation of a new alternative to custody, known as the conditional sentence of imprisonment. This is a term of imprisonment, but one that the offender serves at home rather than in a correctional facility. Since 1996, this new sanction has been widely used by trial judges and has evolved considerably. This chapter explores the nature and evolution of the conditional sentence of imprisonment.

Serving Time in the Community: The Conditional Sentence of Imprisonment
Julian V. Roberts, University of Ottawa

When most people think of imprisonment, prisons come naturally to mind. However, since 1996, many offenders in Canada have been serving terms of custody in the community (see Roberts and Cole, 1999). They have been sentenced to a conditional sentence of imprisonment. Offenders who receive a conditional sentence must obey a number of conditions that are common to all; as well, judges craft specific conditions to fit the individual offender. For example, an offender with an alcohol problem may be ordered to follow an officially recognized treatment program. Many offenders are required to observe a curfew, and some are confined to their residence under a house arrest condition. If the offender violates one or more of the conditions imposed by the court, he or she will be brought back to court for a breach hearing. Unless there was a good reason the condition was violated, the judge will then send the offender to prison for the remaining time on the sentence. Only some offenders are eligible for a conditional sentence; in fact, the *Criminal Code* specifies a number of criteria that must be met before a court can consider imposing this sentence. First, the judge must impose a term of custody. In other words, a conditional sentence can replace only a term of "real jail"; it cannot be used for a case that might otherwise receive probation.

Second, the offence cannot be one of the crimes for which the *Code* prescribes a mandatory sentence of imprisonment. For example, no offender convicted of murder can serve the sentence in the community, as murder carries a mandatory sentence of life imprisonment. Third, the judge must be satisfied that if the offender serves the sentence of imprisonment at home, this will not endanger the safety of the community. In other words, offenders who represent a risk to reoffend are not eligible for this sentence. Finally, the judge must be satisfied that serving the sentence in the community would be consistent with the purpose and principles contained in other sections of the *Criminal Code.*

The conditional sentence has been a source of some controversy over the past few years. To some, it is a legal paradox: an offender is sentenced to a term of custody, but is then allowed to return home, albeit with restrictions on his or her liberty. Critics have suggested that in many cases a conditional sentence is not much different from probation, in that the offender is spending time under supervision in the community. Although a conditional sentence is supposed to be the equivalent of a term of custody (since it is a form of custody rather than an alternate sanction), many people believe that it is much less severe. After all, how can spending time at home be as harsh as being in prison, even if time actually spent in prison will, in most cases, be reduced by release on parole? Opposition has also been aroused when an offender convicted of a serious crime of violence has been sentenced to a conditional sentence.

Some of these criticisms are valid; others seem wide of the mark. As we shall see in this chapter, most (but by no means all) conditional sentence orders include some tough conditions, such as curfews and house arrest. This explains why some offenders are said to prefer a term of "real custody" to a conditional sentence. Since an important Supreme Court judgment in 2000 (*R. v. Proulx*), conditional sentences have become tougher. And, although conditional sentences can be (and in fact are) imposed for very serious crimes such as sexual assault and manslaughter, such cases are quite rare, and there are often important mitigating circumstances present.

On the other hand, advocates of conditional sentencing have argued that a conditional sentence can be as aversive as actual custody. If the offender is serving the sentence in a small community, everyone will know he or she is under a court order, whereas being in prison is more anonymous: the offender may simply have moved. Nevertheless, advocates believe that conditional sentencing represents the future, and that as a society we should not be so eager to imprison people. They point out that Canada has one of the highest rates of incarceration among western nations and that the conditional sentence represents a way to reduce the use of custody in a safe and principled manner.

This chapter summarizes how the conditional sentence of imprisonment has evolved since its introduction in 1996. Created as part of the general sentencing reform, the conditional sentence of imprisonment has evolved considerably, from a sanction that was conceived primarily for property offenders with no, or few, previous convictions, to a disposition that the Supreme Court considered appropriate even for an individual who had assembled a collection of explosive devices, and who, according to consensual expert testimony, represented a threat to the community. In *R. v. Knoblauch*, the Court upheld the imposition of a conditional sentence to be served in a secure psychiatric facility.

The experience of serving a conditional sentence has also undergone a transformation. Most early conditional sentences required offenders to comply with only a few conditions. Today, many (but by no means all) conditional sentence offenders must adhere to strict curfews or live under house arrest.

EFFECT OF CONDITIONAL SENTENCING ON PRISON ADMISSIONS

Perhaps the most basic question about conditional sentencing is whether it has achieved its goal of reducing the number of admissions to provincial correctional institutions. In the early years, some apprehension was expressed that judges would use the sanction to expand, rather than contract, the net of penal control. This does not appear to have happened. Although a small number of conditional sentences have been imposed in cases that formerly would have attracted a term of probation, the overwhelming effect of the introduction of conditional sentencing has been a reduction in the use of custody on a scale unparalleled in western nations. Over the period 1997 to 2001, more than 50,000 individual offenders who would have been sent to prison have served, or are currently serving, their terms of imprisonment in the community (see Roberts and Gabor, 2003). This represents a drop of 13 percent in the rate of admissions to custody over this period.

OFFENCES FOR WHICH CONDITIONAL SENTENCES HAVE BEEN IMPOSED

What kinds of offences typically result in the imposition of a conditional sentence? The answer depends on the province. As can be seen in Table 5.1, the proportion of conditional sentences imposed in 2000/01 for crimes involving violence varied from 12 percent in Prince Edward Island to 43 percent in Manitoba. This suggests that different attitudes to the use of conditional sentencing have arisen among judges across the country, with the inevitable consequence that the probability of an offender receiving a conditional sentence also varies considerably, depending upon the province in which he or she is sentenced.

LENGTH OF CONDITIONAL SENTENCES

Conditional sentences have become longer over the past couple of years. There are several explanations for this change. First, as judges become more comfortable with the sanction, they are likely to use it for a wider range of offences, including some more serious offences that are likely to attract longer sentences. Statistics on the number of conditional sentences reveals a clear increase in the use of conditional sentencing from 1997/98–2000/01. In most provinces, the rate of conditional sentences imposed increased significantly. For example, in Saskatchewan, the rate per 10,000 adults charged rose from 290 to 390 in just four years, an increase of 34 percent. This increase is unaffected by changes in the use of other sanctions.

The second reason for anticipating an increase in the average length of conditional sentences imposed relates to the Supreme Court guideline judgment in *R. v. Proulx*. In the early days of conditional sentencing, most judges appeared to tie the conditional sentence to the term of custody that it replaced. Thus if a judge sentenced an offender to six months in jail and then

Table 5.1 *Conditional Sentences by Offence Category, 2000/01*

Offence Category	P.E.I.	N.S.	Ontario	Manitoba	Sask.	Alberta	B.C.
Violence	12%	28%	33%	43%	38%	26%	24%
Property	52%	30%	38%	28%	37%	46%	37%
Drugs	24%	17%	19%	9%	n/a	20%	27%
Other	12%	25%	10%	20%	25%	8%	12%
Total	**100%**	**100%**	**100%**	**100%**	**100%**	**100%**	**100%**

Source: Correctional Services Program, Conditional Sentencing Special Study, June 2002.

decided that the sentence could be served in the community, the conditional sentence should also be six months in duration.

However, in the *Proulx* judgment, the Supreme Court took the position that the length of a conditional sentence need not be exactly the same length as the term of custody that it replaces (see *R. v. Proulx*, note 5 at para 127). This direction frees judges to impose, for example, a 12-month conditional sentence instead of a 6-month sentence of custody. The trends confirm that the average length of conditional sentences has increased, although the effect is not overwhelming. Table 5.2 demonstrates the shift toward longer conditional sentence orders, by providing the percentage of conditional sentences longer than 12 months in eight provinces. As shown, the proportion of longer orders increased in all provinces, although it was relatively modest in some jurisdictions.

CONDITIONS IMPOSED

Section 742.3(1) of the *Code* prescribes a series of compulsory conditions, applicable to all conditional sentence orders. However, pursuant to s. 742.3(2), judges have the discretion to impose a wide range of other conditions, including abstaining from alcohol, providing for the care of dependants, and attending a treatment program approved by the province.

In addition, according to s. 742.3(2)(f), the court may also order the offender to "comply with such other reasonable conditions as the court considers desirable, subject to any regulations made under subsection 738(2), for securing the good conduct of the offender and for preventing a repetition by the offender of the same offence or the commission of other offences." Any statistical portrait of conditional sentencing must therefore examine the pat-

Table 5.2 *Percentage of Conditional Sentences Longer than 12 Months, 1997/98 to 2000/01*

	1997/98	2000/01
Alberta	17%	32%
Manitoba	14%	23%
Prince Edward Island	3%	10%
Nova Scotia	8%	11%
Quebec	18%	27%
Saskatchewan	14%	18%
Ontario	11%	14%
British Columbia	10%	11%

Source: Correctional Services Program, Conditional Sentencing Special Study, *2002, at 5.*

tern of conditions imposed on offenders and the consequence of these conditions on compliance rates.

Table 5.3 provides data on the conditions imposed in Ontario and Manitoba in 2000/01, the most recent year for which these data are available. The table provides an indication of the kinds of conditions imposed and the differences between two jurisdictions. For example, house arrest was significantly more likely to be ordered as a condition in Manitoba: 47 percent of offenders had this restriction on their liberty, compared to only 10 percent in Ontario. These differences reflect differences in the cases sentenced in the two provinces as well as different judicial attitudes to the use of this sanction.

Table 5.3 *Conditions Imposed on Conditional Sentence Offenders, Ontario and Manitoba, 2000/01*

Condition	Ontario	Manitoba
Abstain from drugs/alcohol	33%	79%
Weapons restriction	19%	22%
Community service	22%	32%
Alcohol/drug rehabilitation	44%	37%
Other treatment program	n/a	55%
Association restriction	35%	43%
House arrest	10%	47%
Curfew	44%	43%
Maintain employment	16%	7%
Maintain residence	47%	48%
Restitution	10%	8%
Education	10%	13%
Other (average number)	100% (3.8)	100% (1.6)

Note: column totals exceed 100% due to imposition of multiple conditions.
Source: *Correctional Services Program,* Conditional Sentencing Special Study, *2002.*

CONDITIONAL SENTENCES HAVE BECOME TOUGHER

Conditional sentences have generally become tougher in recent years. For example, in Ontario, there has been a significant increase in the proportion of offenders on whom a curfew is imposed, rising from less than one in five to almost half the sample in just four years. This increase in the use of one of the most punitive conditions reflects a number of influences.

First, if judges in 2000/01 are using conditional sentences for more serious cases than would have been the case in 1997/98, the imposition of a curfew represents a way of ensuring that these cases are subject to a more severe sanction. Second, one of the unmistakable messages from the Supreme Court in its guideline judgment regarding conditional sentencing was that "conditions such as house arrest or strict curfews should be the norm, not the exception"(*R. v. Proulx*, note 5 at paragraph 36). A conditional sentence is a term of imprisonment and as such should attempt to re-create, in the community, some of the restrictions on an offender's life that prison imposes. If conditional sentence offenders are deemed to be serving a term of imprisonment, perhaps it is only reasonable to expect them to adhere to a curfew.

An expansion of the range of conditional sentences to include more serious cases would necessitate an increase in the number and severity of optional conditions imposed. Higher risk offenders serving sentences in the community require more intense supervision and more rigorous restrictions on their lifestyle. As well, offenders convicted of more serious crimes should face more severe restrictions on their liberty, in order to preserve the codified and fundamental principle of proportionality (see s. 718.1 of the *Criminal Code*). This principle requires that two offenders convicted of crimes of differing seriousness should be sentenced to sentences of variable onerousness. If both offenders are eligible for a conditional sentence, a distinction can be made between them either by varying the duration of their conditional sentences, the conditions attached to their conditional sentences, or some combination of both strategies.

It is reasonable to expect, therefore, an increase in the number and severity of optional conditions imposed on offenders serving conditional sentences. And indeed this is what the data reveal. In Ontario this tendency can be seen most clearly in the increase, over time, in the number of additional conditions imposed. In 1997/98, offenders serving conditional sentences were required to observe on average 2.3 conditions; the number of conditions rose to 3.8 within the brief span of four years. Similarly, in Manitoba, house arrest was imposed in only 5 percent of cases in 1997/98 but almost half the cases in 2000/01. As well, the number of additional conditions increased to the point that the average offender was required to adhere to almost 2 other conditions, in addition to those identified in Table 5.3 and the statutory conditions imposed on all conditional sentence offenders.

SUCCESS RATES OF CONDITIONAL SENTENCES TO DATE

Some critics of conditional sentencing are apprehensive that the offenders serving these sentences may represent a risk to the community. The limited statistics show that the rate of successful completions is quite high, although it has been dropping recently. Thus the successful completion rate of conditional sentence orders in Manitoba fell from 78 percent in 1997/98 to 63 percent in 2000/01. The increase in failure rate is largely accounted for by violations of conditions (see Table 5.4), which rose from 9 percent to 21 percent of all orders, rather than allegations of fresh offending.

Table 5.4 *Outcomes of Completed Conditional Sentence Orders, Manitoba*

	1997/98	1998/99	1999/00	2000/01
Successful completion	78%	79%	71%	63%
Breach with new offence	4%	2%	8%	9%
Breach of condition	9%	8%	18%	22%
Termination (cause unknown)	9%	11%	3%	6%
Total	100%	100%	100%	100%

Source: *Correctional Services Program,* Conditional Sentencing Special Study, *2002.*

A similar trend emerges in Saskatchewan. The rate of successful completion of conditional sentence orders dropped annually from 87 percent in 1997/98, to 85 percent, then to 80 percent, and finally to 77 percent in 2000/01. In all probability this trend also reflects the increased number and severity of conditions. For example, in 1997/98, only 4 percent of conditional sentence orders carried a curfew condition. This percentage rose steadily, and by 2000/01, slightly over one-quarter of offenders were ordered to abide by a curfew. If trends toward lower success rates continue, they will fuel criticism of—and undermine judicial confidence in—the disposition.

RESPONDING TO BREACHES OF CONDITIONAL SENTENCE ORDERS

Offenders who are found to have breached the conditions of their orders face different judicial responses depending on the province in which the offender resides. This issue has generated considerable controversy. The theory underlying any conditional sentence is that it imposes one punishment (community imprisonment), while threatening a more severe one (committal to prison) if the conditions of the imposed punishment are violated.

If the threatened penalty is severe enough, it offers the offender a prudential incentive to respect the conditions of the conditional sentence. It is for this reason that the conditional sentencing literature is replete with references to the "Sword of Damocles" image. Damocles was obliged to remain motionless while a sword hung—suspended by horsehair alone—over his head. He knew that one false move would result in the sword's dropping upon his neck, with unpleasant—and permanent—consequences.

The breach arrangements created by the enabling legislation have been criticized for not providing a sufficiently credible threat (see Roberts, 1997). After all, faced with an unjustified breach, courts have the discretion, under s. 742.6(9) to (a) amend the conditions, (b) suspend the order and commit the offender to custody for part of the remaining time on the order, (c) terminate the order and commit the offender to custody for the remainder of the time to run, or (d) simply do nothing and allow the order to continue.

Section 742.6(9) thus provides judges with a range of responses for the sound reason of allowing a court to respond with some indulgence to minor breaches, or possibly breaches that occur late in the life of the order. Offenders who have been informed of the range of possibilities by their counsel may not share Damocles' sense of imminent threat. Like so many features of the conditional sentence of imprisonment, this one has a cost too; the degree of flexibility can only undermine the deterrent power of a conditional sentence order.

Table 5.5 provides a breakdown of outcomes of those breach hearings in Ontario in which the offender was found to have breached the order without justification. First, however, it may be of interest to note the statistic regarding the outcome of the breach allegation. The percentage of breach hearings in which the allegation was proven has been fairly constant over the four-year period: 74 percent of allegations were proven in 1997/98 and 73 percent in 2000/01. The high percentage of proven breach allegations can be explained by the fact that breaches of conditional sentence orders need only be proved on a balance of probabilities, pursuant to s. 742.6(9) of the *Criminal Code*. This is in contrast to breaches of probation that, since they constitute a new offence, must be proved beyond a reasonable doubt.

As for the response to a proven breach, these data show, for the most recent year, an exact split: half the hearings in which breach of conditions was demonstrated resulted in committal to custody for some period; half the time the offender was permitted to continue serving the sentence in the community, albeit with amended conditions in some cases. It is interesting to note that the Supreme Court direction to judges in *Proulx* ("where an offender breaches a condition without reasonable excuse, there should be a presumption that the offender serve the remainder of his or her sentence in jail")— was seldom followed. The offender was committed to custody for the remainder of the sentence in less than one-quarter of cases (see Table 5.5).

The Ontario data show some modest evidence of an increased judicial inclination over time to respond to breach with committal to custody. In the first two years (1997 to 99), 21 percent of offenders were sent to prison for some period of time; in the two most recent years (1999 to 2001), this rose to 26 percent. The percentage of offenders committed for the duration of the order has been fairly stable over the four-year period. At the end of the day, however, conditional sentence offenders who are found to have breached their orders are as likely to remain in the community as to be committed to prison; this will trouble some observers and criminal justice professionals.

Data from the province of Manitoba are provided in Table 5.6, from which it can be seen that judges in that province have adopted a more rigorous response to breach of conditional sentence orders. In the two most recent years, over three-quarters of offenders found to have breached their orders were imprisoned, and almost half of all proven breaches were sent to prison for the duration of the order. Thus the nature of judicial response to breach varies across the country. Can this variation be explained by characteristics associated with the cases? Is it possible for example, that judges in Manitoba could have been confronted with more serious breaches? It seems unlikely; a more plausible explanation is that the differences reflect variable judicial attitudes to breaches.

CONCLUSION

Although the conditional sentence has been part of the sentencing process in Canada for over six years, we are only just beginning to understand its impact. The answers to some questions are clear. We know that it has reduced the number of offenders going to prison, and we know that most conditional sentence offenders complete their sentences without violating the conditions imposed by the court. However, a number of other questions remain unanswered due to a lack of research. For example, a number of prominent victims' rights advocates have called for conditional sentences to be restricted to property offenders. These individuals argue that imposing a conditional sentence on an offender convicted of a serious crime of violence such as sexual assault causes additional harm to the victim and depreciates the seriousness of the crime. Anecdotal evidence suggests that some victims are very upset when they learn that the offender is able to serve his or her sentence in the community. Of course, satisfying the victim is not the sole purpose of sentencing, but if many victims suffer more because an offender receives a conditional sentence, or because the reason for the imposition of the sentence is not fully explained to the victim, something needs to be done.

We also know little about the supervision of conditional sentence offenders, but here too, anecdotal evidence suggests that there are problems. Conditional sentence supervisors report that they do not have the time to adequately supervise conditional sentence offenders and that some offenders violate their conditions as a result. Judges have been reluctant to impose a conditional sentence in parts of the country where supervision is inadequate. This means that whether any given offender receives a conditional sentence (rather than being sent to prison) may depend on where he or she is sentenced, and that is hardly fair.

Finally, it is important to know more about the experience of offenders serving conditional sentences. Do they take the sentence seriously, or do they, as some have argued, see the sentence as a slightly tougher version of probation? The data presented in this chapter show that, in some parts of the country at least, offenders who breach their conditions do not get sent to prison. Does this send the wrong kind of message to offenders, namely that even if they violate their court-ordered conditions they will get another chance?

Conditional sentencing holds the potential to make the sentencing process more humane and may one day transform the way we think about

Table 5.5 *Judicial Response to Breaches of Conditions, Ontario, 1997–2001*

	1997/1998	1998/1999	1999/2000	2000/2001
No action taken; offender remains in the community	33%	28%	25%	28%
Conditions amended but offender remains in the community	24%	30%	20%	22%
Offender is sent to prison temporarily	16%	23%	25%	27%
Offender is sent to prison for duration of sentence	25%	19%	29%	23%
	100%	100%	100%	100%

Note: columns may not sum to 100% due to rounding error.
Source: Correctional Services Program, Conditional Sentencing Special Study, 2002.

Table 5.6 *Judicial Response to Breaches of Conditions, Manitoba, 1997–2001*

	1997/1998	1998/1999	1999/2000	2000/2001
No action taken; offender remains in the community	30%	18%	5%	5%
Conditions are amended, but offender remains in the community	5%	18%	22%	22%
Offender sent to prison for part of remaining time on sentence	11%	19%	24%	24%
Offender is sent to prison for time remaining on sentence	54%	45%	50%	49%
	100%	100%	100%	100%

Note: table omits "unknown outcome" cases.
Note: columns may not sum to 100% due to rounding error.
Source: Correctional Services Program, Conditional Sentencing Special Study, 2002.

punishment. It may be possible to hold offenders accountable for even quite serious crimes without having to resort to the use of imprisonment. Until the problems that have arisen, however, are resolved, this controversial new sanction must be used with care.

DISCUSSION QUESTIONS

1. *Critics of conditional sentencing, who think it is not an appropriate sanction for serious crimes, have called for Parliament to restrict this disposition to nonviolent offenders. Do you think this is a good idea?*
2. *No research to date has looked at the effect of a conditional sentence on the families of offenders sentenced to a term of custody in the community. How do you think you would feel if a member of your family, with whom you share a residence, was sentenced to serve his or her time at home?*
3. *If you were an offender about to be sentenced and the judge gave you a choice between (a) a 6-month sentence in prison, with some portion of this served in the community on parole, and (b) a 12-month conditional sentence with a curfew and some other tough conditions, which of these two sentences would you choose?*

FURTHER READINGS

Manson, A. 2001. *The Law of Sentencing.* Toronto: Irwin Law.

Roberts, J.V. 2002. The evolution of conditional sentencing in Canada. *Criminal Reports*, 3 (6th series): 267–283.

Roberts, J.V. and Healy, P. 2001. Recent developments in conditional sentencing. *Canadian Bar Review*, 1035–1039.

REFERENCES

R. v. Knoblauch. 2000. 149 C.C.C. (3d) 1. (S.C.C.).

R. v. Proulx. 2000. 140 C.C.C. (3d) 449, 30 C.R. (5th) 1.

Roberts, J.V. 1997. Conditional sentencing: Sword of Damocles or Pandora's box? *Canadian Criminal Law Review*, 2: 183–206.

Roberts, J.V. and Cole, D. (eds.) 1999. *Making Sense of Sentencing.* Toronto: University of Toronto Press.

Roberts, J.V. and Gabor, T. 2003. The Impact of Conditional Sentencing: Decarceration and widening of the net. *Canadian Criminal Law Review*, in press.

CHAPTER 6
Sentencing Disparity

INTRODUCTION

Of all the problems associated with the sentencing process, unwarranted disparity is perhaps the best known and the most intractable. Awareness of sentencing disparity has existed for as long as sentencing itself. It was disparity in sentencing that led Beccaria to write his famous treatise *On Crimes and Punishments*, published over 200 years ago (Beccaria, [1764]). A major impetus behind the radical sentencing reforms introduced in the United States from the 1970s onward was provoked by a desire to reduce wild disparities of treatment from judge to judge. Although these vary from state to state, most reforms involve prescribing a sentence range for each offence. Judges are allowed to sentence outside the range if the case is in some way exceptional.

In Canada, the reforms proposed by the Canadian Sentencing Commission (1987) and those enacted by the federal government in 1996 were aimed, in part, at making sentencing more uniform. Judges in Canada have a great deal of discretion in sentencing many offences. For example, for manslaughter, sentences can legally range from a suspended sentence to life imprisonment. Of course, judges have sources of information to guide their sentencing decisions. These include decisions from the provincial courts of appeal, submissions regarding sentence from the defence and the Crown, precedents, and so on. Nevertheless, many researchers (and some criminal justice professionals) still feel that sentencing disparity is a problem. Before deciding how to resolve the problem of unwarranted disparity in sentencing, it is important to know the extent to which it exists.

Ted Palys and Stan Divorski have carried out perhaps the most careful examination of the phenomenon. They asked a group of over 200 sentencing judges to impose a sentence in a number of cases provided to them. Since the case descriptions were identical for all the judges, any differences in the severity of sentences imposed would have to be a result of the judge and not legally relevant characteristics of the case (such as the offender's criminal record, the amount of money stolen, etc.). The results from Palys and Divorski's study (1986) surprised and indeed shocked many Canadians. Unlike most criminal justice research, the results from this study were published on the front page of *The Globe and Mail*.

Sentencing Disparity

Ted Palys and *Stan Divorski*, Simon Fraser University

Two hundred and six judges of the Canadian Provincial Courts (Criminal Division) took part in this research. Judges from the Yukon and every province but Prince Edward Island were represented in the sample, although judges from Ontario and Quebec composed the majority (66 percent) of participants. Given that there were approximately 1,000 judges of this type at that time, the respondents thus represented approximately a 20 percent sample of all Canadian Provincial Court judges hearing criminal cases. Although not necessarily representative of the whole population of judges at that time, the sample was exhaustive of all those who chose to attend one of eight regional conferences. The extent to which the sample deviated from being representative of the population of judges, and hence was in some ways more homogeneous than the whole population, implies that the disparity observed in the research may well represent an underestimate of the amount of disparity which might actually exist if the whole population of judges, or a more representative sample thereof, had been able to participate. The questionnaire had two major components: (a) a set of sample cases and (b) a number of items that asked judges to report demographic information concerning themselves and their sentencing environments.

THE SAMPLE CASES

Five cases were created, which involved a total of six offenders. For each case, judges were given a full description of the incident for which charges were laid, the circumstances leading up to and surrounding the incident, the offender's reaction to this involvement with the court, the impact of the incident upon the victim, and a detailed pre-sentence report on the offender. The charge(s) was/were noted, as was the plea or finding of guilt of the offender. Judges were asked to (a) impose a sentence for each offender; (b) indicate which case facts were relevant to the sentence; (c) indicate the relative importance of these case facts in determining sentence; and (d) list the legal objectives they were attempting to maximize in choosing their sentence.

A brief synopsis of two cases follows:

1. *Assault Causing Bodily Harm.* The offender was Ray, a 21-year-old, employed, Caucasian male who had no prior record, but who had a reputation for belligerence when drunk. The offence took place in a public bar and was unprovoked. The victim lost an eye in the incident. Ray expressed no remorse.
2. *Break and Enter of a Dwelling House.* Peter was 22 years old, had no prior record, and, although he had had a number of unskilled labour jobs and was viewed positively by his former employers, was currently unemployed after having been laid off. In a planned, daylight adventure, he found an unlocked house with no one home, and took a small amount of cash and jewelry. He was caught almost immediately and readily admitted his guilt.

RESULTS

Table 6.1 summarizes the sentences imposed by the sample judges. The left-hand portion of the table (entitled "sentencing range") shows the most and least severe sentence received by each accused, as well as those sentences which fell at the 10th, 50th, and 90th percentiles. The right-hand portion of the table (entitled "types of sentences") summarizes the proportion of judges in each case who imposed non-incarcerative sentences (i.e., fine, suspended sentence, probation) or sentences involving some incarcerative time in provincial or federal institutions. It should be obvious that there was considerable disparity among judges in the sentences they imposed, although it was also true that the degree of disparity varied from case to case.

DISCUSSION

This research had two objectives. The first was to examine the extent to which a sample of 206 judges of the Canadian Provincial Courts would exhibit variability in the sentences they imposed upon a standard set of five cases. The second research objective was to assess the extent to which this disparity could be accounted for by differences among judges in their (a) personal demographic attributes; (b) sentencing environments; (c) subscription to particular legal objectives; and (d) perceptions of important case facts.

With respect to the first objective, it was clear that substantial disparity was evinced among the sample judges. Given the consistency of these findings with the findings and conclusions of other investigators who have employed alternative methodologies (Hogarth, 1971; Sutton, 1978a and 1978b), it would seem reasonable to conclude that the phenomenon of disparity does indeed exist.

In attempting to account for variability in sentencing, it was found that differential subscription to legal objectives was the most potent predictor of sentence severity, followed closely by the differential importance accorded various case "facts."

Table 6.1 *Sentence Summaries for Five Simulated Cases*

| Case | Sentencing Range | | | | | Types of Sentences | | |
	Least Severe	10th Percentile	Median	90th Percentile	Most Severe	No Incarceration	Provincial Jail	Federal Prison
Ray — Assault Causing Bodily Harm	$500 fine plus 6 months probation	1 month jail plus 2 years probation	6 months jail	1 year 3 months jail plus 2 years probation	5 years prison	4%	92%	4%
Joe — Impaired Driving	$300 fine	$500 fine plus 2 years probation plus community service	3 months jail with TAP recommended and Driver's Licence suspension	6 months jail plus $1000 fine	2 years prison	31%	68%	1%
Peter — Break and Enter	Suspended sentence plus probation	Suspended sentence plus 1 year probation	Suspended sentence plus 2 years probation plus community service	3 months jail plus 1 year probation	1 year jail with TAP recommended plus program training	77%	23%	0%
Michael — Armed Robbery etc.	8 months jail	2 years 6 months prison	4 years 6 months prison	7 years prison	13 years prison	0%	6%	94%
John — Armed Robbery etc.	Suspended sentence	1 year 11 months plus 2 years probation	3 years 6 months prison	7 years prison	13 years prison	1%	24%	75%
Denis — Theft over $200	$1,000 fine and probation	Suspended sentence plus probation	6 months jail	2 years less a day jail	3 years prison	21%	72%	7%

In reviewing the data and discussing the sentencing process with the sample judges, it would seem that case facts, legal objectives, and the sentence exist in some uniform causal sequence (e.g., that a proclivity for particular legal objectives generates a search for particular case facts which in turn leads to sentence) for only some of the judges. Alternatively, it appeared that many, if not most, judges perused case facts, chose salient ones, formulated legal objectives on this basis, and then proceeded to "repackage" case facts in a manner that showed maximal harmony between legal objectives and case facts. This is consistent with earlier research findings that showed the modality of case-by-case variation in judges' sentencing strategies, but also goes beyond this to suggest that the generation of a decision and the justification of the decision are two separate, sequential processes.

But while the analysis above focuses on accounting for sentencing variability in any given case, it should be recalled that the extent of disparity also showed some variability from case to case. The sentences for Peter on the charge of break and enter (which ranged from a suspended sentence and probation to one year in jail), for example, evinced much less disparity than the sentences for John in the armed robbery case (which ranged from a suspended sentence and probation to 13 years in prison). Any complete account of sentence disparity must thus account not only for the existence of disparity in any case, but also its relative existence from case to case.

In this regard, it should be noted first that one variable which did not adequately account for these variations in disparity was the amount of discretion *per se* that judges were allowed. It is noteworthy that it was in the case in which they theoretically had the most discretion—the break and enter, with its maximum possible sentence of life imprisonment—that the judges showed the least disparity. Conversely, in the cases in which the possible sentence range was the lowest—the impaired driving and assault cases—judges' sentences ran the broadest possible gamut. This is particularly noteworthy given that a popular contemporary intervention for sentence disparity—the imposition of sentencing guidelines—is explicit in its rationale of reducing disparity through minimizing discretion.

A more parsimonious explanation places emphasis on differential subscription to particular legal objectives in the various cases. While numerous different legal objectives are recognized within Canadian law, there is not one that bears universal subscription. If one considers the set of these legal objectives, it is easily seen that particular legal objectives often conflict with others in terms of their implications for sentence. Rehabilitative goals are typically associated with non-incarcerative or relatively short incarcerative sentences, for example, while general deterrence and protection of the public argue for longer, more severe sentences. Given that differential subscription to particular legal objectives "explains" sentence disparity in a particular case, then it follows that the relative amount of disparity which emerges in any case will be influenced by the homo- or heterogeneity of legal objectives which vie for attention on a case-by-case basis.

One way to operationalize this degree of homo- or heterogeneity is with respect to the consistency of offender and offence attributes. Where the offender may be viewed relatively positively (e.g., no prior record, no history of violence, victim of circumstance) and the offence as relatively trivial, it seems reasonable to assume that the legal objectives which emerge as dominant will be those involving rehabilitation or the provision of token sanctions to minimize the stigmatic and criminalizing influence of one's interaction with the criminal justice system. Disparity, in other words, would be minimal due to the consensus of objectives. Certainly this was true in the case of Peter, a misguided but otherwise harmless youth who committed a relatively trivial break and enter. Similarly, the commission of a horrific crime by a negative offender (e.g., extensive prior records, history of violence, no remorse) should also lead to relative sentencing uniformity due to the consensus that would exist with respect to legal objectives of incapacitation and protection of the public.

In contrast, the present analysis suggests that disparity will be greatest when offender and offence information are inconsistent, that is, when relatively positive offenders commit horrific acts, or when negative offenders commit more trivial offences. Examples of the former were present in the current research, and substantial disparity was indeed observed. In the assault case, for example, judges were faced with an employed offender who had no prior record, but who committed a violent unprovoked act that involved severe consequences to the victim; sentences ranged from a fine to the maximum of five years in prison. Similarly, John, the armed robber, had no adult record and a stereotypically deprived background, but committed a horrific offence which generated terror and humiliation in two elderly individuals in their own home; his sentences ranged from a suspended sentence to 13 years in prison.

DISCUSSION QUESTIONS

1. *If this much disparity exists, what is the solution? In several American states, judges are bound to follow a sentencing grid. This device provides a sentence range for each offence. The range is fairly narrow (plus or minus six months) and is determined by the seriousness of the crime and the extent of the offender's criminal record. Would the use of a sentencing grid be a good reform in Canada?*

2. *At the time that Palys and Divorski's study was published, it was criticized by some judges for its methodology. These critics argued that since it was just a simulation rather than an actual sentencing hearing, it told us little about the phenomenon. These judges argued that in court, where there is a real offender, recommendations from the defence and Crown, and actual consequences for the accused as well as the judge (his or her sentence could be overturned on appeal), sentencing disparity is far less likely. What do you think of this criticism? Have Palys and Divorski exaggerated the problem by their research method?*

3. *Offenders in Canada are sentenced by professional judges who decide the sentence alone (although they hear submissions from the defence and the Crown). It has been suggested that members of the public should have a more direct say in the sentencing process. One possibility would be to have "juries" of members of the public who would advise judges and even suggest sentences in specific cases. What is your view? Would this reform lead to more or less disparity in sentencing patterns?*

FURTHER READINGS

Hogarth, J. 1971. *Sentencing as a Human Process.* Toronto: University of Toronto Press.

Lovegrove, A. 1997. *The Framework of Judicial Sentencing.* Cambridge, Eng.: Cambridge University Press.

Roberts, J.V. 1999. Sentencing trends and sentencing disparity. In: *Making Sense of Sentencing.* Toronto: University of Toronto Press.

REFERENCES

Beccaria, C. [1764] 1963. *On Crimes and Punishments.* Indianapolis: Bobbs-Merrill.

Canadian Sentencing Commission. 1987. *Sentencing Reform: A Canadian Approach.* Ottawa: Supply and Services Canada.

Hogarth, J. 1971. *Sentencing as a Human Process.* Toronto: University of Toronto Press.

Palys, T., and S. Divorski. 1986. Sentencing disparity. Extracted from Explaining sentence disparity by T. Palys and S. Divorski in *Canadian Journal of Criminology* 28(1):347–361.

Sutton, L.P. 1978a. *Federal Criminal Sentencing: Perspectives of Analysis and a Design for Research.* Report SD-AR-16. Washington, D.C.: U.S. Dept. of Justice.

———. 1978b. *Variations in Federal Criminal Sentences: A Statistical Assessment at the National Level.* Report SD-AR-17. Washington, D.C.: U.S. Dept. of Justice.

CHAPTER 7
Prisoners' Rights

INTRODUCTION

Prisoners should not lose all their rights once they are admitted to custody. Julius Melnitzer has spent time in institutions at all security levels. Following his experiences in Canada's prisons, he wrote a memoir about his experiences. That book, entitled *Maximum, Minimum, Medium*, provides a fascinating look at Canada's correctional system from the inside. As a lawyer with a great deal of experience in the criminal justice system, the author's analysis of life in Canada's prisons is quite unique. This chapter is drawn from his book.

Inhuman Rights
Julius Melnitzer

> Freedom is not divisible; it disappears from a society as soon as it is denied to any member of that society. —Dr. Gabor Maté

After more than eighteen years as a trial lawyer in Ontario, including a decade as a criminal lawyer who served for a time as a Provincial Director of the Ontario Criminal Lawyers Association, I went to jail, a criminal serving a nine-year sentence for fraud.

As a criminal lawyer, I always believed my job ended with my client's acquittal or sentencing. But two-and-a-half years in maximum, medium, and minimum security federal institutions in Ontario taught me that criminal lawyers who abandon their incarcerated clients as spent briefs should rethink their commitment to their profession and their role in society. Here's why.

The civil rights of prisoners are the lowest common denominator of democracy. In jail, correctional supervisors are the judges in internal disciplinary courts where their foot soldiers are the prosecutors (one CS [correctional supervisor] convicted a prisoner in the absence of witnesses because "no guard would take the trouble to write out a charge unless it was true"); permission to telephone a lawyer during business hours hangs on the whim of employees of the State; prisoners do not have access to Bell information or telephone books on their ranges; calls are collect only unless written permission is obtained; and telephone discussions with lawyers transpire in a public place or in a CO's (classification officer's) office in the presence of CSC (Correctional Service Canada) staff.

The apathy of all but a few criminal lawyers as well as the Canadian Civil Liberties Association; the reluctance of a cash-starved Legal Aid system to spend its budget on the convicted; the low levels of education and high levels of illiteracy in the system; and CSC's ignorance and disregard of basic procedural fairness in its day-to-day operations all ensure a trampling of prisoners' rights. Ironically, until a recent court case forced authorities to change the practice, CSC forbade the use of the Inmate Welfare Fund, inmates' money, for legal assistance.

The protection of our democratic core lies in the hands of a few committed activists like the late Order of Canada recipient Claire Culhane and her legacy, the Vancouver-based Prisoners' Rights Group; Ruth Morris from Toronto; Ontario Provincial Court Judges David Cole and Bob Bigelow; prison law practitioners in the Kingston, Ontario, bar; and Queen's University's Faculty of Law's Correctional Law Project, until recently headed by Professor Ron Price, now practising correctional law in the private sector.

This is not a commentary on the rights prisoners should have: that is for the voters and their elected representatives to decide. Nor is it a denial of the relatively humane conditions under which we warehouse the convicted; rather, it speaks to the disregard of due process that pervades our penal system. As sentences get lengthier, paroles become rarer, and more people spend more time in jail, the prevailing attitude seems to be, "Let's feed them and keep them out of the cold." In a democracy, that will not do; so long as society sees fit to give rights to prisoners, it must protect its values even among its exiles. Our failure to do so says much about our penal system's rehabilitative delinquencies.

CSC's response to the public outcry resulting from my tennis partner convicted murderer Philippe Clement's assault on a Gravenhurst woman after his escape from minimum-security Beaver Creek was perhaps my starkest experience with civil rights sacrificed on the altar of public opinion and media hype. In the six months following the public outcry, CSC set out to purge the Creek of violent offenders, many of whom were sent to Warkworth, and some of whom opened their files to me. I was appalled at the haste and lack of justification for the majority of the transfers; in no instance was there an immediate threat of escape or violence, yet none of these inmates were given a chance to contact their lawyers before transfer.

My apprehensions about the panic that had set in with Les Judson [a former warden at Beaver Creek] and his superiors were confirmed orally by some Warkworth COs who were now stuck with these men. One CO put her findings in writing:

> On December 23, 1992, the subject was transferred to higher security
> (Warkworth Institution) as the staff at Beaver Creek had information that
> the subject, along with other perpetrators, had broken into the inmate can-
> teen and stole $3200 worth of merchandise ...

These suspicions were never confirmed. No charges, either institutional or street, were laid against the subject. There is no evidence which ties the subject to this offence. Therefore, there is no valid reason why the security classification on the subject should change. He is still classified as minimum security.

"The subject" was unusually lucky. He was back in minimum within six months. Had his CO been unsympathetic, it would have taken him from twelve to eighteen months to have his grievance processed. And likely, "the subject," who was barely literate, would have had to do it on his own: Legal Aid refused his application, and for three months, his collect calls to lawyers went unanswered.

Apart from "the subject," not a single one of the men summarily ejected from Beaver Creek in the fall of 1992 had made it back to minimum one year later. Even those with lawyers were stymied by the delaying tactics of the Crown in Federal Court and the sluggishness of that court's process.

The greatest price of this arbitrary conduct, apart from the diminution in democratic values, is the cost to society. Many of the cons transferred were the system's successes, the most likely candidates for rehabilitation, men who had spent many years fighting institutionalization and their criminal backgrounds and who had been adjudged, step by grudging step, to have the best potential for a productive return to society.

Wade, a very young-looking, intelligent and self-educated forty-year-old, with two daughters in their twenties and a son in his teens, had fought his way back from tragic alcoholism and drug abuse that led to conviction for two sexual assaults and a twelve-year sentence. He had been a model for other prisoners, a star in every therapeutic program he had taken for seven years. At the Creek, he continued his exemplary ways, working in the kitchen, tutoring other inmates, and minding his own business.

The Parole Board, even in the aftermath of the Clement escape, was sufficiently impressed by Wade's record to grant him unescorted three-day passes to a halfway house in Toronto. On his first pass, he dutifully attended the Clarke Institute of Psychiatry for a psychological assessment; there he told the examining psychologist that he had taken one drink almost a year previous, on New Year's Eve.

Wade's honesty was just the excuse Beaver Creek needed to rid itself of another bothersome high-profile case. Wade was summarily advised that the

Administration had been "informed"—by parties unmentionable, of course— of "derogatory remarks" Wade had made about the deputy warden. Lacking knowledge of his accusers and without access to counsel, Wade had no opportunity to defend himself and was promptly transferred to Warkworth, where he remained until his statutory release in February 1994. CSC's extraordinary powers made a strong impression on me when I reported for transportation to a Kingston hospital for medical testing. The escorting officers politely told me to undress.

"Am I under suspicion for anything?" I asked.

"No," was the quick reply.

My question was deliberate. I had researched the new prison legislation as it related to searches, to discover that "routine" strip-searches were unlawful in the absence of individualized suspicion, except for some carefully circumscribed exceptions that did not apply here.

"Then you've got no right to search me," I asserted.

The officers resolved their confusion by phoning the security office.

"You can't go if you refuse a search," the senior guard told me as he got off the phone.

"Fine," I replied, "I'll go back to my Block." Visions of medical lawsuits and grievances for damages danced in my head.

"The IPSO [internal preventative security officer] says we have to search you anyway."

"You mean that I'm now under suspicion because I insisted on my rights."

"I don't know," said the guard abashedly, "you're the lawyer. I just do what the keeper tells me."

"What are my choices?"

"Go to the hole. They'll strip-search you there." Previous personal experience told me that a request to call my lawyer would not be well received, serving only to heighten suspicion about my refusal to be strip-searched.

I was in a quandary. If I refused, I'd be in the hole. I tried to imagine the write-up on this incident: by the time the IPSO finished, I would doubtlessly be labelled as "under suspicion," CSC's favourite phrase, of trafficking in something or other. I complied, wondering how many thousands of inmates would be searched in ignorance of their rights.

The "cavity search," a fishing expedition through body orifices, is distinguished from assault only by the mandated presence of a doctor and is a more sublime form of intrusion than a strip-search. If a tactile proctological examination doesn't reveal anything, the doctor may use an instrument best described as an anal crank to have a better look through a larger opening.

Refusal to submit to a cavity search is, in a system where random urinalysis testing is common, a virtual admission to drug trafficking. Being labelled as a trafficker is, in turn, an invitation to unremitting harassment, restrictions on visits, and a practical bar to early parole.

Cavity searches are, however, expensive, time-consuming, and embarrassing when fruitless. CSC prefers the "dry cell," where the toilet can't be flushed by the inmate. In Kingston Penitentiary, the nine-by-four windowless cell contains a bed, an eating surface, a steel toilet, and a sink. The lights are on all day, and at night, a bulb strong enough to read by intrudes on sleep, but no books are allowed. The cell is video-monitored twenty-four hours daily, and patrolling guards have an unobstructed vista through a plastic plate on the ceiling. The cell design allows the guards to watch the prisoner's excretions, which remain with him in the uncovered toilet, until the guards find time to come around and secure the evidence.

Just how far down the human rights scale prisoners have fallen can be demonstrated by comparing the dry cell experience with recent court decisions prohibiting police from detaining suspects until they have a bowel movement, enabling authorities to search stool samples for drugs.

Random urinalysis, recently declared constitutional by the courts, is slowly replacing the cavity search and the dry cell, but the tests are no less intrusive, if somewhat more humane.

To those law-and-order aficionados who cheered their way through the last few paragraphs, I merely point out that these methods are designed to prove guilt. Until and if the shit hits the fan, so to speak, the innocent must pay the price with the guilty. The innocent have no recourse if the suspicions against them prove groundless. The irony is that they therefore have far more incentive than the guilty to submit to these barbaric intrusions.

Occasionally, an activist Inmate Committee chairman tries to help inmates assert their rights. The Inmate Committee exists at the discretion of an institution's warden, but now that CSC is legally required to consult with inmates on all matters affecting them other than security, the Inmate Committee is a handy funnel to the population.

The inmate chairman is elected by the population every six months and appoints his own executive. The chairman's capacity to represent the inmates is severely limited, however, because the chairman is himself a prisoner, whose fate hinges on the whims of his keepers.

While politicization is creeping into institutional politics, wardens tend to deal swiftly and severely with chairmen whom they see as rabble-rousers. Shortly before I got to Warkworth, Greg, a fifty-year-old first-timer serving a fourteen-year-sentence for the attempted murder of his wife, was elected chairman. Greying, fatherly, and somehow tweedy in his prison greens, Greg was educated and clever, with a knack for organization.

Greg set out to enforce the Supreme Court of Canada's declaration, in a precedent-setting decision giving prisoners the right to vote, that inmates were entitled to all civil rights other than those that necessarily accompanied the loss of freedom.

To that end, he first presented the Administration with a scheme for effective inmate representation at the grass-roots level. Censorship was his next target: I helped him draw up a grievance against the Administration's refusal to allow the popular Sharon Stone movie *Basic Instinct* into Warkworth; after months of enduring explicitly violent martial arts movies on prison video, I laughed at the exclusion. Simultaneously, Greg hotly protested against the Administration's control and occasional misuse of the Inmate Welfare Fund. The powers-that-be were most unhappy with him.

"They're going to get me, Julius. They don't want a chairman who does anything," Greg told me.

As the tension rose, Greg desperately tried to get in touch with a lawyer; he wrote both to the Ontario Provincial Criminal Lawyers Association, which continued its historical disregard of those who had already paid their bills, and the Canadian Civil Liberties Association, which must have had more popular fish to fry and didn't bother to answer. I finally called my lawyer, Bob Bigelow, who agreed to see Greg on his next visit to Warkworth.

Before Bob could see Greg, the Administration pounced, blaming him for irregularities in the canteen; without explanation, he was hauled out of a visit with his wife and sent to the hole. Soon afterwards, Greg resigned, a non-presence in short order.

Inmate Committee chairmen are not the only targets of the kind of intimidation Greg experienced. Grant, convicted by an internal disciplinary court of possession of a joint after eight offence-free years in the pen, objected to the severity of the penalties for his minor offence. On the street, he would have been fined lightly, at worst; in prison, he lost his single cell in Warkworth's model non-smoking unit, was transferred back to double-bunked Reception, had his pay cut by four levels, lost his job, and spent a week in the hole awaiting Disciplinary Court.

With the law clerk's certificate he had earned in prison from the American Trial Lawyers Association in hand, and with some guidance from me, Grant filed a claim in the Federal Court challenging the severity and multiplicity of his punishments. The attorney general applied to quash Grant's claim, but failed in its summary motion. Grant, who worked in the kitchen, thanked me for my help with a plate of delicately cooked fresh crabmeat that a friendly guard had smuggled in for him.

For a few months I heard nothing more about his case, attributing Grant's silence to the long delays in Federal Court.

"I shut it down," he said six months later, in a hush, averting his eyes.

"Why?" I was sincerely dismayed.

"I've got to do what's right for me. My wife wants me out of here, or at least in camp. I'm on a life beef—they call the shots."

Not yet dislodged from the insulated naïveté of my street days, I had no idea what Grant was talking about.

"They called me in, the unit manager," he went on. "He told me that even if I win, I lose. If I forget it, maybe I get to camp soon."

The threat was not an idle one. And if the unit manager chose to forget his promise once Grant dropped his claim, [the unit manager] could always find new facts to support his change of heart; CSC's power to affect the man's freedom would be as useful in the breaking of the promise as it was in its making.

As I chafed at the injustices, the feelings that drove me as a criminal lawyer came back in spades. In January 1993, I wrote to prison activist Claire Culhane, whose books I had been reading, offering to help in her cause of prisoners' rights. Though my ability to assist was limited by the inaccessibility of research materials, our correspondence continued throughout my incarceration.

CSC's licence to trample human rights stems from its lack of accountability. Politically, the human rights of convicts is hardly an issue with which to blaze to power; an unsympathetic media and public ensure that accountability, where it exists, operates only to inmates' detriment.

Wardens have some discretion in granting passes, escorted and unescorted, as well as work releases; release in serious cases, the ones in the headlines, are the province of the National Parole Board. CSC, through its case management teams and therapeutic staff, makes highly influential recommendations to the board. Wisdom and insight into the human psyche spout from the mouths of twenty-three-year-old COs barely out of community college, secretarial school graduates who have won the CSC promotion competition, or MA students suddenly become "therapists." Their power is frightening and unchecked, often subjective and arbitrary; if quality control or any serious effort at consistency in release decisions and recommendations existed, I couldn't find it in the files I reviewed.

There is little risk for CSC in urging the Parole Board to detain an inmate, but a wrong call for release can have disastrous public relations fallout; thus, it is not surprising that case management teams lean against release. As Jeremiah's CO told him, "Personally, I don't think you should be in here, but I don't want to be the one kicking my lunch bucket down the street." Reid, who had spent seventeen years in prison, observed, "When I got in the system, COs tried to help you. Now, they try to find obstacles to keep you in so they can cover their ass."

CSC's materials are essentially unchallengeable before the Parole Board, a body that the late Chief Justice of Canada's Supreme Court, Bora Laskin, called draconian. The hearings consist of a presentation by the CO, followed by thirty minutes to five hours of untrammeled inmate grilling by at least a two-member board, many of whom are trained only in the fruits of political loyalty and start with the assumption that credibility is not in a criminal's repertoire.

Anything in a CSC report passes for evidence: fact, opinion, hearsay, innuendo, and suspicion—even philosophical musings; reports are in writing, there is no in-person evidence and no opportunity to cross-examine in the quest for liberty. The inmate's lawyer is reduced to an "assistant," usually sitting by without objection, involved only in procedural matters and ten minutes of final arguments. Where evidence favouring release exists, the Parole Board is notorious for capriciously ignoring it, going so far as to reject, without reasons, recommendations from CSC's own professionals. Homespun psychology is regularly expounded as definitive gospel by politically appointed board members, many of them part-time, with little experience and less training: "The offender's response to our questions shows that he has not fully appreciated the consequences of his actions and is not ready for release" are the board's favourite buzzwords.

Always, the spectre of public opinion hangs over the proceedings, twisting the issue of "risk to society," the fundamental question the Parole Board is empowered to decide, into considerations of "how will it look?" Thus, by ignoring the law, the Parole Board assumes the role of lawmaker, affecting a demagogic juggernaut that tramples on concepts of fundamental justice. These concepts are democracy's triggers of accountability, ever so slight a curtsy to an inalienable right—not to freedom, but to the right to fight for it on even ground.

DISCUSSION QUESTIONS

1. *What is meant by the term "due process," and how does it apply to prisoners?*
2. *Is random urinalysis testing acceptable in prison?*
3. *How can the system best ensure that the rights of prisoners are respected?*

FURTHER READINGS

Jackson, M. 2002. *Justice behind the Walls: Human Rights in Canadian Prisons.* Vancouver: Douglas and McIntyre.

Melnitzer, J. 1995. *Maximum, Minimum, Medium.* Toronto: Key Porter Books.

CHAPTER 8
Getting Tough with Young Offenders

INTRODUCTION

Responding to youth crime has been one of the criminal justice priorities for many years now. Routinely, public opinion polls found that, of all components of the system, the youth justice system attracted the most negative ratings from members of the public. The *Young Offenders Act* (which has now been replaced by the *Youth Criminal Justice Act;* see Chapter 9 of this volume) was frequently criticized for not being tough enough. In the search for solutions to rising juvenile crime rates, or even perceptions of rising rates, some people have suggested that we should simply "get tough" with young persons who come into conflict with the law. The experience in the U.S. is helpful in this regard, as many states have introduced tough reforms to their justice systems, including mandatory transfers to adult court and harsh, military-style boot camps. One province in Canada (Ontario) has adopted some of these policies. In this chapter, Dan Gardner, a highly respected investigative journalist with the *Ottawa Citizen,* reports on his research into the effectiveness of punitive youth policies in America.

Responding to Youth Crime: Do "Get Tough" Policies Work?
Dan Gardner, Ottawa Citizen

He's 70 years old, he looks remarkably like Andy Rooney's younger brother, and he's not very happy about where the world is heading. But Jerry Miller isn't the sort of senior citizen who grumbles about "young punks" and the crimes they commit. In fact, what bothers Mr. Miller are the politicians, journalists, and victims' rights activists who think communities can be made safer by getting tough on young offenders. "It's an insane argument," he says, with just a little more sorrow than anger.

In the field of youth corrections, Mr. Miller is a legendary figure. As an author, professor, and head of youth services in three American states, he has dealt with what used to be called "juvenile delinquents" since the days of the Johnson presidency in the 1960s. But it was a single, revolutionary act that made his reputation: In 1970, as chief of the Massachusetts Youth Department, Mr. Miller shut down every young-offender facility and sent the 2,000 inmates back into communities across the state. "We hired a lot of young, college-age staff and we went on a crash program to find and develop alternatives," he recalls. "We came up with about 250 different programs that had never been there before." Sometimes they asked private agencies and groups whether they could take a few kids. They called companies that advertised educational programs on the backs of matchbook covers. Anything to get the teens out of lockup. "We even sent a kid chasing humpback whales with a group from the Massachusetts Institute of Technology."

Only 100 of the teens were kept in a secure environment, mainly small community residences where they were always supervised. The other 1,900 were handed their freedom. It was a daring act at the time. Today, it sounds like pure fantasy.

Not long after Mr. Miller's mass jailbreak, the United States began a profound shift toward more punitive criminal-justice policies. Public attitudes toward offenders grew increasingly punitive. Punishments got more and more severe. Prison populations exploded. For young offenders, the new get-tough attitude meant the helping hand was replaced with the back of the hand. Cities imposed youth curfews. Schools introduced "zero-tolerance" policies on violence that led to automatic expulsions and an increased reliance on the police to settle schoolyard scraps. Programs such as "Scared Straight" took misbehaving kids into prisons to be harangued by inmates about the horrors of life inside. "Boot camps" put them in uniforms to be shouted at by pseudo-drill sergeants. But the most profound change involved "adult time for adult crime"—more and more young offenders were handed adult sentences for certain serious crimes.

So far, Canada's federal government has largely, though not entirely, rejected the fear-and-punishment approach that has prevailed south of the border. But there are many people working hard to change that. The Canadian Alliance party, various police associations, and a handful of populist journalists are all demanding Canada follow the American lead. The government of Ontario has also been pressing for the federal government to adopt U.S.–style policies and has implemented such policies wherever it has jurisdiction.

The tough-on-crime movement is based on a simple idea. "I think there are some young people out there," says David Young, the former Conservative attorney general of Ontario, "who are prepared to take risks ... because the consequences of their aberrant behaviour are minimal. And we'd like to send a message to those young people and all young people that if they commit serious crime, there will be consequences." According to this view, tougher punishments will convince more young offenders to give up crime and deter other young people who might otherwise become juvenile offenders.

In pursuit of this philosophy, Ontario has implemented "zero-tolerance" policies in schools and, in 1997, the province opened Canada's first "boot camp." The Conservative government has also demanded the federal government change the young offender law so that teens charged with some serious crimes would be automatically tried and punished as adults, regardless of their individual level of maturity.

All of these ideas were invented in the U.S. and they're all terribly wrong, says Jerry Miller. Mr. Miller's views are based in part on the results of his own little revolution in the state of Massachusetts. The police, of course, had warned that closing the institutions would mean chaos in the streets. It didn't happen. "We didn't have a single major incident, in terms of a major crime of violence," Mr. Miller says. And the overall rate of juvenile crime, which had been dropping, continued to fall.

Studies have confirmed that the experiment was a success. Generally, the research showed that releasing the young offenders had no effect on crime rates. But a long-term study by the National Council on Crime and Delinquency concluded the reform actually reduced recidivism in a subtle way. "It tended to de-escalate the seriousness of the crimes," Mr. Miller says. "In other words, a kid that was coming out of a reform school, having done a year or a year and a half, when they get in trouble, it's more serious crime. The kids coming out of the community-based (programs) might get in trouble, but (for) lesser things."

Still, it's hard to ignore the fact the U.S. left Mr. Miller's approach in the dust of American history. And since we usually think of abandoned ideas as bad ideas, it's difficult not to assume he must have been proven wrong at some point. In light of the get-tough policies that have swept through the American justice system, surely there must be evidence to show they work? In fact, there is none. If anything, the experience and research of the last three decades has confirmed that creating fear and inflicting pain and punishment are ineffective ways to reform young offenders.

Zero-tolerance policies have been in place for more than a decade. As a result, suspensions and expulsions of students have soared. It hasn't done any good. A recent report on zero-tolerance policies from the Indiana Education Policy Center at the University of Indiana concluded: "There appears to be little evidence, direct or indirect, supporting the effectiveness of suspension or expulsion for improving student behaviour or contributing to overall school safety." Many researchers are convinced that suspending and expelling students is actually worse than useless. The troubled kids who are most often suspended or expelled almost always follow the same pattern: Even in elementary school, they start to fail; they find and hang around with other alienated youths; and their families, which are usually dysfunctional, don't keep tabs on them, and this gives them more and more free time to get into trouble.

For that sort of adolescent, being thrown out of school is only likely to weaken the bonds with school and increase their feelings of alienation. It also gives "troubled youth with little parental supervision more opportunities to socialize with deviant peers," the Indiana report notes. Not surprisingly, "for troublesome or at-risk students, the most well-documented outcome of suspension appears to be further suspension, and eventually school dropout." And since, as research has also shown, the strength of a youth's ties to school are a good predictor of juvenile delinquency, zero-tolerance polices may ultimately increase youth crime rates.

Twenty years ago, Rutgers University criminologist James Finckenauer evaluated the so-called "Scared Straight" programs for young offenders. Juveniles were taken on tours of maximum security prisons by hardened inmates. "This is where you may end up" was the message for the juveniles. Finckenauer found that these programs simply don't work. Since then, the "Scared Straight" approach has steadily expanded throughout the U.S. and elsewhere, but expansion is the only form of success that "Scared Straight" has had. Over and over, research has shown it to be a flop in terms of diverting troubled youth away from a life of crime.

Boot camps are another bright idea that promises more than it delivers. Juveniles sent to boot camps undergo rigorous military-style training, frequently at isolated locations in the countryside, in the belief that exposing teens to strict discipline and overt authority will teach them to respect the law. Research has never borne out the theory. In 2001, a comprehensive report entitled "Youth Violence: A Report of the Surgeon General," was released by the U.S. Surgeon General's office. It was commissioned by the U.S. Congress in response to the Columbine school massacre. The report simply reviewed existing research, some of which stretched back quite some time. It concluded that boot camps not only fail to make a positive difference, they may even increase the rate at which their graduates commit new crimes. A study of Ontario's five-year-old boot-camp experiment found no statistically significant evidence that the boot camp worked better than existing youth justice facilities.

Jerry Miller's belief that most young offenders should be in the community, not isolated in youth facilities, has been put to the test in many different places. Consider the state of Maryland and its next-door neighbour, Washington, D.C. During the 1990s, Washington reduced its state-wide juvenile detention rate by 71%, while Maryland's use of youth detention increased 3%. Over that time, Maryland saw a 15% decline in youth crime compared with a 55% drop in youth crime in Washington, D.C.

Another powerful comparison can be found at home, in the provinces of Ontario and Quebec. Although the federal government is responsible for laws pertaining to young offenders, the provinces and territories administer this legislation according to their own philosophies and priorities. Quebec has traditionally taken a very liberal approach, which focuses not on punishment but on helping kids overcome whatever factors had led them to crime; custody is used only as a last resort. Ontario, on the other hand, has traditionally leaned more toward the use of incarceration and punishment. The contrast in approaches emerges clearly in the rate at which the two provinces sentence young offenders to custody. In Quebec, it's 38 per 10,000 young people. In Ontario, it's 82 per 10,000—a little more than double the rate in Quebec.

If there were any merit to the get-tough philosophy, the were "soft" approach to young offenders should result in higher youth crime rates in Quebec. But that's not the case: The rate of youth crime in Quebec is less than half that in Ontario. Quebec has half as much youth violent crime, less than half the property crime, and less than one-third as many violations of other *Criminal Code* sections (including weapons offences and mischief).

For tough-on-crime advocates, the ultimate weapon in the war on young offenders goes by the slogan "adult time for adult crime." In effect, this policy means denying that young offenders are juveniles at all and treating them as adult offenders. Across the U.S., justice systems have dramatically expanded the range of circumstances in which young offenders can be transferred to adult court and then tried and sentenced as adults. One method is to give prosecutors the option to choose whether a youth will be tried as an adult or not. A more common mechanism, known as statutory transfers, is to simply list a number of serious crimes and require that any youth charged with one of these crimes automatically be treated as an adult.

This is what Canadian advocates of get-tough reforms want. Under existing Canadian law, youths as young as 14 can be punished as adults for serious crimes if it can be shown they are sufficiently mature to fully understand the nature of their actions and take responsibility for them. This arrangement doesn't go far enough for the government of Ontario, among others. The Ontario Tories want all 16- and 17-year-olds automatically tried and punished as adults if they are charged with a "serious offence"—a list that now includes everything from murder to criminal negligence causing death. But if the American experience is anything to go by, that wouldn't be the end of it. "The list [of offences] inevitably grows," says Vincent Schiraldi, president of the Justice Policy Institute in Washington, D.C. and a leading critic of tough-on-crime reforms. The American experience also suggests that after such a law is passed, the minimum age for automatic transfer to adult court is steadily lowered, with the result that more and more juveniles are processed as adults.

Reforms such as these have had a profound impact in the U.S., particularly over the last decade. "From 1992 to 1997, 47 states passed laws making it easier to try kids as adults or otherwise toughening their juvenile codes," says Mr. Schiraldi. Automatic transfers of youths to adult court take place in 28 states. In some instances, the troubling results of such laws make the international news. In one notorious case in 2000, a 14-year-old Florida boy was found guilty of killing a 6-year-old girl. The two had been good friends and the boy, who was unusually large for his age, claimed her death was the result of rough-housing. Even though the boy was only 12 at the time of the killing, he received the same sentence as any 25-year-old, cold-blooded killer: life in prison.

There's no question this is very "tough" treatment. But does it reduce youth crime? All the research suggests not. The first state to embrace this approach was New York, in 1978. Youths aged 13 or older charged with homicide were automatically tried as adults; 14- and 15-year-olds were automatically tried as adults for a variety of serious crimes; and at 16, all youths were considered adults.

Criminologists studied the impact of the New York reforms by looking at arrests of youths for the four years before the change and the six years after. They concluded that the changes had had no effect on crime rates. The same results were found when Florida introduced similar reforms in the 1980s. In fact, a comparison of youth crime trends in the two trail-blazing states of Florida and New York shows no difference from youth crime trends in the nation as a whole: Both states continued to lead the country in youth crime rates. "For most of the 1990s, New York had the highest rate of juvenile crime in the country," notes Mr. Schiraldi. "Florida had the second-highest rate."

Researchers found another case study in Idaho, which, in 1981, started automatically transferring offenders as young as 14 to adult court for serious violent crimes. They compared the number of arrests of youths for the listed crimes in the five years before the change with arrests for the five years after. They also looked at arrest rates in Montana and Wyoming, states that are demographically similar to Idaho but which did not change their laws. The researchers found no evidence that Idaho's tough new laws did any good. On the contrary: After the law was changed, arrests for the listed offences actually increased in Idaho, while the number of arrests for the same crimes in Montana and Wyoming dropped.

Another important study compared two counties in New York State and New Jersey that were part of the same metropolitan area. At the time (1981 and 1982) New York State transferred 15- and 16-year-olds charged with robbery or burglary to adult court; New Jersey treated them as juveniles. This distinction was important since the adult courts of New York focused on punishment and commonly sentenced offenders to prison; the New Jersey juvenile courts focused more on helping young offenders and used incarceration more sparingly.

The study compared how many of these teenagers committed new crimes after they had been released. It found that for the teens convicted of burglary, it made no difference whether the offender had been treated as a juvenile or as an adult. As for the teens convicted of robbery, 76% of those who had gone to adult court were rearrested, compared to 67% of those who had gone to juvenile court. Robbers who had gone through the adult courts were also found to have committed more crimes and to have re-offended sooner than those who had gone to the juvenile system.

In Florida, prosecutors decide whether a teenager will be tried as a juvenile or an adult, and as a result, practice varies greatly from county to county. Researchers compared similar teens who had committed similar crimes but had been sent to different court systems in their respective counties. They found that 30% of teens sent to adult court had re-offended within two years, compared with 19% of those sent to juvenile court. Teens put in adult court also re-offended sooner and at a higher rate than those who had stayed in the juvenile system. They were also more likely to have been rearrested for serious offences.

These studies—and many others like them—were reviewed by the U.S. Surgeon General's office in its 2001 report on youth violence. The report's conclusion was blunt: Treating young offenders as adult criminals is a terrible mistake. "Evaluations of these programs suggest that they increase future criminal behaviour rather than deter it, as advocates of this approach had hoped."

It's easy to understand why tougher punishment doesn't work. For one thing, punishments act as deterrents only if young people actually know about them. But consider that in a recent poll, 91% of adult Canadians described their knowledge of the criminal justice system as moderate to poor. Why would we expect badly educated, alienated teenagers to be better informed? "The right wing keeps saying young offenders know the law," says Graham Stewart, executive director of the John Howard Society. "They have this idea that every scruffy, snot-nosed kid that gets into fights in the street actually spends his weekends in the library poring over law books so he knows exactly what he can get away with." Reality is otherwise.

Teenagers are also unlikely to be deterred by severe punishments because they are by definition immature. They are vastly more impulsive than adults. That isn't a criticism of teenagers, it's a physical reality: Scientists using brain-imaging techniques have discovered that teenaged brains are literally still developing; the capacity to make decisions, still evolving.

So when does a teen become mature enough to assume full responsibility for his or her acts? Some mature faster than others, so it varies from individual to individual. Which is why current Canadian law allows teens to be treated as adults if they commit certain serious crimes—but only if a judge decides the youth in question is mature enough to bear that responsibility. The get-tough approach wipes out this case-by-case method, making transfer to an adult court automatic for any teenager who meets the age and charge criteria—no matter how immature he or she may be.

Another key factor in the failure of punishment is the background of the youths who are most likely to get heavily involved in crime. Overwhelmingly, they come from poor, fractured, abusive homes. "They've been banged off the wall half their lives, or they're living on the street," says Mr. Miller. For these young people, punishment and pain are just a fact of life, like the weather. Worse, the punishment they've experienced has often been arbitrary and unfair. In their experience, it's simply not true that, if you behave well, things will get better. Punishment is just something somebody with power inflicts on you. When the justice system punishes kids like these harshly, they aren't likely to see it as any more meaningful than a beating at the hands of a drunken stepfather.

And punishment can sometimes be even worse than meaningless. When a teenager is caught and sent to a youth justice system that emphasizes help over vengeance, he is told, in effect, that he's got problems that he must straighten out. But if he's convicted and imprisoned as an adult, the message is that he's simply a no-good criminal who must be isolated and punished.

Sociologists call this "labelling" and it's particularly harmful for teenagers who are already alienated from school, family and community—precisely the sort of teenager who often gets in trouble. "You get the system saying the best thing to do with this guy who doesn't feel bonded (to society) is to tell him he's a complete and utter asshole," says Graham Stewart. "All that does is continue to build that sense of not belonging." That experience breeds more and more anti-social behaviour: A true criminal is created.

Unfortunately, neither the evidence nor the explanations have made the slightest difference in developing public policies. American politicians have completely overlooked the research, Mr. Miller says. And when criminologists have objected, they have been dismissed out of hand, or, more often, ignored. The same disregard for research-based evidence can be seen in Canada. In numerous interviews with Canadian tough-on-crime supporters, I asked repeatedly for evidence that their policies actually reduce crime. Not one produced any evidence in support of any policy.

Most startling was a lengthy interview I conducted with David Young. I repeatedly asked the former Ontario Attorney General whether he had evidence to support the many American-style, get-tough reforms that the province has urged the federal government to adopt. He had none. Nor did he seem at all concerned he had none. Evidence was apparently irrelevant to Mr. Young.

For Jerry Miller, these Canadian stories are all terribly familiar, and terribly depressing. "Of all countries to go to look for a model, my God, to go to the United States is bizarre."

For 30 years, Mr. Miller has been fighting a losing battle against the get-tough American model, but he's not giving up. He continues to write and work at his home in the mountains of Virginia. "In the juvenile area, I have no doubt at all that 90% of the kids in institutions could be in a community setting if we attach to them the amount of money that we are spending on them in the institution."

Not many young offenders have benefited from Mr. Miller's vision, but 2,000 kids in Massachusetts did. Many have been in touch. "A lot of them called, or I got letters over the years," he says, suddenly smiling like a grandfather. Then the smile turns to a grin, like Andy Rooney preparing a punch line. "One's an FBI agent," he says, laughing.

DISCUSSION QUESTIONS

1. *Advocates of getting tough with juvenile offenders argue that, if young offenders commit the same kinds of crimes as adults, they should be punished as adults. What is your opinion of this argument?*
2. *What do you think the public's reaction is likely to be to Mr. Gardner's research that seems to show that tough justice for juveniles is ineffective in reducing juvenile crime?*
3. *Some people argue that the age of criminal responsibility should be lowered from 12 to 10, since 10-year-olds commit crimes. What do you think of this policy recommendation?*

FURTHER READINGS

Bala, N., Hornick, J., Snyder, H. and Paetsch, J. (eds.) 2002. *Juvenile Justice Systems: An International Comparison of Problems and Solutions.* Toronto: Thompson Educational Publishing, Inc.

Doob, A. and Sprott, J. 2003. Changing models of youth justice in Canada. In M. Tonry and A.N. Doob (Eds.) *Crime and Justice: A Review of Research.* Chicago: University of Chicago Press.

Varma, K. and Marinos, V. 2000. How do we best respond to the problem of youth crime? In J.V. Roberts (Ed.) *Criminal Justice in Canada.* Toronto: Thomson.

CHAPTER 9
Youth Criminal Justice Act

INTRODUCTION

Until 2003, the treatment of young persons who came into conflict with the law was regulated by the *Young Offenders Act*. That legislation was widely criticized on a number of grounds, including the use of custody for young offenders. Members of the public with little direct experience with the youth justice system tended to criticize the act for being too lenient. Others, including people working in the field and academics, faulted the youth justice system for placing too many young people into open and closed custody. In this chapter, two leading scholars in the field of youth justice examine the implications of the new youth justice legislation with respect to the use of custody as a sanction in youth court.

Regulating the Use of Youth Court and Youth Custody: The *Youth Criminal Justice Act*

Jane B. Sprott, University of Guelph, and *Anthony N. Doob,* University of Toronto

The *Youth Criminal Justice* Act (YCJA) replaced the *Young Offenders Act (YOA)* in April 2003 as the federal legislation governing young persons (aged 12 to 17 inclusive) who violate federal laws. One of the many criticisms of the *YOA* was that many minor cases were brought into youth court, and that too many youths were sentenced to custody (Doob and Sprott, 2003). It is not surprising, therefore, that the preamble to the new legislation suggests that we should have a youth criminal justice system that "reserves its most serious intervention for the most serious crimes and reduces the over-reliance on incarceration for non-violent young persons."

In explaining the need for a new law, the federal Department of Justice, on its Web site (http://canada.justice.gc.ca/en/ps/yj/), lists a number of problems with youth justice under the old *Young Offenders Act,* including the following:

1. The youth justice system lacked a clear and coherent youth justice philosophy.
2. Canada has the highest youth incarceration rate in the western world (for a discussion of this issue, see Sprott and Snyder, 1999).
3. The courts are overused for minor cases that can be better dealt with in other ways.
4. Sentencing decisions by the courts have resulted in disparities in youth court sentencing.
5. The system did not make a clear distinction between serious violent offences and less serious offences.

The first of these points can be seen as the cause of all the others. The second, third, and fifth points describe the undifferentiated manner in which youthful offending is responded to, and the fourth describes another problem: the differential treatment of youth. This chapter examines some of the variation that exists across the country and will then discuss provisions in the *YCJA* that are designed to address these concerns.

USE OF YOUTH COURT

During the first few years of the *YOA,* police appeared to resolve fewer cases outside the system, resulting in an increase in the number of young offenders in youth court (Carrington, 1999). There was also considerable variation across the country with respect to the rate of bringing cases into the youth justice system (Doob and Sprott, 1996). Table 9.1 shows that the overall rate in Canada of bringing cases into youth court in 1999–2000 was 4.17 per 100 youths. The rates in the eastern provinces tend to be somewhat lower than the overall Canadian rate—ranging from 2.71 in P.E.I. to 4.12 in Nova Scotia.

Quebec clearly stands out as the province that brings in the fewest cases— 1.96 per 100 youths in the population. Ontario brings in cases at a rate of 4.28, and the Prairies range from 6.14 in Alberta to 9.41 in Saskatchewan. British Columbia brings in cases at a rate similar to Newfoundland (3.64). The Yukon and Northwest Territories' rates are considerably higher (13.81 and 10.09, respectively) than those of all the other jurisdictions, but Nunavut (4.29) is closer to the Ontario rate.

There is also a tendency for the provinces with the higher overall crime rates to have higher rates of bringing cases into court (see Table 9.1). For example, the Prairie provinces generally have higher crime rates and also bring in more cases. However, this relationship does not hold perfectly. For example, B.C. has the second highest overall provincial crime rate but brings in cases at a rate similar to Newfoundland, the province with the lowest overall crime rate. Quebec has a crime rate similar to that of Ontario, but brings youth to court at a rate less than half of Ontario's (1.96 compared to 4.28). Therefore, it appears that the variation cannot be explained solely in terms of differences in crime rates.

Given the variation that exists—especially between Quebec and the rest of Canada—in the use of youth court, it perhaps is not surprising that Quebec judges are less likely to indicate that they are seeing large numbers of cases that could be adequately dealt with elsewhere (Sprott and Doob, 2002). In a 2001 survey, 73 percent of Quebec youth court judges indicated that they thought that few of the youth court cases could be dealt with adequately outside the youth justice system (see Table 9.2). This stands in contrast to the 44 percent of judges from the rest of Canada who believed that few cases could be dealt with outside the justice system. This difference in judicial perceptions makes sense:

Table 9.1 *Variation in Use of Youth Court: Bringing Cases into Youth Court and the Overall Crime Rate and Violent Crime Rate, 1999–2000.*

Jurisdiction	Youth Court Cases per 100 Youths	Overall *Criminal Code* Crime* Rate (per 100,000)	Overall Violent Crime Rate* (per 100,000)
Canada	4.17	7,655	982
Newfoundland	3.64	5,711	900
Prince Edward Island	2.71	6,686	719
Nova Scotia	4.12	7,571	990
New Brunswick	3.73	6,519	937
Quebec	1.96	6,027	718
Ontario	4.28	6,421	887
Manitoba	7.00	10,723	1,638
Saskatchewan	9.41	12,730	1,663
Alberta	6.14	8,822	1,062
British Columbia	3.64	11,253	1,251
Yukon	13.81	23,540	3,326
Northwest Territories	10.09	27,389	4,722
Nunavut	4.29	21,190	6,074

*Excludes Criminal Code *traffic and other federal statutes.*
Sources: Statistics Canada (2001a and 2001b).

Quebec judges see fewer cases in youth court, so presumably those relatively few cases that they do see are ones that most would agree need to go to youth court.

Comparing Quebec to the rest of Canada obscures some variation in judicial perceptions (see Table 9.3). In the other regions, the majority of judges think that at least half or more of the cases before them could have been dealt with adequately outside the court. These other jurisdictions tend to bring in more cases than Quebec, which likely contributes to the judicial perceptions that larger proportions of cases could be dealt with adequately without recourse to youth court.

THE USE OF CUSTODY IN YOUTH COURT

Perhaps not surprisingly, there is also variation across Canada in the use of custody. Table 9.4 shows that, overall, 34 percent of youth convictions result in a custodial term. Quebec imposes custody on the smallest proportion of cases—27.4 percent—followed very closely by Alberta (28.1). However, when considering the use of custody imposed per 1,000 youths in the population,

Table 9.2 *Judges' Views on the Proportion of Cases That Could Be Dealt with outside of Youth Court*

	Proportion of Cases That Could Be Dealt with Adequately outside of Court			
	Most–All	About half	Few–None	Total
Quebec	9.1%	18.2%	72.7%	100% (22)
Rest of Canada	14.6%	41.7%	43.7%	100% (205)

Source: Doob (2001).

Table 9.3 *Judges' Views on the Proportion of Cases That Could Be Dealt with outside of Youth Court*

	Proportion of Cases That Could Be Dealt with Adequately outside of Court			
	Most–All	About half	Few–None	Total
Atlantic	10.3%	48.3%	41.4%	100% (29)
Quebec	9.1%	18.2%	72.7%	100% (22)
Ontario	11.9%	43.3%	44.8%	100% (67)
Prairies	14.8%	37.0%	48.1%	100% (54)
British Columbia	18.9%	39.6%	41.5%	100% (53)
Territories	33.3%	66.7%	0.0%	100% (3)

Source: Doob (2001).

Table 9.4 *Variation in the Use of Custody, 1999–2000*

	Percent of Guilty Cases Sentenced to Custody	Rate of Custody per 1,000 Youths in Population
Canada	34.0%	9.48
Newfoundland	40.8%	11.55
Prince Edward Island	46.2%	10.42
Nova Scotia	35.7%	10.56
New Brunswick	31.7%	10.32
Quebec	27.4%	4.37
Ontario	39.8%	10.17
Manitoba	27.5%	11.13
Saskatchewan	33.8%	20.91
Alberta	28.1%	12.24
British Columbia	33.7%	8.52
Yukon	48.3%	39.42
Northwest Territories	57.8%	49.55
Nunuvut	26.7%	8.51

Source: Statistics Canada (2001a).

these two provinces have very different rates. While it imposes custody on similar proportions of guilty cases, Quebec has the lowest custody rate of 4.37 per 1,000 youths in the province while Alberta has a relatively high rate of 12.24, due to Alberta's bringing in substantially more cases than Quebec.

Another example of this is Saskatchewan and British Columbia—both impose custody on about one-third of their guilty cases, yet Saskatchewan has a custody rate of 20.91 per 1,000 youths while B.C. has a rate of 8.52.

Other jurisdictions clearly illustrate variation in the percentage of cases found guilty—but less variation than existed in bringing cases into youth court in the first place. Once in the justice system, then, there tends to be less variation. The different rates (per 1,000 youths) of imposing custody across Canada are therefore probably due more to differences in bringing cases into court than to variation in the use of custody as a sanction.

MANY YOUNG OFFENDERS ARE SENTENCED TO CUSTODY FOR MINOR CRIMES

It is also important to look at the types of cases that make up our custodial population. Table 9.5 shows that eight offences (or groupings of offences)

Table 9.5 *Cases to Custody: Quebec, Ontario, and Saskatchewan, 1999–2000*

Most Significant Charge:	Canada		Quebec		Ontario		Saskatchewan	
	#	%*	#	%*	#	%*	#	%*
Theft under $5,000	2,005	9%	242	10.1%	647	7.0%	185	9.2%
Possession of stolen property	1,411	6%	37	1.5%	628	6.8%	163	8.1%
Failure to appear	2,579	11%	123	5.1%	1116	12.0%	276	13.7%
Failure to comply	5,234	23%	418	17.4%	1951	21.0%	321	15.9%
Subtotal	**11,229**	**49%**	**820**	**34.1%**	**4342**	**46.8%**	**945**	**46.9%**
Other thefts	1,011	4%	82	3.4%	388	4.2%	122	6.1%
Mischief/damage	726	3%	40	1.7%	265	2.8%	87	4.3%
Break and enter	2,853	12%	377	15.7%	983	10.6%	283	14.1%
Minor assault	1,521	7%	134	5.6%	808	8.7%	98	4.9%
Total: Sum of eight offences	**17,340**	**75%**	**1453**	**60.5%**	**6786**	**73.1%**	**1535**	**76.3%**
All cases	23,215	100%	2400	100%	9303	100%	2013	100%
Cases to custody per 1,000 youths in the jurisdiction	9.48	4.4	10.2	20.5				

* Percentage of all custodial sentences for which this offence was the most significant charge.

account for the majority of 23,215 custodial sentences in 1999–2000. Theft of property worth less than $5,000 accounted for roughly 9 percent of all cases going to custody. If we add three other relatively minor offences—possession of stolen property, failure to appear in youth court, and failure to comply with a disposition—we find that these four offences account for roughly 48 percent of all cases in which a custodial sentence was imposed. While there is a tendency to think that only the most serious cases result in custodial sentences, these data demonstrate that many custodial sentences are, in fact, imposed for relatively minor cases.

The proportion varies somewhat from province to province and from year to year. But it is safe to suggest that somewhere between one-third and one-half of the youth cases that end up in custody in any province, in any year, have as their most serious charge one of these four offences. When one adds in other thefts, mischief/damage to property, break and enter, and minor assaults, we find that these eight sets of offences account for approximately three-quarters of all cases that end in custodial sentences. Thus, even though more serious offences are, generally, dealt with more harshly by the system (see, for example, Matarazzo, Carrington, and Hiscott, 2001), significant numbers of less serious offences also result in young persons receiving a term of custody.

Table 9.5 supports this pattern of less serious cases accounting for the majority of cases that end in custody for the two largest provinces as well as one relatively small province (Saskatchewan) that incarcerates large numbers of youth.

As we have already noted, Quebec brings far fewer cases to court, per capita, than the other provinces and territories and, as we have seen, places many fewer youths in custody (per capita) than other provinces. It therefore makes sense that the cases that do end in custody tend to be somewhat more serious in Quebec. But even in Quebec, with its relatively sparing use of youth court, a substantial number of youths are placed in custody for relatively minor offences: 61 percent of the cases that went to custody in Quebec had as the most significant charge one of these eight types of offences.

ADDRESSING THESE PROBLEMS WITH THE *YCJA*

One of the *YOA*'s shortcomings was that it contained very weak language regarding when a young person should be sent to youth court (see Doob and Sprott, 1999). For example, although the *YOA* explicitly allowed cases to be dealt with outside the court system, it did so in a very nondirective fashion, using the following language:

> Where it is not inconsistent with the protection of society, taking no measures or taking measures other than judicial proceedings under this Act should be considered for dealing with young persons who have committed offences (*YOA*, Section 3 (d)).

In contrast, the *YCJA* uses much stronger wording to promote the use of alternative measures. The act states that:

> Extrajudicial measures [measures outside the formal court structure] are presumed to be adequate to hold a young person accountable for his or her offending behaviour if the young person has committed a non-violent offence and has not previously been found guilty of an offence (*YCJA*, section 4 (c)).

and

> Extrajudicial measures should be used if they are adequate to hold a young person accountable for his or her offending behaviour and, if the use of extrajudicial measures is consistent with the principles set out in this section, nothing in this Act precludes their use in respect to a young person who (i) has been previously dealt with by the use of extrajudicial measures, or (ii) has previously been found guilty of an offence (*YCJA*, section 4 (d)).

Furthermore, the *YCJA* states that:

A police officer shall, before starting judicial proceedings or taking any other measures under this Act against a young person alleged to have committed an offence, consider whether it would be sufficient, having regard to the principles set out in section 4 [extrajudicial measures, or noncourt alternatives to responding to youth crime], to take no further action, warn the young person, administer a caution ... or, with the consent of the young person, refer the young person to a program or agency in the community that may assist the young person not to commit offences (*YCJA*, section 6 (1)).

In the case of the *YOA*, then, the requirement was only that noncourt alternatives should be considered if they are "not inconsistent with the protection of society." In contrast, under the *YCJA*, approaches that do not involve court are presumed to be adequate for a wide range of cases (cases where the youth has never been to court and is charged with something other than a violent offence). A presumption in favour of a noncourt approach means that an argument needs to be made to bring the case to court. In the absence of such an argument, the presumption is that the case should be dealt with in some other way. And, as the second of these subsections points out, noncourt alternatives can be used even if they have been used before or if on a previous occasion the youth had been taken to court and found guilty. Finally, there appears (section 6(1)) to be a positive requirement on the part of the police to consider noncourt responses to youthful offending, though there are no formal consequences if it turns out that the police do not follow the law in this regard. To summarize, if the *YCJA* fulfils its purpose, the result will be a decrease in the number of young persons in conflict with the law who are brought into youth court.

REGULATING THE USE OF CUSTODY

The provisions in the *YOA* concerning the use of custody were also weak (see section 24(1) to 24(1.1)(b) and (c)). Generally, judges were directed that custody is not to be used unless it is necessary for the protection of the public. But how is the judge to determine when it is necessary? And to tell the judge that noncustodial dispositions are to be used "wherever appropriate" and that custodial sentences are to be used only after the alternatives that are "reasonable in the circumstances" have been considered does not eliminate many alternatives.

The *YCJA*, on the other hand, contains several critical sections relating to sentencing. Section 38 sets out the principles that should guide judges at sentencing, and section 39 lays out the conditions regulating the use of custody. Section 38 states that the purpose of sentencing is to hold a young person accountable through the imposition of just sanctions that have meaningful consequences for the young person and that promote his or her rehabilitation and reintegration into society, thereby contributing to the long-term protection of the public" (section 38(1)).

Judges are then provided with a list of principles to follow when sentencing. One of these principles is that of proportionality in sentencing, which requires judges to impose sentences that are proportionate to the seriousness of the offence and the degree of responsibility of the young person. Another principle is the well-established principle of restraint. This principle requires that the sentence imposed must be the least restrictive one available (*YCJA*, section 38(2)). These two principles are also applicable to adult offenders.

Section 39 of the *YCJA* contains further conditions that must be met before a young offender is committed to custody. Selected sections of section 39(1) are reproduced below:

A youth justice court shall not commit a young person to custody under section 42 (youth sentences) unless

(a) the young person has committed a violent offence;

(b) the young person has failed to comply with non-custodial sentences;

(c) the young person has committed an indictable offence for which an adult would be liable to imprisonment for a term of more than two years and has a history that indicates a pattern of findings of guilt ...

(d) in exceptional cases where the young person has committed an indictable offence, the aggravating circumstances of the offence are such that the imposition of a non-custodial sentence would be inconsistent with the purpose and principles set out in section 38.

Clearly, the language of the *YCJA* is stronger than that of its predecessor, the *YOA*. The new act requires that a sentence be proportional to the seriousness of the offence, for example, rather than suggesting it as a consideration. Section 39 mandates that at least one of four conditions must be met before a custodial sanction can be imposed. The last of these (section 39(1)(d)) is, clearly, the least explicit of the four. However, even this one states that the circumstances must be "exceptional" and that no other noncustodial sentence could be crafted to be consistent with the purpose and principles of sentencing.

Will practices in youth court change once the new act is in force? Although difficult to predict, to some extent it will depend upon the way in which the provinces and territories implement the new legislation and whether crown attorneys, defence counsel, and judges interpret the *YCJA* as representing a major change from the *YOA*.

DISCUSSION QUESTIONS

1. *The authors demonstrate that the official response to young offenders varies from province to province. Some people argue that it is legitimate for practices to vary across the country. Others feel that young offenders should be treated the same regardless of the province or territory in which they happen to live. What is your opinion?*

2. *Sentencing under the* Youth Criminal Justice Act *is quite different from the sentencing of adults, which is regulated by other sections of the* Criminal Code. *What justifications exist for punishing young persons who break the law, according to different principles? Why, for example, do we use custody more often for adults than for juveniles convicted of the same* Criminal Code *offence?*

3. *After reading this chapter, do you think that judges will sentence fewer young persons to custody as a result of the new act?*

FURTHER READINGS

Bala, N. 2002 *Youth Criminal Justice Act.* Toronto: Irwin Law.

Doob A.N. and Sprott, J.B. (In press). Changing models of youth justice in Canada. In M. Tonry and A. Doob (Eds.), *Crime and Justice: A Review of the Research.* Chicago: University of Chicago Press.

Doob, A.N. and Sprott, J.B. 1999. Changes in the sentencing of youth in Canada. *Federal Sentencing Reporter, 11(5)*, 262–268

REFERENCES

Doob, A.N. 2001. *Youth Court Judges' Views of the Youth Justice System: The Results of a Survey.* Ottawa: Department of Justice Canada.

Doob, A.N. and Sprott, J.B. 1996. Interprovincial variation in the use of youth courts. *Canadian Journal of Criminology,* 38(4), 401–412.

———. (1999). Changes in the sentencing of youth in Canada. *Federal Sentencing Reporter,* 11(5), 262–268.

———. (2003).(In press). "Changing Models of Youth Justice in Canada". In *Crime and Justice: A Review of the Research.* (M. Tonry and A. Doob, Eds). Chicago: University of Chicago Press.

Carrington, P. 1999. Trends in youth crime in Canada, 1977–1996. *Canadian Journal of Criminology,* 41(1), 1–32.

Matarazzo, A., Carrington, P.J., and Hiscott, R.D. 2001. The effect of prior youth court dispositions on current disposition: An application of societal-reaction theory. *Journal of Quantitative Criminology,* 17, 169–200.

Sprott, J.B. and Doob, A.N. 2002. Two solitudes or just one? Provincial differences in youth court judges and the operation of the youth courts. *Canadian Journal of Criminology,* 44(2), 165–180.

Sprott J.B. and Snyder, H.N. 1999. Youth crime in the U.S. and Canada, 1991 to 1996. *Overcrowded Times,* 10(5), 1, 12–19.

Statistics Canada (2001a). Youth Court Data Tables 1999–2000. Ottawa: Canadian Centre for Justice Statistics.

Statistics Canada (2001b). Canadian Crime Statistics 1999–2000. Ottawa: Canadian Centre for Justice Statistics.

PART THREE
Victims and the Justice System

CHAPTER 10
Victims of Crime and the Canadian Justice System

INTRODUCTION

Crime victims have, for many years, been overlooked by the criminal justice system. However, more recently, they have come to play an increasingly important role in this system. This is true in Canada as well as in other common-law jurisdictions such as England and Wales and New Zealand. Both the federal and provincial governments in Canada have introduced legislation to provide victims with more services and more "voice" in the processing of criminal cases. In this chapter, the authors, who have worked in the area of victims' policy and practice for many years, explore recent developments with respect to victims in the Canadian criminal justice system.

Victims of Crime and the Justice System

Michelle Grossman, M.A., M.S.W., and *Catherine Kane*, Policy
Centre for Victim Issues, Department of Justice Canada[i]

Both the federal and provincial levels of government in Canada have made significant efforts to improve a crime victim's experience in the criminal justice system. Despite these efforts, many issues related to victims' needs, expectations, and experiences in the criminal justice system require additional attention. This chapter explores several key issues relating to crime victims and the criminal justice system in Canada through an examination of relevant

Canadian legislation and the findings from a selection of recent research on victims and the justice system.

While this chapter does not address the impact of victimization, it is important to recognize that people react differently to events. While one may not expect a victim to be traumatized and fearful following the theft of his or her car, he or she may be just that. At a minimum, he or she will be annoyed and inconvenienced and will seek information from the police and others. More serious and personal violence offences will have far greater impact and longer-term consequences. Victims are tossed into an unfamiliar system in which they do not have a clearly articulated or understood role. A victim is simply one more "case" or one more "witness" for the Crown or judge, but for the victim, this case is his or her only case.

When asked to identify the "players" in the criminal justice system, most people would identify the police, Crown attorney, defence counsel, judge, probation officers or parole officers. Their roles or duties are fairly clear and understood. The legal system generally refers to the "parties" in a proceeding. In a civil proceeding (e.g., a claim for damages for negligence) the parties are referred to as the "plaintiff" and "defendant." The plaintiff is the person "complaining," or alleging a wrong and seeking damages. In criminal proceedings, the parties are the Crown and the accused. It is the Crown that is complaining on behalf of the state (or her Majesty) about a wrong (i.e., a crime) done by the accused. The victim (the person who actually suffered because of this wrong) is not a party.

THE EVOLUTION OF VICTIM "RIGHTS" IN CANADA

In Canada, the emergence of the victim's voice and recognition of the concerns of victims dates back to the early 1970s. Criminal injuries compensation programs, which provided financial awards to victims of crime, originated in some jurisdictions as compensation to police officers injured in the course of their duties and grew to provide limited compensation from the state (i.e., the province) to other eligible victims of violent crime. The federal government, in efforts to encourage the development of such programs in all provinces, provided financial contributions to provinces and established minimum criteria for compensation programs. The federal support for these programs that benefited some victims coincided with government funding for legal aid programs that benefited some accused persons.

By the early 1980s, all Canadian provinces and territories had criminal injuries compensation programs, established by provincial/territorial statute. The programs varied in terms of eligibility and the scope of financial awards. By the early 1990s, many provinces and territories were exploring the effectiveness of criminal injuries compensation programs in meeting the needs of victims in general. While financial assistance is, without question, beneficial, many victims of crime were ineligible and many other needs of crime victims required attention, e.g., information, services, support, and counselling.

While the development of criminal injuries compensation was one sign of the growing recognition that victims of crime deserved assistance, a great deal of credit for raising awareness about victimization is due to the women's movement. Women's advocacy, on behalf of other women who were abused or sexually assaulted but sometimes ignored and discredited by the justice system, coupled with their support, assistance, and protection to abused women, provided an example for others to follow in advocating on behalf of victims of crime in general.

While legislative reforms may benefit victims of crime, it is important to recognize that statutory reform is only one response to crime victims. Services and assistance for victims of crime ranging from emergency or crisis response services, shelters, counselling, victim-witness assistance programs, and specialized services for children and for sexual assault survivors provide practical help and essential support that meet greater needs than legislation meets.

Rather than provide a chronology of the legislative reforms since the late 1980s, which would demonstrate the gradual recognition of the needs of victims of crime, a description of the current provisions in the *Criminal Code* and *Corrections and Conditional Release Act* is set out below. In reviewing these provisions, it is important to understand the distinction between the roles of the federal government versus those of the provincial governments. The federal government is responsible for enacting the criminal law, while the provinces are responsible for the enforcement of the criminal law, the prosecution of offences, and the administration of justice, in general, which includes the provision of services to victims. All provinces and territories have enacted victim legislation addressing matters of provincial responsibility. For example, Manitoba, which was the first province to enact comprehensive victim legislation in 1986, has recently enacted *The Victim's Bill of Rights*. The statute provides rights for victims and obligations on the police, Crown, and other criminal justice players to ensure victims' rights are respected.

While *Criminal Code* reform with respect to crime victims focuses on the period since 1988, it is important to note that the *Criminal Code* has included provisions to permit restitution to be ordered to victims since the 1950s. In addition, the significant reforms to Canada's sexual assault laws in the early 1980s recognized that sexual offence complainants were in need of special considerations. Following Canada's sponsorship of the *U.N. Declaration of Basic Principles of Justice for Victims of Crime* and endorsement by federal/provincial/territorial Justice ministers of the *Canadian Statement of Basic Principles of Justice for Victims of Crime*, both the federal and provincial levels of government pursued legislative reforms.

The description of key *Code* provisions below follows the stages of the criminal process—pretrial, trial, and/or preliminary inquiry, sentencing, and postsentencing.

CRIMINAL CODE PROVISIONS OF BENEFIT TO VICTIMS

Definition of "Victim"

In the *Criminal Code*, "victim" is broadly defined to include "the victim of an alleged offence." *Bill C-79* (1999) added a definition of victim to s. 2 (the general definition section) of the *Criminal Code*. Prior to this amendment, the only definition of victim was found in the section of the *Criminal Code* dealing with victim impact statements. This definition is nonexhaustive and makes no distinction between primary (i.e., the actual victim), secondary (i.e., spouse, parent, co-worker, etc.), or indirect victims of crime. The definition of victim clarifies that the term may properly be used even where no conviction has been entered, acknowledging that the term "victim" does not presume the guilt of the accused.

Consideration of Victim's Safety in Bail Decisions

When a suspect is arrested, the police will determine whether or not the suspect should be detained in custody or released with a promise to appear and sometimes with conditions (commonly referred to as bail). In some cases, these decisions are made by police, in others, by a justice of the peace or a judge. Regardless of who makes the decision to release, most victims want to know the outcome of the decision and also seek assurance that their safety has been taken into account in the making of the decision to release.

Amendments included in *Bill C-79* (1999) require the decision-maker, at various points in the criminal justice process, to ensure "the safety and security of any victim of or to the offence," including:

- that the responsible judicial officer (officer in charge, justice of the peace, or judge) considers the safety and security of the victim in any decision about an accused's bail;
- that where an accused is released pending trial, the judge considers including as a condition to bail that the accused abstain from any direct or indirect communication with the victim and any other condition necessary to ensure the safety and security of the victim; and,
- that the particular concerns of the victim are considered and highlighted in decisions on the imposition of special bail conditions, including in firearms prohibitions and in criminal harassment offences.

Facilitating Testimony

For some victims and witnesses, participating in the judicial proceedings can be intimidating or even frightening. The *Criminal Code* includes several provisions designed to assist victims and to reduce their anxiety. For example:

- providing discretion for the judge to exclude members from the courtroom when necessary for the proper administration of justice;

- allowing a victim or witness who is under 18 years of age, or may have difficulty communicating the evidence by reason of mental or physical disability, to testify outside the courtroom or behind a screen or device that would prevent a view of the accused;
- allowing the admission of videotaped testimony of the victim or witness who is under the age of 18 in specified proceedings, including sexual offences;
- permitting a support person to accompany a witness or victim who is disabled or young (under 14 years of age); and,
- restricting personal cross-examination of young sexual offence victims and personal violence offence victims (under 18 years of age) by a self-represented accused.

Publication Bans

In criminal proceedings, while the general rule is that all proceedings against an accused shall be held in open court, the *Criminal Code* sets out several exceptions to facilitate victims' or witnesses' participation and to protect privacy. Complainants of sexual offences and young victims and witnesses are the primary beneficiaries of these special provisions.

A judge may make an order to protect the identity of any victim or witness, or any information that could disclose his or her identity, if the judge is satisfied that the order is "necessary for the proper administration of justice" (see s. 486(4.1)). An application to the court is made by the victim, witness, or Crown, stating why the order sought is required. The hearing to determine whether the application for a publication ban should be granted may be held in private. The court must consider several specified factors.

In addition, a judge must order a publication ban to protect the identity of all victims of sexual offences and witnesses of sexual offences who are less than 18 years old (s. 486(3), s. 486(4)). In these cases, the judge tells the victim, witness, or Crown prosecutor that he or she may make a request for this protection. If he or she make the request, the judge must order a publication ban.

Provisions for Sexual Offence Victims

In addition to provisions noted above that benefit victims, sexual assault reforms have recognized the unique nature of the offence, the trauma suffered by the victim, and the re-victimization caused by participating in the criminal justice system. The *Criminal Code* provides a clear and common-sense definition of "consent" for the purpose of sexual assault offences. Any nonconsensual sexual activity is a sexual assault and hence proof of lack of consent is an essential element of the offence. Subsection 273.1(1) defines consent as the voluntary agreement of the complainant to engage in the sexual activity in question. Conduct short of a voluntary agreement to engage in sexual activity does not constitute consent as a matter of law. For greater certainty, subsection 273.1(2) sets out specific situations where there is no consent in law.

Restricting the Defence of Honest Belief in Consent

Section 273.2 limits the scope of the defence of honest belief in consent to sexual activity by providing that the defence is not available where the accused's belief arose from the accused's self-induced intoxication, or where the accused's belief arose from the accused's recklessness or wilful blindness, or where the accused failed to take reasonable steps to ascertain whether the complainant was consenting.

Restricting the Admission of Evidence About the Complainant

Sections 276 to 276.5 of the *Criminal Code* govern the admission of evidence regarding a sexual assault complainant's other sexual activity. The *Code* makes it clear that evidence that a complainant has engaged in sexual activity is not admissible to suggest that the victim was more likely to have consented to the sexual activity that is the subject matter of the charge or that he or she is less worthy of belief. The provisions restrict the admissibility of evidence to specific instances of sexual activity, relevant to an issue at trial, and to evidence that has "significant probative value which is not substantially outweighed by the danger of prejudice to the administration of justice." The judge is required to consider a range of factors set out in the *Code* in making this determination. The *Code* also sets out the procedure to be followed and includes provisions to safeguard the victim's privacy including provisions for an *in camera* (closed) hearing, non-compellability of the victim at the hearing, and a publication ban on the proceedings. These provisions are sometimes referred to as the "rape shield" laws.

Protecting the Personal Records of Sexual Offence Victims

Sections 278.1 to 278.9 of the *Code* govern the production of personal records about victims and witnesses in sexual offence proceedings. The provisions place the onus on the accused to establish that the records sought are likely relevant to an issue at trial and require the trial judge to carefully scrutinize applications and determine production in accordance with a two-part process involving a consideration of both the accused's rights to full answer and defence and the victim's rights to privacy and equality. The procedure to be followed is also set out in the *Code* and includes safeguards for the victim's privacy including an *in camera* (closed) hearing, non-compellability of the victim at the hearing, a publication ban on the proceedings and the contents of the application, editing of the records (where ordered to be produced) to delete irrelevant personal information, and the imposition of other appropriate conditions on production.

Sentencing

In 1996, reforms to the sentencing provisions of the *Criminal Code* were enacted. One of these reforms was codification of the purposes and principles of sentencing. Judges are directed to consider a number of objectives when sentencing offenders; two of which are relevant to the interests of victims:

- to provide reparations for harm done to victims or to the community; and,
- to promote a sense of responsibility in offenders and acknowledgement of the harm done to victims and to the community.

Victim Impact Statement

Although there are only two parties in a sentencing hearing, the offender, represented by defence counsel, and the state, represented by the Crown, the victim of the crime nevertheless has a role to play. Most countries permit crime victims to submit a statement to the court detailing the impact that the crime has had upon their lives. Some American states go even further and allow victims to make recommendations to the court about specific sentences. This is not permitted in Canada.

In 1988, the *Criminal Code* was amended to permit the court to consider a victim impact statement (VIS), and, since 1995, the *Code* has required the court to consider a victim impact statement at the time of sentencing. The victim impact statement describes the harm done to or loss suffered by the victim of the offence. The form of the statement must be in accordance with procedures established by a victim impact statement program designated by the lieutenant governor in council of the province.

In order to improve the utility of victim impact statements, the victim impact provisions in the *Criminal Code* were amended in 1999. The amendments:

- ensure that the victim is permitted to read a victim impact statement at the time of sentencing if he or she wishes to do so;
- require the judge to ask, before imposing sentence, whether the victim has been informed of the opportunity to prepare a victim impact statement;
- authorize adjournments to permit a victim to prepare a statement or to submit other evidence to the court about the impact of the crime;
- require that victim impact statements be considered by courts and Review Boards following a verdict of not criminally responsible on account of mental disorder; and,
- clarify that at proceedings to determine whether an offender sentenced to life in prison should have his or her parole eligibility reduced (s. 745.6 hearings), the information provided by the victim may be oral or written.

Victim Surcharge

A victim surcharge is an additional penalty automatically imposed on offenders at the time of sentencing unless the accused seeks an exception due to undue hardship. It is collected and retained by the provincial and territorial governments and used to help fund programs, services, and assistance to victims of crime within their jurisdiction. The victim surcharge was included in the 1988 amendments to the *Criminal Code* and proclaimed in 1989 along with regulations setting out the applicable amount. Amendments in 1999 fixed the amount of the surcharge and provided for automatic imposition upon conviction. The surcharge is 15 percent of any fine imposed on the offender. If no fine is imposed, the surcharge is $50 in the case of an offence punishable by summary conviction and $100 in the case of an offence punishable by indictment; or an increased surcharge, at the discretion of the judge, in appropriate circumstances.

Restitution

Restitution may be ordered by the court, on its own motion, or to cover readily ascertainable pecuniary damages including those resulting from bodily injury (not pain and suffering). There are no criminal enforcement provisions; enforcement of restitution is the victim's responsibility.

Victims and the Correctional System

The *Corrections and Conditional Release Act (CCRA)* governs Correctional Service Canada (CSC), which is responsible for supervising offenders sentenced to more than two years in custody, and the National Parole Board (NPB), which is mandated to determine whether to release offenders into the community. The act contains specific provisions authorizing the release of some offender-related information to victims who register with CSC and request information.

Anyone can request publicly available information such as the offence for which an offender was convicted, the sentence length, and eligibility dates for temporary absences, day parole, or full parole. Victims of crime, as defined in the *CCRA*, may register and request additional information that may include the penitentiary where the offender is serving the sentence; the date of a Parole Board hearing; the nature of the conditions attached to any work release, parole, statutory release, or temporary absences; as well as whether the offender is in custody and, if not, the reasons. Victims may request ongoing information and must ensure that CSC and NPB have their current address for this purpose.

Victims may also provide information to the Correctional Service and National Parole Board. Victim Liaison Officers within CSC generally receive requests for information from victims and provide information to them. Victims may request to attend Parole Board hearings as observers and may also have access to the decision registry of the National Parole Board. Victims may prepare and submit victim impact statements, describing the physical, emotional, and financial impact of the offence upon them, to the Parole Board. Recently, National Parole Board policy has been revised to permit victims to read or otherwise present the victim impact statement at the hearing.

Victims and Life Sentences

Offenders convicted of murder are sentenced to imprisonment for life. Most such offenders, however, become eligible for parole after serving a number of years in prison. In many cases, victims and/or their families express a desire to know when the offender in their case becomes eligible for parole, or has a parole hearing. Most prisoners serving life sentences with no parole for at least 15 years are eligible to apply for a jury review of their parole eligibility date. The provision in the *Code* that permits such an application is sometimes referred to as the "faint hope clause." Often, the families of murder victims express a desire to know when the offender in their case makes an application under this provision.

To ensure that information is provided to victims about life sentences, the *Criminal Code* requires a judge to state, for the record and for the benefit of surviving victims, that an offender convicted of murder who has received a life sentence may apply for a reduction in the number of years before he or she is eligible to apply to a court for parole after serving at least 15 years of the sentence. In addition, at proceedings to determine whether an offender should have his or her parole eligibility reduced (s. 745.6 or "faint hope clause" hearings), the information provided by the victim may be oral or written, at the option of the victim.

As mentioned earlier, legislative reform has addressed some victim needs and, while further reforms have been called for, such reforms should be supported by research that examines both the effectiveness of the existing legislation and the broader needs of victims.

CURRENT RESEARCH—SELECTED KEY ISSUES

As an exhaustive review of the myriad of issues relating to victims of crime is beyond the scope of this chapter, a selection of issues is presented below.

Victim Needs

The needs of victims range from the general to the specific and may be dependent, in many cases, on the type of victimization experienced and the characteristics of the individual victim. Victims identify financial needs, emotional needs, practical needs, and needs related to personal safety and security to varying degrees and in varying circumstances. However, research indicates that the need for information is amongst the most critical and universal needs expressed by victims of crime (e.g., Wemmers, 2002; Fattah, 1997).

Faced with the labyrinth of the criminal justice system, victims frequently have no concept of how best to navigate through the system. In most cases, accused persons have defence lawyers who ensure that the defendant is made aware of the details of the case. While many victims may mistakenly believe the Crown attorney to be their personal lawyer, the Crown acts on behalf of the state, not the victim. Nevertheless, victims should not have to hire their own lawyers to protect their interests or assist them through the system and do not typically do so. Consequently, victims of crime must rely on the various criminal justice system officials to provide the appropriate information necessary to keep victims apprised of how their case is proceeding and progressing.

Plea Negotiations

Plea negotiations (or plea bargains) may not immediately come to mind when reviewing topics related to victims of crime. However, the practice of such negotiations has a significant impact on crime victims. A plea bargain is defined as a "negotiated agreement between the defence and the prosecution in a criminal case. Typically, the defendant agrees to plead guilty to a specified charge in exchange for an oral promise of a lower sentence." (Lectric Law Library). Plea-bargaining is important since about 90 percent of criminal cases are resolved through guilty pleas, many of which are the direct outcome of plea negotiations between Crown and defence (Verdun-Jones and Tijerino, 2002).

Verdun-Jones and Tijerino (2002) report that a victim's role in plea-bargaining in Canada is virtually nonexistent, despite the critical effect that the results of such an arrangement may have directly on the victim. They explain that although plea negotiations play an integral role in the criminal justice process in Canada, they in fact "have no formal legal status and are not subject to direct judicial regulation." (pg. 5)

A victim's exclusion from this pretrial procedure may contribute to his or her negative perception of the criminal justice process. Agreements made between the Crown and the defence without the input or, at a minimum, the knowledge of the concerned crime victim may contribute directly to a victim's dissatisfaction with the criminal justice system. On the other hand, a guilty plea avoids the need for victims to participate in trial proceedings, an activity which they may find traumatizing and re-victimizing.

Verdun-Jones and Tijerino (2002) suggest that although formal involvement in this process may prove to be difficult, simple steps such as being informed of the plea negotiation before it takes place, as well as representation of a victim's views by the Crown at the time of the plea negotiation, may serve to satisfy the wishes of many crime victims. Furthermore, they note that in 1987, the Canadian Sentencing Commission made a number of recommendations related to the issue of plea negotiations, several of which addressed victims' involvement in the process. However, to date, these recommendations have not been implemented.

Verdun-Jones and Tijerino's report examines the current legislative and judicial responses to plea-bargaining within Canada and identifies the negative consequences that flow from the lack of any formal process for the regulation of this practice. The report also identifies four potential models for the participation of victims in the plea-bargaining process and provides recommendations regarding the possible way forward for this process in Canada.

Verdun-Jones and Tijerino's extensive review of the literature in this area illustrates the need for further research regarding the role of the crime victim and the practice of plea negotiations in Canada.

Victim Impact Statements

Victims' experiences with victim impact statements were the focus of an exploratory study conducted by Meredith and Paquette for the Policy Centre for Victims Issues (Department of Justice Canada) in 2000. This research involved the implementation of six focus groups. Although each focus group was small, and limitations in terms of participant selection precludes generalization of the findings, the study did raise a number of issues with respect to victim impact statements and the need for further exploration of this provision.

A summary of findings from the report, based on the limited study sample, revealed that, "participants' perceptions of what victim impact statements are supposed to accomplish were twofold. The first perceived goal was that the statements should allow victims to have a say in the sentencing process by presenting to the court how the crime has affected their lives" (2001, pg. 6). The second perceived goal, as reported by many of the study participants, was to "have an effect on the sentence actually imposed in their cases." (pg. 6) While many of the participants acknowledged "that judges must take into account a number of factors in reaching their decisions on sentencing," many of the study participants were, in retrospect, "sceptical that their statement had had any such effect.... Some participants reported a cathartic effect from preparing their statements." (pg. 6)

Most participants were aware of their right to read their statements aloud, and there was strong support among participants for this right.

Participants in five of the six groups were generally positive about their experiences with victim impact statements, "despite frequent doubt that these statements had any significant effect on the sentences imposed" (p. 10).

Among the benefits ascribed to the process of completing and submitting a statement were the following:

- It allows victims to vent their anger;
- It allows victims to confront the accused in a safe environment;
- It enables victims to include in their statements information that they were prevented from providing in their testimony;
- It allows victims to bring to the court's attention the total impact of the offence regardless of the specific charges; and,
- Some offenders, as a result of hearing the victim impact statement, may come to think more seriously about the harm they have done (p. 10).

It was interesting to note that one group, almost in its entirety, was not satisfied with their experiences with completing a victim impact statement. According to the summary report of the focus group study:

Some group participants reported considerable frustration with the court process when sentences were imposed which they perceived to have been negotiated prior to submission of their VISs. In these cases, they were confident that no account had been taken of their experiences as victims, and resented the system's seeming disregard for the effort which went into preparing their VISs (p.12).

It is clear that there remains considerable room for further exploration and research in the area of victim impact statements in terms of their intended purpose, their actual use, and the resultant satisfaction at their implementation by victims, offenders, and criminal justice professionals alike (see Roberts, 2003 for a review of the research into the use of victim impact statements at sentencing).

Restorative Justice

Restorative justice, as an alternative to more traditional retributive methods of criminal justice, has received increasing attention in Canada and elsewhere. The subject has been the focus of much recent research, especially in regards to victims of crime.

Wemmers and Canuto (2002) reviewed the literature that specifically examined victims' perceptions and expectations of restorative justice as well as their experiences in a restorative justice system. The authors examined these three concepts as related to victims and restorative justice to determine whether restorative justice programs adequately address victims' needs.

The report used the following definition: "Restorative Justice is a process whereby all parties with a stake in a specific offence come together to resolve collectively how to deal with the aftermath of the offence and its implications for the future" (p. 1). In a "Fact Sheet" on restorative justice produced by the Policy Centre for Victim Issues, Department of Justice Canada, restorative justice is defined as, "one way to respond to a criminal act" where the emphasis is put "on the wrong done to a person as well as the wrong done to the community." The definition continues by asserting, "Restorative Justice recognizes that crime is both a violation of relationships between specific people and an offence against everyone—the state." The Fact Sheet also states that "the fundamental principle is that restorative justice must not re-victimize the victim in any way," and that "the process and the outcome should not cause further harm."

Among the conclusions reached by Wemmers and Canuto as a result of their selected examination are the following:

- Victims generally are in favour of restorative justice practices provided participation is fully voluntary.
- Restorative justice programs provide victims with notification of the developments of their case and an opportunity to ask for restitution.

- Victims are quite content to hand over certain responsibilities, such as punishing offenders, to criminal justice authorities.
- Victims participate in restorative justice programs to seek reparation, help the offender, confront the offender with the consequences of the crime, and ask questions such as why the offence was committed.
- Victims' expectations are an important determinant of victim satisfaction.
- When compared to victims whose cases were handled in the traditional criminal justice system, there is no clear evidence to conclude that victims in restorative programs are any more or less satisfied (p.35).

Despite these and other conclusions reached in the report, Wemmers and Canuto state that "Clearly restorative justice programs are not a panacea for victims" (p. 35). Furthermore, the authors note that "more research is needed that compares and contrasts the impact of different restorative justice programs on victims" (p.36).

CONCLUSION

The need to consider the criminal justice system from the perspective of the victim is clear. While the role that crime victims play in this system is not as apparent as those of others in the criminal justice system, it is important that crime victims receive the attention and consideration they deserve. Although the role of the victim in the justice system has received increased attention in both the research literature and in policy and legislation, more work remains. Further exploration of the needs and concerns of victims is necessary, as are continuing efforts to evaluate the benefits of the progress already made (or initiatives already taken) to improve the criminal justice system.

DISCUSSION QUESTIONS

1. *Do you think that the legislative provisions described in the chapter provide an adequate level of involvement for victims, or should the role of the victim be further expanded?*
2. *Some victims' rights advocates suggest that crime victims should be able to include a recommendation about the sentence in their victim impact statement. Others respond that victims should not have this right as it will lead to more variability in sentencing. What do you think?*
3. *In Canada, plea negotiations have no formal legal status and are not subject to direct judicial regulation; nevertheless, they play an integral role in the criminal justice process. In Canada, a victim's role in plea-bargaining is virtually nonexistent despite the critical effect that the results of such an arrangement may have directly on the victim. How do you think this issue might be resolved in order to provide more satisfaction to victims, while preventing infringement of an accused's rights?*

FURTHER READINGS

Barrett, Joan M. 2000. *Balancing Charter Interests: Victims' Rights and Third Party Remedies*. Toronto: Carswell.

Burns, Peter. 1992. *Criminal Injuries Compensation* (Second Edition). Toronto: Butterworths Canada Ltd.

Roach, K. 1999. *Due Process and Victims' Rights: The New Law and Politics of Criminal Justice*. Toronto: University of Toronto Press.

Young, A.N. 2001. *The Role of the Victim in the Criminal Process: A Literature Review—1989 to 1999*. Victims of Crime Research Series. Ottawa: Department of Justice Canada.

REFERENCES

Canadian Sentencing Commission. 1987. *Sentencing Reform: A Canadian Approach*. Ontario: Ministry of Supply and Services Canada.

Department of Justice Canada. 2001. *Restorative Justice Fact Sheet*. Ottawa: Policy Centre for Victims Issues.

Fattah, E.A. 1997. From crime policy to victim policy: The need for a fundamental policy change. In M. McShane and F.P. Williams III (Eds.), *Criminal Justice: Contemporary Literature in Theory and Practice* (pp. 75–91). New York and London: Garland Publishing, Inc.

Lectric Law Library. http://www.lectlaw.com/def2/p053.htm.

Meredith, C. and Paquette, C. 2001. *Summary Report on Victim Impact Statement Focus Groups*. Victims of Crime Research Series. Ottawa: Department of Justice Canada.

Roberts, J.V. 2003. Victim impact statements and the sentencing process: Recent developments and research findings. *Criminal Law Quarterly* (In Press).

Verdun-Jones, S.N. and Tijerino, A.A. 2002. *Victim Participation in the Plea Negotiation Process in Canada: A Review of the Literature and Four Models for Law Reform*. Report for the Policy Centre for Victim Issues. Ottawa: Department of Justice Canada.

Wemmers, J. 2002. Restorative justice for victims of crime: A victim-oriented approach to restorative justice. *International Review of Victimology*, 9, 43–59.

Wemmers, J. and Canuto, M. 2002. *Victims' Experiences with, Expectations and Perceptions of, Restorative Justice: A Critical Review of the Literature*. Victim Issues Research Series. Ottawa: Department of Justice Canada.

ENDNOTES

[i] The views expressed in this chapter are those of the authors and do not necessarily represent the organizations for which they work.

CHAPTER 11
Victim Impact Statements

INTRODUCTION

Victims provide input into the sentencing process by means of the Victim Impact Statement (VIS). In this form submitted to the court, the victim describes the effect of the crime on his or her life. Crime victims have been overlooked in the criminal justice system until fairly recently, but all common-law jurisdictions now allow victims to have some input into the sentencing process.

That said, victim impact statements have been criticized on a number of grounds. Defence counsel sometimes object to the contents of these statements, which at times can be quite emotional. Some commentators argue that victim impact statements should not be allowed because they may result in the court's imposing a harsher sentence on the offender. In fact, there is little evidence that this happens because judges are trained to consider only information that is relevant to the sentencing decision. For example, if the victim wrote in the victim impact statement that the offender should go to prison for a long time, the judge would disregard this opinion, as victims are supposed to restrict themselves to information about the effects of the crime and are not allowed to make sentence recommendations.

Although victim impact statements are now an important component of the sentencing process, little is known about the way that judges use these statements at sentencing. In this chapter, Judge Renaud draws upon the case law and his experiences to explain how he incorporates the victim impact statement into his sentencing decisions. Judge Renaud is a very experienced member of the judiciary who has written many articles on various aspects of the sentencing process.

Victim Impact Statements: The View from the Bench
Mr. Justice Gilles Renaud, Ontario Court of Justice

> I will never forgive you for stealing the only thing I have had from my
> mother!

With those words, perhaps the most memorable I have ever heard in a courtroom, I came to understand fully the impact that a crime can have on a
victim. The speaker was a thirty-something single man who had never met his
mother, and whose only link with her was a letter in which she set out something of her life. It had been stolen during a residential burglary and later
destroyed for no reason at all. If I learned anything that day, it was that no
written victim impact statement can adequately convey the sense of loss or
violation of any victim, the loss that is obvious in the eyes of those who have
suffered. Although I had studied the legislation and the major cases, I knew
that I had much to learn about the experiences of victims of crime.

In this chapter, I describe the dynamics at play when victims seek to
express how they now view themselves and the world they live in. My intention is to point out all of the considerations I consider when assessing the
impact of a crime on a victim. To do so, I will attempt to "walk you through"
my thought process when I evaluate a victim impact statement.

1.   WHAT IS THE SENTENCING OBJECTIVE?

The starting-point must be to identify what should *not* influence the determination of the sentence. In this respect, I must remind myself that I cannot be
motivated by a desire to avenge the loss or harm inflicted on the victim. In
other words, although retribution is a legitimate principle of sentencing,
vengeance is not. This was made clear in a well-known judgment, *R. v. C.A.M.,*[i]
in which the Supreme Court distinguished retribution from vengeance in the
following way (at para. 80):

> Retribution in a criminal context, by contrast, represents an objective, rea-
> soned and measured determination of an appropriate punishment which
> properly reflects the moral culpability of the offender, having regard to the
> intentional risk taking of the offender, the consequential harm caused by
> the offender, and the normative character of the offender's conduct. Fur-
> thermore, unlike vengeance, retribution incorporates a principle of
> restraint; retribution requires the imposition of a just and appropriate pun-
> ishment, and nothing more.

2. WHO MAY APPROPRIATELY DISPLAY EMOTION?

It would be improper for a judge to be influenced by the emotions that may arise as a result of the victim impact information. The selection of an appropriate sentence is a rational exercise, albeit one that may include the evaluation of highly emotional experiences. By permitting the reception of such information pursuant to s. 722 of the *Code*, Parliament has indicated that courts must be sensitive to the plight of those who have been harmed or who have suffered a loss. Indeed, many Court of Appeal judgments feature a section titled "Impact on the Victims and their Families." One example is found in *R. v. D. (D.)*[ii] at paras. 10–13. Nevertheless, victim impact statements should not be the foundation for appeals to emotion.

When considering victim impact information, I attempt in most cases to examine the comments of the victim, and the harm or loss that he or she has suffered, at the beginning of my judgment. There are three reasons for this. First, I believe that this tends to bring out and to underscore the aggravating elements of the crime (such as the loss suffered by the victim) while introducing the observations of the victim. Second, it appears to be the best way to recognize that it is first and foremost a member of the community who has suffered harm. In many instances, the victim impact statement is the only means of demonstrating how the vitality of the community has been undermined. And, third, presenting the victim impact statement permits me to evaluate the reaction of the offender to this information about the effect of the crime. On occasion, I have reduced what might otherwise have been the sentence in response to what appears to have been a sincere expression of regret during the reading of my judgment.

3. HOW CAN MERE WORDS ON PAPER EXPLAIN THE LOSS THAT ONE HAS EXPERIENCED IN FATAL CASES?

Perhaps the most difficult cases to sentence are those involving the loss of life. In considering the great tragedy that has occurred, I must be mindful of all of the aspects of the loss suffered by the family and friends of the victim. On the other hand, I cannot overlook those instances in which there is no one present to mourn the loss of life that has resulted from the offence. In one instance in Ottawa, a person who had recently arrived in Canada was killed by an impaired driver. The victim had no known relatives. As a result, at sentencing, the trial judge resorted to the device of thinking out loud of what his life had been, and how the dreams and hopes he must have had were now destroyed, and how his loss would be felt by his family and friends.

No matter how we approach the situation, however, the problem remains the same: how may mere words adequately describe the loss of life? How can someone capture on paper the terrible consequences for the victim's family and friends? These questions bring to mind the case of *R. v. Winning*,[iii] in which the offender was convicted of second-degree murder. In that judgment, the court used the following words to describe the loss: "While the victim impact statements reflected the enormous tragedy to the victim's family ..." (at para 7).

Of course, they cannot. Hence, anything said by a trial (or appellate) court in respect of the harm suffered by the victim(s) must reflect the reality that we can only attempt to understand the harm inflicted and the loss that has been incurred.

4. DOES THE VICTIM IMPACT STATEMENT SERVE TO PROVIDE UP-TO-DATE INFORMATION ABOUT THE CONSEQUENCES BROUGHT ABOUT BY THE CONDUCT OF THE OFFENDER?

Yes, it does. *R. v. B. (R.H.)*[iv] provides an example of a victim impact statement describing how the victim continues to suffer as a result of the criminal actions of the offender, even though more than three decades have passed since the crime was committed. As we read at para. 14, "The victim impact statement indicates that the victim continues to suffer as a result of these assaults." The victim in this case had been subjected to repeated indecent assaults over a number of years when she was a very young child. This type of information must be evaluated and the impact of that harm may not be overlooked, but it must not be given disproportionate weight or importance.

5. MAY THE VICTIM-IMPACT STATEMENT(S) PROVIDE MORE THAN ONE PERSPECTIVE ON THE OFFENCE AND THE OFFENDER?

Again, the answer is yes. A not too uncommon situation is encountered in the judgment of *R. v. Simcoe.*[v] The offender pleaded guilty to manslaughter in the death of her father. In summary, it was argued on behalf of the offender that she attacked her father with a large kitchen knife, stabbing him repeatedly on the arms, as a consequence of a sexual assault he committed upon her while she was sleeping; her capacity to defend herself had been impaired by quite excessive drinking. The victim died as a result.

Para. 5 notes how "the trial judge had ... victim impact statements from two of the appellant's siblings and from a grandchild of her father as well as a letter from the appellant's maternal grandmother." Para. 9 further states the following: "The appellant's siblings were angry at [her] for what she did and did not believe that she had been sexually abused by their father." Although nothing more is said on the subject, in particular on the subject of the comments of other relatives, one can easily imagine that some of the close relatives of the deceased, being also the close relatives of the offender, might well be supportive of her, especially in light of the evidence that the victim had most foully abused his daughter over a lengthy period of time. On the other hand, it is not surprising to find close relatives who denounce the death of the victim and who are quite vocal in condemning the offender.

What is the court to do in such cases? One course of action is simply to take pains to place the comments on a spectrum, ranging from fully supportive to totally opposed to any leniency, and then to identify the appropriate factors that permit a balanced and fair view of the comments of all of the victims.

6. ARE VICTIM IMPACT STATEMENTS NECESSARY IN THAT NOTICE MAY BE TAKEN OF THE HARM DONE TO THE VICTIM(S) BY MEANS OF COMMON-SENSE INFERENCES?

In certain instances, I ask myself whether the information set out in the victim impact statement is not superfluous? May not the trial court take notice of the fact, as a common-sense inference, that when a person is run down by an impaired driver that individual has suffered great mental anguish and will no doubt fear future injury of the same nature? Must information be advanced to support the obvious belief that a victim of a sexual assault will be fearful of future molestation?

In this respect, *R. v. D. (D.)*[vi] sets out the following comment at para. 10: "As expected, the appellant's conduct has resulted in untold grief and misery for the children and their families. The lives of four families have been shattered; four children have been robbed of their youth and innocence; four children have been permanently scarred and possibly damaged psychologically for life. This is attested to in the victim impact statements filed at the sentence hearing."

7. DO VICTIM IMPACT STATEMENTS SHIFT THE BURDEN OF PROOF BORNE BY THE PROSECUTION?

The short answer is no. Trial judges must be mindful at all times that the Crown must establish beyond a reasonable doubt any aggravating fact that is disputed by the defence, and that may result, if proven, in a harsher sentence for the offender. Accordingly, it will always be useful to receive information setting out the presence of any "significant detrimental effect" the crime may have brought about, to use the language of para. 4 of *R. v. Boston.*[vii]

8. MAY VICTIM IMPACT STATEMENTS PERMIT THE INTRODUCTION OF ADDITIONAL AGGRAVATING ELEMENTS?

There is no simple answer to this question, as additional pieces of evidence are occasionally received, after protest from the defence, as a result of a successful application by the Crown to introduce formal proof of the overlooked elements of proof. On other occasions, the courts refuse to hear such late information.

R. v. Jackson[viii] illustrates one of the concerns regarding victim impact statements. As set out at para. 41, the police officer who was shot at twice during the course of a drug investigation "... indicated that, in his opinion, the appellant had deliberately lured [the victim] to follow him 'for the sole purpose' of shooting him. He explained his belief that although the appellant could easily have escaped, the appellant had deliberately 'egged' him on." It is easy to see the potentially harmful consequences that may befall the offender if the victim impact statement results in introducing aggravating elements that were not previously disclosed or advanced in the Crown's case.

Paragraph 50 of the judgement holds that "from a procedural perspective, the statement did not follow the *Criminal Code* provisions concerning the filing of a victim impact statement, and the sentencing procedure mandated by the *Criminal Code* does not provide for or contemplate the making of the kind of statement at issue here." It is submitted that this refers, in part at least, to the inclusion of the information not relating to the shooting incident and the "egging on."

9. IS THE INFORMATION SET OUT IN THE VICTIM IMPACT STATEMENT SIMPLY AN UNFAIR DUPLICATION OF THE EVIDENCE LED AT TRIAL?

This is a major concern that defence counsel raise from time to time. Once again, *R. v. D. (D.)*[ix] is of assistance in making plain the potential prejudice that an offender may suffer if the victim impact statement results in an unfair duplication of aggravating information. Indeed, para. 11 reads in part: "One boy speaks of the fear he felt while being sexually assaulted, a fear surpassed only by the terrifying prospect of being thrown over the appellant's 30th-floor balcony should he dare disclose."

Although it is appropriate for the victim to state what he or she feels with respect to the crime, the sentencing judge must indicate that mere repetition of information heard at trial will not result in this material's being given greater weight.

10. WHAT ARE CONCERNS ABOUT THE VICTIM IMPACT STATEMENT AND SECONDARY HARM SUFFERED BY THE FRIENDS AND FAMILY OF THE VICTIM?

At para. 11 of *R. v. D. (D.)*[x] are the following passages from the victim impact statement. Firstly, "The boy's mother ... explains how she herself was molested as a child by her father and how the appellant's conduct has caused her to live her son's pain and re-live her own pain. In her words, 'this has taken many years from my son's life and I know this will hurt me for the rest of my life.'"

Secondly, note that "The child's father speaks about his son's emotional problems and the symptoms that appeared with the onset of abuse, including withdrawal, misbehaviour and bed-wetting. He also talks about the amount of time the family has spent taking their son to doctors to try 'to get a handle on his emotional problems' and how he himself suffers from bouts of depression and ongoing stomach problems as a result of all that has happened."

It does not appear that any principled reason can be advanced to prohibit the submission of this type of information. Thus, I should consider it but I must always be mindful not to award it too much importance in the ultimate decision.

11. MUST IT BE TAKEN FOR GRANTED THAT THE DIFFICULTIES ENCOUNTERED BY THE VICTIM ARE SOLELY (OR CHIEFLY) THE RESULT OF THE HARM SUFFERED?

This is a problem that I and other judges encounter quite often, and it is very vexing. Our concern is that a certain element of aggravation will be assigned to a factor that may be the result of other stressors or factors. For example, if we return again to *R. v. D. (D.)*,[xi] we note at para. 12 that "another boy reports that the appellant's misconduct has left him angry, nervous and scared … According to his parents, the child is filled with anger and frustration and he sometimes becomes 'belligerent' and 'outright mean.' His schoolwork has suffered and his marks have dropped considerably. He has a hard time focusing on his studies and difficulty sleeping."

The degree and quality of the evidence advanced by the prosecution in that case results in little opposition to that kind of comment. However, the concern is that the same kind of comment may be advanced in a case in which the link between the violence inflicted and the resulting harm may not be so self-evident. What is the sentencing court to do in such a case? In light of the duty cast upon the Crown to prove all aggravating factors beyond a reasonable doubt, will it be proper to accept these types of assertions without question?

By way of illustration, note as well *R. v. M. (P.)*[xii] at para. 7: "C. filed a lengthy victim impact statement describing how the events had affected her whole life including her poor relationship with female peers, her promiscuity with men, her lack of trust of men and the subsequent breakdown of her sexual relationship with her husband." Without in any way questioning the merits of the harm described in the case, one can easily foresee that in a given case, an offender might wish to contest that all of these consequences are the direct (and sole) result of the wrongdoing. In such a case, judicial economy might well be compromised, leaving aside the fundamental concern of not re-victimizing the victim. How the resolution of such a conflict may be brought about remains to be seen.

12. CAN VICTIM IMPACT STATEMENTS SERVE TO PREDICT FUTURE HARM?

This is also a vexing question. For guidance, I turn to the words of Justice Moldaver at para. 36 of *R. v. Boston*[xiii]:

In this respect, while there may have been a time, years ago, when offenders like the appellant could take refuge in the fact that little was known about the nature or extent of the damage caused by sexual abuse, that time has long since passed. Today, that excuse no longer holds sway. The horrific consequences of child sexual abuse are only too well known.

In other words, in some types of cases, trial judges are entitled to accept, without formal proof, the suggestion of the victim that future harm will take place. In other cases, this is not so obvious. For example, must it be taken for granted that a victim of fraud, of theft, will suffer further secondary harm such as the loss of his or her business, or bankruptcy, because of what took place?

In an effort to answer this question, I refer to *R. v. Dobis*.[xiv] Mr. Dobis was an employee in a position of trust with Electro Canada. He commenced stealing from the company less than a year after being made accounting manager. His thefts and fraud continued for more than three years. His dishonest conduct consisted of two different components—direct thefts for deposit into his personal accounts and thefts to participate in a "get rich" scheme with an eye to reaping more than US$10 million. The amount stolen under both schemes was very large—about $286,000 and $1.9 million, respectively.

Paragraph 34 records that "the victims of the crimes suffered terribly. The company was crippled; its survival, including the jobs of 250 people, is still in jeopardy. Moreover, the long-term goals of the family owners of the company have been rendered fragile." Perhaps a more direct means of making plain the potential for harm is to quote from one victim impact statement:

> ... I bought Electro Canada Limited, a small electrical products manufacturing company with 20 employees, in 1979. For the next twenty years, my wife and I diligently worked long hours, lived modestly and managed the Company conservatively, virtually debt free, reinvesting all of the profits in the Company, in order to grow Electro Canada, which was to provide our retirement pension and an inheritance for our six children. *All of this was put in doubt, and remains in doubt today,* because of the respondent's crimes. [Emphasis added]

It is not at all certain how the sentencing court is to assign aggravating weight to such information.

13. CAN VICTIM IMPACT STATEMENTS EXPRESSLY QUANTIFY THE LOSS SUFFERED?

A recent case, *R. v. Bogart*,[xv] provides a rare example of a victim impact statement expressing in real terms the loss suffered. Dr. Bogart was found guilty of a massive fraud against the Ontario Health Insurance Plan (OHIP), having fraudulently billed the plan of $923,780.53 over seven years. Both in amount and duration, this case ranks as one of the largest scale frauds ever committed against OHIP.

The valuable objective information recorded at para. 23 stated:

> Some people believe that a fraud on government or a government agency is a victimless crime. This view assumes that governments have deep pockets on which to draw to recover the loss. But a fraud like the one committed by the respondent causes many costs to our public health care system and those who rely on it. The victim impact statement filed by the Ministry of Health showed that the money stolen by the respondent could have financed over 30,000 well baby care visits, over 40,000 routine prenatal care visits, or more than 50,000 routine visits to the elderly in nursing homes. Providing such comparisons undoubtedly makes it easier to understand the full scope of the wrongdoing.

14. WHEN SHOULD VICTIM IMPACT STATEMENTS BE INTRODUCED IN EVIDENCE?

One of the concerns often raised by defence counsel surrounds the late introduction of victim impact statements. Defence counsel argue that they cannot know how the information therein will affect the trial judge's perception of the seriousness of the crime.

In this respect, note *R. v. O'Quinn et al.*,[xvi] at para. 38:

> In my view, there is some ambiguity about what transpired before Justice Culver at the pre-trial meeting. I find it difficult to accept defence counsel's characterization of the pre-trial discussion as one in which Justice Culver gave an "unequivocal" statement of the sentence he would impose. The opinion expressed as to sentence was conditional upon a collective plea by all four accused, which did not transpire. It was conditional upon receipt of favourable pre-sentence reports. It was made in the absence of full information, as Justice Culver had neither the victim impact statements nor the relevant case law.

Note as well the timing issue as it developed in *R. v. Jackson*,[xvii] as set out at para. 40. After both Crown counsel and the appellant's counsel had made their submissions with respect to sentencing, Crown counsel stated: "Your Honour, I have just been advised that [the victim, a police officer] would like to address the court." Counsel for the appellant objected. The trial judge permitted [the officer] to be sworn and to make a statement.

15. HOW MUCH INFORMATION IS APPROPRIATE IN A VICTIM IMPACT STATEMENT?

Another danger associated with these statements is that too much information is being provided too late in the proceedings. In this vein, note *R. v.*

Holub.[xviii] Paragraph 10 sets out that "the trial judge read the hundreds of victim impact statements that were submitted." This led him to conclude that "without question, the fraudulent process, employed by all three accused, caused proven deprivation and the loss of hard-earned money, as well as embarrassment and humiliation, all in return for no money's worth." One can easily imagine the concerns arising if this type of information was provided quite late in the sentence hearing.

CONCLUSION

In this chapter I have attempted to address certain questions that I, and no doubt many other judges, might entertain when assessing victim impact statements. Although not an exhaustive review of our thought processes nor an exhaustive analysis of the case law on the subject of victim impact statements, the chapter instead explores some of the insights that govern our decision-making.

I consider the submission of a victim-impact statement to be a vital element in sentencing, and I often comment on the absence of such information. Although these statements often do not influence the selection of the sentence to any significant degree, they have the potential to assist the trial judge in understanding fully, so far as is possible, how much the children of the deceased miss their father, or to what extent the surviving spouse finds it difficult to shop alone for Christmas gifts for the children and so on. The criminal court needs to hear and to understand these events and emotions.

DISCUSSION QUESTIONS

1. *If you were a crime victim, would you want to complete a victim impact statement for the judge to consider?*
2. *Some victims would like to make a direct recommendation about sentencing, although this is not allowed under the current VIS scheme. Do you think that under exceptional circumstances victims should be allowed to make sentence recommendations?*
3. *What problems might arise if victims were allowed to recommend a sentence for the judge to impose?*

FURTHER READINGS

Meredith, C. and Paquette, C. 2001. *Summary Report on Victim Impact Statement Focus Groups.* Ottawa: Department of Justice Canada.

Roberts, J.V. 2003. Victim impact statements and the sentencing process: Recent developments and research findings. *Criminal Law Quarterly,* in press.

Young, A. 2001. *The Role of the Victim in the Criminal Process: A Literature Review—1989 to 1999.* Ottawa: Department of Justice Canada.

ENDNOTES

i (1996), 105 C.C.C. (3d) 327

ii [2002] O.J. No. 1061, 58 O.R. (3d) 788, 157 O.A.C. 323, 163 C.C.C. (3d) 471 (C.A.)

iii [2002] O.J. No. 578, 155 O.A.C. 236 (C.A.)

iv [2002] O.J. No. 2345 (C.A.)

v [2002] O.J. No. 884, 156 O.A.C. 190 (C.A.)

vi [2002] O.J. No. 1061, 58 O.R. (3d) 788, 157 O.A.C. 323, 163 C.C.C. (3d) 471 (C.A.)

vii [2002] O.J. No. 887, 156 O.A.C. 129, 58 O.R. (3d) 460 (C.A.)

viii [2002] O.J. No. 1097, 163 C.C.C. (3d) 451, 158 O.A.C. 289, 58 O.R. (3d) 593 (C.A.)

ix [2002] O.J. No. 1061, 58 O.R. (3d) 788, 157 O.A.C. 323, 163 C.C.C. (3d) 471 (C.A.)

x [2002] O.J. No. 1061, 58 O.R. (3d) 788, 157 O.A.C. 323, 163 C.C.C. (3d) 471 (C.A.)

xi [2002] O.J. No. 1061, 58 O.R. (3d) 788, 157 O.A.C. 323, 163 C.C.C. (3d) 471 (C.A.)

xii [2002] O.J. No. 644, 155 O.A.C. 242 (C.A.)

xiii [2002] O.J. No. 887, 156 O.A.C. 129, 58 O.R. (3d) 460 (C.A.)

xiv [2002] O.J. No. 646, 163 C.C.C. (3d) 259, 157 O.A.C. 83, 58 O.R. (3d) 536 (C.A.)

xv [2002] O.J. No. 3039 (C.A.)
[2002] 167 C.C.C. (3d) 390
[2002] 162 O.A.C. 347
[2002] 61 O.R. (3d) 75

xvi [2002] O.J. No. 2016, 159 O.A.C. 186, 59 O.R. (3d) 321 (C.A.)

xvii [2002] O.J. No. 1097, 163 C.C.C. (3d) 451, 158 O.A.C. 289, 58 O.R. (3d) 593 (C.A.)

xviii [2002] O.J. No. 579, 155 O.A.C. 278, 163 C.C.C. (3d) 166 (C.A.)

CHAPTER 12
Responding to Domestic Abuse

INTRODUCTION

One of the most serious crimes that has become more visible in recent years is the domestic abuse of women. For many decades the problem remained hidden. Now, as a result of research such as the Violence Against Women survey conducted by Statistics Canada in 1993, we know that it is a truly national problem and that the official statistics underestimate the true extent of violence against women in their own homes. Responding to domestic violence has therefore become a criminal justice priority in this country as elsewhere. In this reading, the authors explore the policing response to domestic violence and point out some important limitations of this approach.

Immigrant Women's Perceptions of the "Policing Solution" to Woman Abuse

Sandra Wachholz, University of Southern Maine, and Baukje Miedema, Dalhousie University

Over the last two decades in Canada there has been a growing interest in developing a more aggressive criminal justice response to woman abuse. Fueled by a desire to emphasize the criminal nature and seriousness of woman abuse, various jurisdictions have adopted a variety of new police programs and policies to address the problem, with mandatory charging policies resting as the cornerstone of many of these initiatives.[i] As such, police intervention in woman abuse cases has become one of the primary responses to this deeply structural social problem.

Although the notion and practice of increased police intervention in woman abuse cases has received wide support among various state officials and women advocates, it is identified by many as a limited and inherently problematic approach that can do little to deter such violence or alter the socioeconomic conditions that sustain woman abuse (Currie and MacLean, 1992; DeKeseredy and MacLeod, 1997). Clearly, police intervention in these cases does send important messages about the serious criminal nature of woman abuse and it does provide victims with some level of immediate protection. However, increasing numbers of studies provide evidence of the limited role that initiatives such as mandatory arrest policies can play in reducing woman abuse. Few arrests are ever prosecuted, and there is evidence to suggest that in some instances certain individuals are more frequently violent if they are arrested (e.g., Martin and Mosher, 1995). Concomitantly, various studies report a trend in "dual arrest" where the female victims of abuse are also arrested by the police—a practice which some suggest points to the overenforcement of mandatory arrest policies (Martin, 1997).

While there is a growing body of critiques of the current police practices designed to address woman abuse, very few studies in Canada have examined women's perceptions of and willingness to invoke police intervention. This is unfortunate, for as Martin and Mosher (1995:3) argue, criminal justice intervention in woman abuse cases can often bring a multitude of harms to women, "particularly those who are socially and economically marginalized."

One group that is thought to be especially resistant to police intervention given the multiple levels of oppression that many endure is immigrant women. To date, however, much of the information about their perceptions of police intervention in woman abuse cases has been biographical, anecdotal, or "secondhand" in nature and has generally focused on the views of immigrant women who reside in large, urban areas (MacLeod et al., 1993). This has left many important questions unanswered. For example, given the added level of isolation that many immigrant women who reside in rural areas endure, do they fear that police intervention in cases of woman abuse will generate even greater isolation for them?

This chapter reports findings from interviews with 48 immigrant women in an effort to explore their perceptions of police intervention in woman abuse cases. Approximately one-third of the participants indicated that they had been abused by a partner or husband while residing in Canada.

Like the unfolding layers of an onion, many of the women indicated that they held a number of fears about police intervention in woman abuse cases, and they identified a myriad of harms that could and often do occur pursuant to police involvement in such situations. The concerns and feelings that the women expressed about police intervention reflect, at some level, many of the emotional responses and dynamics that arise for women when they experience woman abuse. For example, a significant number of the women stated that calling the police could isolate them from their friends and community, foster feelings of disempowerment, and place them in a position where they are forced to interact with someone whom they may not trust, but who has power over them. Such findings reflect a pattern, as DeKeseredy and MacLeod (1997:4) would argue, where "well-intentioned responses to woman abuse can actually add to the experiences of uncertainly, isolation, unequal power dynamics, unfairness and low self-esteem that ... women suffer at the hands of their abusers." This chapter reviews these findings and highlights some of the many reasons why the "policing solution" to woman abuse can do little to address the needs of this population.

SUPPORT FOR THE POLICING SOLUTION TO WOMAN ABUSE

As Loader (1997:11) notes, "those who seek to mobilize more or 'tougher' policing as a response to crime find themselves swimming with the emotional tide." Clearly, over the last two decades in Canada the emotional tide has been flowing toward greater and more aggressive police intervention in woman abuse cases. Government reports, the media, and academic journals are replete with arguments advocating such action (Martin and Mosher, 1995). Victims' and women's advocate groups have played an important role in ushering in state-based reforms against violent men. Frustrated by the police's historical neglect of woman abuse, these advocates have worked to secure more decisive police action in cases of woman abuse (Davis and Smith, 1995; Martin and Mosher, 1995). The culmination of support for a more aggressive criminal justice response to woman abuse has produced legal initiatives such as mandatory arrest and no-drop prosecutorial policies.

It is important to note that while there is significant support for the law and order, police solution to crime in general, and to woman abuse in particular, a burgeoning collection of research has pointed to the rather limited role the police can play in reducing crime. For example, numerous studies now suggest that increasing the number of police officers and reducing police response times to crime scenes have made little difference to crime rates (Bayley, 1994; Loader, 1997). In turn, as noted earlier, the mandatory arrest policies that have arisen across Canada have done little to reduce the incidence of woman abuse (Morley and Mullender, 1992). However, even against the weight of this evidence, general public sentiment continues to be "marked by high 'fantasy content' regarding what the police can and should do" (Elias, 1987, cited in Loader, 1997:3).

The increased emphasis and faith in police involvement in woman abuse cases is, in part, thought to be driven by liberal, legal ideology. The promotion of aggressive police intervention is premised on the belief that by treating woman abuse like other assaults, female victims will be afforded more equality of opportunity to justice. Justice demands, according to liberal philosophy, "that those who are similarly situated receive similar treatment" (Martin and Mosher, 1995:15). However, the "policing solution" not only resonates well with the tenets of liberal, legal philosophy, but it is also congruent with current neoconservative, law-and-order ideologies regarding crime control. Within this belief system, the police are thought to be a viable and critical means to reduce crime.

Marginalized groups may be less willing to accord respect and authority to the police as a result of certain experiences that they have had with them. In this regard, many immigrant women may be quite resistant to police intervention in situations of woman abuse given their experiences with the police in Canada and in their countries of origin. The harm that police intervention may foster based on immigrant women's socioeconomic vulnerability may also function as a disincentive to calling the police.

Studies based on predominantly non-immigrant populations have found that many abused women do not believe that arrest and incarceration can effectively address woman abuse. Chalmers and Smith (1988), for example, report that only 6% of the 106 battered women in their study regarded police involvement as the best means to end woman abuse. The overwhelming majority of these women considered the provision of shelters and public education to be more desirable than police intervention.

In one of the few Canadian studies designed to examine abused immigrant women's perceptions of police intervention in woman abuse cases, Martin and Mosher (1995) found that the 11 women in their study held strong reservations about the police and about their ability to deal effectively with male violence against women. As revealed through in-depth interviews, the women were united by their experiences of abuse and by their shared fear of police intervention.

Even in the wake of such fear, six of the women contacted the police. The participants did not, however, lend their full support to the mandatory arrest, no-drop prosecutorial policy adopted by the police and courts in Toronto.[ii] Seven of the 11 women felt that the abuser should always be charged, but only one woman indicated that she liked the policy of mandatory arrest in combination with a no-drop prosecutorial policy. The overwhelming majority of the women felt the victims of woman abuse should have the right to dismiss charges against their abusers.

Various documents produced by organizations and government bodies also suggest that abused immigrant women are often afraid to invoke police intervention (Currie, 1995; MacLeod and Shin, 1990). As a case in point, Godin (1994) notes that some abused immigrant women may be reluctant to call the police given that they have immigrated from a country where the police were seen as part of an oppressive state. This account is not, however, based on an empirical study.

Little empirical research has been undertaken to examine immigrant women's perceptions of the "policing solution" to woman abuse even though immigrant women represent a significant percentage of the Canadian population, accounting for approximately 16% of the female population in 1991 (Statistics Canada, 1996). As a step toward addressing this problem, this chapter explores the experiences of immigrant women and, in particular, abused immigrant women.

METHODOLOGY

Six focus groups involving 48 women were held in different locations ranging from small towns to larger cities across New Brunswick in 1997. The groups were co-facilitated by the researchers and took place in a diverse range of locales: offices of volunteer organizations, church basements, and living rooms. Each group began with the presentation of two case vignettes. The first vignette described a situation where a woman was being abused and the participants were asked to imagine that she was a native-born citizen residing in their country of origin. They were then encouraged to describe how women in their country of origin generally deal with woman abuse. The second vignette described a situation that was similar to the first, but in this instance the abused woman was an immigrant who had lived in Canada for five years. The participants were again asked to describe how the woman might deal with the situation, assuming that she was from their country of origin. The case vignettes inevitably led to discussion about the utility and effectiveness of police intervention in woman abuse cases. It is important to note that the case vignettes allowed the women to talk about their abuse in the third person, if they wished to do so.

PROFILE OF THE PARTICIPANTS

The women had immigrated to Canada from many parts of the world: Africa, South East Asia, the Middle East, Latin America, and Europe. Almost all of the women had accompanied their husbands to New Brunswick where, in most instances, the husband had secured a job. In a few cases the women came to marry a Canadian citizen or they came to work, generally as nannies. In fact, the majority of women could be characterized as "reluctant immigrants." They were immigrants or refugees who came solely because their husbands wanted to move to Canada. Approximately one-third of the participants indicated that they had been abused by a partner or husband while residing in Canada; the abuse included one or more of the following injurious behaviours: physical abuse, sexual abuse, psychological abuse, emotional abuse, financial abuse, and spiritual abuse. None of the women stated that they had contacted the police.

RESULTS

As DeKeseredy and MacLeod (1997) have noted, many governmental policies established to address woman abuse have had the unanticipated consequence of limiting women's choices and increasing their fear. Reflecting this, virtually all of the immigrant women who participated in the focus groups expressed a variety of concerns and fears about the "policing solution" to woman abuse. They indicated that in many instances, police intervention could actually worsen the problem of abusive relationships, e.g., social isolation, unequal power dynamics, and male control. Thus, police intervention was generally viewed by the participants as a response that could foster harm and suffering. This was in turn compounded by the women's socioeconomic vulnerability as immigrant women and by their status as residents of a predominantly rural province where the immigrant population is small.

The findings are discussed in four sections which correspond to dynamics that surround woman abuse: (i) social isolation, (ii) unequal power dynamics, (iii) control and surveillance, and (iv) uncertainly and insecurity. Each section begins with a succinct discussion of a given dynamic and then explores the interface between the dynamic and data from the focus groups. It is worth noting that while each dynamic is presented separately, they are not mutually exclusive.

1. Social Isolation

Social isolation is one of the dynamics that often characterizes the lives of women who experience woman abuse. In some instances a woman may be forced by a controlling partner or husband to separate herself from potential sources of support and friendship, while in other situations factors such as embarrassment and fear may compel a victim of woman abuse to withdraw from her family, friends, and community (Kirkwood, 1993). Thus, for a variety of reasons, "violence encourages isolation" (Thorne-Finch, 1992:3).

The experience of social isolation was, in fact, part of the lives of a significant number of the participants in the focus groups. Over half of the women stated that they were reluctant to contact the police as doing so meant that they might face even greater levels of loneliness. Most of the women who expressed this concern (N=17) stated that invoking police intervention could bring dishonour and shame to an immigrant woman's husband, family, and ethnic community, and thus could sever their relationships with those who could assist and support them. Reflecting this concern, one woman stated, "My husband is a very proud man. If I called the police I would hurt his pride and my family's honour."

Almost all of the participants indicated they felt that woman abuse was a personal matter that should be handled privately within the family through mediation. As one woman stated, "You can't go around to the police or courts with a family matter or even a quarrel between friends." As such, sustaining loyalties to one's husband, family, and community was often cited as taking precedence over calling the police, and it was identified as a means to avoid isolation.

As seven women noted, the prospect of contacting the police was particularly frightening given that they already felt a great deal of social, cultural, and linguistic isolation as residents of New Brunswick, a province where the immigrant population is relatively small. In 1991, only 3% of the residents of

New Brunswick were immigrants while in Ontario, in that same year, 24% of the population were born outside Canada (Statistics Canada, 1996). To complicate matters even further for immigrant women in New Brunswick, there are virtually no culturally specific programs or services for those who experience woman abuse. The few programs that do exist in Canada for abused immigrant women are generally located in large urban cities such as Victoria, Montreal, and Toronto. Thus, given the scarcity of programs and the small immigrant population in New Brunswick, police assistance was seen by a number of the participants as an action that would only compound their social isolation.

2.   Unequal Power Dynamics

Woman abuse is an expression and mechanism of the structural oppression of women (Kirkwood, 1993; Barnett and LaViolette, 1993). At the core of this problem is male domination over women, which occurs across the institutional structures of society and within women's daily lives (Thorne-Finch, 1992). For a number of the participants, the prospect of calling the police appeared to hold, at some level, the potential to create or re-create the unequal power dynamics that surround woman abuse. One-third of the women said that they would not seek police assistance in cases of woman abuse as such action meant that they would have to interact with someone whom they feared and did not trust, but who held power over them. Their fear of the police appeared to be based, in part, on their perceptions of and experiences with police practices in their country of origin. As Currie (1995:36) has explained:

> In some cases, the experiences of ethnocultural minority community members with the police may result in a view of the police as repressive and discriminatory. Police may have been experienced in the past as corrupt, undisciplined and discriminatory. In the cases of refugees or immigrants from authoritarian states, the police may have been direct agents of oppression—taking part in torture, disappearance and murder.[10]

In this regard, ten of the women stated that in their country of origin the police often oppress and assault citizens. These women were reluctant to use the police in Canada out of fear that an officer would use his or her authority to engage in physical force with either the victim or offender in woman abuse cases. The following statements made by various women reflect this fear: "If you call the police they may beat up your husband"; "If you call the police you may be in even more trouble as the police officer may be a batterer himself."

Reflecting yet another concern about the power differential between themselves and the police, approximately one-third of the participants said that they would not invoke police intervention as they feared the police would ridicule and discredit their claim of abuse—a fear shared by non-immigrant women as well (Home, 1994). This feeling of distrust appeared to be related, in part, to their status as women. Lamenting the fact that most police officers are male, one woman stated, "If I called the police they would laugh at me and ask, 'Why did you marry him?'" This was a particularly pronounced concern for several of the women who were married to non-immigrant men. They feared that the police would be more inclined to believe their husbands because they had been born in Canada.

Finally, one-fifth of the women said that their fear of encountering racist treatment by Canadian police was another factor that would inhibit them from reporting woman abuse. In such instances, the police were seen as in a position to use their power over immigrant women to inflict racist practices. One woman felt, for example, that the Canadian police operate on "some very stereotypical ideas [about immigrant women]." This woman went on to state that most police assume that immigrant women are abuse victims who are capable of enduring victimization, a practice that may offer immigrant women less protection.

For a variety of reasons, then, many of the participants in the study felt that invoking police assistance would place them in a position where they would have to deal with someone who wielded power over them, but whom they did not trust. Thus, as one woman stated, "that would be the last thing you would do, go to the police."

3. Control and Surveillance

As Kirkwood (1993:63) notes, "Control by one over another exists when one person has greater influence over the other's behaviour or perspectives than does that person herself." In situations where abuse is occurring between a couple, male control over the female victim is a central aspect of the relationship. The needs, wants, and behaviour of the female partner are often profoundly influenced by the demands of an abusive male (DeKeseredy and MacLeod, 1997; Kirkwood, 1993).

A number of the participants spoke openly about the controlling behaviour of their partners. One woman stated, "You have to follow him no matter what." As another woman said, "I just followed my husband ... like a dog." Thus, for many of these women, seeking police intervention was an action that could expand rather than reduce the level of social control that was already part of their lives. Calling the police meant that they might encounter individuals who would attempt to assert control over their needs, wants, and destiny.

In particular, one-fourth of the participants stated that they feared calling the police as such action might ultimately bring them into contact with immigration authorities that could deport them and their families. As one woman stated simply, "[if I called the police] I would be deported." Although a woman who is a landed immigrant is protected from deportation if her sponsorship breaks down pursuant to woman abuse, many of the women in the study did not know this. To further complicate matters, several women indicated that some abusive spouses threatened to withdraw sponsorship if they reported the abuse. Such threats, as Jang et al. (1990:2) have argued, are a means to keep women silent and are a "way to maintain power and control over them."

Child protection officials were cited by five of the women as another state authority that they feared and thought might intervene in their lives if they contacted the police. These women feared that their children might be removed from their home under the assumption that they could not provide a safe environment for them, a finding that has appeared in other studies of immigrant women (Martin and Mosher, 1995). Reflecting this fear, one woman lamented, "The [abused] woman is already so vulnerable ... and then they take her children away, they say that you are an unfit parent for the children." For this woman (and others), police assistance in woman abuse cases was seen as having the potential to invoke various forms of state surveillance and control over themselves and their families.

Fear of losing control over the decision about how to deal with the behaviour of an abusive male emerged as another reason why several of the women would not contact the police in situations of abuse. Six of the participants indicated that they would not call for law enforcement assistance given the expanded police power to arrest in domestic abuse cases that has been in place in New Brunswick since 1987. The women who expressed resistance to New Brunswick's mandatory arrest policy generally felt that it was far too inflexible, reduced their control over a situation, and would do little to end the violence. Lamenting the loss of control over a situation that could occur for a woman pursuant to the mandatory arrest policy in New Brunswick, one woman stated, "Everyone has the right to tell you when you are abused and send you to whatever service exists ... everyone has the right to tell you, you know, your husband is abusing [and then make an arrest]." As this woman's words indicate, useful police intervention was not equated with mandatory arrest.

4. Insecurity and Uncertainty

Women who are the victims of abuse often experience a number of challenges to their physical, emotional, social, and financial well-being as a result their partners' violent and controlling behaviour. As such, battered women's lives are often surrounded by a host of insecurities. For many of the participants, calling the police was perceived as an action that could only compound the insecurities and uncertainties that are part of the lives of abused immigrant women. In this regard, over half of the women indicated that they would not seek police intervention in situations of woman abuse as such assistance would only create or exacerbate their socioeconomic vulnerability and insecurity.

In particular, 13 of the participants feared they would incur long-term financial insecurity if they called the police given their economic dependency

on their partners. Invoking law enforcement assistance meant that their partners could be arrested and might subsequently lose their jobs. If this happened, as one woman said, you would have to become a welfare recipient
"and eventually you [would] decide you are better off with him."

Clearly, fear of encountering financial problems at the outset of leaving
an abusive partner is a concern shared by non-immigrant women as well.
However, the risk of incurring economic insecurity is generally greater for
immigrant women given the multiple levels of oppression that many experience. Across Canada, immigrant women are over-represented in low-paying
jobs (Status of Women Canada, 1997). They often face, as Martin and Mosher
(1995:25) have underscored, "a discriminatory workplace which siphons them
into job ghettoes characterized by low pay and lack of job security." These factors, in combination with the Canadian government's unwillingness to
accredit various foreign diplomas, credentials, and degrees, foster economic
marginalization for immigrant women (Miedema and Nason-Clark, 1989).

With respect to the employment status of the participants, the majority
worked within the home in unpaid labour. Of those who were employed, 70%
worked in part-time, low-wage service industry jobs. Many of the women
stated that they would have difficulty supporting themselves financially if
they separated from their partners. The concerns that they raised about their
ability to achieve financial independence were tied, in large part, to their circumstances as immigrant women. It is important to note, however, that many
of the women's situations were compounded by the fact that they were
residing in small, rural communities with relatively high unemployment
rates.

In summary, then, there are many reasons why immigrant women are
reluctant to invoke police assistance in cases of woman abuse. While the
"policing solution" to woman abuse has won the support of police departments and various other groups across Canada, virtually all the participants in
this research felt that it could do little to address the needs of abused immigrant women. In light of this fact, in the words of one woman, you simply
"don't go outside to the police or to the law."

DE-CENTERING THE POLICING SOLUTION TO WOMAN ABUSE

As the sessions revealed, most of the participants viewed police intervention
as a form of assistance that could only add to the harm and suffering that
immigrant women experience as a result of woman abuse. The "policing solution" rests, however, at the heart of the state's response to the deeply structural problem of woman abuse (Currie, 1995; Currie and MacLean, 1992). The
focus of this solution is on detecting and addressing individual fault. In the
process, it functions to individualize and depoliticize woman abuse. As Currie
and MacLean (1992:25) state, "Wife beating has been transformed from a critique of patriarchal power to demands for protection from male power. While

the latter is a documented real need, the problem is that its satisfaction has been equated with justice for women."

In light of these concerns, a growing number of critics have argued that the "policing solution" needs to be de-centered from its position as the eminent solution to woman abuse. The notion of "de-centering" refers to a process, as Carol Smart (1989:5) explains, where an emphasis is placed on thinking about nonlegal strategies to address social problems and on discouraging "... a resort to law as if it holds the key to unlock women's oppression." De-centering the "policing solution" is thought to hold the promise of creating an environment where greater emphasis would be placed on thinking about ways to address the forms of structural oppression that work to condone and sustain woman abuse, which would thus signal a movement back toward the transformative demands of the battered women's movement.

The process of de-centering the "policing solution" was, in fact, strongly endorsed by the immigrant women who participated in the focus groups. As one woman said, "This help from the government or whatever, it is not really solving your problems, it's just splitting [up families]." Thus, rather than suggesting there should be more "law and order" state-controlled responses to woman abuse, the women called for the introduction of various forms of structural reform and community-based initiatives to address the abuse that immigrant women experience.

With respect to structural reform, several of the women called for the development or enhancement of social policies that would function to reduce immigrant women's socioeconomic inequality. Their suggestions included, for example, access to job training programs that would meet the specific ethno-cultural needs of immigrant women; governmental accreditation of foreign credentials; free, accessible, and long-term language training programs; and universal social welfare programs that would provide affordable housing and adequate living allowances. Reflecting on these needs, one woman stated: "In a lot of cases, the [immigrant] woman has to stay in an abusive relationship because they don't have employment and welfare doesn't give her enough earnings to support the family and to pay the rent and to live on her own ... An immigrant woman needs a lot ... there's a lot of things that have to be done and need to be done."

In terms of community-based initiatives, the participants proposed various prevention and intervention strategies that were designed to address the particular needs of immigrant women. Notably, none of the strategies that they proposed emphasized increased policing and punishment of male abusers. Instead, they generally focused on community partnership initiatives to deal with abuse. For example, several of the women proposed that every immigrant and refugee organization should have ongoing education and information sessions about woman abuse. In particular, several of the women called for increased collaboration between immigrant and refugee agencies and woman abuse projects and shelters. In discussing this collaborative effort, some of the women noted that it would be very useful if women from battered women shelters were to make presentations in settlement and language programs. The use of videos, as an important visual aid for those struggling with French and English, was identified as a valuable way to discuss woman abuse.

With respect to intervention strategies, conflict resolution mechanisms such as family or community mediation were cited as the preferred means to deal with woman abuse, and many of the women spoke of the historical and cultural use of such techniques in their country of origin. Reflecting an interest in mediation, one woman stated, "I feel the government should first of all try to make sure that they don't approach [the couple] to break up ... instead maybe they should try and give counseling to both ... give them six months or four months." Many of the participants shared this view and thus called for the creation of more culturally specific counseling and support services for both abusive immigrant men and the victims of abuse—women and children.

The nature of the strategies proposed by the participants suggests that police intervention does not represent an appropriate solution to woman abuse for this population. Rather than mobilizing the police, social policies to address immigrant women's socioeconomic oppression, mediation, and community education partnerships were identified by virtually all of the participants as the most desirable way to deal with immigrant woman abuse.

CONCLUSION

The participants felt that police intervention could only enhance the pain and suffering of abused immigrant women. It was considered to be a response that could actually replicate, at some level, the conditions and experiences that surround abuse: isolation, inequality, control, and unequal power dynamics. Many of these conditions, as the participants suggested, are even more complex and problematic for immigrant women who reside in a predominantly rural province such as New Brunswick where there are few culturally specific services and the immigrant communities are small. Clearly, the voices of the participants shed light on how a well-intentioned state response such as the "policing solution" can perpetuate rather than reduce harm. What is needed, as these women and others have argued, are social policies and program initiatives that would "... explore new ways of living, relating, helping and supporting [immigrant women]" (DeKeseredy and MacLeod, 1997:68).

DISCUSSION QUESTIONS

1. *Where do you stand on the question of mandatory charging? Do you think the state has a right to prosecute an alleged offender even if the victim wishes to discontinue proceedings?*
2. *What do you think of the alternate strategies advocated by the authors in this chapter? Are they likely to prove more useful for victims and effective for offenders?*

3. *Do you think that more specialized police and court services for visible minority or ethnic victims of domestic abuse are a good idea? Such specialized courts already exist for Aboriginal offenders and offenders with drug addictions.*

FURTHER READINGS

Erez, Edna. 2000. Immigration, culture conflict and domestic violence/woman battering. *Crime Prevention and Community Safety. An International Journal* 2:27–36.

Wachholz, Sandra and Miedema, Baukje. 2003. Gendered silence: Immigrant women's access to legal information about woman abuse. In M. Sterling, A. Cameron, N. Nason-Clark, and Baukje Miedema (Eds.), *Understanding Abuse: Partnering for Change.* Toronto: University of Toronto Press.

REFERENCES

Barnett, Ola W. and LaViolette, Alyce D. 1993. *It Could Happen to Anyone: Why Battered Women Stay.* London: Sage Publications.

Bayley, D. 1994. *Police for the Future.* Oxford: Oxford University Press.

Chalmers, Lee and Smith, Pamela. 1988. Wife battering: Psychological, social, and physical isolation and counteracting strategies. In Tigar McLaren (Ed.) *Gender and Society: Creating a Canadian Women's Sociology.* Toronto: Copp Clark Pittman.

Currie, Dawn H. and MacLean Brian D. 1992. Women, men and police: Losing the fight against wife battery in Canada. In Dawn H. Currie and Brian D. MacLean (Eds.) *Rethinking the Administration of Justice.* Halifax, Nova Scotia: Fernwood Press.

Currie, Dawn H. 1995. Battered women and the state: From the failure of theory to a theory of failure. *Journal of Human Justice* 1:77–96.

Davis, Robert and Smith, Barbara. 1995. Domestic violence reforms: Empty promises or fulfilled expectations. *Crime and Delinquency* 41:541–552.

DeKeseredy, Walter S. and MacLeod, Linda. 1997. *Woman Abuse: A Sociological Story.* Toronto: Harcourt Brace.

Elias, N. 1987. *Involvement and Detachment.* Oxford: Oxford University Press.

Godin, Joanne. 1994. *More than a Crime: A Report on the Lack of Public Legal Information Materials for Immigrant Women Who Are Subject to Wife Assault.* Ottawa: Department of Justice Canada.

Home, Alice. 1994. Attributing responsibility and assessing gravity in wife abuse situations: A comparative study of police and social workers. *Journal of Social Service Research* 19:67–84.

Jang, D., Lee, D., and Merolle-Frosch, R. 1990. Domestic violence in the immigrant community and refugee community: Responding to the needs of immigrant women. *Response to the Victimization of Women and Children* 13:2–7.

Kirkwood, Catherine. 1993. *Leaving Abusive Partners*. London: Sage Publications.

Loader, Ian. 1997. Policing and the social: Questions of symbolic power. *British Journal of Criminology* 48:1–18.

MacLeod, Linda and Maria Shin. 1990. *Isolated, Afraid and Forgotten: The Service Delivery Needs and Realities of Immigrant and Refugee Women Who Are Battered*. Ottawa: Health and Welfare Canada.

MacLeod, Linda, Shin, Maria, Hun, Queenie, Samra-Jawanda, Jagrup, Rai, Shalen, and Wasilewska, Eva. 1993. *Like a Wingless Bird: A Tribute to the Survival and Courage of Women Who Are Abused and Speak Neither English nor French*. Ottawa: Department of Canadian Heritage.

Martin, Dianne L. and Mosher, Janet E. 1995. Unkept promises: Experiences of immigrant women with the neo-criminalization of wife abuse. *Canadian Journal of Women and the Law* 8:3–44.

Martin, Margaret. 1997. Double your trouble: Dual arrest in family violence. *Journal of Family Violence* 12:139–157.

Miedema, Baujke and Nason-Clark, Nancy. 1989. Second class status: An analysis of the lived experiences of immigrant women in Fredericton. *Canadian Ethnic Studies* 21:63–73.

Morley, Rebecca and Mullender, Audrey. 1992. Hype or hope? The importation of pro-arrest policies and batterers' programmes from North America to Britain as key measures for preventing violence against women in the home. *International Journal of Law and the Family* 6:265–288.

Smart, Carol. 1989. *Feminism and the Power of Law*. London: Routledge.

Statistics Canada. 1996. *Profiles: Total Immigrant Population*. Ottawa: Minister of Supply and Services Canada.

Status of Women Canada. 1997. *Gender and Immigration: Some Key Issues*. Ottawa: Policy Directorate.

Thorne-Finch, Ron. 1992. *Ending the Silence: The Origins and Treatment of Male Violence Against Women*. Toronto: University of Toronto Press.

ENDNOTES

[i] For purposes of this study, woman abuse is defined as consisting of the following injurious behaviours perpetrated against a woman by a man who is either her husband or common-law partner: physical abuse, sexual abuse, psychological abuse, emotional abuse, financial abuse, and spiritual abuse.

[ii] No-drop prosecutorial policies prohibit the victims of woman abuse from being able to take action that would lead to the withdrawal of criminal charges once they have been filed against an abusive male.

PART FOUR
Voices of Actors in the Criminal Justice Process

CHAPTER 13
The Role of the Prosecutor

INTRODUCTION

Most people are familiar with the role and function of a defence counsel: to argue the accused's side against the case of the state. This means rebutting evidence where possible and advancing the interests of the accused right through to the sentencing hearing, in the event of a conviction. At the sentencing hearing the defence will propose a sentence that would be in the best interests of the accused, and representation of the accused may not stop here if an appeal of the conviction or sentence is launched. The role of the Crown is less well known, however. Some victims come to court to testify against the accused and are surprised to learn that the Crown's job is not to represent *their* specific interests, but rather to prosecute the case on behalf of the state. This is not to say that the victim will be ignored, although that does happen on occasion. Today, the criminal justice process attempts to keep the victim apprised of developments in the case and will attempt to incorporate the interests of the accused where possible and appropriate. At the end of the day, however, the criminal trial has only two official parties: the state and the accused.

In this reading, Brian Manarin, an experienced Crown attorney in the province of Ontario, draws upon his experience to provide a portrait of the role of the Crown or prosecutor. He discusses the various decisions that confront a Crown counsel, such as the determination of the charge to be laid (including whether it is in the public interest to proceed with a prosecution at all), the issue of bail for the accused person, and submissions on sentencing.

Prosecution and the Exercise of Discretion in Everyday Practice[i]

Brian Manarin

The vast majority of all allegations of criminal misconduct in Canada are prosecuted in the lower level provincial division courts. If one pictures an inverted funnel, with the provincial courts representing the wide opening and the Supreme Court of Canada representing the narrow spout, a better appreciation of just how busy the provincial courts really are should emerge. It is with this in mind that this article is written. As such, the reader should assume that the dynamics of prosecution in everyday practice are best described by drawing from this unique and industrious forum.

The Crown attorney (and any assistant Crown attorney in his or her charge) is a lawyer whose responsibilities involve the preparation and prosecution of cases for alleged criminal and quasi-criminal offences occurring within the province in which he or she is employed. Although countless statutes come into consideration when allegations of criminal conduct are made, the pre-eminent legislation that governs the prosecution of criminal offences in Canada is known simply as the *Criminal Code*.[ii] Contained within this lengthy federal statute is a detailed sketch of what Parliament considers to be acceptable and unacceptable conduct in civilized Canadian society. The *Criminal Code* of Canada can be viewed as the catalyst, in some form or fashion, behind all criminal prosecutions that take place in the country.

The majority of prosecutors earn their living in the courtroom. Their lot in life focusses largely on the search for the truth in the context of the trial process. However, it should also be clearly recognized that many issues that are integral to the administration of justice are dealt with far from the courtroom. Although certainly not an exhaustive list, other prosecutorial responsibilities include the drafting of court documents and providing professional advice to the police, related agencies, and the general public on criminal matters. In addition, prosecutors must possess a thorough knowledge of criminal law and procedure and the rules of evidence, as well as a strong comprehension of the workings of the *Canadian Charter of Rights and Freedoms*,[iii] the supreme law of the land. Last, but not least, the prosecutor must bring superior judgment and a healthy degree of common sense to his or her workday duties.

In order to better appreciate what distinguishes a prosecutor from any other type of lawyer, reference should be made to the actual role of the prosecution in the trial process. The parties to any criminal prosecution are Her Majesty the Queen on the one side and those accused of committing the offences on the other (Wijesinha and Young, 1978:1). The prosecution must ensure that the accused receives a fair trial. The end goal is not to register a finding of guilt, but rather, it is to come to a just result born out of the evidence presented at trial. Without a doubt, the best definition of the role of the Crown can be found in the often-quoted words of Mr. Justice Rand of the Supreme Court of Canada in the case of *Boucher v. R.*[iv] wherein he stated the following:

> It cannot be over-emphasized that the purpose of a criminal prosecution is not to obtain a conviction; it is to lay before a jury what the Crown considers to be credible evidence relevant to what is alleged to be a crime. Counsel have a duty to see that all available legal proof of the facts is presented: it should be done firmly and pressed to its legitimate strength, but it must also be done fairly. The role of the prosecutor excludes any notion of winning or losing; his function is a matter of public duty: in civil life there can be none charged with greater personal responsibility. It is to be efficiently performed with an ingrained sense of the dignity, the seriousness, and the justness of judicial proceedings.

The goal of every prosecutor is to meet the high standards that Justice Rand emphasized in his classic statement on the subject. However, prosecutors are human and thus subject to the same foibles and fallibility as any other person in any other walk of life. Putting aside one's passions to make way for moderation and impartiality is a constant effort.[v] Maintaining neutrality does not, however, translate into a lacklustre effort on the part of the prosecution. To the contrary, the Crown counsel, like any other advocate, is entitled to advance his or her position forcefully and effectively.[vi]

In contrast, the role of the defence counsel is to be openly partisan toward his or her client. It is well understood that the defence has a duty to protect the client from being found guilty of a criminal offence and, to that end, the defence may rely on all the available evidence and defences so long as they are not false or fraudulent. Therefore, the defence is not obligated to assist the prosecution at trial. In fact, the defence is entitled to assume an entirely adversarial role toward the prosecution.[vii] Whereas the prosecution must disclose the case in its entirety to the defence, the defence need not state in advance what specific response (i.e., defence) will be made to the accusation, who the witnesses are, or what they will say on the witness stand. Distilled to its most fundamental, a person accused of committing a crime is presumed to be innocent until the prosecution proves his or her guilt beyond a reasonable doubt. Because of this, an accused person has a right to remain silent and, in doing so, avoid the potential for self-incrimination. The burden of proving guilt always rests squarely on the shoulders of the prosecution.

By emphasizing the distinction between the prosecution and the defence, the trial process as well as the various responsibilities of the prosecutor should be more easily understood. In order to illustrate the typical duties and obligations of a prosecutor practising in the provincial courts, the remainder of this article will concentrate on, in general terms, three areas that would be dealt with regularly during a normal week in the office of the Crown attorney: (1) charge screening and disclosure; (2) bail hearings; and (3) sentencing. The trial process itself will not be dealt with in any direct way.

CHARGE SCREENING AND DISCLOSURE

Although there is an immediate need for policing in Canadian society, there is not a concurrent need to prosecute all alleged offenders. The decision to continue or terminate a prosecution is among the most difficult Crown counsel must make (*Crown Policy Manual*, 1994:1). It is at this early stage of the proceedings that prosecutors would do well to remember the following words of wisdom:

> A Crown attorney must be ever alert to prevent abuses of the criminal process. He must stand independent between the accused and overzealous police. He must recognize and prevent vexatious or multifarious charges being laid or prosecuted. He must recognize unworthy or vindictive complainants and not become wittingly or unwittingly an instrument of persecution. He must remain objective, exercising his own discretion and judgement, especially in cases that have caused public outrage or incensed his community. Cases that have political overtones, cases that have attained a great deal of publicity, or cases that appeal to prejudices, such as race or religion, must be dealt with in the same fashion (Bynoe, 1968:102).

Screening occurs when the prosecution receives its brief of the allegations from the agency—usually the police or an individual—responsible for laying the charge or charges. Screening is an ongoing process and must be done before a date is set for a preliminary inquiry or trial. Each charge is screened to decide, among other things, the following: (1) whether there is a reasonable prospect of conviction; (2) whether it is in the public interest to discontinue a prosecution even though there is a reasonable prospect of conviction; (3) whether the proper charge has been laid; (4) whether the investigation is complete; and (5) whether an offer of diversion should be made to the accused (*Crown Policy Manual*, 1994:2).[viii]

If there is no reasonable prospect of conviction, then a prosecution must be terminated. The test is an objective one that considers the availability and admissibility of evidence, the credibility of witnesses, and the viability of any apparent defences. After considering the issue of reasonable prospect of conviction, the public interest must be contemplated. Although deciding what is in the public interest can be a daunting task for a seasoned prosecutor, or even the courts for that matter, certain questions should be asked regularly when a charge is being tested on the anvil of the screening process:

- Is the incident in question grave or trivial?
- What are the victim's views?

- What is the age and health, both physical and mental, of an accused or witness?
- Would public confidence in the administration of justice be maintained by the screening decision?
- Are issues of national security or international relations involved?
- What is the degree of culpability for the accused in the grand scheme of the particular offence being alleged?
- Is there a prevalence of this type of offence being committed in the community?
- Would a conviction be unduly harsh or oppressive in relation to this particular accused person?
- Has the accused co-operated in the police investigation, or is he or she willing to do so now?
- How strong is the Crown's case?
- How old are the allegations?
- How long and costly will the prosecution be compared with the likely sentence for the crime?
- Are alternatives to prosecution available? (*Crown Policy Manual*, 1994:4–5)

Although police officers are required to have a sufficient working knowledge of criminal law to allow them to make arrests and lay charges, it is Crown counsel who must ultimately decide whether the proper charge has in fact been laid or whether another charge should be substituted at the screening stage. Depending on the situation, recommending that the police change a charge can often result in reducing duplicate charges since one single action can result in the commission of many criminal offences. In other circumstances, substituting one charge for another can save valuable resources by keeping a case within the jurisdiction of a provincial division judge. Additionally, when more subtle legal nuances are assessed by the prosecutor, a keen eye for detail can result in the police laying a more or less serious charge than they originally contemplated.

Until an investigation is complete, neither an accused person nor a prosecutor can truly appreciate the strengths or weaknesses of a particular case. As such, the prosecutor must be satisfied that all avenues of a police investigation have been exhausted. If such is not the case, then Crown counsel must direct the police to complete the areas of the investigation that are incomplete. In this regard, the prosecution should invite the opinion of defence counsel to see if there have been other oversights by the police.

Finally, regarding the screening of criminal charges, Crown counsel has the opportunity to divert a charge away from the criminal justice system. This means that no prosecution will proceed, and the person accused of the offence will not acquire a criminal record. Historically, a prosecutor has always had the discretion to refuse to invoke the various judicial procedures envisioned by the *Criminal Code* and withdraw a charge or charges against an accused.

Presently, diversion programs have been devised by the attorneys general, lieutenant-governors in council, or their respective designates in each province and are collectively recognized as "alternative measures" by the *Criminal Code*.[ix] Generally speaking, if an accused person admits to his or her involvement in the commission of an offence and does not wish a trial, alternative measures may be used by the prosecutor to deal with that person if, in so doing, it would not be inconsistent with the protection of society. The interests of society and those of the victim are weighed in the balance. Similarly, the interests of the accused are fully protected. This is accomplished by (1) ensuring that he or she fully and freely consents to the alternative measures, and (2) ensuring that a trial is actually held if that is what the accused desires.

Alternative measure programs may involve the diversion of charges for mentally disordered accused, prostitutes and their patrons, native Canadians, young offenders,[x] as well as a host of other minor (and generally first-time) offenders. Each diversion requires the completion of some program or act of contrition that satisfies the prosecution's terms and conditions. By offering alternatives, the offender will be discouraged from offending again and avoid acquiring a criminal record. Also, the state is spared the necessity of expending scarce resources.

BAIL HEARINGS

The issue of bail, or "judicial interim release" as it is described in the *Criminal Code,* means the release from custody of accused persons so that they can maintain their liberty while awaiting trial. Although, in certain circumstances, a police officer or a justice of the peace can arrange a person's release (Trotter, 1992:Chapter 2), this article will concentrate on bail hearings conducted in court where a prosecutor is called upon to make a decision whether an accused person should be detained in custody until guilt or innocence is determined by a judge.

Picture, if you will, bail court on a Monday morning where, in addition to the normal volume of weekend arrests, there have been raids on illegal establishments and final "take-downs" of various special police crime prevention projects resulting in further large-scale arrests. As you can imagine, the ability to make intelligent, fair, and informed decisions as to release or detention can be an overwhelming task. Digesting the allegations pertinent to each accused person, considering the positions of the police, defence, and complainants, and considering strategy for the bail hearings requires a cool head and a large measure of confidence.

The outcome of a bail hearing is often pivotal to the outcome of the case itself. Statistics have shown that over 80 percent of all charges dealt with in the provincial division courts result in guilty pleas (Martin, 1993:15). Experience has shown that persons detained without bail are much more likely to plead guilty so that they may start serving their sentence immediately. Justice through trial seems much less appealing when a person is waiting for his or her "day in court" without a release on bail. As such, it is perhaps at the bail hearing where the prosecutor is under the most intense pressure to be firm but fair.

What are the fundamental concerns at a bail hearing? It is clear that an accused person will be granted a form of bail unless the prosecution can show why the detention of the accused person is justified. In fact, it is required by law that the least onerous form of release be granted to an accused person unless the prosecution can show why a more stringent form of release should be imposed.[xi] However, there are six situations that can shift the onus to the accused to show why his or her detention is *not* justified. Five of these six situations are relevant to a provincial division bail hearing and generally concern the following:

1. Has the accused person allegedly committed another indictable offence while on release?
2. Has the accused person allegedly committed an offence involving organized crime for which the maximum punishment is imprisonment for five years or more?
3. Has the accused person allegedly committed an indictable offence and is not ordinarily resident in Canada?
4. Has the accused person allegedly failed to attend court as required on a previous outstanding release or failed to otherwise live up to the terms of the previous release?
5. Has the accused person allegedly committed or conspired to commit an offence involving the production, trafficking, or importation of certain controlled drugs?[xii]

Whether the burden is on the accused or prosecution, three different areas of concern are consistently addressed at a bail hearing: (1) Is the accused person's detention necessary to ensure his or her attendance in court in order to be dealt with according to law? (2) Is the accused person's detention necessary for the protection or safety of the public? (3) Is the detention necessary to maintain confidence in the administration of justice, having regard to all the circumstances, including the apparent strength of the prosecution's case, the gravity of the nature of the offence, the circumstances surrounding its commission, and the potential for a lengthy term of imprisonment?[xiii]

Although the sections of the *Criminal Code* are clear on when a prosecutor may seek to detain a person in custody until trial, these criteria should not be applied automatically. By erring on the side of caution, Crown counsel is often falling short of the standards that are expected from his or her office. The following three examples illustrate the point.

Example #1
A refugee claimant from Cuba has come to Canada to escape the repressive Castro regime of which he was a vocal opponent. He has left family and

friends behind. Six months into his stay in Canada, he finds himself charged with a street robbery that occurred in an area of Toronto that is plagued by this type of offence. The identity of the perpetrator of this crime is clearly an issue at trial. No significant injuries were suffered by the victim. Although the accused person has no real roots in the community, he has no criminal record and has two sureties who will guarantee his release on bail and who will, in addition, offer a cash deposit.

Although protection of the public as well as the fact that this offence generally commands a lengthy term of imprisonment upon conviction are important issues to be considered, the foremost concern in this situation tends to be whether this accused will flee if granted bail. With no ties to the community, it would appear that flight from prosecution should be a concern. Should Crown counsel simply point out that because the accused is not normally resident in Canada, he should be detained, and it is up to the accused to show why he should be released? Or do the facts require more detailed consideration?

Although the accused has not yet established himself in Toronto, the prosecution clearly is aware that he has come to Canada to escape his homeland. Why would a person return to a country in which he knows he is not welcome? Although this type of offence must be denounced, it is equally clear that there are weaknesses in the Crown's case because the identification of the culprit is not certain. The fact that the accused has no criminal record, despite being in Canada only for a short time, bodes well for his release. It would appear that this is a case in which the Crown could, given all these circumstances, suggest a form of release without abdicating its duties as a minister of justice.

Example #2

The police are called to a residential dwelling, the scene of an earlier domestic assault by a husband on his wife. The accused was drinking heavily at the time of the incident but is now sober and remorseful. The accused has no criminal record, and the police discover from family sources that his behaviour was an aberration likely stemming from the loss of his job. Although there are no apparent injuries, the victim is concerned that her husband broke a sacred trust between them, and she fears that he may repeat this conduct if he is granted bail. The victim is financially dependent on her spouse and has two small children to care for. The accused has a surety who will allow him to live at his home, far away from the family abode, while awaiting trial. He will also get the accused some treatment for what appears to be an alcohol problem.

Society's general abhorrence for spousal assault cannot be overstated. What was once considered a problem to be worked out within the family is now understood to be a serious criminal offence that brings with it significant criminal sanctions. Both police and prosecutors realize that an inordinate number of homicides result from domestic violence. However, the truly objective prosecutor must not be influenced by his or her disgust for certain alleged conduct. Although it is totally understandable that the spouse may fear a repetition of the abuse, all indications reveal that this assault was an isolated incident.

The fact that a strong surety has come forward who can put some physical distance between the abuser and the victim should also alleviate certain concerns. Even though there are many arguments as to why this type of offence is a more serious form of violence, the fact remains that, except for the spousal abuse/violence toward women issue, Crown counsel would really have no choice but to immediately concede that this accused person is a candidate for bail. Although the protection of the victim can only be achieved in certain situations by denying the abuser any form of release, in this case, a carefully crafted bail order would meet the ends of justice.

> Example #3
> The accused person is on a police release for communicating for the purpose of engaging in prostitution. One of the terms of his release is that he abide by a curfew that requires him to be in his place of residence between 11:00 p.m. and 6:00 a.m. every day. He is seen by the police to be staggering down the road at 3:00 a.m. on the day in question, and, upon investigation, it is discovered that he is in violation of his curfew. The accused is clearly guilty of failing to comply with a fundamental condition of his release. Although this is a reverse-onus situation, the accused seeks another bail and can produce a substantial surety to the court. At the time, the accused has no criminal record.

It is often easy to fall into the habit of rationalizing that since an accused will, in all likelihood, be found guilty at trial of the offence for which he desires bail, the notion of release pending that foregone conclusion is somehow now inappropriate. Clearly the strength of the prosecution's case is an important consideration when deciding whether bail is a viable option, but in a situation such as in this example, other factors must be considered. This accused would, but for his subsequent curfew violation, be a candidate for the alternative measures program in regard to his prostitution-related offence. As for the curfew violation itself, despite the fact that violating a release condition is a serious offence, it is highly unlikely that, upon conviction, the accused would ever be sentenced to a period of custody. As such, a detention order at the accused's bail hearing would be overly harsh given what he could expect as a just punishment for either or both offences. This being the case, sound judgment would dictate a further release for this accused person, but with more restrictive conditions.

SENTENCING

Arguably nothing is more vexing for a prosecutor than making submissions on sentence. By definition, the accused now stands guilty as charged as a result of a guilty plea or after being found guilty at trial. In either situation, the accused is at his or her most vulnerable, and so is the Crown counsel. The former is vulnerable because the passing of sentence can result in the loss of liberty as well as the stigmatization of the offender for years to come. The latter is vulnerable since the quality of justice is often measured by the submissions of the prosecution on sentence. A lack of impartiality at this most emotional stage of the proceedings can tarnish the entire office of the Crown attorney, not just the reputation of the individual prosecutor. It is for this reason alone that the role of Crown counsel has been measured on the strength of the following statement: "With the result, as with the verdict at the trial, he is enormously unconcerned" (Humphreys, 1955:748).

Being unconcerned about the outcome of a prosecution should not be interpreted as being apathetic, which could mean that Crown counsel had relinquished his or her responsibility for a just sentence. Thus, historically, the prosecution is expected to display a lack of concern at the end as well as the beginning of the trial process, to acquit itself without feeling or animus in order to dispassionately reach a just conclusion.

The purpose and principles of sentencing are now largely incorporated into the *Criminal Code* of Canada.[xiv] Entire texts have been written on the subject of sentencing, and it is not the intention of the author to delve into the legal details of this complex area. Suffice it to say that sentencing hearings are almost entirely fact-generated. Therefore, no two proceedings are ever exactly the same, despite efforts to treat like offenders in similar fashions. One area of sentencing that is worthy of special comment pertains to the conditional sentence.[xv] Recent amendments to the *Criminal Code* have resulted in a new type of sentence in Canada. When a person is convicted of an offence that does not have a minimum term of imprisonment spelled out in the *Criminal Code*, the court may order that the offender serve the sentence in the community. The sentence must be less than two years imprisonment, and the court must be satisfied that the offender will not be a danger to the community. Finally, the court must be satisfied that serving the sentence in the community would be consistent with the fundamental purpose and principles of sentencing as set out in the *Criminal Code*.

The advent of the conditional sentence in 1996 means that offenders who traditionally went to jail are now increasingly serving their sentences in the community subject to, as one might expect, various conditions. So far, it has been difficult for many prosecutors to accept the conditional sentence as a viable alternative to traditional incarceration, for two reasons: (1) it is hard to appreciate how the value systems in Canadian society have shifted so dramatically in recent times that Parliament has allowed offenders who would have been jailed before to serve their sentences in the same community whose trust they violated; (2) due to scarce resources, the administration of criminal justice is ill-equipped to monitor or prosecute those offenders who do not live up to the conditions of their sentences in the community.

A shortcoming of the conditional sentence is that many judges, defence counsel, and prosecutors view it as a second-class form of punishment. It is bandied about more as a tool for plea-bargaining purposes than as a legitimate form of sentence. On anecdotal evidence alone, the disparity between the imposition of a conditional sentence upon a guilty plea as opposed to after a trial appears to be glaring.

How should Crown counsel remedy the misuse of the conditional sentence? The answer is obvious. The prosecution has a positive duty to apply the law as expressed by Parliament and to actively urge conditional sentences upon the court whenever the circumstances dictate. This would be in keeping with the highest traditions of the Crown and entirely consistent with the expected objectivity that goes with the office. To lead by example is to conscientiously discharge the duties of the prosecution.

CONCLUSION

The provincial division courts are the lifeblood of the criminal justice system. They have been variously described as ungovernable battlefields and as arenas of remarkable cohesion. No matter what particular view is held, there is no denying that the prosecution plays an essential role in making the busiest of all Canadian courts a functional role model for the administration of justice. By maintaining an objective frame of mind, Crown counsel will continue to uphold a cornerstone of the adversarial process. It is not always an easy task.

DISCUSSION QUESTIONS

1. *As noted in the introduction to this reading, criminal justice is attempting to become more sensitive to the needs of crime victims. Some people have suggested that, prior to making a plea bargain with an accused, the Crown should seek and obtain the approval of the victim. Do you think this is a good idea?*
2. *As Mr. Manarin notes, the accused in a criminal trial is not obligated to take the stand to testify. In some cases, it would make the Crown's task easier if the accused were compelled to testify. What is your reaction to changing the rules of evidence to compel the accused to testify if the Crown so desires?*

FURTHER READINGS

Brockman, J., and G. Rose. 1996. *An Introduction to Canadian Criminal Procedure and Evidence*. Toronto: Nelson Canada.

Stenning, P.C. 1994. Current issues concerning the court process. In *Canadian Criminal Justice*, 2nd ed., Curt T. Griffiths and Simon N. Verdun-Jones (Eds) (pp. 279–350). Toronto: Harcourt Brace Canada.

REFERENCES

Bynoe, B.C. 1968. The role and function of Crown counsel. 3 C.R.N.S. 90.

Crown Policy Manual. 1994. Policy # C.S.-1, Charge Screening, January 15.

Humphreys, C. 1955. The duties and responsibilities of prosecuting counsel. *Criminal Law Review* 739:748.

Martin, G.A. 1993. *Report of the Attorney General's Advisory Committee on Charge Screening, Disclosure, and Resolution Discussions.* Toronto: Queen's Printer for Ontario.

Trotter, G.T. 1992. *The Law of Bail in Canada.* Toronto: Carswell.

Wijesinha K., and B.J. Young. 1978. *Aids to Criminal Investigation.* Scarborough: Panju Canada Ltd.

ENDNOTES

[i] The comments found herein are solely those of the author, made in his personal capacity.

[ii] R.S.C. 1985, c. C-46, as amended.

[iii] S. 33, Part I of the *Constitution Act, 1982,* being Schedule B to the *Canada Act 1982* (U.K.), 1982, c. 11.

[iv] *Boucher v. R.* (1955), 110 C.C.C. 263 at 270.

[v] *R. v. Bain* (1992), 10 C.R. (4th) 257 at 264 (S.C.C.), wherein Mr. Justice Cory recognizes that passions are not easily stilled, even when considering counsel for the Crown: "they, like all of us, are subject to human frailties and occasional lapses ... I do not make these observations in order to be critical of Crown Attorneys. Rather they are made to emphasize the very human frailties that are common to all, no matter what the office held."

[vi] *R. v. Daly* (1992), 57 O.A.C. 70 at 76, para. 32 (C.A.).

[vii] *R. v. Stinchcombe* (1991), 68 C.C.C. (3d) 1 at 7 (S.C.C.).

[viii] Contained therein is a more exhaustive list of considerations that must be addressed by the Crown attorney's office.

[ix] *Supra* note 1, ss. 716, 717.

[x] *Young Offenders Act,* R.S.C. 1985, c. Y-1, s. 4, as amended.

[xi] *Supra* note 1, s. 515(1).

[xii] Ibid., s 515(6).

[xiii] Ibid., s. 515(10).

[xiv] Ibid., ss. 718–718.2.

[xv] Ibid., ss. 742–742.7.

CHAPTER 14
The Role of the Defence Counsel

INTRODUCTION

One of the critical professions in the criminal justice system, and the one with which people may be most familiar (if only from court shows on television), is the defence counsel. Although we are quite familiar with defence lawyers, this does not necessarily mean that we have a good understanding of their role in the criminal justice system. In this chapter, Paul Burstein, an experienced criminal defence lawyer practising in Toronto, discusses the professional life of a defence counsel and addresses a question he is frequently posed.

The Importance of Being an Earnest Criminal Defence Lawyer
Paul Burstein of the Ontario Bar

As a criminal defence lawyer, I am often asked by friends and family whether it bothers me to work so hard in the defence of someone who I know is guilty. For reasons that I hope to make clear a little further on, I have never found this to be a very difficult question to answer. However, the other day my seven-year old daughter asked me a slightly different question, one that I found myself struggling to answer.[i] She asked me how it was that I could defend bad people. My daughter's question led me to rethink the soundness of the explanations that I had long offered to critics of criminal defence lawyers. Fortunately, after some long periods of thought I managed to once again come to terms with this skepticism with respect to the importance of criminal defence work for our society.

In order to emphasize the importance of what criminal defence lawyers do, I think it is necessary to first explain what it is that we do. Simply put, criminal defence lawyers represent people who find themselves accused of crimes. As a result of the proliferation of television legal dramas, most people mistakenly perceive a defence lawyer's job to begin and end with the trial. In fact, most of a criminal defence lawyer's time is spent helping clients long before their cases actually get to trial. Indeed, the vast majority of criminal cases do not ever go to trial. Although the numbers have varied over the past couple of decades, no more than 5 to 10 percent of criminal charges are resolved by way of a trial. If so few criminal cases result in trials, what are all those criminal defence lawyers doing hanging around the courthouses? It may sound trite, but they are trying to help their clients stay out, or get out, of jail.

THE CLIENT AT THE POLICE STATION

Typically, a criminal defence lawyer's "job" begins long before the client's case even gets to trial. In fact, a criminal defence lawyer often becomes involved in a case even before the client goes to court. In Canada, s. 10(b) of the *Canadian Charter of Rights and Freedoms* provides that:

10. Everyone has the right on arrest or detention
    (b) to retain and instruct counsel without delay and to be informed of that right ...

Canadian courts have interpreted this constitutional right to mean that the police must tell someone who has been arrested that he or she can immediately contact a lawyer for free legal advice.[ii] Where a "detainee" (i.e., a person who has been detained) requests to speak to a lawyer, our courts have also held that the police are obliged to help that detainee get in touch with a lawyer right away, such as by providing him or her with a phone and a phone book.[iii] For those detainees who call a lawyer from the police station (not all of them do), the defence lawyer will almost always urge the detainee to assert his or her right to remain silent. Contrary to a popular misconception, it is not only the guilty who "confess" to the police while being held in detention.

It is not at all uncommon for the "innocent"[iv] to provide the police with a false confession. It is even more common for detainees who are not guilty of the charge to provide the police with an account of the events that is confused or mistaken. After all, these people are being held in custody and are being interrogated by very skilled and experienced questioners. More often than not, those police interrogators will confront the detainee with overblown claims of a case against the person in the hope of stimulating some sort of incriminating statement.

Accordingly, in an effort to prevent the creation of unreliable "confessions," our law guarantees a detainee the right to remain silent upon arrest. It is the defence lawyer's job to not only remind the detainee of this right during that first phone call but also help the detainee build the courage to maintain that silence in the face of any subtle or confrontational police questioning. In my experience, the vast majority of police officers, when told by the criminal defence lawyer of the detainee's desire to remain silent, will do the honourable thing and refrain from questioning that detainee any further. Fortunately or unfortunately, not all clients, no matter how many times they come in contact with the criminal justice system, seem to be able to learn what it means to SHUT UP![v]

RELEASE OF THE CLIENT ON BAIL

The other task of a criminal defence lawyer during that first phone call from the police station is to attempt to persuade the police to allow the client-detainee to be released on bail. While the police will usually have already made a decision in this regard, there are times when a defence lawyer's input can help satisfy the arresting officer that it is appropriate to release the detainee directly from the police station. If not, the defence lawyer will ask where and when the client-detainee will be brought to court for a hearing before a justice of the peace to determine whether or not the client should be released on bail. The *Criminal Code* requires that a person who has been arrested, and who has not been released at the scene or at the police station, be brought before a justice of the peace within a day or so of the arrest for a bail hearing. Many believe that the bail issue is the most important one in the criminal process. Given the long delays that occur between the time of the arrest and the time when a trial can be held, some people will have a strong incentive to plead guilty to their charge(s), even when they are not in fact guilty, simply to avoid a lengthy wait in a pretrial remand facility for their trial date.

In preparation for a bail hearing, a defence lawyer will need to help his or her client to find a surety; that is, someone who is willing to pledge a sum of money as a guarantee of that person's ability to supervise the detainee if released. In many cases, defence lawyers also must function as social workers or counsellors and help arrange for their clients to obtain treatment, secure employment, or re-enroll in school, as the justice of the peace will want to know that the client won't be sitting at home and watching soap operas until the trial date arrives. I cannot tell you how many times I have been in bail court and have heard the expression "the devil finds work for idle hands."

DEFENCES

Win or lose, the bail hearing does not end the case for a person who has been charged with a criminal offence. The next stage in the process involves trying to determine whether the client has a defence to the charge(s) he or she faces. At the risk of grossly oversimplifying what I do, criminal defences can generally be divided into two categories; namely, factual defences and legal defences. The factual type of defence involves a challenge to the evidence that the police have gathered in the course of the investigation that resulted in the charge(s) against the client. Perhaps the witness is lying? Maybe he or she implicated the accused in order to benefit himself or herself, such as through a lesser sentence for his or her own charges or for a monetary reward? Maybe the eyewitness is mistaken? As noted elsewhere in this volume (see Chapter 19), eyewitness identification is notoriously unreliable.

The other type of defence, the legal kind, focuses on whether or not what the person is accused of doing should be considered "criminal." For example, there may be no dispute that my client shot her husband, but it may have been in self-defence and, thus, legally justified. In trying to determine what, if any, defence a client may have to a criminal charge, the defence lawyer will need to gather information relevant to the case. That information will come from the police reports and witness statements, which the prosecutor is legally obliged to disclose to the defence in advance of the trial,[vi] as well as any information the client and other potential witnesses might be able to provide. (This is known as the Crown providing "disclosure" to the defence.) In addition, the defence lawyer may have to do some research into the law that governs the features of the client's case; for example, whether the police have engaged in an illegal search, whether self-defence includes the defence of one's property, or whether two lovers in a parked car are in a "public place." Once the defence lawyer has determined the nature and extent of the available defences, the lawyer is ready to advise the client how next to proceed.

At this juncture, the client is presented with two options: plead guilty in the hope of obtaining a more lenient sentence from the court as a reward for sparing everyone the time and expense of a trial *or* schedule a date to have a trial at which time the client can plead "not guilty" and contest the prosecutor's case. As noted above, in the vast majority of cases, persons charged with criminal offences will opt to have their lawyer try to negotiate a plea bargain with the prosecutor (see Chapter 4).

The term "plea bargain" connotes exactly what it means; namely, in exchange for giving up the right to a full-blown trial, the accused receives the prosecutor's recommendation for a more lenient sentence than would normally be sought if that accused had been convicted after a trial. This bargaining is often done at the prosecutor's office and is sometimes mediated by a judge. Upon learning the bottom-line offer of the prosecutor, a defence lawyer must always seek the input of the client before accepting or rejecting it. When asked by clients whether I would take the plea bargain if I were in their shoes, I am always left to explain that my risk–benefit analysis of trial versus guilty plea will, by definition, be different than theirs. As I tell them, given the nature of my work, I am quite used to spending my days in jail and am quite comfortable hanging around with criminals. If, on the other hand, the client is one of the minority who decide to reject the plea bargain in favour of a trial, the court will schedule a trial for some time down the road.[vii]

PREPARING FOR TRIAL

Preparing a case for trial is very much like producing a film or a play. First, you have to develop the story on which the play will be based. By this, I certainly do not mean that lawyers help clients fabricate stories in order to avoid conviction. I am simply referring to the development of the narrative that takes into account the evidence that the defence lawyer believes will be accepted by the jury (or judge) at the end of the case *and* that is consistent with innocence. In a nutshell, that is what a criminal defence lawyer does in representing a client at a trial; develop an "innocence" narrative to compete with the "guilty" narrative constructed by the police. For instance, the police may not have interviewed all of the potential witnesses, some of whom may not only cast doubt on the claim by others that a client is the guilty party, but also may shed light on the true identity of the perpetrator.

The development of a competing narrative is, however, no easy task. By the time a defence lawyer becomes involved in a case, the prosecution narrative has already been constructed. The raw material (i.e., the evidence) is rarely still sitting at the scene waiting to be collected and examined. Nevertheless, a defence lawyer must visit the scene of the crime to discover the competing innocence narrative. Perhaps the one feature of criminal defence work that is fairly reflected on television is the sleuthing that criminal defence lawyers do in the preparation of their clients' cases.

I recall going to a seedy hotel in downtown Toronto in preparation for a murder case where my client, a young female prostitute, had been charged with stabbing her customer to death. The case was about whether she had acted in self-defence. Thus, her opportunities to escape would play a critically important role in the jury's decision. After waiting for the elevator for 10 minutes down the hall from the room where the stabbing had occurred, I decided to take the stairs back down to the lobby. It was only then, when I saw that the staircase had been locked (apparently to prevent prostitutes from servicing clients in the stairwell and thereby avoiding the $50 room charge) that I better understood why my client would have felt that there was no means of escaping her attacker.

The next element of the trial drama is the cast of characters, and some are indeed characters. Who are the people who will tell the story to the jury? What is their background? Are they neutral and impartial, or do they have an axe to grind with the client? Do these people have a criminal record or a history of substance abuse? Usually, as part of the disclosure, the defence lawyer will be given this sort of information about the proposed witnesses. However, in some cases, a defence lawyer must hire a private investigator to go out and gather information about the witnesses. Unfortunately, even with the assistance of a private investigator, a criminal defence lawyer will never have the investigative resources that were (and are) available to the police and prosecutor. This is one of the principal justifications for insisting that the prosecutor bear the burden of proving guilt beyond a reasonable doubt, rather than asking the accused to prove that he or she is innocent.

With the storyline developed and the cast of characters defined, the defence lawyer must then turn to "directing" the play. In stark contrast to television legal dramas, most criminal defence lawyers do not simply stand up after the prosecutor finishes questioning a witness and begin cross-examination of that witness. Cross-examination must be carefully thought out and planned so that it does not do more harm than good. Moreover, it is important for a criminal defence lawyer to maintain the jury's interest in the case: important points that arise in the middle of a long and meandering cross-examination of a witness will be lost. In an effort to help maintain the jury's interest, lawyers will also try to think of ways to illustrate the testimony of the witnesses, such as by diagrams, photographs, or computer simulations. The ultimate efficacy of the "production" in the courtroom will depend on the time invested in its planning.

CONSTITUTIONAL ISSUES

While the outcome of the majority of trials depends upon the narratives created by the witnesses and the evidence, some trials are not about who did what, where, why, and to whom. Occasionally, a trial will instead focus on the law itself. One of the most famous Canadian examples is the trial of Dr. Henry Morgentaler. Most Canadians recall that in 1988 the Supreme Court of Canada declared that anti-abortion laws violated s. 7 of the *Canadian Charter of Rights and Freedoms*.

What most lay people do not appreciate, however, is that this ruling was made in the context of Dr. Morgentaler's trial on criminal charges for performing abortions. Dr. Morgentaler never denied that he had performed the abortions on the women in contravention of s. 251 of the *Criminal Code*. Instead, his defence focused on the constitutional validity of the law itself. In other words, Dr. Morgentaler's lawyer argued that it did not matter whether or not his client had done what the prosecutor was alleging because even if he had done those things, the *Charter* prohibited the Government of Canada from making it a crime to do those things.

Section 52 of the *Constitution Act, 1982*, affectionately known by lawyers as the "supremacy clause" states:

> 52(1) The Constitution of Canada is the supreme law of Canada, and any law that is inconsistent with the provisions of the Constitution is, to the extent of the inconsistency, of no force or effect.

In plain English, this means that the Canadian Government is not entitled to make laws that violate the rights that are set out in the *Canadian Charter of Rights and Freedoms*. Accordingly, a trial judge has the power to strike down a provision of the *Criminal Code* that is inconsistent with the *Charter*, just as the Supreme Court of Canada did when it struck down s. 251 of the *Code* in Dr. Morgentaler's case. This means that a lone criminal defence lawyer, armed with nothing more than a solid legal argument, can "make" (or, rather, unmake) law, a feat not possible even for the prime minister.

It was not long into my career as a criminal defence lawyer before I started to raise "section 52" challenges to criminal laws that I (and my clients) felt were oppressive and unfair. In 1993, about a year and half after being called to the bar, I launched a challenge to Canada's criminal prohibition on marijuana on behalf of a client who was charged with growing some plants in his house for his own personal use. As a result of a very good plea bargain that quickly followed that challenge, the court was never given the opportunity to decide the issue. However, less than two years later, I became involved, with my friend and mentor Professor Alan Young, in another challenge to Canada's criminal prohibition on marijuana that has wound its way to the Supreme Court of Canada. Should the Supreme Court of Canada agree with our reasoning as to how the law violates the rights enshrined in s. 7 of the *Charter*, the Court would declare the law to be "of no force or effect" pursuant to the supremacy clause in s. 52 of the *Constitution*. This would mean that our client would be acquitted of the marijuana offences with which he was charged back in 1995. More importantly, though, it would also mean that no other Canadian could henceforth be convicted of breaking this law because the law itself will be effectively erased from the books.

In some instances, criminal defence lawyers will instead challenge only the scope of a particular criminal law, as opposed to the law itself. For example, in the marijuana case, one of the alternative arguments is that the criminal prohibition on cannabis, as it is referred to in the legislation, should be limited to the type of cannabis that can be used by people to get high. While it may sound silly to think that people could be convicted of having hemp, a non-intoxicating form of cannabis, the law is unfortunately not so clear. Indeed, the drug analyst who testified at the trial admitted that based on the testing protocol, he would willingly certify a piece of hemp clothing as cannabis as the clothing would contain all of the elements that the law required for something to be certified as cannabis. Rather than compelling the court to strike down the law, this argument would simply require the court to redefine the law in a way that would produce a more appropriate definition of the "crime" being challenged.

In a similar vein, I was also involved with Alan Young in a challenge to the breadth of the criminal law that prohibited the "Thornhill Dominatrix" from offering her clients sado-masochistic services for hire. She had been charged with operating a common bawdyhouse on the basis that the sado-masochistic services were the equivalent of criminally proscribed sex-for-hire. On the strength of expert evidence concerning its sociological, psychological, and cultural dimensions, we argued that the nature and purpose of "S and M" activities is not sexual but rather psychological stimulation; namely, the thrill associated with the anticipation and experience of pain (and/or humiliation).[viii] Therefore, we argued, the criminal prohibition should not apply as it was properly limited to activities that were specifically aimed at providing sexual stimulation in exchange for money. Despite the inferential support to the argument provided by prior case decisions, the courts reaffirmed their monopoly on being paid to administer punishment.

My involvement in these various constitutional challenges also highlights another important feature of being a criminal defence lawyer; namely, the need (or opportunity) to study new disciplines beyond the confines of law. For the constitutional challenge concerning marijuana, I had to educate myself on the psychopharmacological, sociological, criminological, botanical, and historical perspectives on the criminal prohibition of marijuana. For the Dominatrix case, I had to become versed in the culture of "S and M" in order to be able to explain it to the court and, more importantly, to be able to demonstrate why the stereotypical perception of this practice is misguided.

For other cases, I have had to learn about psychiatry, literature, chemistry, toxicology, biology and even entomology (i.e., the study of bugs). This pursuit of knowledge can be a burden of the criminal defence lawyer's job. Indeed, I recall having to spend all of my Friday evenings, for weeks on end, sitting on a stool in the cramped office of our engineering expert in the "Just Desserts" murder case being taught all about digital image processing in preparation for the case. Then again, this is probably one of the great benefits of being a criminal defence lawyer: the opportunity to learn about things in the world to which I might never otherwise have been exposed.

DEFENDING PEOPLE WHO MAY WELL BE GUILTY

Despite the very long hours, the limited financial rewards, and the general lack of respect from the public, most of the time I love my job. I meet interesting people, learn fascinating new things, and visit places I would otherwise likely never have gone. In many ways, the job of a criminal defence lawyer is exotic and exciting.

Having explained why someone might want to be a criminal defence lawyer and what it is that criminal defence lawyers do, I am left to answer the questions as to how I could defend someone whom I "know" is guilty. To begin with, it is important to remember that our criminal justice system, while good, is far from perfect. One need only pay heed to the increasing number of wrongful convictions that are emerging in Canada (and especially in the United States). Indeed, look back to the media coverage of the arrest of Guy Paul Morin, a man we now know to be innocent of the murder with which he was charged. Back in 1985, the public "knew" he was guilty. It was not until almost a decade later that the public realized its mistake. Perception is not reality.

The only way to help reduce the number of wrongful convictions is to ensure that the system never cuts corners, no matter how heinous the crime. If someone is really guilty, the system should be able to arrive at that determination in a fair and just manner; that is, by following the same rules it always does. Everyone must be subject to the same set of rules, no matter who he/she is what he/she has been accused of doing. There are many countries where that is, unfortunately, not the case. In those places, the rules depend upon who you are or whom you know. These are governments that exist, in part, because there are no defence lawyers to challenge the arbitrary detention and imprisonment of those people whom these governments label as "criminals." While Canada is a long way off from that paradigm, we must never take for granted our rights and freedoms nor those whose job it is to defend our rights and freedoms. Defending the "guilty" is a necessary part of ensuring that we all continue to enjoy our rights and freedoms.[ix] In short, defence lawyers keep the criminal justice system honest.

That still leaves me with my daughter's question of how I can defend "bad" people, as opposed to people who have been accused of doing a bad thing. Why is it that "bad" people should benefit from all of my hard work as a criminal defence lawyer? Why should someone who has a long history of violating other people's rights be entitled to the same rights and freedoms as everyone else? For better or for worse, ours is a criminal justice system that seeks only to punish people for what they have done, not who they are. It has to be that way.

Consider what it would mean to base our punishment decisions on whether a person was "good" or "bad." Even in such a system, it would be unfair to punish those who were bad through no fault of their own; for example, those who suffered from fetal alcohol syndrome or those who had grown up being physically abused in group homes after being abandoned by their families. This would mean that we could punish bad people only after having a trial to determine if they were bad by choice or by circumstances. If we did not care to make that distinction, we would have to be prepared to charge all those who may have contributed to the person's crime of being bad, such as parents, schools, peers, and government. Of course, when I explained all of this to my daughter, she was quick to agree and remind me that I should therefore be the one serving her detention at school because it is my fault, not hers, that she was bad. Spoken like the daughter of a criminal defence lawyer.

DISCUSSION QUESTIONS

1. *Consider this chapter in light of the preceding chapter written by a prosecutor. How does the role of a defence counsel differ from that of a prosecutor?*
2. *How has your conception of the role of the defence counsel changed as a result of reading this chapter?*
3. *Some people think that the system is too protective of the rights of the accused. Others believe the opposite, that the state has too much power in prosecuting accused persons. What is your opinion?*

FURTHER READING

Greenspan, E. 1980. The role of the defence counsel in sentencing. In B. Grosman (Ed.), *New Directions in Sentencing*. Toronto: Butterworths.

ENDNOTES

i Being the father of Courtney, age 7, and Nikki, age 4, has taught me more about how to ask, and how to answer, "tough" questions than my many other experiences in the criminal law sphere.

ii *R. v. Bartle* (1994), 92 C.C.C.(3d) 289 (S.C.C.).

iii You would be amazed at how many first-time detainees go about choosing the defence lawyer who will represent them by simply going to the section in the yellow pages that lists "criminal lawyers" and starting at the As. You would, no doubt, be equally amazed at how many criminal defence lawyers were named "AAAAAAAAAASmith" at birth!

iv Whether they are "factually" innocent (i.e., did not do what the police have alleged) or "legally" innocent (i.e., have not done something that actually amounts to a crime).

v For example, in *R. v. Manninen* (1987) 34 C.C.C.(3d) 385 (S.C.C.), one of the seminal cases on the "right to counsel" in Canada, the accused, a "rounder," is savvy enough to assert his right to speak to a lawyer when arrested on a robbery charge. However, he then proceeds to engage in the following dialogue with the arresting officer:

Q. Where is the knife that you had along with this (showing the accused the CO_2 gun found in the car) when you ripped off the Mac's Milk on Wilson Avenue?

A. He's lying. When I was in the store I only had the gun. The knife was in the tool box in the car.

Q. What are these for?

A. What the fuck do you think they are for? Are you fucking stupid?

Q. You tell me what they are for, and is this yours? (showing the grey sweatshirt)

A. Of course it's mine. You fuckers are really stupid. Don't bother me anymore. I'm not saying anything until I see my lawyer. Just fuck off. You fuckers have to prove it.

vi See *R. v. Stinchcombe* (1991), 68 C.C.C.(3d) 1 (S.C.C.).

vii The lag between the "set date" and the trial can range up to a few years. The length of the delay is dependent upon the jurisdiction and upon the nature of the case; more complicated cases require more court time and, thus, are harder to slot into already very busy schedules.

viii Apparently, much like bungee-jumping, skydiving, or white-water rafting.

ix Throughout history, criminal defence lawyers have been accused of being unpatriotic. In one of the most eloquent descriptions of the importance of defence lawyers, Henry Brougham, defending Queen Caroline on charges of adultery before the English House of Lords many centuries ago, said: "An advocate, in the discharge of his duty, knows but one person in all the world, and that person is his client. To save that client by all means and expedients, and at all hazards and costs to other persons, and, among them, to himself, is his first and only duty; and in performing this duty he must not regard the alarm, the torments, the destruction which he may bring upon others. Separating the duty of a patriot from that of an advocate, he must go on reckless of consequences, though it should be his unhappy fate to involve his country in confusion." (Trial of Queen Caroline, by J. Nightingale, vol. II, the Defence, Part I (1821), at p.8).

CHAPTER 15
The Role of the Judge

INTRODUCTION

Many people think that judges simply supervise trials and sentence convicted offenders, but they have a great deal more to do than that. Judges are required to perform many varied judicial functions over the course of a typical day. In addition to their in-court activities, they may supervise pretrial conferences, meet with lawyers, see police officers about search and other kinds of warrants, write judgments (quite lengthy at times), and stay current with a large number of areas of the law. The professional life of a judge is not helped by the backlog of cases. In this reading, a very experienced provincial court judge in one of Ontario's busiest courts describes a typical day in his professional life.

A Day in the Life of a Provincial Court Judge
Judge David P. Cole, Ontario Court of Justice, Toronto

I became a lawyer in 1975, practising exclusively as criminal defence counsel until my appointment as a judge of the Ontario Court of Justice (Provincial Division)[i] in 1991. What follows is a narrative of a typical day in one court at the Metro East (Scarborough) Court facility in Toronto, with its major phases, players, and communications with one another and before the bench. In order to better understand what happens in a judge's life, the following is an explanation—from one judge's perspective—of some of the "Realpolitik" as various court personnel and myself go about our various duties in dealing with accused.

When I arrive at the court building each morning, I find on my desk in my office the list of the cases scheduled to be heard that day (the "docket"). On the day that I shall describe (September 1, 1998), I had to deal with the following charges: failing to appear (Mr. Ashbury); impaired driving (Ms. Andrus); breach of probation (Mr. Burns); assault (Mr. Fisher); mischief to private property/prowl by night (Mr. Goode); and two young offenders, K.B. and R.S.[ii]

Crown attorneys are full-time or contract lawyers currently employed in the Scarborough Crown attorney's office. On this particular day, Ms. Crisante[iii] was the Crown assigned responsibility for prosecuting all the new cases on the trial list. Normally—though, regrettably, by no means always—the trial Crown is given the Crown files ("briefs") for preparation the afternoon before the court hearing.

The paperwork for even the simplest of cases is often quite voluminous. For example, the charge of failing to appear against Mr. Ashbury was legally quite simple: Could the Crown establish to my satisfaction that Mr. Ashbury had an obligation to appear in court and that he had failed to do so? Once the Crown could prove these things, the *Criminal Code* directed that Mr. Ashbury would be found guilty of this offence unless he could establish that he had a lawful excuse for not appearing. However, there is considerable paperwork necessary to prove such a charge; at a minimum, the Crown would need certified copies of the form of the accused's release on bail, a certified copy of the charge that he failed to appear, and a certificate of the court clerk indicating that he had not appeared on the scheduled date. The trial Crown would then have the responsibility for checking to see that the investigating police officer (or, in this case, the accused's probation officer) had included all the necessary documents in the brief. Failure to do so would likely result in an aborted prosecution.

The Crown brief for the impaired driving charges against Ms. Andrus might, depending on the facts and issues raised, be several centimetres thick. It would usually contain the statements of police officers and civilian witnesses, a computer printout of the accused's breath readings, reports from a toxicologist explaining the significance of those readings, and a videotape of some of the time she was in the police station. Also likely to be included would be photocopies of precedents from other cases that Crown counsel thinks the defendant might submit in arguing her case.

Unlike some European systems in which the presiding judge is deeply involved in investigating every detail of cases from their outset, the Canadian justice system is designed in such a way that the judge is supposed to know as little as possible about the cases he or she is assigned. Thus, I would not usually see much, if any, of this paperwork prior to the trial. Similarly, fairly elaborate steps are taken to ensure that I would not be assigned to try cases of which I have any previous knowledge.

Before going into court, I normally do not look at the docket of the new cases I am about to try. On this day the only cases with which I was familiar ahead of time were those concerning the two young offenders, K.B. and R.S. I had already started these cases on prior occasions, and these were the only cases to which Mr. Kerr, the other Crown listed on the court docket, had been assigned. As the day developed, he dealt with some of Ms. Crisante's cases in order to maximize efficient use of court time. She prepared herself to respond to arguments that defence counsel in Ms. Andrus's impaired driving case (driving with over .80 milligrams of alcohol per millilitre of blood) announced at the last minute that he was going to raise.

Duty counsel are lawyers mandated to provide advice or advocacy services to accused making their first appearance or in bail court.[iv] They are not usually assigned to trial courts. Because the Scarborough court has a great many accused who tend to be unfamiliar with Canada's justice system,[v] officials of the Ontario Legal Aid Plan have assigned five duty counsel to the courthouse on a daily basis. One of these is supposed to act as a "standby" duty counsel, in part being available to assist unrepresented accused appearing in trial courts.

As the first item of business, the Crown usually calls up the cases that defence counsel or the investigating police officer has not spoken to her about, to find out the status of the cases. When Mr. Burns's case was called, he told me that he had not been able to arrange for a lawyer to represent him on the charge of breaching a probation order because he could not afford the $25 fee to process his application for legal aid. He asked to have his case adjourned. I examined the paperwork, which disclosed that Mr. Burns was charged with not paying the restitution that was part of a previous probation order. It also revealed that he had agreed several months earlier that he would proceed to trial on September 1 regardless of whether he had counsel. If I were to find Mr. Burns guilty, he faced the possibility of going to jail (depending on the circumstances of the breach and his previous record). Nevertheless, given his previous indication that he was prepared to proceed to trial without counsel, I ruled that unless there was some extraordinary reason for him to have another chance to get a lawyer, I would not grant a further adjournment.

Mr. Burns then told me that since the charge had been laid, he had paid off the outstanding order for restitution. At this point, Crown counsel intervened, saying that her brief indicated that while partial restitution had been made, a balance of $200 remained outstanding at the time the brief had been prepared, and that unless she received further information, she was not prepared to withdraw the charge. Mr. Burns said, "My old lady took a hundred dollar money order down to my p.o. [probation officer] last week."

I told the accused that while, in his mind, it might be true that he had "fixed it ... with his p.o.," could he please explain how he could have done this while $100 apparently remained outstanding? In response, Mr. Burns simply stared at the floor. The Crown explained to the accused that the probation officer had caused the accused to be charged because, in the probation officer's opinion, Mr. Burns had wilfully declined to complete paying restitution when he was in a position to do so. I told Mr. Burns that it was up to the

Crown, not his probation officer, to decide whether the charge would be proceeded with, but that we should wait for the probation officer to arrive at court (due to pressure of work, they are almost always late) to further update the Crown.

Mr. Burns then told me that he could not wait because he had to go to work and asked what he "would get ... if I cop [plead guilty] to the charge." Such an inquiry by an accused is quite common and raises several difficult issues for the court system. First, while I told Mr. Burns that I would not and could not tell him in advance what I might do if he were to plead guilty, strictly speaking, this was not true. There are many cases in which I am consulted in advance if a plea bargain is contemplated. I did not feel comfortable doing so in this case because Mr. Burns had neither his own counsel nor duty counsel to advise him. For this reason, I sent him off to the duty counsel office in the hope that the standby duty counsel might be able to advise him. Unfortunately, he returned to court a few minutes later, saying that he had been told that the standby duty counsel was busy and would not be available for some time, if at all.

Surprising as it may sound, many accused enter pleas of guilty despite the fact that they may have legal or factual defences to the charge. They decide for their own reasons, which often seem very sensible to them, that they are not interested in presenting a defence. As a judge, I cannot accept a plea unless the accused makes an informed waiver of his or her rights and is prepared to admit to all the elements necessary to support the Crown's case. In this case, had Mr. Burns insisted on pleading guilty, because he was not represented by counsel, I would have conducted what is termed a "plea comprehension inquiry," reviewing with him his understanding of his right to contest the allegations and his willingness to admit to each element of the Crown's case. If he had balked at any stage, I would likely have struck the plea and remanded the case to another trial date. The practical difficulty that arises is that on the next date, the accused may go through the same process, this time pretending that he is making an informed waiver and conceding the elements of the case just so he can get it over with.

Luckily, by this time, Mr. Burns's probation officer arrived. Crown counsel suggested that the case be "held down" to allow the parties the opportunity for some brief discussion. Although I was not privy to discussions among the accused, the probation officer, and Crown counsel, they eventually presented me with a compromise. Mr. Burns's case would be adjourned for thirty days. If he voluntarily performed twenty-five hours of community service prior to the return date by way of extra punishment for not having done what he was supposed to do, the parties agreed that the criminal charge would be withdrawn on the next appearance.

This case neatly illustrates several of the time allocation dilemmas regularly faced by the criminal justice system (and the extent to which the professionals are driven by the need to use court time as efficiently as possible). Given the relative unimportance of this case compared with the others on the list, the Crown likely had very little interest in prosecuting Mr. Burns that day, particularly since, being unrepresented, his case would probably take about ninety minutes to try. According to the Ministry of the Attorney General's current guidelines, a court day is supposed to consist of eight hours of trial time.[vi] After extensive discussion in our court's delay reduction committee, our trial co-ordinator has been instructed to "load" fourteen hours of trial time per day into a court such as 404. This is based on assumptions—well understood by court professionals though not by some accused and the general public—that a substantial number of cases will not proceed to trial despite having been scheduled as if they would be. As will be learned from what follows, Mr. Burns's case was the first of several that day to be diverted away from a trial.

All of this was now compounded by the fact that by the time the trial date came up, Mr. Burns's probation term had expired, thus making the agreement negotiated on the court date virtually unenforceable. If Mr. Burns did not perform the agreed-upon community service, all that could be done when his case next came before the court (on September 30) would be to process the original charge of breaching his probation by failing to make restitution. Once again, Crown counsel assigned to 404 court on that date, facing another list containing at least fourteen hours of cases, would not likely have much interest in prosecuting the charge. And so it goes ...

Did Mr. Burns know or guess some or all of this? Did he put off the day of reckoning by luck or by design? I do not know for sure. Ironically, in our adversarial system, the judge in the courtroom is usually the person who knows the accused the least. Apart from the brief series of questions I asked in response to his request for an adjournment, I am not supposed to engage in much dialogue with an accused. (And if Mr. Burns had had counsel there to represent him, he would likely have stood mute, leaving it up to his lawyer to speak on his behalf.) Because of this, over the years, I have learned to try as hard as I can to resist the quite human temptation to speculate and judge without sufficient evidence.

Although this is usually an acceptable way of proceeding on a given day, problems can and do occur when cases are not completed on the same day that they start. This is particularly the case when the evidentiary portion of a trial must be remanded to another day. This happened in the case of Ms. Andrus. The accused's lawyer brought a pre-trial motion to dismiss the charges on the basis that she had not been given her constitutionally guaranteed right to counsel.[vii] Because of the time needed to deal with the cases ahead of hers, her case could not be started until the afternoon (this is quite typical). The evidence called by counsel for the accused on the motion to stop the proceedings (on the basis that her *Charter* rights had been violated) was completed. In reply, most of the evidence of the main police officer was given. Unfortunately, because of insufficient time, the remainder of his testimony (including cross-examination by the defence) had to be deferred to March 4, 1999. After taking ten minutes of court time to twist the trial co-ordinator's arm and those of the lawyers, this was the earliest date that the time required could be matched with the schedules of the witnesses, the lawyers, and myself.[viii]

In such cases, in addition to taking what I hope are accurate notes of what is said by each witness as he or she gives his or her evidence, as soon as I leave court at the end of the day, I try to make notes immediately of how I am responding to the evidence as it is unfolding (recognizing, of course, that my preliminary impressions may change during the case). This includes such things as whether I think there is an adequate connection between Fact A and Fact B, why certain questions have not been asked (or properly answered), and, most importantly, what I think of the witnesses' credibility. While I try not to make up my mind until I have heard all the evidence and the lawyers' submissions, the reality of the situation is that given these lengthy delays and the danger of wrongly convicting an innocent person, most judges in this position would be more likely to acquit when the case is resumed six months later. This kind of ongoing resource problem is something that all court professionals are well aware of, and that is likely why the Crown seemed resigned or disappointed while the defence seemed quietly elated.

Why were more consecutive days not scheduled to avoid such unreasonable delays? This is a constant systemic problem that could be solved if more resources were available. As a result of aggressively pre-trying cases, efforts toward reducing the backlog of cases have been more successful in Scarborough than anywhere else in the province.[ix] However, despite repeated requests, no more resources are likely to be made available in the near future. As a result, cases such as this one will tend to "slip through" the system.

What happened in Ms. Andrus's case was this: as soon as defence counsel decided that he wished to launch a "right to counsel" constitutional challenge, the court rules required him to serve a formal "Notice of a Constitutional Question" on the Crown and with the court. This notice must be filed at least fifteen days prior to the trial date in order to give Crown counsel an opportunity to prepare to respond to the motion. He did not do so, asking that I permit him to proceed with his motion despite his failure to file it on time (which I have the power to do). He claimed that the reason he did not do so was simple inadvertence on his part. Crown counsel responded by saying that this was "too bad. The rules are there for a purpose. I am sick and tired of defence counsel going about their business as if the rules don't exist."

While I appreciated defence counsel's apparent candour, how did this help me in deciding whether to allow him to argue the motion? Although I have not seen him for many years, defence counsel is known to me as someone whose word can be accepted. Was he subtly reminding me, as an ex-defence counsel, that I, too, might have made such a slip and that I should not show him up in front of his client? Was he signalling me that he wasn't really serious about the motion and was just going through the motions of presenting a defence? (After all, "right to counsel" issues are probably the most frequently argued motions under the *Charter*. A counsel as experienced as himself surely would have spotted the issue earlier. From what I know of the case to date, that should have been easy.) Or was he signalling perhaps that his client was not paying him as quickly as he would have liked and that he was "playing hardball" with her, refusing to file the motion until she had completed paying his retainer?

And how should I have responded to the Crown's position? Should she, as soon as she realized that the defence had filed a motion, have filed a written application to dismiss it as being beyond the time frame allotted by the rules of procedure? That is doubtful unless this was an extremely serious case, and apart from the clerk in the office making sure that the motion was put in the Crown brief, no one in the Crown's office would have looked at the motion until late on August 31. What if the motion ultimately turned out to be valid and the charges were dismissed for a breach of the accused's constitutional rights? Should I have refused to hear it simply because it was not filed on time?

What have I learned about this for the future? Should I be more careful with this particular lawyer if I see him in the future? Should I modify my practice in such cases to penalize counsel for sloppy conduct by saying that I will hear only out-of-time motions if they agree to pay for a complete transcript if the case has to be remanded to another date? Or might that only penalize the poor? Should I have ordered a transcript (recognizing that, unlike Crown or defence, no one has ever formally told me that I am on a limited budget, though I know this to be the case) so that I am not forced to rely on my substantive notes of the evidence when the case is resumed?

The court clerk occupies a very important position. In addition to ensuring that all the various court documents are located and brought to court each day by the scheduled start time, his or her job is to ensure that each time I make an order, it is accurately reflected in the court records. This may be as simple as ordering that a case be remanded to another date, or it may be very complicated, such as ensuring that varying terms of imprisonment or probation are properly apportioned to each charge. As I write this, the newspapers have reported an apparently appalling case in which an accused wrongly spent a week in jail. This took place despite several supposedly fail-safe procedures designed to protect against this very kind of miscarriage of justice. Apparently someone had ticked off the wrong box on a court form designed to record judicial orders. Instead of recording that the accused had been given a year to pay his fine of $1000, it was recorded that the accused had been sentenced to jail for a year. No one, including the justice of the peace who made the order, noticed the mistake.

In order to protect against this very type of error, many of the orders that I make—particularly penalties of various forms—are presented to me at least twice for signature: once when the court clerk writes up what I have said, and again when the formal order has been typed. On a very busy day, I might be asked to sign upward of fifty orders. Although I suppose I could refuse to sign them until I have an opportunity to check them against my notes, the reality is that if I do that, everything will be delayed. If I delay signing remand papers for incarcerated accused, the jail will refuse to accept them, which means that the backlog of incoming prisoners to the jail at the end of the day will be extensive. If I decline to sign probation orders immediately, those placed on probation may tire of waiting and leave the court, not knowing when and where they are supposed to report next. Because I have realized that it causes all kinds of problems if I stop to read each paper in detail, like many other judges, I have tacitly condoned the practice of agreeing to sign them as they are prepared. The result is that I am constantly having such papers thrust at me throughout the day, even when I am on the bench trying to concentrate on the proceedings. In practice, this means that the judge relies heavily on the court clerk and the support staff who type the orders to ensure their accuracy.

The problem does not end there. Despite the best efforts of the court personnel, errors get made because the staff simply are not trained to pick up some types of errors. This week, our court probation officer saw me about a case from some months ago. She pointed out that I had clearly made an error by imposing a period of probation in circumstances in which I had no power to do so. I did not spot the error at any stage (the day had been a particularly busy one), nor did the lawyers (who had urged this disposition on me). What is even sadder is that the accused, a man of limited intelligence, was clearly in no position to realize that he had been improperly dealt with.

According to ministry statistics, in 1997, I dealt (however briefly) with some 2400 cases. Like other judges, I often worry about cases in which I may have made mechanical errors (such as errors writing the warrant) which may have resulted in an improper process being applied (or not applied[x]) against an accused.

As I have previously mentioned, the trial co-ordinator has been instructed to put more cases onto a trial list than can actually be dealt with. What happened with the rest of the cases is a good illustration of how this kind of daily gamble works.[xi]

While Ms. Crisante was outside the courtroom "brokering" Mr. Burns's case, as usually occurs, she was also able to plea-bargain or divert all but Ms. Andrus's case. Some of the cases were relatively simple for her to deal with. In Mr. Fisher's case, the alleged assault victim (complainant) did not turn up at court, which happens in about 40 percent of cases. There may be many reasons for this: the complainant may have moved since the charge was laid on December 30, 1997, and may not have received the mailed subpoena; or the complainant may simply have decided that, having called in the police to intervene, he or she is not interested in proceeding with the charge.[xii]

Even when complainants do come to court, as occurred in Mr. Goode's case, they may tell the Crown that they would be satisfied with a reduced charge. In that case, Mr. Goode, the accused, while drunk[xiii] and despondent about breaking up with his girlfriend, had hung around her townhouse one night intending to persuade her to resume their relationship. When she spurned his advances, he smashed the windshield of what he assumed was her new lover's car. In fact, the vehicle belonged to, as I was told, "her religious advisor."[xiv] What the ex-girlfriend wanted was an order for the accused to stay away from her. What the male complainant wanted was the cost of repairing his car. After verifying that the accused had lived up to the term of his bail order that required him not to communicate with his ex-girlfriend, Crown and defence counsel jointly proposed that I order the accused to post a "peace bond." In exchange for having the charge withdrawn, the accused would promise to keep the peace and be on good behaviour for one year. If he did not live up to the conditions of the order (staying away from the two complainants and making restitution for the windshield), he would stand to lose $500 (the amount of the peace bond) and would be liable to be prosecuted for being in breach of the bond. All parties left the courtroom hand in hand.

Mr. Ashbury's case raised different issues. Given the carnage on our roads, police forces tend to be very intolerant of suspected drunk drivers. Even where there are few signs of impairment and the accused's breath reading is just over the limit (as happened here), police are under instructions to lay charges rather than sending the accused home in a cab. Because of aggressive lobbying by groups such as MADD (Mothers Against Drunk Driving), for many years, Crown counsel have been under a directive to prosecute vigorously all drinking and driving charges. In part because of their lobbying, the severity of the mandatory minimum penalties has been increased considerably.

Unlike most other criminal charges, large numbers of middle-class people are charged with drinking and driving offences. As they wish neither the inconvenience of being without a licence (up to a year for a first offender) nor the stigma of a criminal record, they are often prepared to invest considerable resources in defending themselves against these charges. Thus, in most cities, there are specialist defence counsel who devote much of their practices to defending drinking drivers.[xv] They frequently employ expert toxicologists whose role is to uncover technical flaws in the Crown's case.

Once again, Crown counsel was faced with a dilemma that day. As only one other court had offered help (by now it was about noon), she could not send out Mr. Ashbury's case (or that of Ms. Andrus) to another court. Thus, she was virtually forced to enter into a plea bargain with Mr. Ashbury's very skilled defence counsel. Although I was not present during the plea bargaining (which all happened in Crown counsel's office), having done it myself for some sixteen years, I can imagine that the conversation went something like this (salty language deleted):

Crown: If I agree to drop the charge of failing to appear, will your client plead to the over .80?

Defence: Forget it, I've got my tox [expert toxicologist] on standby, and he'll be able to provide "evidence to the contrary."

Crown: Well, in that case, I'll proceed on both, one at a time. Even if I lose one, if we don't finish today, you'll just have to come back. I've got to get something out of this.

Defence: You might lose both. You know these charges have been going since '92, and they might get thrown out for undue delay.

Crown: Yeah, but that's only because your client disappeared and wasn't re-arrested until '97. Besides, you haven't filed a motion under the new rules, so you can't argue it anyway.

Defence: Judge Cole will let me abridge the time. You know these ex-defence counsel ....

Investigating Officer: Look, I've got better things to do than watch you two try to out-macho one another. I've been talking to the accused outside. He isn't a bad guy. He's got no other driving record that I know of and the [breath] readings were pretty low. I'm not interested in blood. I'll be content as long as he gets a big fine.

Crown: All right, with this reading, the new directive allows me to let him plead to careless driving under the provincial *Highway Traffic Act*. But he'll have to plead to the fail to appear.

Defence: Sounds good to me. At least, this way, he'll keep his licence. Give me ten minutes to talk to him.[xvi]

The bargain ultimately proposed was as follows: the Crown would allow the accused to plead guilty to the lesser charge of careless driving. Both parties would agree that the accused should be fined $1000. The accused would plead guilty to failing to appear; in exchange, Crown counsel would agree not to ask for jail but would join in asking for a fine of $300. The accused would be given six months to pay.

According to the rules that are expected to guide me, I may depart from plea bargains if I find them offensive, but, in order for all parties to know what to expect, I normally go along with them. I was entirely content to do so in this case. On the basis of what I was told (unlike some other cases, the first I heard of the contents of the plea bargain was in open court), the proposed disposition seemed entirely sensible, having been made by experienced counsel well aware of the strengths and weaknesses of their case.

During the time that Ms. Crisante had been negotiating outside court, Crown counsel Mr. Kerr was speaking to the continuing cases of the two young offenders (R.S. and K.B.) assigned to me. I describe these two cases in some detail not because young offenders are generally more violent (that is a myth unfortunately perpetuated by those who seek to make political hay through scaremongering), but because they illustrate the range of cases with which I deal on a daily basis.

In February 1997, I found R.S. guilty of armed robbery and aggravated assault. The accused had begun to demonstrate a variety of disturbed behaviours from about age ten. He was hospitalized from time to time, complaining that he had visual hallucinations and that demons were controlling him. He identified his parents as persecutors and from time to time had little to do with them, withdrawing to his room for days on end. One night in June 1996, just after his fourteenth birthday, he told his father he was going to the neighbourhood convenience store. He concealed a knife in his jacket, which he brandished at the proprietor. The accused fled the store, having taken fifty cents that happened to be sitting on the counter top. He was pursued by a friend of the proprietor. As they reached the other side of the road, R.S. was tackled to the ground. He stabbed his pursuer several times, necessitating some forty stitches. Some of the victim's scarring was permanent.

The accused was arrested a few minutes later. When he was taken to the police station, he gave some coherent responses to questions asked by the officers. Sometimes, however, he spontaneously broke into monologues, claiming that "Kurt Cobain told me that the guy in the store was the Devil, and that I had to kill him or I would go to hell forever."

At first, there were questions about whether the accused was fit to stand trial. After some period of assessment in a psychiatric facility, during which he was assessed as suffering from a severe form of schizophrenic disorder, he was stabilized on medication so that he was deemed fit to stand trial. As the doctors who assessed him considered that he had been insane at the time he committed the offences, he raised the defence of insanity at his trial. I rejected that defence[xvii] and sentenced him to two and a half years.

The *Young Offenders Act*[xviii] provides that an accused in these circumstances has the right to have his status reviewed every six months. R.S. has insisted on availing himself of that right (I suspect because it gives him a day out of the facility he is being held in) despite the fact that, for many months, he refused to take the medication that he so obviously needed. In his untreated state, he was prone to assaulting other prisoners and staff, which of course meant that he could not put together any release plan that had any hope of success. According to a report that was forwarded to me as part of his review, progress seemed to have been made. He was now taking a medication that agreed with him (many schizophrenia medications have unpleasant side effects), and the social workers reported that he had become much easier to manage. Through his counsel, he agreed that his case should be remanded for another six months. I assumed that if his counsel felt that R.S.'s progress was sufficient, he would request a substantial hearing, at which time I could be asked to release him on probation.

The second young offender I dealt with that day was K.B. She was born in another country, and her father died in an accident when she was a few months old. Because her mother objected to that society's deeply rooted custom that women should not remarry, she elected to come to Canada, leaving the 6-month-old K.B. in her grandparents' care. Although K.B. saw her mother every year for a few weeks, she did not live with her until she was six years old. Both agreed that, as unfortunately happens so frequently in these situations, mother and daughter did not bond well. This was compounded by the fact that soon after they began to live together, the mother became involved with a man she ultimately married.

Sometime after K.B. started high school, she began to go through normal teenage rebellion, albeit in a very moderate form. Her parents objected to the fact that she began to go out with J.C., a boy from a different culture. They told her that she could not continue the relationship. There were fights, often of a physical nature, between mother, stepfather, and daughter.

In April 1998, the parents told K.B. that she would be grounded until she stopped seeing J.C. The young couple met secretly and persuaded one another that the only way out was for them to murder her parents and get their money so that they could flee to the United States, where they "could live happily ever after."[xix] After discussing this for a few days, K.B. let J.C. into her house in the middle of the night. By pre-arrangement, he had a mask and was armed with a large knife that he had taken from home. He crept into the parents' bedroom and started to slash at them while they were sleeping. He nearly severed the mother's thumb and stabbed both parents numerous times, fortunately not fatally. All the while, K.B. remained outside the room, listening to what was going on. After J.C. escaped, the police were called.

As the parents were initially unclear as to who their assailant was, K.B. was asked by the police to provide a description of the intruder. She told them that it was a "black youth with a Jamaican accent."[xx] On the basis of her description, the police conducted an investigation. As the case had attracted some public attention, they issued a public warning containing this description and handed out fliers to neighbours warning them to be vigilant. Two days later, K.B. was questioned again, and this time she admitted that she had lied. J.C. was arrested and charged with attempted murder. (Ironically, he had confessed to his parents, who had assisted him in disposing of the knife and mask. They, too, were arrested and charged with obstructing justice.)

As this was an important case, one Crown counsel was immediately assigned to all three cases. The Crown applied to have J.C. transferred to be tried as an adult (he was fifteen); that hearing would take place before another judge at Scarborough court.[xxi]

Crown counsel Mr. Kerr realized from the outset that he had considerable legal hurdles in the prosecution of K.B. The only evidence against her on potential charges related to the attempted murder of her parents was her own confession to the police. Because the officers dealing with the case had not been fully trained in taking statements from young offenders, they had taken the incriminating statement from her as though she had been an adult. Unbeknown to these officers, the Supreme Court of Canada had recently insisted on very high standards of informed waiver before a statement taken from a young person could be admitted into evidence. It did not take long for Mr. Kerr to realize that he could not use K.B.'s statement to convict her.

The only other way the Crown could hope to convict K.B. would be to call J.C. as a witness against her. This could be very risky for the Crown. If J.C. was called without the Crown's knowing what he might say on the stand (he would likely refuse to co-operate with the Crown unless he got some benefit from it), he could say anything, some of which might hurt the Crown's case against K.B. If he was to be a co-operative witness, the Crown would likely secure his co-operation only by agreeing to some reduced charge against him, which it was not prepared to do given the circumstances and the severity of the injuries caused. For these reasons, Crown counsel proposed (and defence counsel was only too happy to accept) to proceed only on a charge of public mischief (lying to the police).

Although I was not the scheduled pre-trial judge on the day the parties came to their proposed plea bargain, they asked to see me in chambers. This happens regularly at the Scarborough court. The lawyers "judge shop" as part of their plea bargain, seeking to find a judge who will agree in advance to commit himself or herself to a range of sentence.[xxii] They told me that the Crown would ask for a sentence of twelve to eighteen months, but that I should make some allowance for the amount of pretrial custody that the accused would have served by the time I ultimately sentenced her. The defence would ask for probation, arguing that the amount of pre-trial custody was equivalent to some ten months,[xxiii] and that was sufficient given her age and Parliament's view of the seriousness of the offence, as expressed by the maximum possible penalty of two years. I agreed that counsel were in the range and that so long as mental health assessments (which I would order as soon as she pleaded guilty) were not devastating, I would not exceed the sentence sought by the Crown.

The accused entered her plea of guilty that same day, and the case was remanded so that mental health assessments and a pre-disposition report (a social history of the accused prepared by a youth probation officer) could be obtained. On September 1, the parties made their formal submissions based on the facts and what was disclosed in the various reports. Having heard what they said, I told the lawyers that I needed time to think about what they had said and put the case over until after my next chambers day on September 4.[xxiv]

During the sentencing hearing, a joint victim impact statement was filed on behalf of both parents. I accepted it because both parties agreed that it should be filed. As I thought more about the case, I wondered if I should have done so. The report documented the devastating impact their daughter's behaviour has had on the parents' lives. They are both physically and mentally unable to work; it appears that because they cannot pay their mortgage, they will lose their home, their only form of substantial saving. However, because of what the accused pleaded guilty to, I was not, strictly speaking, sentencing her for her part in causing harm to her parents. I concluded that what happened on that awful night only provided the backdrop for the lies that she told the police. As a result, I decided that I should factor in the victim impact statements only to the extent that they would give me some sort of clue to the accused's likelihood of re-offending (the psychiatric report concluded that it was low) and because they told me that her parents were not prepared to offer her any support at this time.

On September 10, I gave oral reasons,[xxv] sentencing the accused to ten months of open custody,[xxvi] followed by twelve months' probation. The lengths of the various terms were tailored around the accused's schooling (school is a real strength for her). Like R.S., she could come back to ask me to review her status after six months of open custody.

This, then, is part of a day in the life of a busy court. It is usually intense, sometimes tragic, always human, and endlessly fascinating. It may even be socially useful.

ENDNOTES

i At the time of writing, the Provincial Division of the Ontario Court of Justice comprises about 260 judges, about 180 of whom preside over 95 percent of the criminal cases in the province.

ii Initials are used because the *Young Offenders Act* provides that no young offender's name may be published.

iii As of the date of writing, this particular Crown's office employs almost 50 percent women, up from about 30 percent when I started as a judge in Scarborough in 1991. This reflects the general trend in the Ontario bar, where now over 50 percent of recent graduates are women. Unfortunately, this has not yet happened on the bench. Only in British Columbia has the percentage of women judges in large court systems come anywhere near to achieving parity. Currently in Ontario, the percentage of Provincial Division women judges is still less than one-third, and even fewer in the Superior Court.

iv Unfortunately, some provincial legal aid plans are insufficiently funded to provide this important (and highly efficient) service. Duty counsel services (for adults) are confined to telephone advice upon arrest.

v Scarborough tends to be a magnet for refugee claimants, visitors, and new immigrants. Although there is no precise figure that fully and accurately captures this phenomenon, some indication of the diversity of the population in the court's catchment area is reflected in the fact that in fiscal year 1997, court interpretation services were offered in fifty-four languages. On some days, two or three interpreters for the same languages are necessary.

vi I have no idea where the bureaucrats come up with this notional figure. To allow for the movement of prisoners from remand centres to the court (some may be transported as much as 40 km through rush-hour traffic), experience demonstrates that it is almost impossible to start a trial court before 10:00 a.m. Because it is very difficult for court reporters to be able to concentrate for longer than about ninety minutes at a time, on the best of days, morning court goes from 10:00 a.m. to 1:00 p.m. with a fifteen- to twenty-minute break. Court normally resumes at 2:00 p.m., again with an afternoon break. Court usually recesses at 4:30 p.m. to allow court staff to finish their paperwork and prisoners to be returned to their remand centres.

vii Section 10(b) of the *Canadian Charter of Rights and Freedoms* provides: "Everyone has the right on arrest or detention to retain and instruct counsel without delay and to be informed of that right." The Supreme Court of Canada has generally interpreted this to mean that an accused should have the right to telephone a lawyer as soon as practicable following arrest or detention. Police forces have responded to this by providing private access to duty counsel or a private lawyer by telephone from the police station.

viii The reason that this cumbersome process took place on the record in open court was that, in fact, there were some earlier dates available. Knowing that the case was already on the verge of being dismissed for taking too long to come to trial, everyone (including myself in an oblique way) felt the need to protect his or her position by saying that, while he or she could be available, it was the other party's "fault" that they could not take advantage of those dates. Some of the final compromises were interesting. The police officer had to telephone his staff sergeant to get approval to come to court on a date he was scheduled to be away, thereby being eligible to "pick up a court card," entitling him to be paid at double the normal shift rate. He was obviously delighted. Defence counsel and the accused were also content because they could defer the potential day of reckoning by another six months (if convicted, Ms. Andrus stood, at the very least, to lose her licence for a year). Crown counsel, who is currently working part-time, seemed mostly concerned to adjourn this to a date when her child-care needs could be accommodated (so that another Crown attorney would not be forced to take over the case). For myself, March 4 was a scheduled "chambers day," a regularly scheduled time during which I am supposed to read the approximately 500 pages of case law, legislative updates, and other items of interest that cross my desk each week, or to write judgments or articles (such as this one). One of my concerns was whether the trial coordinator could find me another chambers day.

ix Since January 1996, as a result of the police, the Crowns, the Legal Aid Plan, and the judges finding new resources or diverting existing staff, we have cut our backlog by 32.5 percent. However, because we have done so well, the bureaucrats have deemed that we are no longer on the chronic list of courts experiencing extreme delays, and it has been difficult for us to argue that our Crown and judicial complement should be maintained. As a result, both complements have been somewhat cut back, and we are beginning to slip again, as this delay signifies.

x An example of this arose here. As I was typing this article, I realized that in the case of Mr. Ashbury's charge of failing to appear, I should have at least considered whether to impose a 15 percent victim surcharge to his $300 fine under the *Criminal Code*. These surcharges are to be applied to raise money for various forms of victim support services. Neither the Crown nor the clerk drew this to my attention, and I simply neglected to raise the issue.

xi I leave it to the reader to consider whether this fits the definition of a "working" criminal justice system. Some observers have questioned whether it is "a system" at all.

xii   This seems particularly to be the case in charges of wife assault. Consistent with data from other jurisdictions, recent Toronto figures suggest that about 40 percent of complainants do not appear for trial. (Anecdotal evidence from Crowns who prosecute such cases puts the figure even higher.) This is the case despite police and prosecutorial directives mandating "no-tolerance" responses to such incidents.

xiii There is some consensus among criminal justice professionals that alcohol or drugs figure in about 75 percent of criminal offences.

xiv   What he was doing there at 11:00 p.m. on a Saturday night was not made clear to me. Sometimes criminal court offers wonderful opportunities for creating fantastic fiction à la Marquez or for reciting Shakespearian verse à la Rumpole!

xv   The going rate in Toronto for some of the top counsel at the time of writing is about $5000 per case, not including the costs of various experts. It may even be higher in areas of the country where there is no public transit. Accused people willingly pay this fee because of the economic and social costs of doing without a licence.

xvi   Variants of this type of conversation occur every day. Depending on the exhaustion level of the lawyers, more bargaining (some would call it haggling) can take place over the amount of the proposed fine. Interestingly, the lawyers would be unlikely to bargain about the length of time the accused should have to pay the fine. For his part, the accused might be less concerned about the amount of the fine; he would likely be more concerned about how long he would have to pay it. This illustrates one of the fundamental differences between lawyers and accused. The former tend to be more concerned about form, while the latter tend to be more concerned with substance.

xvii Insanity pleas are quite rare. This is the only one I have had since my appointment. On the other hand, dispositions of "not criminally responsible" (another type of mental impairment defence) are relatively frequent. I probably hear one (usually on consent of both parties) about once every two months.

xviii On April 1, 2003, the *Young Offenders Act* was replaced by the *Youth Criminal Justice Act*. The processes here remain the same under the new law.

xix   K.B. later told the police that one of her other motivations for the offence was that her stepfather had sexually assaulted her on several occasions. She refused to provide the police with any further information and indicated that she did not wish to have her stepfather charged.

xx   The racial stereotyping is particularly troubling.

xxi   Obviously, that judge and I refrain from talking with one another about our respective cases. Given the seriousness of the matters, each of us might have to solicit the advice of our colleagues who, as always, are generous with their advice. We have agreed to handle this by leaving the lunchroom whenever the other wishes to discuss the case with another colleague.

xxii Appellate courts across the country have been very clear that, because plea bargains so obviously give the impression that what happens in open court merely rubber-stamps what has been worked out in advance (the very term "plea bargain" is frowned on by the appellate courts, and judges usually prefer to use such neutral phrases as "pretrial discussions"), the judge should decline to agree to any particular sentence and agree only, if at all, to a particular range or type of sentence. Frankly, this is observed daily in the breach in busy provincial courts. Many of us consider that if we do not agree to precise plea bargains, our lists will likely be even more backlogged. Luckily, in this case, the parties came to me with a range of sentence rather than a precise sentence proposal.

xxiii Although I do not, as a matter of law, have to make any allowance for pretrial custody in the sentence ultimately imposed, the Supreme Court of Canada has said that an allowance should normally be made on a "two-for-one basis." In other words, for each day spent in pretrial custody, two days should be taken off the normally appropriate sentence.

xxiv In fact, in addition to my chambers day, I spent a lot of time reading and thinking about this case throughout the Labour Day weekend. The judicial life may seem "cushy" to outsiders (our salaries are good, our pensions are excellent, we get six weeks of holidays and up to thirty-six chambers days per year, and we cannot be fired except in the most extreme circumstances). However, most judges I know spend much of their weekends and some of their holidays preparing for upcoming cases.

xxv Like most judges, I would dearly like to be able to take the time to write thorough reasons, addressing in detail the facts, the arguments of the lawyers, and case law. Unfortunately, the constant time pressures are such that this can rarely be done. In 1998, I have been able to do this in only five cases (which is, in fact, quite a high number compared to many other judges).

xxvi Open custody (open only to young offenders, not adults) is a form of halfway house. If the accuseds live up to the rules of the facility (they are fairly tightly supervised), they may be permitted to go out for specified activities (such as going to school or work) or to attend rehabilitative programs. If they misbehave, they may be placed in secure custody.

CHAPTER 16
The Role of the Probation Officer

INTRODUCTION

When most members of the public think about the criminal justice professionals who run the justice system, lawyers, judges, and police officers come most readily to mind. Probation officers have a lower public profile than these other professions, yet in many respects their role in the criminal justice system is critical because most offenders are sentenced to community-based sanctions. As you will learn in this chapter, written by Karen Middlecoat, an experienced probation officer in Ontario, members of the probation service supervise offenders on probation, offenders serving conditional sentences of imprisonment in the community, and provincial parolees.

Supervising offenders is a challenging task. Although the probation officer must ensure that the court-ordered conditions of the probation order or conditional sentence order are observed, the offender also needs assistance in taking steps toward rehabilitation. When a condition of a probation order or conditional sentence order appears to have been violated, the probation officer must decide whether to return the offender to court. This is a difficult decision since it may well result (particularly if the offender is serving a conditional sentence) in the imprisonment of the offender.

The Probation Officer's Report
Karen Middlecoat, Probation Officers' Association of Ontario

Several years ago a distinguished justice at the Superior Court of Ontario was invited to be a guest speaker at a professional development day for probation and parole officers. He praised us for helping troubled individuals in times of dwindling social resources and expressed almost bewildered admiration for us. In fact, he confessed, "To be honest with you, when judges don't know what to do with someone, we put them on probation." The feelings of relief and validation in the room were practically palpable: finally, a judge was acknowledging what we had known all our professional lives.

CASELOAD OF A PROBATION OFFICER

In Ontario, approximately 1,000 probation officers supervise approximately 75,000 individuals, comprising about 20,000 young persons and 55,000 adults. Young persons, aged 12 to 17, are actively supervised as alternative measures cases, probation cases, and open custody residents. Adults, aged 18 and older, are probationers, conditional sentence cases, and provincial parolees. Probation officer caseloads vary significantly from small towns to major cities, and the duties of probation officers vary widely across the province. In parts of northern Ontario, probation officers have smaller caseloads, but are required to fly into remote areas to see clients. In Toronto, probation officers have adult caseloads that average approximately 120 clients; young person probation officers may have fewer clients but their responsibilities are more extensive, as they maintain ongoing contact with parents, schools, and counselling agencies.

Generally, most probation officers supervise adult offenders, who are defined as persons 18 years of age or over on the date of their offence. Adults report to probation officers for several reasons, but most are supervised on a probation order. This is a legal document requiring the offender to comply with certain conditions for a specific period of time. An adult probation order cannot exceed three years, although some offenders can be on probation continuously for several years, if judges continue to place them on probation each time they are sentenced. Probation orders have four standard conditions:

1. The offender shall keep the peace and be of good behaviour;
2. The offender shall appear before the court when required to do so by the court;
3. The offender shall notify the probation officer before any change of name or address; and
4. The offender shall notify the probation officer before any change of education or employment.

In addition, judges can impose other conditions designed to respond to the specific needs of the particular offender. For example, a court can order an offender to reimburse the victim or perform unpaid work for the community. Probationers may also be ordered not to go to certain locations. An example of this type of condition would be one prohibiting the offender from entering certain premises where the offence occurred. Someone found guilty of shoplifting could be forbidden from entering the store where the offence was committed; a man convicted of assaulting his wife could be prohibited from returning to the marital home; or a woman convicted of Communicating for the Purpose of Prostitution could be barred from entering a part of the city after the judge's specifying the perimeter of the prohibited area.

Ensuring That the Conditions of Probation Are Observed

Despite the obvious intent of the probation conditions to assist offenders while deterring them from committing further offences, these same conditions are fraught with enforcement difficulties. The enforcement of probation conditions is an important part of a probation officer's job. According to the *Criminal Code* of Canada, an adult has breached probation when he or she has failed or refused to comply with a probation condition "without reasonable excuse." Therefore not every violation of probation results in the offender's return to court, and probation officers make the final decision whether or not to charge an individual with breaching a probation order.

Discretion is often exercised regarding the reporting condition (the obligation to report to a probation officer) of a probation order, as it is the most common optional condition and therefore the most often violated. Probation officers will rarely charge a client when one or two appointments have been missed, even if the reason is one of simple forgetfulness. However, if the offender establishes a pattern of missing scheduled appointments after having repeatedly been cautioned, a probation officer will pursue a charge as this is clearly unreasonable. In the case of high-risk offenders, the probation officer would not wait for a pattern to be established as the safety of a victim or the general public would be of paramount concern. Conversely, if there are extenuating circumstances, a probation officer may choose not to charge an individual even if the reporting condition has been violated.

Difficulties can arise in some circumstances when the offender has mental health problems and doesn't understand the importance of keeping appointments. In these cases, a "reasonable excuse" is somewhat evident, but the probation officer will not take the risk of leaving such an individual in the community without some sort of ongoing supervision. Instead, the probation officer will override the reasonable excuse rule, err on the side of caution, and lay a breach of probation charge in order to protect the individual and the community, especially if medication or the lack thereof was of particular concern.

The case of Benjamin illustrates this issue. Benjamin was a 30-year-old who suffered from a bipolar affective disorder and refused to take medication. He was also in a wheelchair due to the amputation of both his legs following a suicide attempt at a subway station. He was on a two-year probation order for Fraud Accommodation and Assault, resulting from a hotel stay for which he refused to pay and, when confronted by hotel staff, spitting on one of the employees. Benjamin was ordered to report to a probation officer as often as directed, but had no fixed address and could not be contacted. The probation officer made contact with Benjamin's parents and left messages for Benjamin, as he would phone his parents occasionally to ask for money. Benjamin called his probation officer twice and flatly stated that he had no intention of reporting. The probation officer decided to charge him for not reporting and issued a warrant for his arrest.

Approximately three months after the warrant was issued, Benjamin was arrested again in a hotel room for damaging furniture and smashing mirrors. He was sentenced in court several months later and received more probation with a condition to attend for psychiatric counselling. Unfortunately, he never reported and within two months had committed suicide. In this case, the probation officer had realized that Benjamin, given his medical condition, would probably never report or attend psychiatric counselling regardless of how many probation orders he was given or how many times he was charged with breaching probation. Yet the probation officer still charged him in an attempt to protect Benjamin from himself and to fulfill probation services' responsibility to the community and to the justice system. Unfortunately, doing all the right things did not ultimately help Benjamin.

Community service work, which requires the offender to perform volunteer work, can cause problems if the offender has full-time employment as well as other responsibilities that limit his or her ability to complete the hours ordered. Occasionally community service work has been ordered on offenders who are long-distance truck drivers, construction workers who work twelve-hour shifts, single mothers with full-time jobs, and young offenders in school with homework and part-time jobs. Individuals in these categories have difficulty in performing the work ordered by the court.

Even more problematic is community service work that is imposed on individuals, such as sex offenders and persons with disabilities, who are difficult to place in a community service work agency. Community Service is equally imposed on individuals who are capable of performing the hours but who choose not to perform the prescribed hours.

When community service becomes problematic, the probation officer must consider all the facts and decide whether or not to charge the offender, keeping in mind that the *Criminal Code* states that a breach of probation has been committed when the offender has failed or refused to comply with probation "without reasonable excuse." Charlene and David illustrate examples of the discretion that a probation officer will exercise regarding community service work enforcement.

Charlene was a 36-year-old single mother of a six-year-old girl. She had been convicted of shoplifting and ordered to perform 100 hours of community service work at a rate of 10 hours per month during a one-year probation order. However, because she had a full-time job, Charlene had only limited time on weekends to perform community service at the food bank to which she had been assigned. She managed to perform community service every month but never completed the prescribed monthly rate of 10 hours. At the expiration of her probation Charlene had completed only 68 of the 100 hours ordered, and so her probation officer decided to exercise her discretion not to return her to court. Given Charlene's circumstances, she had made a reasonable effort towards complete her Community Service work.

Conversely, David was a 20-year-old, convicted of possession of stolen property. He lived with his parents, who were aware of his offence and his probation term with its requirement to perform 100 hours of community service work at a rate of 10 hours per month during a one-year probation order. For the community service, David was placed at a church that provided hot meals and beds to homeless people. David was not in school and worked sporadically for a friend's roofing business when work was available. David failed to perform any hours for the first three months, citing forgetfulness, work opportunities, and vague references to insufficient time. He was cautioned that if he failed to begin his hours he would be returned to court and charged with failing to perform community service work at the monthly rate.

During the third quarter of probation David performed a total of 22 hours and in the final three months completed another 15 hours, for a total of 37 hours. He was returned to court, found guilty of not completing community service work, and given another year's probation with a condition to perform a fresh set of 100 hours of community service work. One may assume that the judge's intention was to let David know that he could not avoid the imposition of community service work; certainly David knew now that he had a second conviction on his criminal record. During his second probation order, David performed 53 hours, but his employment situation had not changed and his reasons for incompletion remained vague and unsubstantiated. He was again returned to court and fined $400 with no more probation or community service work.

Restitution

The court's intention when imposing a restitution condition is more straight-forward, yet the "reasonable excuse" clause raises much more complex issues. When the amount of money is relatively small and the offender's ability to make restitution is established, then restitution is usually paid and no enforcement is necessary. However, if the amount is considerable and the offender is unable to pay the entire amount, then he or she is practically set up for failure and subsequent enforcement.

Although the probation officer could exercise discretion and not breach the individual if the "reasonable excuse" clause is applicable, all restitution cases have victims, unlike community service work, for example, and the recipients are persons who have no recourse to reclaim their money except via the courts. In these cases, probation officers are very reluctant to deny the victims their entitlement to see the offender held accountable for non-payment. For this reason the offender will be brought back to court, and a judge will decide what the appropriate response to non-payment should be.

The case of Edward is a good example of the way in which a court's best intentions can miscarry, creating a dilemma for the probation officer. Edward was a 46-year-old man convicted of defrauding his landlord of approximately $30,000. Edward was sentenced to the maximum of three years' probation to allow him as much time as possible to repay the victim. However, the court's restitution condition read as follows:

> ...to pay restitution at a monthly rate until the restitution is paid in full. A monthly amount will not be specified but a payment must be made each and every month until probation expires.

Unfortunately, the order did not stipulate that the full amount of restitution was to be paid by the end of the probation period, and as no monthly rate was given, the offender made a monthly payment, by money order, of one cent. In an attached letter that accompanied his first payment, the offender made it clear that he was not breaching the restitution condition in any way and even acknowledged that, although he had to pay four dollars every month to purchase a money order, he would still pay only one cent monthly to the victim.

Although the probation officer had the option to return the case to the original judge and request a variation in the payment schedule, the effort may not have gained the desired result, and the offender, or his attorney, could express an objection to a more onerous payment system. Nevertheless, the probation officer was able to advise the victim that financial recovery was available to him through a civil court action. The victim agreed to pursue this remedy but expressed great frustration at the expense of time and money to regain his own money.

Another example of an unsuccessful restitution case is that of Frank, a 33-year-old convicted of Mischief to Private Property. Following an argument in a bar, Frank left the establishment and vandalized his opponent's truck. He was convicted and ordered to pay $1,800 restitution over a two-year probation period. Frank lived in the basement apartment of his parents' home but had very little interaction with them, as his parents were aware that Frank sold drugs while receiving disability income. However, they felt somewhat protective of Frank as he had developed some brain damage from years of drug use and could not maintain regular employment. Over the two years of probation Frank reported regularly but insisted that the victim would just keep the $1,800 as his insurance company would cover the cost of the repairs. Frank was advised repeatedly that he had still been held responsible by the court for damages and had a legal requirement to compensate the victim.

While on probation for Mischief, Frank was arrested and convicted of cocaine possession and sentenced to two weeks imprisonment and one year probation. Upon expiration of his first probation order, Frank had paid only $350 of the total restitution and was returned to court for breaching probation. At the time of his trial Frank stated that he could not afford to pay the stipulated amount due to his limited income on disability, but had done the best he could. He was acquitted of the charge of breach of probation.

Cases such as Edward's and Frank's reinforce probation services' ongoing desire not to be utilized as collection agencies by the courts; however, when restitution is successful, it communicates a worthwhile lesson for the offender and provides the victim with a sense of closure rarely experienced by other victims in the justice system.

Enforcing Conditions That Restrict an Offender's Lifestyle

Ironically, the easiest violations of probation to prove are also the most difficult on which to obtain convictions; these are the "lifestyle" conditions. Such conditions include requiring the offender to abstain from alcohol or drugs, or to see a mental health professional on a regular basis. Violations of these abstinence- or treatment-related conditions are often discovered by the police, who apprehend the individual in an intoxicated state, or by the probation officer, who can determine a client's compliance with psychiatric treatment though a phone call to the relevant mental health professional.

Although the offender's noncompliance can be clearly established, determining that the offender breached the condition "without reasonable excuse" is very difficult, as some judges may consider substance abuse and mental illness medical conditions over which an individual has little control. As a result, a court that imposes a probation condition prohibiting the offender from consuming alcohol or nonprescribed drugs can unintentionally bring the offender back into the system. Furthermore, requiring the offender to seek treatment for substance abuse, psychological difficulties, or even spousal abuse does not guarantee that the offender will comply with the condition, and a return to court for a breach of the treatment condition may hold the offender accountable without addressing the underlying problem that gave rise to the offending.

The most common cases are those like George's, involving substance abuse. George was a 48-year-old convicted of assault. After consuming alcohol, George slapped and pushed his wife, who called police. He was found guilty and placed on probation for 18 months with a condition to attend counselling for partner assault. However, the court acknowledged that alcohol was a factor in the assault and added a condition on the probation order that instructed the offender "to consume alcohol moderately." Unfortunately, no one advised the court that George was in fact an alcoholic, and that by his standards, moderation in alcohol consumption was not in all likelihood the standard that the court intended. The probation officer could not send George to alcohol counselling as only partner abuse counselling had been ordered, and George expressed no interest in going voluntarily. Therefore, although the probation officer arranged partner abuse counselling and cautioned George that failure to complete the program would result in a breach, his inherent problem of alcohol abuse remained untreated.

Probation orders that require the offender to "abstain absolutely from the purchase, possession, or consumption of alcohol" also cause enforcement difficulties for probation officers. Monitoring these conditions is simply not possible, and violations are rarely discovered unless the offender is in public and arrested by police. Interesting exceptions, however, are cases like Harry, an admitted alcoholic, who was found guilty of impaired driving. He was fined $1,200, placed on probation for one year, required to attend a program, and prohibited from drinking for one year. Harry was self-employed in his own well-established renovations company and stated that he could not attend any residential program but agreed to attend weekly AA meetings held at the probation office.

Within a few months, Harry's wife notified the probation officer that Harry had been violating his abstinence condition. As she was the only person who could testify that Harry had been drinking, she was advised that she would be required to attend court as the sole witness. Immediately she stated that she would not go to court to testify against her husband. When the probation officer indicated that the incidents would be discussed with Harry at his next appointment, she begged the officer not to say anything to Harry as he would know she had informed the probation officer of his violations. In these cases, probation officers are placed in difficult positions between confronting the offender and violating his wife's request for secrecy, and should the probation officer have returned Harry to court to hold him accountable for violating his abstinence condition, the case still risked a withdrawal if the sole witness, Harry's wife, failed to testify. Furthermore, once Harry's probation order expired, he would be able to resume drinking and cease attending AA meetings, and one could only hope that the program would have had a sufficiently positive effect on him to encourage him to seek out meetings in the community voluntarily.

Treatment and counselling conditions raise similar concerns, and no offence is a better example than domestic assault. Ian was a 32-year-old convicted of assaulting his wife. He was prohibited from returning home until he had completed a program for partner assault and had obtained written permission from his wife allowing him to return home. Ian attended two sessions of the 16-week program then stopped, stating that he had no time to go. He was charged by the probation officer, returned to court, found guilty, and ordered to attend the program again. Again he failed to complete the sessions and began harassing his wife by phone calls and unscheduled visits. She called police and again Ian was returned to court. He was sentenced to thirty days in jail and probation for one year, with a condition, for the third time, to attend counselling. He failed to attend the program and within weeks had seriously assaulted his wife, breaking her arm and nose. He was incarcerated for eight months, but despite three probation orders, counselling conditions and custodial sentences, Ian believed that his right to see his wife superseded any legal authority that stipulated otherwise. Cases like Ian's are common in the justice system, and despite the thorough work of police, probation officers, and the courts, Ian's wife and women like her continue to live in fear.

Indeed, all cases that involve high-risk offenders, high-need offenders, or persons with serious charges require more intensive supervision from the probation officer. Within the past five years, procedures regarding the supervision of sex offenders, domestic assault offenders, and mental health and substance abuse cases have become more complex and stringent, stressing ongoing contact with the offenders, victims, and treatment agencies. Although probation officers recognize the necessity of these standards, the resulting escalation in workload has detracted from their time spent with lower-risk clients, some of whom form a bond with their probation officers and grow to rely on them for support and guidance. Many probation officers choose their profession because they enjoy human interaction and genuinely want to "help people." Ironically, the ones they may be able to help the most are the ones with whom they can't spend enough time, due to ever-increasing workloads and the court's reliance on community supervision as the most frequently used sentencing option.

CONDITIONAL SENTENCE OFFENDERS

Probation officers also supervise offenders serving conditional sentences of imprisonment. Conditional sentences were introduced in 1996 as an additional sentencing option to fill the void between probation and incarceration (see Chapter 5). Conditional sentence offenders have committed a crime that warrants imprisonment but, because the court does not consider them a threat to the community, they are allowed to serve the sentence at home. Some examples are offenders who have committed serious frauds or violent offences, but who may have full-time jobs and families to support.

The conditions of probation orders are also standard on conditional sentences, but the reporting condition that is optional on probation orders becomes a mandatory condition for a conditional sentence. Notably, the only additional mandatory condition on conditional sentences prohibits the offender from leaving the province without written permission from the probation officer. One major difference between probation orders and conditional sentence orders is that the latter will often include a condition of house arrest that confines the offender to his or her home, except for court-authorized exceptions. Unfortunately, when judges list exceptions beyond work, religious services, and medical emergencies, house arrest loses much of its perceived effectiveness. The recent case of John illustrates this problem.

John was given a one-year conditional sentence for aggravated assault and assault causing bodily harm against an ex-girlfriend and her new boyfriend. He was placed under house arrest but among the exceptions to confinement was permission to shop for groceries. This exception gave John free rein to be in the community, as he would have a ready explanation for any absence from home. Conditions with exceptions of this kind create problems for the probation officer and do not enforce the intended restrictions.

Theoretically, the enforcement of conditional sentences is intended to be a much swifter process than probation enforcement, but in practice this is generally not the case. Unlike an alleged breach of probation, which is an entirely new criminal charge, an alleged breach of a conditional sentence simply results in a court hearing, during which the onus is upon the offender to prove he or she did not violate the conditional sentence. If a breach is deemed to have occurred, the presiding justice has four options:

1. Take no action;
2. Change the optional conditions;
3. Suspend the conditional sentence and direct that the offender serve a portion of the unexpired sentence in custody with the balance to resume upon release; or
4. Terminate the conditional sentence and direct that the offender serve the full balance of the conditional sentence in custody.

Unfortunately, the conditional sentencing process is in its legal infancy, and the implications of conditional sentence conditions are still being discovered. An example is the case of Lloyd, who received a one-year conditional sentence for assaulting his wife for the second time in three years. Lloyd was ordered to attend partner abuse counselling and to complete it by the end of his conditional sentence. Due to an extensive waiting list and some delays on Lloyd's part, he began the program nine months after the conditional sentence started. Lloyd attended every session until his conditional sentence expired, at which point four sessions remained outstanding. Lloyd refused to complete the program but could not be breached by the probation officer as no balance remained on the order that could be converted to custody.

YOUNG PERSONS

Probation for young persons offers many of the options available to adults; however, the maximum period of time for young person probation is two years, rather than the three years for adults. Although the same issues exist for monitoring and enforcing young person orders, a notable distinction is the influence of peer groups, an effect seen regularly among young persons whose offences involve co-accused who, occasionally, are fellow gang members.

Mark was a 17-year-old found guilty of theft over $5,000 and possession over $5,000. He had stolen his parents' car, and when police found him in a parking lot with two friends hours after the car had been reported stolen, all three were charged, although Mark's two co-accused eventually had their charges dropped. One of Mark's conditions prohibited him from having any contact with his two friends; however, information from the police indicated that Mark had stolen the car as part of his initiation into a gang and had met his friends to show successful completion of his task. Mark denied any connection to a gang during interviews with his probation officer, and the requisite loyalty to his group overrode any court-imposed nonassociation condition or any threat of enforcement that his probation officer could make.

Generally the courts impose as few conditions as possible on young persons, favouring the restorative and rehabilitative aspects of probation as they relate to the offence. However, some conditions become onerous and present the probation officer with clear challenges.

Nagenthan was a 17-year-old found guilty of theft under $5,000 as a result of shoplifting a portable CD player from an electronics store. He was placed on probation for one year and prohibited from entering the electronics store. Nagenthan was also ordered to take classes in English as a Second Language. Although he was 17 at the time of the offence, he had turned 18 by the time of sentencing and had already graduated from Grade 12, with plans to attend college the coming September. Because the ESL condition had no relevance to his offence and conflicted with his college schedule and part-time job at a local restaurant, the probation officer exercised his discretion and advised Nagenthan that the ESL condition would be set aside providing that the youth continue his education and employment.

Another notable difference between adult and young person supervision is the involvement of parents. The probation officer must establish contact with the parents or guardians to ensure that information is being exchanged regularly. However, some parents have the misplaced belief that once their child has been through the justice system and now has a probation officer to whom he or she must report and legal requirements with which to comply, discipline issues and behavioural problems at home will be corrected. Sadly, this is not the case. Probation officers explain to parents that, as agents of the court, they can only enforce the conditions of probation and offer the youth some guidance, not guarantee improvements in the youth's behaviour. Probation officers will often receive calls from parents complaining that their child is out late, not doing house chores, or not telling them where he is going or with whom he is socializing. Indeed, a parent once called her son's probation officer and complained that he was still leaving dirty dishes in the kitchen sink and not cleaning his room, despite being on probation!

Obviously the probation officer has no authority over the young person in these circumstances, although some parents believe that probation officers could fix problems in one year that had developed over the previous 16. Conversely, some probation orders will require the youth to "be amenable to the routine and discipline of the family home," and in many cases this stipulation will bring some sort of clear expectations into the household, especially if the probation officer meets with the youth and his parents and writes a contract that all parties sign.

Regrettably, this well-intentioned condition may not achieve its desired results, as in the case of Paula, a 16-year-old found guilty of assaulting her mother, who refused to give Paula money. Paula was placed on probation for

18 months and required to report to a probation officer, write a letter of apology to her mother, reside at home and be amenable to the routine and discipline of the home. The probation officer met with Paula and her mother and wrote out a contract with four rules regarding curfew, chores, phone privileges and respectful behaviour.

Approximately five months later, Paula's mother advised the probation officer that the home situation was deteriorating and rules were not being followed. At the next probation appointment Paula admitted that she was breaking rules but that her mother was becoming too unreasonable. The probation officer suggested family counselling but Paula refused. The probation officer then arranged for Paula and her mother to attend the next appointment together; however, Paula's mother called the officer within a few weeks and advised that money and jewellery were missing and that Paula's whereabouts were unknown.

Clearly the probation officer's difficult decision was whether to wait and hope that Paula would resurface, thus avoiding her re-involvement in the court system with more criminal charges, or to issue a warrant for her arrest and have police actively look for her and prevent her from any harm she could encounter on city streets. By the next week Paula's mother called the officer. She'd heard from friends of her daughter's that Paula was staying with various acquaintances and had no intention of returning home. Paula's mother was becoming extremely anxious about her daughter's safety and questionable companions, and the officer decided to issue the warrant. Paula's mother was advised and encouraged to tell Paula's friends of the warrant with the hopes that Paula would contact the probation officer. True enough, Paula called her officer to question the existence of the warrant, but refused to attend the local police station to address the outstanding charge, and stated unequivocally that she had no intention of returning home.

Months later Paula was arrested for shoplifting and the outstanding warrant came to light. Paula was found guilty of both offences and despite her mother's statement that she would accept Paula back home, Paula told the court she did not plan to return home. She was given another year's probation, instructed to report as required, and live at a residence approved by her probation officer. As Paula had had no approved residence since her mother's, any friend's house or city shelter became an approved residence as the alternative was the street. Paula continued to report satisfactorily and was advised that the probation officer would be calling the residences she provided to confirm her housing. However, by the expiration of probation, Paula was 18 with no fixed address, no employment and no family support, despite the best intentions and efforts of probation services. Fortunately, not all cases end as bleakly as Paula's, and when an individual does appear to have benefitted from probation supervision, the officer feels a rare sense of success, as in the case of Rick.

Rick was a 25-year-old factory worker convicted of assault, arising from a fight outside a bar. He was placed on probation for one year with conditions to report as directed, maintain employment, and not be on the premises where the offence had been committed. Rick reported regularly and complied with conditions but the probation officer suspected that Rick had an alcohol problem, among other issues. However, she could not engage him in meaningful conversation. At the third appointment, the probation officer asked Rick about his activities and interests, and he expressed surprise that the probation officer would care about subjects that did not relate to probation supervision. She responded that he seemed somewhat troubled and unhappy, and she was willing to listen if he felt like talking. He again expressed surprise, but offered little response. However, over the next few appointments, he spoke about his estrangement from his family, with the exception of his only sister who lived in British Columbia, and even spoke fondly about his cat, Sully. He mentioned AA meetings that he'd attended in the past but had not found helpful, and wasn't interested in resuming them.

The probation officer's next contact with Rick was a phone call. He was in a phone booth and admitted he'd been drinking. He planned to withdraw all his money from his bank account, buy alcohol, rent a motel room, and commit suicide. The probation officer asked what had happened, but Rick simply stated that he was fed up with life. As the probation officer continued to talk to him, she waved down a colleague passing in the hallway and wrote a note explaining the ongoing emergency. Rick's probation officer managed to learn Rick was in a phone booth near his bank, the bank's location, and even what he was wearing. At one point, Rick stated, "I know what you're trying to do, but it won't work." The probation officer reminded him that his life mattered, to his family, his sister, and even his cat, which would be abandoned and neglected without him.

In the meantime, the probation officer's colleague had relayed Rick's description and whereabouts to police, and eventually, officers located Rick in the phone booth and transported him to hospital. Rick remained there for a few days and, upon his release, reported to his probation officer. He could not verbalize any event that had led to his suicidal thoughts, but had felt a general depression that became exacerbated by his alcohol consumption. Nevertheless, he thanked his probation officer for helping him that day and revealed that, after he returned home from hospital, he phoned his sister in British Columbia and resumed contact. As Rick's probation came to an end, he decided that he was going to use his banked savings to move to British Columbia to be near his sister, who was happily expecting him. A few months after Rick's probation terminated, his probation officer received a postcard. Rick was living with his sister temporarily, working at a landscaping company, and had attended two AA meetings. He ended the note by thanking the probation officer again for caring. She heard from him only one more time: he sent her a Christmas card that year, enclosing a photograph of him and Sully.

Although cases like Rick's are somewhat outnumbered by less successful ones, these are the cases that make the probation profession worthwhile, and the opportunities to make a difference, and the challenges therein, never cease. Many cases are never resolved the way the courts intend and probation officers wish, but the desire to help individuals who've made mistakes to move beyond them and get their lives back in order remains. Like the judge at the professional development day, probation officers may not always initially know what to do with their offenders either, considering the challenges of each case and the complexity of the probation officer's roles. We are responsible for ensuring that the offenders comply with their conditions; for returning them to court when those conditions are violated; for providing support, counselling, and direction to assist in rehabilitation, thereby reducing recidivism; and to keep the victims and general public protected at all times to the best of our abilities. As long as probation officers continue to accomplish these goals, they continue to derive satisfaction from knowing they are doing the right thing.

DISCUSSION QUESTIONS

1. *From reading this chapter, what in your view is the hardest part of the job of being a probation officer?*
2. *In your opinion, do probation officers have too much discretion, not enough discretion, or about the right amount of discretion in terms of dealing with offenders?*
3. *From what you have read, what is the primary function of a term of probation?*

FURTHER READINGS

Abadinsky, H. 1997. *Probation and Parole: Theory and Practice.* Upper Saddle River, N.J.: Prentice Hall.

Bottomley, K. 1990. Parole in transition: A comparative study of origins, developments, and prospects for the 1990s. In M. Tonry and N. Morris (Eds.), *Crime and Justice: A Review of Research,* Volume 12. Chicago: University of Chicago Press.

Petersilia, J. 1998. Probation and parole. In M. Tonry (Ed.), *Oxford Handbook on Crime and Punishment.* Oxford: Oxford University Press.

CHAPTER 17
Life Prisoners

INTRODUCTION

When a "snapshot" profile of the federal prison population was taken, lifers accounted for almost one in five inmates. This chapter tells the story of one female life prisoner, in her own words. Gayle was 43 when she was sentenced to life imprisonment with no possibility of parole until she had served 10 years. The chapter contains extracts from two interviews with Gayle. The first was conducted while she was still in prison (in 1990), the second in the community after she had been released on parole (in 2001). A life sentence never ends; although most prisoners sentenced to life will eventually be released on parole, they will be on parole for the rest of their natural lives.

GAYLE'S STORY

Life sentences are cruel. I mean, they give you a sort of mandatory [sentence of life imprisonment]. You serve a certain amount of time, but that doesn't mean anything …. the hoops you have to jump through … Even a National Parole Board member told me, "If you ask me to tell you what I did ten years ago, I wouldn't be able to tell you, so I find it hard to ask somebody if they have remorse over something they did ten years ago." And that's ten years; can you imagine what the life–25 guys [life imprisonment with no parole until twenty-five years have been served in prison] are like? It's beyond reality. Before the death penalty was abolished, second-degree was seven years instead of ten, so after five years you were eligible for day parole; three years, you're out on passes. Now that is fairly logical; a reasonable amount of time. Before the death penalty was abolished, the number of first-degree and second-degree convictions, as a percentage of all homicides, was only in the twenties; twenty-seven percent, or something. The rest were manslaughter convictions. And right after the death penalty was abolished, the total numbers turned

around. As a matter of fact, manslaughter convictions were only nineteen percent of all homicide convictions; the rest were first- and second-degree.

I think every case has to be taken individually. In my case, I don't see how
putting me in prison is justified at all. I have to say that, honestly, because I'm
not a threat to society, number one. I'm a totally productive person, and, I
mean, you could force me to work for the government for twenty years. That
would be penalty enough. You know, I mean, I could be productive. You could
say to me, "Okay, for ten years fifty percent of your salary has to be donated
to this family you offended." I could be productive. Why lock me up and tell
me to behave like a seven-year-old kid and take away every kind of value that
I have? Or try and take it away. All it does is make me bitter. I have no respect
for any authority in this system.

What society has to understand is that people don't go out and say, "I'm
going to go out and kill somebody tonight." That is not the reality. Four out
of five murders are murders that are committed on people they know: family
or close friends. All the research has been done. They already know all that.
And the murder during the commission of a crime, say an armed robbery or
something, well, I really don't know; I don't know if prison is really the
answer there either. Because, why does that person want to take money and
stick a gun in somebody's face? But nobody cares about why. Putting people
in prison isn't going to change that kind of attitude, especially because they
are desensitized persons in the first place. They don't give a fuck. They go out
and they couldn't care less how you're feeling at all about what they're going
to do. So putting them in prison and not caring about them is not going to
teach them how to care. It doesn't make sense.

The only people who should be in prison in my estimation are people
who cannot control themselves from one moment to the next and sexual
offenders who need intensive therapy. And an institutionalized environment
is the only place they're going to actually be able to get it, where you can control them and make sure they're going to do it. What's wrong is wrong, but
how can I compensate? I cannot bring the person back, so the only thing I can
do is try and be as productive a person as I can.

[*This second interview with Gayle took place at her home in the Lower Mainland in
the spring of 2001.*]

To help prepare for my parole application, I knew I needed to do a couple
of things. The authorities agreed to call in a woman psychologist and I saw her
for three years, so that was great. The other thing is I knew I needed to have
some kind of pass experience behind me before I could go up for day parole.
I finally got a pass to go to Simon Fraser University to pick up my certificate
in Liberal Arts. That was my first pass. Other than that there was not a lot
done that I did, it was my sisters who campaigned feverishly among friends
and family to get letters written. I had about sixty-five letters to the parole
board. I had a tremendous amount of support. Plus I had to find a halfway
house. Since I was federal that was the big dilemma. I didn't want to go to the

only one available for women, because it was under provincial jurisdiction. When different halfway house people would come in, I would talk to them to see if they would accept a woman. Seven Steps was the only one. I knew some people that were there and they had lifers there. They were willing to take me for a three-year duration, so everything was sort of set for me to be successful at my first parole hearing. What happened was they granted me an unescorted temporary absence for thirty days. During that time, I applied for parole right from Seven Steps and I was granted day parole based on the thirty-day performance.

A friend of mine went with me to be there as support at the parole board hearing. Des Turner is a retired gentleman who became interested in prison and parole issues after my sister had spoken to him about my case. Because you're a lifer you have to have three board members there. Naturally they ask you questions about whether or not you have remorse and what your feelings are about everything, and so on and so on. They felt that I was quite aggressive at the time. I tried to be as calm as I could, but of course I was quite anxious. That hearing versus the hearing later on when I went to get my full parole after I had served three years on day parole—I went to the board then and they commented on how calm I was and what a change had come over me and they felt that I was really showing signs of being rehabilitated. I basically said, "Well, I'm not inside, that's why I'm calm." It's so simple and it's so obvious, but it's not obvious to people who don't know what it's like to serve time.

I had to see a parole officer, originally once a week and then once every two weeks, and then once a month for two years. In the third year it was every second month. Now I see her every three months. I've been very fortunate. I had an excellent parole officer the first time around and I had him for two years. He was really good, very supportive and didn't seem to be overly suspicious; he took me at my word. Then I had another gal and she was pretty good. I have another woman now and she's very good. As far as making suggestions, they really didn't have to make a lot of suggestions with me because I already had my family support and jobs lined up. I was already working towards things. I basically reported to them on what I was doing. Things were still there for me. I had my family and friends there. Everybody sort of welcomed me back. I had a car. I got a job within four months. I wanted to finish my degree so I did that first at SFU.

But I didn't feel like I was back. I didn't feel like I belonged. I thought that ... it was amazing to me that if I felt like that after having a full life, a full career, a family, and everything before, what would happen with people that have nothing? I always said it was a little bit harder for me in some respects to go inside because I was leaving so much behind. Whereas other people were leaving very little anyway. But returning after a certain period of time, for me it was seven years, I found myself quite paranoid, which is something that most lifers talk about. I didn't feel that I belonged. My son had to remind me to buy new clothes, to change, to get in step with things. I couldn't have cared less because I got used to wearing the same thing every day. As long as it was clean, I didn't care. I'm still like that. Basically, my family is still saying, "Why don't you get dressed up?" So that's something that I lost which was actually, in my opinion, a good thing to lose because it was so superficial. In effect, the real world is like that. The real world wants to see you keep up with the fashion and look a certain way.

Then driving, I found it very strange because the things that I had left behind weren't there. A lot of the buildings were gone and the streets had changed. Some were one way. There were new highways, new bridges. I had a difficult time in the beginning to find my way around—I'd get turned around very easily. If there was an accident or if I saw a policeman pull somebody over, I would just start shaking. I was terrified of being pulled over and sent back, even though I had no reason, I wasn't doing anything, but I had that great fear. So that part of me, it took me about two years before I felt that I belonged here. Up until then I didn't feel I belonged. It's a hard thing to describe what I mean by that. I don't really know how to describe it other than I didn't feel safe, I didn't feel a part of this world anymore, I was still inside. In some respects, part of me always will be inside.

There's a saying, *"You may be out of prison but the prison is never out of you."* What happened was I just sort of went back to being who I was in a way: getting into business, getting back into the industry that I was in before, rushing around, having family dinners, shopping—a regular sort of life. But part of me still was involved with what was going on, because I felt so indebted, and I still feel indebted, to people inside who helped me through that time; we shared an existence that was akin to what people share in the trenches during wartime.

One of the things that is vitally important for me occurred when I was in Kingston at the Prison for Women (P4W). Prior to going inside, I worked in an industry that was male-dominated. I had male children, was married, had a lot of friends who were men, I wasn't really trustful of women. I realized, through speaking with the psychologist and so on, that I had quite a bit of suspicion and resentment towards women. One of the reasons was being part of one race and part of another; I was rejected quite a bit. I only had certain friends who accepted me at that time. This is a historical thing; things aren't like that any longer, but they were like that then. If I'd be called names, racial slurs, it would be mainly by other girls because that's who your peer group is. When I went to Kingston I learned very quickly, it was like a thunderbolt that struck me, how women were so wonderful to one another. All of these women who had come from terribly abusive homes and conditions of extreme poverty, who are illiterate, a lot of them, who didn't have families who were supportive of them, who really had nothing and no chances, were like sisters to one another, were like mothers to one another, took care of each other, found time to do the most incredible, creative things and give everything they had to each other. When somebody was in trouble, for instance, this one young woman, Corine, who is dead now, when she slashed we would hide her so she wouldn't be taken to the hole. We'd try and bandage her up and keep her quiet. The one time this same young woman, when the guards came to take her to the hole, everybody in the top tier came out. That's twenty-five women who came out and stood outside their cells and said, "No, you're not taking her." That kind of solidarity, that kind of concern, willing to stick your neck out, literally, because they could bring in the storm troopers, was such an example of love for one another. I gained so much respect for women that I never had before I went inside. They cared a great deal for me and so fasted when I was fasting, alongside me, to support my efforts to get back to B.C.

When I went to Matsqui institution, we still wrote to one another. I still contributed articles to the *Tight Wire*, the prison newspaper there, and the articles, as I read them now, were full of a huge amount of rage and anger. Then when I got to Matsqui there were a few guys who weren't happy to have a woman there. Part of them was threatened I guess, part of them thought that I had privileges because I could wear my own clothes, even though I didn't have access to a lot of the things that they had access to, but they didn't see it like that. The majority of guys were extremely good to me, treated me like a sister, very protective. I was probably the safest woman in Canada at the time. There were a lot of fellows who needed someone to talk to and they couldn't talk to a guy about problems they were having with their wife or girlfriend because they'd be considered wimps and cry-babies, but they'd talk to me. We'd talk for long periods of time about what was going on, so I got very close. When things were happening to me, when they tried to ship me out and served me with an involuntary notice, the lifers group signed a petition to try and keep me there.

They tried to ship me to Burnaby Correctional Centre when they just opened it. I didn't want to go to the provincial prison because, number one, the conditions were terrible there compared to what I had. I had open visiting privileges, all the programs, the hobby shop. I would have had nothing. Also, I knew that my chances of parole and getting in a halfway house were a lot better if I stayed in the federal system versus going to provincial. So, I certainly didn't want to go. They served me with an involuntary transfer notice to say, "No, you're going, whether you want to or not." The lifers group signed a petition, the student union guys signed petitions to show their support for me at Matsqui. That was amazing. They didn't have to do that. It wasn't my suggestion, they just did it on their own. I was part of the student council at that time, and part of the lifers group. I was on the board of the lifers group. I had been nominated for the prisoners' committee as hospital rep even though I was denied the opportunity to run by the warden. The guys showed me a tremendous amount of respect. We had a lot of solidarity between us. Their issues I understood very well, particularly the lifers. Because there were so many of them, we could really do a lot of things and share opinions about things. It broadened my view on the whole prison system. I saw the differences in the men's systems versus the women's. I saw the differences in the way the staff treated men versus the way the staff treated women. I was quite amazed that guys could basically swear a lot of times and not get charged whereas a woman, all she had to do was give somebody a dirty look and she could be charged with threatening.

I was in the hospital unit at Matsqui so I saw a lot of the prisoners being brought in for medical treatment. They came in from all the different prisons in the region. In particular there was one fellow who had a tremendous number of headaches. He was an aboriginal fellow, one of their best carvers. What happened was he was diagnosed with an inoperable brain tumour. He was in a tremendous amount of pain. Before that, he was only getting Tylenol. If you were not a prisoner, you would have gone to a regular doctor, probably had a CAT scan. After a certain period of time, they would have discovered that and you would certainly have been relieved of your pain. So he suffered a tremendous amount until they finally agreed, and this was after two or three tests, that he did have a brain tumour. I was with him right until he died. I'd go into his room, which was next to mine, and clean his room for him just because he couldn't stand to have guards around. Seeing the differences between what happened to him and what would happen to other people outside, it was so obvious that it wasn't right.

There was Craig Hill, who was in a wheelchair. Claire Culhane [a prisoners' rights advocate] was instrumental in finally getting him out on Royal Prerogative of Mercy. He was a young man who couldn't do much for himself since he was very debilitated, dependent on his wheelchair, and couldn't stand alone without leaning against the wheelchair; nevertheless, the parole board said that since he could still stand he was still a danger to society, and had denied him again. I was charged with disobeying a direct order because I had gone into a prisoner's bedroom when I heard him fall, to pick him up. That was another thing, in a regular situation you would naturally go to help your neighbour who had fallen, and you knew they were very sick. I think there were four or five fellows who died during the time I lived in the hospital. So, as soon as you are a prisoner, you're treated differently. I was amazed that it went right through the so-called health care as well. I saw the same thing with the women in Kingston; if they slashed, they went to the hole first, not to the hospital to get fixed.

Do I see the prison system as having improved over the years? One step forward, two steps back. If I look at myself, I was so naïve that I thought as soon as you walked inside the door the most important thing would be to be productive, to work on everything you could do to make yourself a better person so that when your time came to walk out the door you would be better prepared, whether it was addressing some physical problem you had, or an emotional or a mental instability, or whether or not it was gaining training or going to school, or learning something concrete that you could use in the outside world. But, no. As a matter of fact, anybody who achieves anything inside does it despite the system, not because of the system. Especially now, they have all these programs that are six weeks long, and they shuffle people through. They are just numbers to prove that they are taking all these so-called programs. Cognitive skills: how to think properly, anger management.

To give you an idea, I remember in Kingston they brought this anger management course in. They decided that I was one of the people that needed to take this. There were seven of us in the class. After the first class of anger management, because you're naturally bringing up a lot of issues that make you angry, you've got nobody to deal with the issues, so within twenty-four hours I was the only one who wasn't charged with having a fit of temper or whatever.

Along with anger management there should be assertiveness training. There are two sides of the coin. How do you deal with issues that are beyond your control? How do you sort out which are beyond your control and which you can do something about, maybe not immediately but step by step, and then you can achieve some kind of relief from the frustrations that you're feeling? The way that it's taught was basically point the finger: it's all your fault, so you're the one who needs to control things and realize that you're wrong. I used to tell women "you have a right to be angry, you have a reason to be angry." There are times when anger is a totally normal human response. I guess this is the problem with the prison system. Once you're a prisoner, you're a prisoner. You're not a person anymore.

When Lucie McClung [the new commissioner of Correctional Service Canada] says the Canadian prison system is the best system in the world, it means, obviously, that the prison systems around the world are really brutal and terrible. We already know that. To say that the Canadian system is best in the world is a crock. They may have one part of it that may be a good idea but they don't expand it enough. In other words, in the women's system they decide to build all these regional facilities and they were going to have all these beds for women to have children with them. Well, they now have more segregation beds than they have ever had; in fact, they have about ten times more beds in maximum security than they do for women with children. So they've downplayed, cut back that whole program in favour of having more and more maximum-security beds. They're continually going towards a more controlled model. Even the healing lodge, which was originally a great concept—it was supposed to be an aboriginal healing lodge with aboriginal staff, and everything went around treatment or healing concepts—now it's moved towards a control model. The staff is gradually being replaced with CSC staff.

There's one healing lodge: Maple Creek, Saskatchewan—the Okimaw Ohci Healing Lodge. That's right, that was where Yvonne Johnson was and where Rudy Wiebe went to visit her when they were working on her book *Stolen Life, The Journey of a Cree Woman*. To give you an idea, she was doing quite well there. I have a lot of respect for Yvonne, she's been through a lot. She wanted to address some of the problems about being abused as a child. She went through tremendous abuse. The elders there now didn't feel that the healing lodge was the appropriate place to deal with it. Well, where else for

God's sake if not the healing lodge? It's supposed to be a place for healing. So what do they do? She agreed to go to Sask Pen, to the women's unit to deal with some issues. She gets there ... I got a letter from her a couple of weeks ago. She gets there, no programs, she's now being warehoused. She can't get back to the healing house so she's in a men's penitentiary right now.

I wasn't invited to the closing of P4W [The Prison for Women, which housed federal female offenders]. Correctional Service Canada (CSC) wouldn't pay for any travel expenses to the people who were invited. They were supposed to invite all the original task force members to be there but they weren't going to pay for their travel, which I thought was interesting. So it ended up being mostly CSC people with the big celebration for closing P4W. Meanwhile, now the women actually have it worse in some respects. They're separated into small groups in four different regions and there are so many staff there and there is a coercive kind of tactics going on. Women are afraid to speak out. They tell me that they can't even write a letter without a guard over their shoulder saying, "Well, I don't think you should write that." They don't know what their rights are, they don't know how to access them. Right now they are always threatened that they'll be sent to a men's SHU (Special Handling Unit) if they step out of line. Unfortunately, I think there are thirteen women in the SHU in Prince Albert, and they call it a women's unit. I think, out of the thirteen, eleven are aboriginal women. All the women from P4W should have gone to the regional facilities. Number one, there's no reason for any of the women to be in maximum security in men's facilities. They have enough beds in the regional facilities. What they need to do is move the minimum-security women out of the regional facilities and into the community.

There's a huge amount of money being spent in corrections, as everybody knows, over one and a half billion dollars a year now. Most of it is in salaries. If you look at the people that are doing the so-called programs, they're all guards, basically. Not many of them have any real qualifications. I know that they say they like to have somebody with a year's university, but that really doesn't say anything about training, does it? So there are no programs going on inside except for the ones CSC calls programs. Unfortunately, the people who are taking those so-called courses aren't learning anything that they can use in the outside world. In other words, their certificate in living skills or anger management doesn't help them get a job, it doesn't train you to get a job. It gives you no education. The university program was really the only thing that people serving long sentences could do and continue on and increase their learning and their knowledge versus other programs. If you're finished in six weeks and you're doing a life sentence, what good is a six-week program? By the time you're ready to move along you'd have to retake the program.

Meanwhile, you have to take all of these things, otherwise they won't recommend you to parole. People are forced into taking things that they know aren't helping them a damn bit and there's no continuity to anything on the outside, so it's a dead end. They go to the board and they've got all these tick marks opposite their name but it hasn't increased their ability to function in the outside world in the slightest. There are some parts of the programs, I'm sure, that are good, but overall they're costly and don't really help the person to reintegrate and become a better member of society.

What they need is real training for people. If they have a vocational program such as the machine shop, it should be identical to the one outside. So when the person goes through the program they have an actual certificate that is equivalent to something they would achieve outside. So they can go out and get a job and make enough money to keep their families relatively well or at least get some place. At this point in time it is very difficult to get a job. It was even difficult for myself. The only reason I was able to was because I had some friends who were able to get me on. It was not an easy thing—and I had a lot of training. If I had been able to get new training, I would have gone into a new area, but I wasn't able to get anything like that.

People coming out of prison can totally appreciate how scary it must be for people who've never been to a prison, never talked to anybody who has been in prison. They think that all prisoners are dangerous or all former prisoners are dangerous. Prisoners need to come out into the community and speak at community centres and volunteer their time, and have some kind of normalization period so that both the public and the prisoner can get used to one another again. The fact is that everybody's going to get out of prison, we all know that. You need to have halfway houses because they have structure there. They have hours that you have to be in and hours that you can be out. There need to be more services, though, transportation and so on for people coming out so they know how to get along and get around. People who live in communities who don't want prisoners as a group might consider having transition houses where they have a mix of people. There are lots of street people and battered wives, for instance, who have a lot in common with women coming out of prison. They've all had a lot of the same experiences. Transition houses could accommodate some, but there needs to be more safe housing, period. You want the neighbourhood to be safe, too. It's a matter of screening the people that come into the halfway house. That's very important. I can appreciate people not wanting to have a serial criminal in their midst, I can totally appreciate that. But somebody who has been incarcerated one time in their life, there's no reason to think that they can't make it on the outside and can't contribute to a better society again. It's an irrational fear that the public has about what a criminal is.

I had never been to prison before, I didn't know anybody in prison. I was busy with my life, working and raising my family, and I thought that anybody who is in prison must have done something wrong and that's why they were there, and assuredly they'd be there learning some kind of a trade or getting more education, and learning how to become a better person and when they got out they would be able to get a job and get on with their life. If they didn't want to work and they wanted to have it easy, which is my idea of what people were trying to do that ended up in prison, then they'd go back and that's what they deserved. That's how naïve I was. I honestly thought that people went inside and learned how to become better people, that's what they were doing in there. In fact, that's so far from the truth it's very, very sad and depressing. All that money is wasted. Instead of somebody going inside to try and increase their knowledge, go to school, do a trade, all that happens is you learn how to exist and survive in prison. That means you learn how to cope with the constant pressure to put on a face that is acceptable to the administration and to get along with other people that you might have never met in your whole life but who are also in prison.

You're caught up with trying to stay in touch with the real world outside, which is your family and friends and community, and living in the world of prisons that is a totally unreal world. Nobody in the outside world could imagine what it is like never to feel safe in your own shower, never to feel safe or be able to sleep through a night. A lot of the people who are inside are there because they have never been able to communicate or build relationships. One of the reasons is because they're illiterate. They are full of fear all the time, they're fearful of not being able to do something correctly, they never build any confidence and just do what they need to do to survive. The money that is being spent—you could hire teachers to go in and teach. Never mind guards to teach. Guards should just be doing what they're trained to do and that's guarding. All the rest of the people inside could be going to classes, could be researching, and going back to when they were kids and trying to figure out what it is that they wanted to do with their lives.

I'm a lot calmer now, mainly because I don't have the stressors any more. I don't have to worry about the door slamming in my face. I feel very sad about what's happened to people that I know inside, people that are still there. It forces me to maintain contact because I feel that a lot of those people helped me to get through the time. I want to try and be there for them, even in a limited way. I belong to a group called Strength in Sisterhood Society. It's a group of former prisoners and prison advocates and supporters that try to provide a voice for women. We attend different conferences and we do a lot of speaking engagements, write letters to Parliament. We network with other women's organizations and justice groups across the country. I still go to West Coast Prison Justice Society, which is another non-profit society that was formed while I was still inside at Matsqui. They provide legal information to prisoners and produce a newsletter that talks about current cases. I've done radio shows; for example, we did the Prison Justice Day special on August 10th on CBC. I've also done quite a few newspaper interviews and comments, things like that.

The other side concerns my own family and what their needs are, and trying to be there for them as well. Without a doubt I'm a better person because of the prison experience. I'm a lot more compassionate and understanding, less judgmental. I think with 16 percent of the female federal prison population serving sentences for life and 15 percent of the men, you've got a population that is growing, aging, and which could be contributing in so many ways; but instead they're being used primarily to keep the prisons calm.

I think it's so necessary for lifers to keep in touch with one another to see what's going on in each region, to see what's available when they do get out, just to find out what everybody's doing.

Lifers are a very close-knit group of people. As soon as you meet somebody else who is doing life, you know what it means, and you want to know that they're safe and hopefully that they are doing okay. I know that the women I've gone in to see when I was in Kingston were so happy that I'm doing well. It gives them a great incentive to know that they can get out and they can do it.

DISCUSSION QUESTIONS

1. *Does anything in this chapter change the perceptions that you have of offenders sentenced to prison for life?*
2. *In your view, is there enough emphasis on rehabilitation in Canada's prisons?*
3. *Some people argue that prison should be reserved for offenders who represent a clear danger to the community, and that offenders such as Gayle should be punished in the community (see Chapter 23). Others take the position that prison is a useful sanction even for offenders who do not represent a threat to society. Which position is closest to your own?*

FURTHER READINGS

Melnitzer, J. 1995. *Maximum, Medium, Minimum.* Toronto: Key Porter Books.

Murphy, P., Johnsen, L., and Murphy, J. 2002. *Paroled for Life. Interviews with Parolees Serving Life Sentences.* Vancouver: New Star Books.

Murphy, P. and Johnsen, L. 1997. *Life–25: Interviews with Prisoners Serving Life Sentences.* Vancouver: New Star Books.

PART FIVE
Current Issues in Criminal Justice

CHAPTER 18
Racial Discrimination in the Criminal Justice System

INTRODUCTION

No issue arouses quite as much concern among criminal justice policy-makers and members of the public as discrimination. A justice system that treats different categories of offenders in different ways is no justice system at all. Conducting research on the treatment of racial minorities in the criminal justice system is very challenging, in large measure because an individual's ethnicity is not generally recorded in most criminal justice statistics. In this chapter, Scot Wortley and Andrea McCalla review the research that has explored the treatment of black suspects, accused persons, and offenders by the criminal justice system in Ontario. They also place this work in an international context, for the problem of discrimination plagues the justice systems of all western nations.

Bias against Black People in the Ontario Justice System
Scot Wortley and *Andrea McCalla*, University of Toronto

Statistics on race and crime are rarely collected and disseminated in Canada. However, the information that is available suggests that black people are greatly overrepresented in the criminal justice system. For example, although black people make up only 2 percent of the Canadian population, they represent 6 percent of those held in federal penitentiaries (see Wortley, 1999). The federal incarceration rate for black Canadians (146 per 100,000) is almost five times higher than the rate for whites (31 per 100,000). This overrepresentation is even greater in Ontario. Although blacks constitute only 3 percent of the province's population, recent figures suggest that they represent 12 percent of all admissions to federal prisons in the region (Solicitor General of Canada, 1997) and 15 percent of all admissions to provincial correctional facilities. The Ontario incarceration rate for blacks is a striking 3,686 per 100,000 population, compared to only 706 per 100,000 for whites (Commission on Systemic Racism, 1995:89). Although Canada often prides itself on being a more racially tolerant country than our neighbour to the south, the racial disparities revealed by these Canadian incarceration statistics are very similar to those found in American prison data (Tonry, 1995; Mauer, 1999).

Why are black people overrepresented in Canadian prison statistics? One possible explanation is that the Canadian criminal justice system is biased against black people. Indeed, community activists, defence lawyers, and academics have frequently argued that both the police and the courts discriminate against blacks and other visible minorities (see Foster, 1996; Henry, 1994). Criminal justice representatives, on the other hand, vehemently deny charges of racism and claim that the system is colour-blind. The chief of the Toronto Police Service recently reiterated this opinion when he stated that: "There is no racism ... We don't look at, nor do we consider the race or ethnicity, or any of that, as factors of how we dispose of cases, or individuals, or how we treat individuals" (*Toronto Star*, 2002:A14). Similar denials are often expressed by Ontario criminal court judges and prosecutors (Commission on Systemic Racism, 1995). Proponents of this "no-racism" argument frequently make the claim that blacks are overrepresented in prison statistics because they simply commit much more crime than individuals from other racial groups (see Worthington, 2002; Goldstein, 2002; Willbanks, 1987). The heated debate between the advocates of these two competing explanations erupted—once again—after the *Toronto Star* released a series of articles alleging police bias against blacks (Rankin et al., 2002a; 2002b) at almost the same time the city was suffering from a rash of violent homicides involving young black offenders and victims (Blizzard, 2002; Goldstein, 2002). The purpose of this chapter is to provide a brief review of recent research documenting discrimination against black people at all stages of the Ontario criminal justice system. We conclude with a discussion of the various strategies that might reduce racism in the justice system and highlight the need for additional research on this important—and very controversial—topic.

PERCEPTIONS OF CRIMINAL INJUSTICE

During the 1980s, allegations that the criminal justice system was racially biased were easily dismissed by governmental officials as representing the unfounded opinions of "radical" black activists. It was argued that the vast majority of black and other visible minority citizens had complete confidence in the police and criminal courts. However, subsequent research has illustrated that perceptions of racial discrimination are quite widespread. In 1994, the Commission on Systemic Racism in the Ontario Criminal Justice System conducted a survey of over 1,200 Toronto adults (18 years of age or older) who identified themselves as either black, Chinese, or white. Over 400 respondents were randomly selected from each racial group. The survey results indicate that three out of every four black Torontonians (76 percent) believe that the police treat members of their racial group more severely than they treat white people. Furthermore, 60 percent of the black respondents also felt that members of their racial group are treated worse by the criminal courts. Interestingly, the findings also indicate that perceptions of racial bias are not restricted to the black community. Indeed, over half of the white respondents (56 percent) reported that they think black people are treated worse than others by the police and a third (35 percent) think blacks are treated worse than others by the courts (see Wortley, 1996).

Additional research suggests that a high proportion of black youth also perceive that the criminal justice system is discriminatory. For example, a 1995 survey of 1,870 Toronto high school students found that over half of the black respondents (52 percent) felt that the police treat members of their racial group much worse than they treat the members of other racial groups. By contrast, only 22 percent of South Asians, 15 percent of Asians, and 4 percent of whites felt that they were subject to discriminatory treatment (Ruck and Wortley, 2002). Similarly, another high school survey, conducted in 2000, found that 74 percent of black students believe that members of their racial group are more likely to be unfairly stopped and questioned by the police than the members of other racial groups. This opinion was shared by only 31 percent of South Asians, 27 percent of Asians, and 13 percent of whites (see Tanner and Wortley, 2002). It should be noted that, in all three of the studies discussed above, racial differences in perceptions of criminal injustice could not be explained by racial differences in social class or other demographic factors.

Findings such as these have caused various government and criminal justice representatives to admit that the "perception" of discrimination exists in Ontario and that, at the very least, the criminal justice system suffers from a serious "public relations" problem. These findings have also motivated various police organizations to implement programs designed to improve relationships with various minority communities (see Stenning, 2003). However, there is still considerable debate about the cause of these perceptions of racial bias. Critics of the justice system feel that perceptions of discrimination reflect reality and are rooted in the lives of black people.

On the other hand, the conservative view is that perceptions of injustice are inaccurate and caused by other factors such as peer socialization and exposure to stories about racism in the American media. One popular explanation is that most black people in Canada are immigrants who come from countries—like Jamaica or Nigeria—where the criminal justice system is corrupt, brutal, and oppressive. As a result, many black people have based their opinion about the police and the courts on their experiences in their home country. The hypothesis is that second- and third-generation blacks, who have been raised in Canada, will have a much better opinion of the Canadian justice system. Research, however, suggests that the opposite is true. Recent immigrants, in fact, perceive much less discrimination in the Canadian justice system than immigrants who have been in Canada for a long period of time. Indeed, blacks who were born in Canada tend to have far worse perceptions of the police and the criminal courts (see Ruck and Wortley, 2002; Tanner and Wortley, 2002; Wortley et al., 1997). How can we explain this finding? Are perceptions of discrimination based on personal and/or group experiences? To answer this question we must turn to the empirical data.

Racial Profiling

Cecil Foster, in his book documenting the experiences of Caribbean immigrants to Canada, maintains that the police frequently stop, question, and search people of West Indian descent for "DWBs—driving while being black" violations (Foster, 1996:5). Foster's words reflect the belief, widespread among Canada's black population, that law enforcement and customs officials needlessly interrogate and harass black people solely because of their racial background (see Henry, 1994). Are black people more likely to be stopped, questioned, and searched by the police than people from other racial backgrounds? Official data from both England (Bunyan, 1999) and the United States (see Engel et al., 2002; Harris, 1997) suggest that they are. In England, for example, the passage of the *Police and Criminal Evidence Act (PACE)* gave the police the authority to stop and search persons or vehicles on the reasonable suspicion that they would find drugs, stolen goods, or other prohibited items. However, the *PACE* legislation also mandated that the police make a written record of the racial background of all people who are subjected to police stops and searches. Police statistics from 1997–98 reveal that black people are stopped and searched at a rate of 142 per 1,000, compared to 45 per 1,000 for Asians and 19 per 1,000 for whites. Overall, the English data suggest that blacks are 7.5 times more likely to be stopped and searched by the police than whites (Bunyan, 1999; Brown, 1997).

Unfortunately, unlike in England and the United States, police forces in Canada are not required to record the race or ethnicity of the people they stop and/or search. Thus, official police statistics cannot be used to investigate the presence or absence of racial profiling. However, other forms of investigation have uncovered evidence that racial profiling may exist in this country as well. For example, James (1998) conducted intensive interviews with over 50 black youth from six different cities in Ontario. Many of these youths reported that being stopped by the police was a common occurrence for them. There was also an almost universal belief that skin colour, not style of dress, was the primary determinant of attracting police attention. James (1998:173) concludes that the adversarial nature of these police stops contributes strongly to black youths' hostility toward the police.

Although ethnographic studies such as this one provide great detail about police encounters and document the "lived experiences" of black youth, they are based on rather small, non-random samples. They thus risk being dismissed as "anecdotal" and not truly representative of police behaviour. However, similar evidence of racial profiling has been recently uncovered by two surveys that utilized much larger, random samples. To begin with, a 1994 survey (described above) of over 1,200 Toronto residents found that black people, particularly black males, were much more likely to report involuntary police contact than either whites or Asians. For example, almost half (44 percent) of the black males in the sample reported that they had been stopped and questioned by the police at least once in the past two years. In fact, one-third (30 percent) of black males reported that they had been stopped on two or more occasions. By contrast, only 12 percent of white males and 7 percent of Asian males reported multiple police stops (see Wortley, 2003a).

Multivariate analyses reveal that these racial differences in police contact cannot be explained by racial differences in social class, education, or other demographic variables. In fact, two factors that seem to protect white males from police contact—age and social class—do not protect blacks. Whites with high incomes and education, for example, are much less likely to be stopped by the police than whites who score low on social-class measures. By contrast, blacks with high incomes and education are actually more likely to be stopped than lower-class blacks. Blacks professionals, in fact, often attribute the attention they receive from the police to their relative affluence. As one black respondent stated: "If you are black and you drive something good, the police will pull you over and ask about drugs" (Wortley, 2003a).

A recent survey of approximately 3,400 Toronto high school students (Tanner and Wortley, 2002) further suggests that blacks are much more likely than people from other racial backgrounds to report being subjected to random street interrogations. For example, over 20 percent of the black students in the study report that they have been stopped and searched by the police on two or more occasions in the past two years, compared to only 8 percent of whites, 5 percent of Asians, and under 5 percent of South Asians. Similarly, over 40 percent of black students claim that they have been physically searched by the police in the past two years, compared to only 17 percent of their white and 12 percent of their Asian counterparts (see Table 18.1).

However, the data also reveal that students who engage in various forms of crime and deviance are much more likely to receive police attention than students who do not break the law. For example, 81 percent of the drug dealers in this sample (defined as those who sold drugs on 10 or more occasions in the past year) report that they have been searched by the police, compared to only 16 percent of those students who did not sell drugs. This finding is consistent with the argument that the police focus exclusively on suspicious or criminal activity when deciding to make a stop—not the personal characteristics of citizens. The data further reveal that those students who spend most of their leisure time in public spaces (e.g., malls, public parks, nightclubs, etc.)

Table 18.1 *Percent of Student Respondents Who Report That They Were Stopped and Searched by the Police in the Past Two Years, by Race*

	Black	White	South Asian	West Asian	Asian	Hispanic	Other
Not Searched	59.7%	83.5%	89.7%	92.6%	88.3%	80.0%	78.7%
Searched Once	16.9%	8.5%	5.6%	4.4%	6.3%	10.3%	9.5%
Searched 2 or More Times	23.4%	8.1%	4.7%	3.0%	5.5%	9.7%	11.8%
Sample Size	474	1,289	605	405	129	145	263

$x^2=231.850$; df=12; p <.001

are much more likely to be stopped by the police than students who spend their time in private spaces or in the company of their parents. This leads to the million-dollar question: do black students receive more police attention because they are more involved in crime and more likely to be involved in leisure activities that take place in public spaces?

While our data reveal that white students have much higher rates of both alcohol consumption and illicit drug use, black students report higher rates of both minor property crime and violence. Furthermore, both black and white students report higher rates of participation in public leisure activities than students from all other racial backgrounds. These racial differences, however, do not come close to explaining why black youth are much more vulnerable to police contact. In fact, after statistically controlling for criminal activity, drug use, gang membership, and leisure activities, the relationship between race and police stops actually gets stronger. Why?

Further analysis reveals that racial differences in police stop-and-search practices are actually greatest among students with low levels of criminal behaviour. For example, 31 percent of the black students who *have not* engaged in any type of criminal activity still report that they have been stopped and questioned by the police on two or more occasions in the past two years, compared to only 6 percent of white students in the same behavioural category. Similarly, 21 percent of black students with no deviant behaviour report that they have been physically searched by the police, compared to only 4 percent of whites who report no deviance (Wortley and Tanner, 2002). Thus, while the first survey, discussed above, reveals that age and social class do not protect blacks from police stops and searches, this study suggests that good behaviour also does not shelter blacks from unwanted police attention.

These findings have two major implications. First, because the black community is subject to much greater police surveillance, blacks are also much more likely to be caught when they break the law than white people who engage in the same forms of criminal activity. For example, 65 percent of the black drug dealers in the above high school study report that they have been arrested at some time in their life, compared to only 35 percent of the white drug dealers. Imagine that 10,000 people live in a high-density community in downtown Toronto. Imagine further that half of the residents of this community are black and the other half are white. Let us also assume that an equal number of the black and white residents (250 from each group) sell illicit drugs on a regular basis. If, due to racial profiling, black residents are more likely to be stopped and searched by the police, black drug dealers in this neighbourhood will be more likely to be detected and subsequently arrested than white offenders. For example, if 50 percent of the black residents are randomly searched, compared to only 10 percent of the white residents, this searching practice should yield 125 black arrests and only 25 white arrests.

Interestingly, the race-crime statistics (125 black arrests compared to only 25 white arrests) produced by such biased search practices would probably be used to justify the use of racial profiling (i.e., we found more black than white offenders; therefore, our profiling strategy must be correct). Racial profiling can become a self-fulfilling prophecy. This example helps illustrate how arrest statistics may have more to do with law enforcement surveillance practices than actual racial differences in criminal behaviour. In sum, racial profiling may help explain the overrepresentation of minorities in arrest statistics (DeLisi and Regoli 1999; Klinger 1997).

However, it should be noted that research also suggests that the police almost never arrest citizens who are not involved in some form of criminal activity. This may lead to the conclusion that racial profiling is harmless: if you don't break the law, you will not be arrested. However, the second major consequence of racial profiling is that it serves to further alienate black people from mainstream Canadian society and reinforces perceptions of discrimination and racial injustice. Indeed, research strongly suggests that black people who are frequently stopped and questioned by the police perceive much higher levels of discrimination in the Canadian criminal justice system than blacks who have not been stopped. Interestingly, being stopped by the police does not appear to increase perceptions of injustice for whites or Asians (Wortley et al., 1997). Being stopped and searched by the police, therefore, seems to be experienced by black people as evidence that race still matters in Canadian society.

POLICE USE OF FORCE

Highly publicized American cases of police violence against black people serve to reinforce the perception that North American police officers are biased against members of the black community. However, high-profile cases of police brutality involving black victims are not limited to the United States. The names of people such as Albert Johnson, Lester Donaldson, and others are frequently used to illustrate that police use of force is a problem faced by blacks in Canada as well (see Pedicelli, 1998). Unfortunately, allegations of racial bias with respect to the police use of force are extremely difficult to research. Official documentation regarding citizens killed or injured by the police is simply unavailable to Canadian researchers (Goff, 2001). However, an examination of news stories suggests that blacks are indeed highly overrepresented among those killed or injured by the police in Ontario (see Pedicelli, 1998, for a detailed review of selected cases from both Montreal and Toronto). For example, between 1978 and 2000 we were able to identify—through media coverage—34 separate shootings in which citizens were either killed or severely injured by the police in Toronto. Nineteen of these cases (56 percent) involved black victims, 10 (29 percent) involved whites, and 5 (15 percent) involved people from other racial backgrounds. Additional analysis reveals that 13 of the 23 people (57 percent) who were shot and killed by the police during this time period were black. Although overall numbers are low, the fact that black citizens represent over half of those killed or injured by the police is disturbing—particularly when you consider the fact that they make up only 6 percent of Toronto's total population.

These findings, however, do not constitute "proof" that the Toronto police are racially biased with respect to the use of force. Indeed, the fact that these cases resulted in few criminal charges (and no convictions) could be seen as evidence that these shootings were justified. This interpretation is consistent with American research (see Fyfe, 1988) that suggests that, once situational factors (e.g., whether the suspect had a gun or was in the process of committing a violent felony) have been taken into account, racial differences in the police use of force are dramatically reduced. Nonetheless, until such detailed research is conducted within Canada, questions about the possible relationship between race and police violence will remain.

THE ARREST SITUATION

Recent observational studies of police–citizen encounters conducted in the United States suggest that, controlling for criminal conduct, race is unrelated to the police decision to arrest (see Delisi and Regoli 1999; Klinger 1997). In other words, the police rarely arrest citizens, regardless of their race, unless there is clear evidence that a crime has been committed. Once again, it must be noted that similar studies have not been conducted in Canada. However, recent Canadian evidence suggests that race may influence police behaviour once an arrest has been made. An analysis (Rankin et al., 2002a) of over 10,000 Toronto arrests—between 1996 and 2001—for simple drug possession reveals that black suspects (38 percent) are much more likely than whites (23 percent) to be taken to the police station for processing. White accused, on the other hand, are more likely to be released at the scene. Once at the police station, black accused are held overnight, for a bail hearing, at twice the rate of whites. These racial disparities in police treatment remain after other relevant factors—including age, criminal history, employment, immigration status, and whether or not the person has a permanent home address—have been taken into statistical account. Studies that have examined the treatment of young offenders in Ontario have yielded very similar results (Commission on Systemic Racism, 1995).

RACE AND BAIL

The bail decision is recognized as one of the most important stages of the criminal court process. Not only does pretrial detention represent a fundamental denial of freedom for individuals who have not yet been proven guilty of a crime, it has also been shown to produce a number of subsequent legal consequences. Controlling for factors such as type of charge and criminal record, previous research suggests that offenders who are denied bail are much more likely to be convicted and sentenced to prison than their counterparts who have been released (see Reaves and Perez, 1992; Friedland, 1965). Thus, racial disparities in pretrial outcomes could have a direct impact on the overrepresentation of Aboriginal and black people in Canadian correctional statistics. Indeed, the Manitoba Aboriginal Justice Inquiry found that Aboriginal accused were more likely to be denied bail and more likely to spend lengthier periods in pretrial detention than non-Aboriginals (see Hamilton and Sinclair, 1991). Similarly, an examination of 1,653 cases from the Toronto courts, conducted on behalf of the Commission on Systemic Racism in the Ontario Criminal Justice System, revealed that blacks are less likely to be released by the police at the scene and the police station (see Roberts and Doob, 1997: Table 12). This disparity is particularly pronounced for those charged with drug offences. Indeed, the study found that almost one-third of black offenders (31 percent) charged with a drug offence were held in detention before their trial, compared to only 10 percent of whites charged with a similar offence. This profound racial difference remains after other relevant factors—including criminal history—have been statistically controlled (Roberts and Doob, 1997).

A second Toronto-area study provides additional evidence of racial bias in pretrial decision-making (Kellough and Wortley, 2002). This research project tracked over 1,800 criminal cases, appearing in two Toronto bail courts, over a six-month period in 1994. Overall, the results suggest that 36 percent of black accused are detained before trial, compared to only 23 percent of accused from other racial backgrounds. Race remains a significant predictor of pretrial detention after statistically controlling for factors associated with both flight risk (e.g., employment status, home address, previous charges for failure to appear, etc.) and danger to the public (e.g., seriousness of current charges, length of criminal record, etc.).

Additional analysis, however, suggests that black accused are more likely to be detained because they tend to receive much more negative "moral assessments" from arresting officers. Moral assessments refer to the subjective personality descriptions that the police frequently attach to show-cause documents. The data suggest that police officers, on average, spend more time justifying the detention of black than white accused. Clearly, this is evidence that police discretion extends from the street and into the courtroom—at least at the pretrial level. Finally, the results of this study suggest that rather than managing risky populations, pretrial detention is a rather important resource that the prosecution uses (along with over-charging) to encourage (or coerce) guilty pleas from accused persons. Those accused who are not held in pretrial custody, by contrast, are much more likely to have all of their charges withdrawn.

It is interesting to note that, even when they are released on bail, black accused are still subjected to greater court surveillance. Controlling for legally relevant variables, black accused out on bail tend to receive significantly more release conditions—including curfews, area restrictions, and mandatory supervision requirements—than whites. Since blacks are subject to a greater number of release conditions and are more likely to be arbitrarily stopped and investigated by the police (see evidence on racial profiling above), it is not surprising to find that blacks are greatly overrepresented among those charged with breach of condition offences (Kellough and Wortley, 2001).

RACE AND SENTENCING

International research on racial differences in sentencing has produced mixed results. Some studies have found that minorities are treated more harshly, others have found minorities treated more leniently, and some find no difference in sentencing patterns for racial minorities (Cole, 1999). A similar pattern of results emerges from sentencing research involving Aboriginal offenders (see La Prairie, 1990). Relatively little Canadian research has focused on the sentencing of blacks or other racial minorities. Those studies that do exist, however, point to the possibility of racial discrimination, for certain offences at least. For example, Mosher's (1996) historical analysis of the Ontario courts, from 1892 to 1930, reveals that black offenders experienced much higher rates of conviction and harsher sentences than their white counterparts. Multivariate analyses of these data reveal that observed racial differences in sentencing severity cannot be explained by other legally relevant variables (Mosher 1996:432). More recently, the Commission on Systemic Racism in the Ontario Criminal Justice System compared the sentencing outcomes of white and black offenders convicted in Toronto courts during the early 1990s. The results of this investigation revealed that black offenders convicted of drug offences were more likely to be sentenced to prison. This racial difference remains after other important factors—including offence seriousness, criminal history, age, and employment—have been taken into statistical account. Toni Williams (1999:212) concludes that "this finding indicates that the higher incarceration rates of black than white convicted men is partly due to judges treating them more harshly for no legitimate reason." However, Roberts and Doob (1997) note that the commission's research suggests that the effect of race is statistically weaker at the sentencing stage than at earlier stages of the justice process and appears limited to drug offences.

Clearly, research on racial differences in sentencing is at an early stage in Canada. One factor that has yet to be examined is the impact of the victim's racial background. For example, American research suggests that, regardless of their own race, individuals who victimize white people are treated more harshly by the courts than those who victimize blacks and other racial minorities (Cole, 1999). This fact might help explain why minority offenders—who usually victimize people from their own racial background—sometimes appear to be treated more leniently at the sentencing stage. It is also important to stress that Canadians should be wary about adopting American-style "tough on crime" policies. Indeed, recent American studies suggest that, rather than overt discrimination by individual judges at the sentencing stage, the overrepresentation of minorities in prison populations is the result of the creation of both "mandatory minimum" and "three strikes" legislation (Tonry, 1995; Mauer, 1999; Cole, 1999).

Race and Corrections

As with other stages of the criminal justice system, very little Canadian research has examined the treatment of racial minorities within corrections. However, consistent with studies on the police and the criminal courts, the research that has been conducted suggests that some forms of racial bias exist behind prison walls. The Commission on Systemic Racism in the Ontario Criminal Justice System, for example, found that while racist language and attitudes plague the environments of many Ontario prisons, and racial segregation is often used as a strategy for maintaining order, correctional officials do not acknowledge that racism is a significant management problem (Commission on Systemic Racism, 1995). Commission researchers also found evidence of racial bias in the application of prison discipline. Black inmates are significantly overrepresented among prisoners charged with misconducts—particularly the types of misconducts in which correctional officers exercise greater discretionary judgment. This fact is important because a correctional record for such misconducts is often used to deny parole and limit access to temporary release programs. Indeed, exploratory research suggests that black and other racial minority inmates, controlling for other relevant factors, are somewhat more likely to be denied early prison release (Mann, 1993; Commission on Systemic Racism, 1995).

Unfortunately, Canadian research has yet to explore possible racial discrimination in parole decisions within federal correctional facilities. Commission researchers highlighted the fact that current rehabilitation programs do not meet the cultural and linguistic needs of many racial minority inmates (Commission on Systemic Racism, 1994; 1995). The current correctional system, it is argued, caters to white, Euro-Canadian norms. The treatment needs of black and other racial minority prisoners are either unacknowledged or ignored. Ultimately, inadequate or inappropriate rehabilitation services for minority inmates may translate into higher recidivism rates for nonwhite offenders—a fact that may further contribute to their overrepresentation in the Canadian correctional system.

CONCLUSION

This chapter began by noting that the majority of Ontario's black population believes that the criminal justice system is biased against blacks. A brief review of the empirical evidence suggests that these perceptions are not unfounded. Research conducted within the province has consistently uncovered evidence of discrimination in policing, the courts, and corrections. With the possible exception of policing, racial disparities at any one stage of the criminal justice process are not huge. However, in our opinion, the additive effect of discrimination throughout the system has a major impact on the black community. Clearly, research to date strongly suggests that racial discrimination, along with higher rates of criminal offending, can help explain the overrepresentation of blacks in correctional statistics.

Nonetheless, most Canadian criminologists acknowledge that much more research is needed. For example, more studies—incorporating both official and unofficial data—are needed to explore racial differences in police stop-and-search practices, police use of force, arrest decisions, and complaints against the police. Larger studies—including a wider array of criminal offences—are needed to explore racial differences in pretrail detention, conviction rates, and sentencing. Additional correctional research, particularly at the federal level, is also needed to examine racial differences in parole decisions and access to suitable rehabilitation programming. Finally, good evaluation research is required if we are to properly explore the impact of programs that have been designed to reduce racism within the Canadian justice system. For example, numerous strategies—including community policing initiatives, cultural sensitivity training, formal antiracism regulations, and campaigns to recruit officers from racial minority communities—have been implemented by police forces across the country. However, these programs have not been evaluated in a scientific manner by external researchers (see Stenning, 2003). How do we know if these programs are working or if they are simply window-dressing designed to convince the public that issues of racism are being addressed?

Future research on racism in Canada, however, is greatly hindered by the current ban on the collection and dissemination of race–crime statistics (see Wortley, 1999). We believe this type of information is needed to further explore the treatment of different racial/ethnic groups. The primary justification for the current ban is that information on the racial background of criminal offenders might be used to reinforce racial stereotypes and justify discrimination within all sectors of Canadian society. Unfortunately, there is very little evidence that the current ban on race-crime statistics actually prevents people from drawing a connection between race and criminality. An Ontario survey found that many residents believe that black people are responsible for a disproportionate amount of crime (cited in Roberts, 2002). These beliefs are likely based more on media coverage of crime (from both Canada and the United States) than exposure to official crime data. Indeed, recent Canadian studies suggest that the vast majority of news coverage involving blacks is related to criminal activity (see Wortley, 2003b; Henry and Tator, 2000). Furthermore, race-crime statistics from other countries are freely available to those who want to put forth racially based theories of crime causation (Rushton, 1988). In sum, we feel that while the current ban on race-crime statistics has little impact on public beliefs about the relationship between race and criminal behaviour, it has served to prevent a more effective investigation of possible racist practices within the Canadian criminal justice system.

We conclude with a caution. Recently, conservative critics have charged that research that documents racism within the justice system does more harm than good. They argue that publicly discussing evidence of racism creates distrust, damages relationships with specific minority communities, and lowers morale among criminal justice personnel (*Toronto Star*, 2002:A14). We could not disagree more. Good, objective social research does not create social problems—it merely documents them. The discomfort of having to talk about racism—and deal with it in the policy arena—should not be used as an excuse to prevent further research in this area.

DISCUSSION QUESTIONS

1. *The authors argue that routinely collecting criminal justice statistics that include the race of the individual would be a good idea. What do you think?*
2. *If systemic discrimination against black people exists in the criminal justice system of Ontario, what, in your opinion, should be done about the problem? Which remedies are worth considering?*
3. *One solution involves taking radical steps to increase the number of visible minority criminal justice professionals, including police officers, lawyers, and judges. How effective do you think this solution is likely to be?*

FURTHER READINGS

Commission on Systemic Racism in the Ontario Criminal Justice System. 1995. *Report of the Commission on Systemic Racism in the Ontario Criminal Justice System*. Toronto: Queen's Printer for Ontario.

Wortley, Scot. 1996. Justice for all? Race and perceptions of bias in the Ontario criminal justice system—A Toronto survey. *Canadian Journal of Criminology* 38:439–467.

Wortley, Scot, Macmillan, Ross, and Hagan, John. 1997. Just Des(s)erts? The racial polarization of perceptions of criminal injustice. *Law and Society Review* 31:637–676.

REFERENCES

Blizzard, Christina. 2002. A crisis of their own choosing: Black leaders insist it's racial profiling, not black-on-black violence. *Toronto Sun*. November 1:16.

Brown, David. 1997. *Pace Ten Years On: A Review of the Research*. London: Home Office.

Bunyan, Tony. 1999. The cycle of U.K. racism: Stop and search, arrest and imprisonment. *Statewatch* 9:1–4.

Cole, David. 1999. *No Equal Justice: Race and Class in the American Criminal Justice System*. New York: The New Press.

Commission on Systemic Racism in the Ontario Criminal Justice System. 1995. *Report of the Commission on Systemic Racism in the Ontario Criminal Justice System*. Toronto: Queen's Printer for Ontario.

Commission on Systemic Racism in the Ontario Criminal Justice System. 1994. *Racism Behind Bars: The Treatment of Black and Other Racial Minority Prisoners in Ontario Prisons—Interim Report of the Commission on Systemic Racism in the Ontario Criminal Justice System*. Toronto: Queen's Printer for Ontario.

DeLisi, Matt, and Bob Regoli. 1999. Race, conventional crime and criminal justice: The declining importance of race. *Journal of Criminal Justice* 27:549–557.

Engel, Robin Shepard, Calnon, Jennifer M., and Bernard, Thomas J. 2002. Theory and racial profiling: Shortcomings and future directions in research. *Justice Quarterly* 19(2):249–273.

Foster, Cecil. 1996. *A Place Called Heaven: The Meaning of Being Black in Canada*. Toronto: HarperCollins.

Friedland, M.L. 1965. *Detention Before Trial: A Study of Criminal Cases Tried in the Toronto Magistrate's Court*. Toronto: University of Toronto Press.

Fyfe, J.J. 1988. Police use of deadly force: Research and reform. *Justice Quarterly* 5(2):165–205.

Goff, Colin. 2001. *Criminal Justice in Canada*, 2nd ed. Scarborough: Nelson Thomson Learning.

Goldstein, Lorrie. 2002. It's not racist to fight violent crime. *Toronto Sun*. October 29:16.

Hamilton, A.C., and Sinclair, C.M. 1991. *Report of the Aboriginal Justice Inquiry of Manitoba*. Winnipeg: Government of Ontario.

Harris, David. 1997. Driving while black and all other traffic offences: The Supreme Court and pretextual traffic stops. *Journal of Criminal Law and Criminology* 87:544–582.

Henry, F. 1994. *The Caribbean Diaspora in Toronto: Learning to Live with Racism*. Toronto: University of Toronto Press.

Henry, Frances, and Tator, Carol. 2000. *Racist Discourse in Canada's English Print Media*. Toronto: Canadian Race Relations Foundation.

James, Carl. 1998. "Up to no good": Black on the streets and encountering police. In Victor Satzewich (Ed.), *Racism and Social Inequality in Canada: Concepts, Controversies and Strategies of Resistance*. Toronto: Thompson, 157–176.

Jefferson, Tony, and Walker, M. 1992. Ethnic minorities in the criminal justice system. *Criminal Law Review* 81:83–95.

Kellough, Gail, and Scot Wortley. 2002. Remand for plea: The impact of race, pre-trial detention and over-charging on plea bargaining decisions. *British Journal of Criminology* 42(1):186–210.

———. 2001. Risk, moral assessment and the application of bail conditions in Canadian criminal courts. *Paper presented at the 2001 International Meeting of the American Law and Society Association*. July 2–7, Budapest, Hungary.

Klinger, David. 1997. Negotiating order in patrol work: An ecological theory of police response to deviance. *Criminology* 35:277–306.

La Prairie, Carol. 1990. The role of sentencing in the over-representation of aboriginal people in correctional institutions. *Canadian Journal of Criminology* 32:429–440.

Mann, C.R. 1993. *Unequal Justice: A Question of Color*. Bloomington: Indiana University Press.

Mauer, Marc. 1999. *Race to Incarcerate*. New York: The New Press.

Mosher, Clayton. 1996. Minorities and misdemeanours: The treatment of Black public order offenders in Ontario's criminal justice system—1892–1930. *Canadian Journal of Criminology* October:413–438.

Pedicelli, Gabriella. 1998. *When Police Kill: Police Use of Force in Montreal and Toronto*. Montreal: Vehicule Press.

Rankin, Jim, Quinn, Jennifer, Shephard, Michelle, Simmie, Scott, and Duncanson, John. 2002a. Singled out: An investigation into race and crime. *Toronto Star*. October 19:A1.

———. 2002b. Police target black drivers. *Toronto Star*. October 20:A1

Reaves, B., and Perez, J. 1992. *Pre-trial Release of Felony Defendants*. Washington, DC: U.S. Department of Justice.

Roberts, J.V. 2002. Racism and the collection of statistics relating to race and ethnicity. In W. Chan and K. Mirchandini (Eds.), *Crimes of Colour*. Peterborough: Broadview Press, 101–112.

Roberts, Julian V., and Doob, Anthony. 1997. Race, ethnicity, and criminal justice in Canada. In M. Tonry (Ed.), *Ethnicity, Crime, and Immigration: Comparative and Cross-National Perspectives*, Volume 21. Chicago: University of Chicago Press, 469–522.

Ruck, Martin, and Wortley, Scot. 2002. Racial and ethnic minority high school students' perceptions of school disciplinary practices: A look at some Canadian findings. *Journal of Youth and Adolescence* 31(3):185–195.

Rushton, Phillipe. 1988. Race differences in sexuality and their correlates: Another look at psychological models. *Journal of Research in Personality* 23:35–54.

Solicitor General of Canada. 1997. *Basic Facts About Corrections in Canada: 1997 Edition*. Ottawa: Public Works and Government Services Canada.

Stenning, P. 2003. Policing the cultural kaleidoscope: Recent Canadian experience. *Police & Society* 7:21–87.

Tanner, Julian, and Scot Wortley. 2002. *The Toronto Youth Crime and Victimization Survey: Overview Report*. Toronto: Centre of Criminology.

Tonry, Michael. 1995. *Malign Neglect: Race, Crime and Punishment in America*. New York: Oxford University Press.

Toronto Star. 2002. There is no racism. We do not do racial profiling. *Toronto Star*. October 19:A14.

Wilbanks, William. 1987. *The Myth of a Racist Criminal Justice System*. Belmont, CA: Wadsworth.

Williams, Toni. 1999. Sentencing black offenders in the Ontario criminal justice system. In J.V. Roberts and D. P. Cole (Eds.), *Making Sense of Sentencing*. Toronto: University of Toronto Press, 200–216.

Worthington, Peter. 2002. Oh, the deadly irony of it all: Violence shows cops right. *Toronto Sun*. October 30:40.

Wortley, Scot. 2003a (Forthcoming). The usual suspects: Race, police contact and perceptions of criminal injustice. *Criminology*.

Wortley, Scot. 2003b. Misrepresentation or reality: The depiction of race and crime in the Canadian print media. In Bernard Schissel and Carolyn Brooks (Eds.), *Marginality and Condemnation: Critical Criminology in Canada*. Halifax: Fernwood Press, 55–82.

Wortley, Scot. 1999. A northern taboo: Research on race, crime, and criminal justice in Canada. *Canadian Journal of Criminology* 41(2):261–274.

Wortley, Scot, Macmillan, Ross, and Hagan, John. 1997. Just Des(s)erts? The racial polarization of perceptions of criminal injustice. *Law and Society Review* 31:637–676.

CHAPTER 19
Miscarriages of Justice

INTRODUCTION

Many members of the public believe that the justice system is tilted toward protecting the rights of the accused, with the result that guilty parties escape conviction. In reality, however, innocent accused persons are sometimes convicted of crimes that they did not commit. This is particularly disturbing when the conviction results in a long prison sentence, as was the case for David Milgaard. Criminologists have recently begun to explore the causes and consequences of wrongful convictions. In this reading, two Canadian researchers who have explored this issue in depth discuss the question of wrongful convictions.

Wrongful Conviction in Canada
Myriam Denov and *Kathryn Campbell*, University of Ottawa

In Canada, the criminal justice system is based on the adversarial model, which involves two parties, the state and the accused. As a result of the criminal trial between competing parties, the "truth" eventually emerges. At least that is the theory. The numerous procedural safeguards in place are presumed to protect the innocent from both unintentional and/or intentional errors on the part of the police, prosecutors, or judges. Unfortunately, the cases of wrongful conviction in Canada call into question the ability of our criminal justice system to convict the guilty and acquit the innocent. The devastating ordeals of wrongly convicted Canadians, such as Donald Marshall Jr., David Milgaard, Guy Paul Morin, Thomas Sophonow, Steven Truscott, Jamie Nelson, and others, serve as powerful reminders of the flaws of the justice system.

These cases highlight the need to examine the factors that contribute to the conviction of the innocent.

The objective of this chapter is to explore the causes and consequences of wrongful convictions, as well as the government responses to the problem. First, the chapter examines the many individual and systemic factors that appear to contribute to wrongful convictions. Second, relying on in-depth interviews with two Canadians who have been wrongly convicted, the effects of wrongful conviction on both the individual in question, as well as their families, are highlighted. Finally, the state responses to wrongful conviction are addressed, including s. 690 of the *Criminal Code*, commissions of inquiry, and government approaches to compensation.

THE PREVALENCE OF WRONGFUL CONVICTIONS

Justice may miscarry in two ways: an innocent accused may be found guilty, or a guilty person may be acquitted. The focus of this chapter will be on those cases where an innocent individual is wrongly convicted of a crime. Until relatively recently, wrongful convictions were thought to be a rare occurrence (Carrington, 1978). However, recent research has demonstrated that, while the number of wrongful convictions is largely unknown (and possibly unknowable), estimates of the frequency of such miscarriages range from very few cases each year to 20 percent of all convictions (Holmes, 2001). A study conducted at a maximum-security prison for the National Association of Parole Officers in Britain revealed that as many as 6 percent of the inmates in that prison may have been wrongly convicted. The association believed that this figure was typical of other British prisons (Carvel, 1992). There is no reason to believe that the rate of wrongful conviction is any lower in Canada.

Causes of Wrongful Conviction

Research has revealed that wrongful convictions do not occur as a result of one individual making a single grave mistake. Instead, several individual and systemic factors may, either alone or in concert with each other, contribute to wrongful convictions (Castelle and Loftus, 2001). These factors include eyewitness error, erroneous forensic science, false confessions, the use of jailhouse informants, professional and institutional misconduct, and racial bias.

Eyewitness Error

Psychologists have long demonstrated that, due to normal deficiencies in the human memory process, eyewitness identification is inherently unreliable (Sanders, 1984). In fact, eyewitness error, which is often the sole or major evidence of guilt in criminal cases, appears to be the single most important factor leading to wrongful convictions in the United States and the United Kingdom (Huff et al., 1986). According to the U.S. National Institute of Justice study (Conners et al., 1996) 24 out of 28 wrongful convictions occurred at least in part from erroneous eyewitness identification. Eyewitness errors may happen for several reasons, including suggestive police interviewing, unconscious transference, and the malleability of confidence (Castelle and Loftus, 2001). Suggestive police interviewing may occur if the police communicate information to eyewitnesses that subsequently influences and ultimately contaminates their testimony.

In Canada, suggestive police interviewing led to the initial convictions of Donald Marshall Jr., David Milgaard, and Thomas Sophonow. In each of these cases, witnesses were pressured by police to the point where they abandoned their original testimony and gave false evidence (Anderson and Anderson, 1998). Unconscious transference is said to occur among witnesses when a person seen in one situation is confused or recalled as a person seen in another situation (Loftus, 1979). The malleability of confidence refers to the pliable nature of a witness's certainty of their testimony. Research has demonstrated that witnesses who identify a suspect from a police lineup or group of photos are far more confident of their choice if given positive feedback from authorities, even in casual conversation (see Wells and Bradfield, 1998).

Most jurors, unaware of the unreliability of eyewitness identification, may place unwarranted faith in its accuracy (Sanders, 1984). In Ontario, defence lawyers are prevented from calling upon experts to discuss the frailties of eyewitness identification. While judges are supposed to inform the jury of the limitations of such evidence, this happens infrequently (Bayliss, 2002). The questionable accuracy of eyewitness testimony, coupled with the fact that it is often heavily relied upon by criminal justice personnel, makes eyewitness identifications a significant contributor to wrongful convictions.

Erroneous Forensic Science

Erroneous and fraudulent forensic science has also been linked to wrongful convictions. In some cases, inadvertent human error, sloppiness, exaggeration, misinterpretation, and bias may work to contaminate evidence, whether in the forensic laboratory or at the crime scene (Castelle and Loftus, 2001). More disturbing, however, are those cases in which forensic scientists deliberately tamper with evidence. For example, Stephanie Nyznyk, a laboratory technician working out of the Centre for Forensic Sciences in Ontario, suppressed information that hair and fibre samples used by the prosecution to successfully convict Guy Paul Morin of murder had been contaminated and should have been discarded as evidence (Anderson and Anderson, 1998).

False Confessions

A confession is often viewed as the most powerful piece of evidence that the prosecution can bring against an accused. Juries are said to believe a defendant who confesses to a crime, regardless of other evidence pointing to the contrary (Leo and Ofshe, 1998). While most find it difficult to believe that anyone would confess to a crime he or she has not committed, research indicates that this may not be such a rare phenomenon. For example, of 62 wrongly convicted individuals who were exonerated by DNA evidence in the United States, Scheck, Neufeld, and Dwyer (2000) found that 15 of these individuals originally confessed to the crime. To understand how innocent people can come to confess to crimes that they did not commit, it is important to examine police interrogation techniques.

The Canadian case of Christopher Bates, who was wrongly convicted of murder in 1993, provides a telling example of an individual who gave a false confession to police. Bates was arrested and charged with the murder of a shopkeeper who had been killed and robbed of 90 dollars. While in police custody, Bates was interrogated, threatened, and tortured for 17 hours. He was told that if he did not confess, his children would be taken by child protection authorities. After many hours of physical and psychological torture, Bates agreed to sign a declaration linking him to the robbery. Bates explained that the extreme fear for his life pushed him to sign the declaration. His false confession played an important role in his conviction. He spent five and a half years in a maximum-security prison for a murder he did not commit.

The Use of Jailhouse Informants

The use of jailhouse informants may also play an important role in the conviction of the innocent. In such cases, prisoners provide information to law enforcement officials in exchange for money, property, or leniency in sentencing. The use of jailhouse informants is strongly embedded in the culture of the criminal justice system as a means of securing a conviction. Of the 13 Illinois death-row inmates found to be wrongfully convicted, five—or nearly 40 percent—were prosecuted using the testimony of jailhouse informants (Armstrong and Mills, 2000). Further, it is unfortunately apparent that jurors give great weight to confessions allegedly provided to jailhouse informants. American studies indicate that, for the average juror, there is not much difference between the manner in which he or she receives and weighs a confession given to a police officer and a confession given to a jailhouse informant (Cory, 2001).

In Canada, the case of Guy Paul Morin illustrates the serious dangers of relying on jailhouse informants. In 1985, Guy Paul Morin was arrested and charged with the murder of a young child. While Morin was jailed without bail, two jailhouse informants, who were facing charges of sexual assault and assault, respectively, came forward claiming that Morin had confessed to the crime. This was the only direct evidence of Morin's guilt (Kaufman, 1998:546). Both informants received reduced penalties as a result of their testimonies. Morin was convicted, in part because of their testimony, but his conviction was reversed on appeal. The informants retestified at Morin's second trial, where he was convicted. Through DNA evidence, Morin was later found to be innocent and was subsequently released from prison.

The risks involved with relying on jailhouse informants are obvious. In his report on the wrongful conviction of Thomas Sophonow, Justice Cory described jailhouse informants as a "uniquely evil group" who "should as far as it is possible, be excised and removed from our trial process" (Cory, 2001). Informants may have much to gain and little to lose by providing false testimonies to authorities. It is thus essential that this relatively common practice within the justice system be subject to limited use and informants be prohibited from testifying.

PROFESSIONAL AND INSTITUTIONAL MISCONDUCT

Unprofessional conduct on the part of the police, the prosecution, and the judiciary is an important contributing factor to convicting the innocent (Huff et al., 1986). As a first point of entry into the criminal justice system, the police play a pivotal role in deciding whom to charge and in obtaining evidence to support a charge. In building their case against a suspect, the police may suppress, lose, misinterpret, or overlook evidence that supports the defendant's claim of innocence. Such errors may occur through prejudicial identification lineups, misuse of informants, solicitation of false confessions, and reliance on poor forensic science. Such unprofessional behaviour may be well-intentioned and motivated by a sincere desire to strengthen the case against a suspect who professionals are "convinced" is guilty.

This process is often referred to as "tunnel vision" on the part of criminal justice professionals, whereby the guilt of one particular suspect is assumed and evidence is then manipulated by authorities through a number of questionable practices to prove that guilt. Whether tunnel vision occurs among police officers or the prosecution, authorities may become so focused on one particular individual that they may make deliberate attempts to destroy that individual's alibi and eliminate all other potential suspects from the investigation (Schreck, 2002).

Professional misconduct may also occur in the form of withholding evidence considered favourable to the defence. The Canadian justice system prohibits police and prosecutors from pursuing a prosecution while withholding evidence that supports a claim of innocence. A prosecutor has a duty to learn about evidence favourable to the defence that may be in police possession and ensure the disclosure of all such information to the defence (Lockyer, 2002). Withholding evidence not only raises ethical questions about prosecutorial conduct but also may inevitably contribute to wrongful convictions (Rosenberg, 2002)

The Canadian case of Donald Marshall Jr., who was wrongly convicted of the murder of Sandy Seale in Nova Scotia in 1971, provides some disturbing examples of the police and the prosecution failing to disclose information crucial to an accused's defence. Ten days following Marshall's conviction for the murder of Sandy Seale, a witness (Jimmy MacNeil) came forward to police declaring that he had seen Roy Ebsary, not Donald Marshall Jr., stab Seale. The police failed to thoroughly investigate the assertion of this witness. Moreover, according to the Marshall Inquiry (Royal Commission, 1989), MacNeil's claim was never disclosed by police to either Marshall's defence counsel or to the Halifax Crown counsel assigned to handle Marshall's appeal of his conviction. Had this information been presented to the Court of Appeal, it is likely that a new trial would have been ordered (Royal Commission, 1989). Similarly, the prosecution failed to inform Marshall's defence counsel of statements of several witnesses whose stories tended to corroborate Marshall's account of the events of the murder (Wall, 1992). Marshall spent 11 years in prison for a crime he did not commit. Roy Ebsary was tried and later convicted of this murder.

While the practices of individual police officers and prosecutors are highly significant, it is essential to examine the larger institutional context within which wrongful convictions occur. Martin (2001) identifies three institutional factors that may contribute to convicting the innocent. These include the high-profile nature of a case, which pressures authorities for a quick resolution; the marginalized status of the accused as an "outsider"; and that the case rests on evidence that is suspect or inherently unreliable. When all three factors are present within the institutional context, there may be a greater likelihood that authorities will pressure a defendant into a false confession, overlook the initial reluctance of an eyewitness, believe an unreliable jailhouse informant, or fail to disclose favourable evidence—all of which may precipitate a wrongful conviction.

The case of David Milgaard, who was wrongly imprisoned for 22 years for the rape and murder of Gail Miller in 1970, provides a powerful example of police and institutional misconduct, as well as tunnel vision on the part of prosecutors. The high level of public anxiety provoked by this brutal crime put great pressure on the police to make an arrest. Milgaard, who was labeled as an impulsive and marginalized troublemaker, became the target. The case against him was based on questionable evidence, obtained through police intimidation. Approximately six years following Milgaard's release from prison, DNA testing established his innocence. Another individual, a serial rapist who was living blocks away from the murder scene, was subsequently convicted of the crime in 1999.

Racial Bias

Several factors may help to explain why racial minorities are disproportionately represented among those wrongly convicted. These factors include institutionalized racism, erroneous cross-racial identification, stereotyping, and extreme social disadvantage. Racism is a complex set of ideologies, attitudes, and beliefs claiming racial superiority, and sometimes involving racial discrimination and disadvantage for ethnic minorities (Cashmore, 1996). Institutionalized racism, which can be unintentional or deliberate, refers to the

> collective failure of an organization to provide appropriate and professional service to people because of their colour, culture or ethnic origin. It can be seen or detected in processes, attitudes and behaviours which amount to

discrimination through unwitting prejudice, ignorance, thoughtlessness, and racist stereotyping which disadvantage minority ethnic people (Macpherson, 1999:28).

In this sense, race is built into the structure of our economic, political, and legal institutions, thus contributing to differential opportunities and differential treatment of racial groups within these institutions. This places racial minorities at a severe disadvantage, making them vulnerable to miscarriages of justice.

While little Canadian research has addressed the link between race and wrongful conviction, the prominent case of Donald Marshall Jr., a Mi'kmaw Aboriginal who was wrongly convicted of the murder of Sandy Seale, illuminates the ways in which race is embedded in the Canadian criminal justice system. The Royal Commission on the prosecution of Donald Marshall Jr. acknowledged that Marshall had been wrongly convicted and imprisoned because, *inter alia,* he is Mi'kmaw:

> The tragedy of the failure is compounded by the evidence that this miscarriage of justice could and should have been prevented, or at least corrected quickly, if those involved in the system had carried out their duties in a professional and/or competent manner. That they did not is due, in part at least, to the fact that Donald Marshall Jr. is a Native (Royal Commission, 1989:1).

The Royal Commissioners' principal finding in their report was that a two-tier system of justice existed in Nova Scotia—a system that responded differently depending on the status, wealth, and race of the person investigated (Royal Commission, 1989, Vol. 1:220). Donald Marshall Jr., as a Mi'kmaw, was on the bottom of the second tier (Turpel/Aki-Kwe, 1992). Marshall's second-class treatment was noted by the Commissioners, who found that Marshall's defence counsel failed to provide an adequate standard of professional representation to their client (Royal Commission, 1989). His lawyers, who had access to whatever financial resources they required, conducted no independent investigation, interviewed no Crown witnesses, and failed to ask for disclosure of the Crown's case against their client. The Marshall case demonstrates how, within the Canadian context, institutionalized racism, stereotyping, and social disadvantage may indeed contribute to miscarriages of justice.

EFFECTS OF WRONGFUL IMPRISONMENT

The negative effects of incarceration on those serving long terms of imprisonment have been well documented. According to Sykes (1958), the "pains of imprisonment" include the deprivation of liberty, goods and services, heterosexual relationships, autonomy, and security. However, not all prisoners experience these deprivations in the same way. In the case of the wrongly convicted, these negative effects are likely exacerbated by the miscarriage of justice that caused the prisoner's detention. In order to illustrate the effects of imprisonment on the wrongly convicted, as well as their families, we draw upon in-depth interviews with two Canadians who were wrongly convicted: Jamie Nelson was wrongly convicted of a sexual assault and served over three years in prison, while Christopher Bates served over five years for a murder he did not commit.

Identity

A prison sentence constitutes a "massive assault" on the identity of those imprisoned (Berger, 1963). This assault is said to be especially difficult on first-time inmates who must contend with the sudden and abrupt shift in their social situation (Schmid and Jones, 1991). In order to protect themselves and their identity, prisoners are often compelled to adopt a provisional or "suspended identity" during the period of their incarceration (Schmid and Jones, 1991). Jamie Nelson explains the importance of taking on a "new" and temporary identity in prison to ensure his survival:

> I had to build up that extra protection in prison. The other layer of Jamie
> wasn't there ... I couldn't be Jamie. I had to be someone that I'm not,
> somebody that will fight, somebody that will push, somebody that doesn't
> give a fuck. I had to wear certain hats to survive.

However, the situation becomes highly complex for those wrongly convicted. Not only are these individuals forced to take on a prison identity that defines them as criminals when they are in fact innocent, but also, they may be compelled to create a further identity, given the nature of their conviction. Jamie Nelson, who was wrongly convicted of a sexual assault, explains:

> I developed a second story right away. I certainly didn't want anybody to
> know I was in custody for violently raping a woman. My second story was
> "I beat somebody up that was trying to break into my house." I had to
> create a good enough lie that could explain away me going to prison for
> five to seven years ... so, it was a pretty grisly tale. I kicked him in the head
> a few times with steel boots, you know, I beat him up bad. That was my
> second story.

Nelson maintains that he could only show his true identity as an innocent man in the presence of parole board members who were to determine his fate:

> I had to wear a different hat when I was with the people that made the dif-
> ference [prison administration]. That's when I wore the Jamie hat—when I

was in front of the panel [prison administration]. I never once deviated from my claim of being innocent. And that was the only time that I got to wear that hat ... I could be Jamie, behind that door, because they could not release anything to the population. I knew I was safe in that room, in that environment. It was when I was living in the community as an inmate that I ... needed to wear those different hats.

Resistance

Being wrongly imprisoned appeared to produce an unfaltering resistance to all aspects of prison life. Throughout their incarceration, both Nelson and Bates resisted being labeled as a criminal and maintained their innocence to the prison administration. The constant pronouncement that they had been wrongly convicted was frequently perceived by authorities as an inability to adapt to the prison environment and an example of the denial of their offence. As Bates notes

> I was obsessed about my case ... I was wrongly convicted. [My case manager] kept on making reports, "the guy just denies and denies and denies, he keeps talking to you about his case, case, case"... My classification officer told me, "Jesus, you've got to stop doing this, you're never going to get out ... The parole board takes this as if you're denying the crime ... that you're not healed ... you're not fixed ... You have to admit to the crime in order to fix your problems." Sorry! I'm not guilty! I'm not denying. I'm just telling you the truth.

This unwavering resistance often created further difficulties. Nelson, who was wrongly convicted of sexual assault, maintained his credibility and status as an innocent man by refusing to apply for parole and refusing to participate in prison programs for sexual offenders. He explains:

> I was clinging to my innocence ... I started to get myself in trouble because I wouldn't even apply for parole. You don't have to apply, it's a damn privilege last time I looked at it. I didn't want it, because I'd have to be that guilty man. So I wouldn't even apply, but then that started to go negatively against me. [They would say to me] "What are you hiding?"

His refusal to self-identify as a "sex offender" and refusal to participate in prison sex-offender programs eventually led to his being placed in segregation:

> [The administration] told me that I was going to the sexual behaviour program ... and I said, no I wasn't. I made it clear to them that the only way

that they would have me go to that program was that somebody had to drag me to it. So they ended up keeping me in the hole six months.

Loss of Freedom and Consequences for the Prisoner's Family

The losses experienced by those wrongly convicted were profound. These included loss of freedom and the loss of their former identity and sense of self:

I lost me, is what I lost … my identity, who I am … The way I viewed life.

However, the most significant loss appeared to be the loss of family. Nelson, whose three children were apprehended by child protection authorities when his wife suffered a breakdown during his incarceration, explains the devastation of losing his family:

What it affected was my nuclear family—wife and my children, my family. It completely devastated that. We lost our home … I lost my kids … I lost the care and guidance and companionship of my dad. We were extremely close. I lost that … the hardest part about being an inmate was the loss of the family.

Furthermore, the hardships that accompany losing one's family through incarceration also affect the families themselves. Not only are they deprived of the emotional support of their loved one and forced to deal with the reality of having a family member in prison, but they also may be deprived of an essential source of income (Ferraro et al., 1983). As Nelson explains:

[My wife], she was left living with the reality of being single, with four children, a mortgage, hydro, the groceries, and other accoutrements that go with having four young children: one in school, needing to work, needing to deal with babysitters and, oh yeah, my husband's in prison.

The effects of a wrongful conviction and imprisonment are clearly devastating for the individual and his or her family. In response, the state has proposed several methods of redress.

STATE RESPONSES TO WRONGFUL CONVICTION: ISSUES OF REDRESS AND COMPENSATION

When a miscarriage of justice has occurred, the wrongly convicted have levels of recourse available to them in order to rectify the miscarriage of justice. These areas of redress include s. 690 of the *Criminal Code*, sometimes referred to as the "mercy clause," and financial compensation.

Section 690 of the Canadian *Criminal Code*

As it stands currently, s. 690 of the Canadian *Criminal Code* enables individuals who maintain that they have been wrongly convicted to apply for a review of their case. Canada relies on the Criminal Conviction Review Group of the Department of Justice to undertake such reviews. The criteria of eligibility regarding application for a conviction review are quite narrow. First, individuals who are eligible must have been convicted of an indictable or serious offence or sentenced under the dangerous- or long-term offender provisions of the *Criminal Code*. Second, these individuals must also have exercised all of their rights of appeal through the various courts, a process that can take many years. Finally, there must be new matters of significance that were not previously considered by the courts or arose after the conventional avenues of appeal had been exhausted (McFadyen, 2002).

The review process is lengthy and may take many years. Once all of the relevant information has been compiled and investigated, legal advice is prepared for the federal minister of Justice to make a decision. While the minister does not make decisions regarding guilt or innocence, if he or she is satisfied that a miscarriage of justice has occurred, a recommendation is made with respect to one of the following remedies: (1) ordering a new trial or hearing; (2) ordering a new appeal proceeding; or (3) referring any question to the Court of Appeal for its opinion.

Few applications are made each year to the minister of Justice. For example, in 1990, 27 applicants completed the review process, but none were offered remedies (Rosen, 1992). One reason for these small numbers may be the arduous application process involved. Moreover, some wrongfully convicted individuals have challenged the relevancy of applying to the government for "mercy." As David Milgaard questions: "Why ask the Canadian government to give you mercy for something that you haven't done? I refuse." (Milgaard, 2002).

Given the many impediments to filing an application, it is not surprising that the federal government has responded with amendments to this provision. Recently enacted, *Bill C-15A* represents an attempt to make the conviction review process more open and accountable (*Canada Gazette,* 2002). These amendments to the *Criminal Code* (sections 696.1–696.6)[i] will affect conviction review and seek to

- clearly state when a person is eligible for a review;
- specify the criteria under which a remedy may be granted;
- explain in regulations the process of review and how one applies for a review;
- expand the minister's power to include the review of summary convictions;
- provide investigative powers to those investigating cases on behalf of the minister, allowing investigators to compel witnesses to testify and documents to be produced.

In order to enhance independence of these reviews, a senior individual from outside the department will be appointed to oversee such applications (Department of Justice, 2000).

While these amendments will likely address some flaws in the system with regard to who is eligible for review and the criteria according to which a remedy is granted, it is questionable whether they will attain the "degree of transparency and public accountability" that the government is attempting to achieve. As a means of redress, a s. 690 review may still be inaccessible to many and limited in its application.

Commissions of Inquiry—Issues of Compensation

When a wrongful conviction occurs, individuals often attempt to seek financial compensation for the harm they have suffered. While the awarding of compensation is an attempt by the government to rectify a miscarriage of justice, such awards are small consolation for the devastation to family, credibility, livelihood, and mental health that a wrongful conviction entails. In Canada, historically it has been through the work of various royal commissions or commissions of inquiry that the judiciary and the public at large have become aware of flaws in the criminal justice process. To date, three commissions of inquiry have occurred in Canada to address the circumstances surrounding wrongful convictions. The Marshall Inquiry, which emanated from the wrongful conviction of Donald Marshall Jr., had a broad mandate to review and assess the administration of criminal justice in Nova Scotia and to "make recommendations" to help prevent such tragedies from happening in the future (Royal Commission, 1989). The report contained findings of fact as well as specific recommendations that addressed a variety of diverse issues including the role of the police and Crown attorneys; ways to ensure more equitable treatment of blacks and Aboriginals in the criminal justice system; and new mechanisms to deal with future cases of wrongful convictions (Royal Commission, 1989).

Both the Kaufman Inquiry into the wrongful conviction of Guy Paul Morin and the Sophonow Inquiry,[ii] were mandated to examine police and forensic investigations and criminal proceedings that may lead to wrongful convictions. Taken together, the inquiries recommended changes to police procedures regarding evidence gathering, reliance on jailhouse informants, and enhanced disclosure of evidence to the defence.

There have been other cases of wrongful convictions where compensation was awarded by the courts in the absence of commissions of inquiry. In these cases, provinces have recognized errors in the administration of justice and have awarded compensation. However, these awards are difficult to obtain and come only after many years of legal and political wrangling. Problems continue to plague this process with respect to decisions around who is considered deserving, of how much, and under what circumstances. Ultimately, financial compensation, regardless of the amount, does little to rectify the emotional, social, and financial damages wrought by a wrongful conviction.

CONCLUSION

It is clear that serious individual and systemic factors contribute to judicial errors in Canada. The complexities surrounding eyewitness error, false confessions, racial bias, jailhouse informants, and professional misconduct highlight the need for further in-depth research and study. Moreover, existing state response of redress appear unable to adequately confront and tackle these issues. For example, recent amendments to s. 690 of the *Criminal* Code in our view fall short of achieving their stated goals of enhanced transparency and accountability. Moreover, the commissions of inquiry that seek to address the issue of prevention are often disappointing, as their recommendations are rarely fully implemented. From time to time the media draw our attention to the issue of wrongful conviction, through highly controversial and publicized cases. However, attention to the issue is often fleeting and fails to result in long-term change. Piecemeal reforms introduced to address individual errors are insufficient. There must be greater accountability among agents of the criminal justice system as a whole. Programs of education will allow these individuals to become more aware of how the consequences of their actions may contribute to wrongful convictions. As well, the voices of the wrongly convicted themselves need to be heard. It is only by listening to their accounts and experiences that the true extent and impact of the problem will be understood.

DISCUSSION QUESTIONS

1. *Parole authorities often require a prisoner to accept responsibility for his or her crime before being granted parole. Can you explain the problems that this creates for prisoners serving time for crimes that they did not commit?*
2. *In light of what you have read in this chapter, do you think the Canadian criminal justice system does enough to prevent wrongful convictions?*
3. *Do you think that creating a review body independent of the courts and the federal Department of Justice would be a useful way of uncovering wrongful convictions?*

FURTHER READINGS

Anderson, B., and Anderson, D. 1998. *Manufacturing Guilt: Wrongful Convictions in Canada*. Halifax: Fernwood.

Huff, C.R., Rattner, A., and Sagarin, E. 1996. *Convicted but Innocent: Wrongful Conviction and Public Policy*. Thousand Oaks, California: Sage Publications.

Westervelt, S., and Humphrey, J. 2001. (Eds.) *Wrongly Convicted: Perspectives on Failed Justice*. New Jersey: Rutgers University Press.

REFERENCES

Armstrong, K., and Mills, S. Ryan. 2000, February 1. "Until I can be sure": Illinois is first state to suspend death penalty. *Chicago Tribune*, February 11.

Anderson, B., and Anderson, D. 1998. *Manufacturing Guilt: Wrongful Convictions in Canada*. Halifax: Fernwood.

Bayliss, D. 2002. *The Impact of Canadian Inquiries into Wrongful Conviction*. Paper presented at the conference on Wrongful Conviction: Experiences, Implications and Working towards Justice. Ottawa: University of Ottawa.

Berger, P. 1963. *Invitation to Sociology: A Humanistic Perspective*. Garden City, New York: Doubleday Anchor Books.

Canada Gazette. 2002. *Regulations Respecting Applications for Ministerial Review—Miscarriages of Justice*. Part 1, volume 136, no. 39. Ottawa: Queen's Printer.

Carrington, F. 1978. *Neither Cruel nor Unusual*. New Rochelle, New York: Arlington House.

Carvel, J. 1992. Many prisoners could be wrongly jailed. *Guardian Weekly*, April 5.

Cashmore, E. 1996. *Dictionary of Race and Ethnic Relations*. London: Routledge.

Castelle, G., and Loftus, E. 2001. Misinformation. In S. Westervelt. and J. Humphrey (Eds.), *Wrongly Convicted: Perspectives on Failed Justice*. New Jersey: Rutgers University Press.

Conners, E., Lundregan, T., Miller, N., and McEwan, T. 1996. *Convicted by Juries, Exonerated by Science: Case Studies in the Use of DNA Evidence to Establish Innocence after Trial*. Washington, DC: National Institute of Justice.

Cory, P. 2001. *Commission of Inquiry Regarding Thomas Sophonow*. Manitoba Justice, Province of Manitoba.

Department of Justice, Canada. 2000. *Highlights of the Omnibus Bill*. Ottawa: Communications Branch, Department of Justice.

Ferraro, K.J., Johnson, J.M., Jorgensen, S.R., and Bolton, F.G. 1983. Problems of prisoners' families: The hidden costs of imprisonment. *Journal of Family Issues*, 4(4):575–591.

Holmes, W. 2001. Who are the wrongly convicted on death row? In S. Westervelt and J. Humphrey (Eds.), *Wrongly Convicted: Perspectives on Failed Justice*. New Jersey: Rutgers University Press.

Huff, R., Rattner, A., and Saragin, E. 1986. Guilty until proven innocent: Wrongful conviction and public policy. *Crime and Delinquency*, 32(4):518–544.

Kaufman, F. 1998. *Commission on Proceedings Involving Guy Paul Morin*. Executive Summary and Recommendations. Toronto. Ministry of the Attorney General.

Leo, R., and Ofshe, R. 1998. The consequences of false confessions: Deprivation of liberty and miscarriages of justice in the age of psychological interrogation. *Journal of Criminology and Criminal Law,* 88:429–496.

Lockyer, J. 2002. *Disclosure of Evidence.* Paper presented at the conference on Wrongful Conviction: Experiences, Implications and Working towards Justice. University of Ottawa.

Loftus, E. 1979. *Eyewitness Testimony.* Cambridge: Harvard University Press.

MacFadyen, M. 2002. *Criminal Conviction Review Group: 690 Review Clause.* Paper presented at the conference on Wrongful Conviction: Experiences, Implications and Working towards Justice. University of Ottawa.

Macpherson, S.W. 1999. *The Stephen Lawrence Inquiry: Report of an Inquiry by Sir William Macpherson of Cluny.* London: The Stationery Office.

Martin, D. 2001. The police role in wrongful convictions: An international comparative study. In S. Westervelt and J. Humphrey (Eds.), *Wrongly Convicted: Perspectives on Failed Justice.* New Jersey: Rutgers University Press.

Milgaard, David. 2002. *The Voices of the Wrongly Convicted. Innocents behind Bars.* November 16. Association in Defence of the Wrongly Convicted. Toronto, Ontario.

Rosen, P. 1992. *Wrongful Convictions in the Criminal Justice System.* Ottawa: Library of Parliament, Parliamentary Research Branch.

Rosenberg, M. 2002. *Public Inquiries—the Process and the Value.* Innocents behind Bars. November 17. Association in Defence of the Wrongly Convicted. Toronto, Ontario.

Royal Commission on the Donald Marshall Jr. Prosecution. 1989. Commissioners' Report. Halifax: Nova Scotia.

Sanders, R. 1984. Helping the jury evaluate eyewitness testimony: The need for additional safeguards. *American Journal of Criminal Law,* 12:189–220.

Scheck, B., Neufeld, P., and Dwyer, J. 2000. *Actual Innocence.* New York: Doubleday.

Schmid, T. and Jones, R. 1991. Suspended identity: Identity transformation in a maximum security prison. *Symbolic Interaction,* 14 (4):415–432.

Schreck, A. 2002. Commissions of Inquiry. Paper presented at the Conference on Wrongful Conviction: Experiences, Implications and Moving towards Justice. University of Ottawa.

Sykes, G. 1958. *The Society of Captives.* Princeton, New Jersey: Princeton University Press.

Turpel/Aki-Kwe, M. 1992. Further Travails of Canada's Human Rights Record: The Marshall Case. In J. Manette (Ed.), *Elusive Justice: Beyond the Marshall Inquiry.* Halifax: Fernwood.

Wall, B. 1992. Analyzing the Marshall Commission: Why it was established and how it functioned. In J. Manette (Ed.), *Elusive Justice: Beyond the Marshall Inquiry.* Halifax: Fernwood.

Wells, G., and Bradfield, A. 1998. Good you identified the suspect: Feedback to eyewitnesses distorts their reports of the witnesses' experience. *Journal of Applied Psychology,* 83:360–376.

ENDNOTES

ⁱ These amendments came into effect on November 25, 2002.

ⁱⁱ Thomas Sophonow underwent three trials for the murder of Barbara Stoppel in 1981. After a mistrial and two successful appeals, Sophonow was acquitted and received an apology from the Saskatchewan government.

CHAPTER 20
Responding to Sex Offenders

INTRODUCTION

Sex offenders provoke more concern among members of the public than any other category of offender. This is particularly true when the crime is murder and the victim a child. When terrible crimes such as these occur they attract intense media attention, and politicians seek to make changes to the criminal justice system to ensure that society is adequately protected. Of the reforms launched in recent years, few have attracted as much attention as the concept of sex offender registries. The Canadian criminal justice system now has sex offender registries at the federal and provincial levels. In this chapter, Mary Campbell, a correctional policy expert, describes the registries that have been created in Canada within the past few years.

Sex Offender Registries: Sign Here Please, and Don't Forget to Stay in Touch
Mary E. Campbell of the Ontario Bar

Great public and political concern about sex offenders has led to a number of policies designed to reduce the risk to society. One such policy involves creation of a database, with a requirement that known sex offenders must register so that authorities can know where these ex-offenders are living. Prior to the mid-1980s, sex offender registries were a largely unknown concept in Canada and abroad—a handful of American states adopted registration schemes in the 1960s, but with little fanfare (e.g., California 1944, Nevada 1961, Ohio 1963, Alabama 1967). Sex offenders were tried, were sentenced, completed their sentences, and resumed some degree of anonymity in their daily life. The offender's criminal record would remain in existence, subject to any later pardon or form of executive clemency. In Canada, criminal records are maintained in the Canadian Police Information Centre (CPIC), an electronic database that can be accessed only by police for investigative or court proceedings. In a very real sense, CPIC functions as a "registry" of all criminal records.

But by the early 1990s, three events occurred, one in Canada and two in the United States, that changed the ways in which we thought about the reintegration of sex offenders into the community. The Canadian event was the tragic abduction and murder of a young boy named Christopher Stephenson in 1988. He was lured away from a shopping centre, sexually assaulted, and murdered by Joseph Fredericks, a man who had spent most of his life bouncing back and forth between the mental health and criminal justice systems and was a known sex offender. At the time of the murder, Mr. Fredericks was on a "registry." He had been released from penitentiary under the form of conditional release then known as "mandatory supervision" (now called "statutory release"), and was under a requirement to report to the police and to a parole supervisor. Thus Mr. Fredericks was effectively on two "registries": CPIC by virtue of having a criminal record, and the rosters of both Correctional Service Canada and the National Parole Board by virtue of being a conditionally released inmate. But one afternoon, he headed to the mall and committed his terrible crime. The community and the country were understandably outraged.

At the same time that the Coroner's Inquest into the death of Christopher Stephenson was unfolding in Ontario, two other pivotal events developed. The first was the passage in 1990 (in Washington State) of various highly publicized reforms to the management of sex offenders, including a sex offender registry. The other was the creation of a similar registry in 1994 in New Jersey following the death of young Megan Kanka at the hands of a convicted sex offender who had been living next door to the victim at the time of the crime. Taken together, these events contributed to growing public concern about the problem of sex offending in North America. There was enormous pressure in Canada to strengthen Canadian laws in relation to sex offenders and to adopt the American responses, including registries.

FEDERAL ACTION

In examining the Canadian response, it is important to bear in mind two key distinctions between the American and Canadian criminal justice systems. The first, as noted above, is the existence of CPIC, which has no national counterpart in the United States. Thus, Canada has since 1962 operated a national "registry" of all convicted offenders. Any police officer anywhere and anytime can enter an individual's name and obtain a record of all convictions, not just sex offences. Confirmation of the match can be made through fingerprints.

The other key distinction is the existence in Canada since 1949 of legislation that allows for the indefinite (or lifetime) incarceration of offenders who are deemed to present a serious risk to society. These provisions, now the Dangerous Offender (DO) sections of the *Criminal Code*, allow courts at the time of sentencing to order the indefinite incarceration of high-risk offenders, if certain criteria are met. The vast majority of those offenders who have been detained as DOs are sex offenders. Washington State had no such legislation when it adopted its various legislative measures in 1990 to better control sex offenders; the offender could be sentenced only to a fixed term of imprisonment.

Thus, while there was significant pressure to adopt the American reforms, an examination of the Canadian system indicated that there was less need to do so. Federal, provincial, and territorial ministers responsible for criminal justice nonetheless asked their officials to examine ways in which the Canadian system could be improved. An interdepartmental working group of Justice, Health, and Solicitor General officials formed in 1993 undertook an extensive review of issues relating to child sexual abuse. A federal/provincial/territorial working group on high-risk offenders was formed the same year and developed a 16-point action plan. This resulted in

- the development of a "screening system" for use by voluntary sector agencies and other groups working with children, to better screen potential volunteers and employees who would be working with children;
- the creation of a "Long-Term Offender" designation in the *Criminal Code* to allow postsentence community supervision of sex offenders for up to 10 years, recognizing that sex offender recidivism tends to occur over longer periods of time than non-sex offending;
- amendments to the Dangerous Offender provisions to streamline and focus the proceedings; and
- the creation of a new "peace bond" in s. 810.1 of the *Criminal Code*, to permit supervision of persons suspected of being at risk to commit a sex offence against a child.

The specific issue of creating a sex offender registry along the lines of the U.S. models was researched, reviewed, and rejected.

PROVINCIAL REGISTRIES

The public and political pressure to create a national sex offender registry did not, however, disappear. By 2001, six provinces had created or announced their intention to create a registry. The registries were largely directed at sex offenders, though in at least one case, the registry was aimed at "high-risk offenders," however that was to be defined. Even among those aimed at sex offenders, however, there wasn't complete consistency about what should be included.

Ontario was the only province to fully operationalize a registry system. *"Christopher's Law,"* named after Christopher Stephenson, was proclaimed in force on April 23, 2001. The preamble to the act stated its purpose:

> The people of Ontario believe that there is a need to ensure the safety and security of all persons in Ontario and that police forces require access to information about the whereabouts of sex offenders in order to assist them in the important work of maintaining community safety. The people of Ontario further believe that a registry of sex offenders will provide the information and investigative tools that their police forces require in order to prevent and solve crimes of a sexual nature.

The act requires any person living in Ontario and who has been convicted of a specified sex offence to register with local police. Other persons required to register are those found guilty of such an offence but given an absolute or conditional discharge, and those persons charged but found not criminally responsible on account of mental disorder.

Offenders have 15 days in which to register after moving to the province, completing their custodial sentence, or their final court appearance, if it results in a noncustodial disposition. There is no obligation in the act for police, courts, or corrections officials to notify offenders of the registration requirement. However, failure to register (without lawful excuse) is punishable on first offence by a fine of up to $25,000 and/or imprisonment for up to one year, and on second or subsequent offence by a fine of up to $25,000 and/or imprisonment for up to two years less a day. Depending on the nature of the "registrable offence," the required registration period is either for 10 years or life. Reregistration is required if the offender moves and, in any case, annually. Information on the registry is intended primarily for police use, but can be used as the basis for public notification of the presence of a sex offender in the community. Anecdotal reports so far indicate a high uptake in initial registration.

British Columbia passed the *Sex Offender Registry Act* in April 2001 just prior to dissolution of the legislature for an election. The new government indicated its intention to pursue similar legislation, but as of the fall of 2002 had not done so. The April 2001 legislation was intended to proceed in two phases. Phase One was to compile in one database information from courts and corrections databases about sex offenders. Phase Two was to include mandatory registration by convicted sex offenders—the same catchment as Ontario but also extended to persons with outstanding charges for sex offences or convicted by a court outside Canada, as well as young offenders. The list of sex offences was also broader, including nonsexual offences with a sexual motive or nature, such as break and enter, trespassing at night, criminal harassment, and kidnapping and forcible confinement. The objectives of the act were summarized in s. 3, which stated that the minister "may establish a sex offender registry for the purposes of (a) law enforcement, (b) crime prevention, and (c) public safety."

Alberta also announced its intention to create a registry, although references were to a somewhat ambiguous "high-risk offender" registry as well as to a "pedophile registry." On May 15, 2001, the premier announced that a registry of convicted offenders would be established "if the concept is deemed feasible following a two-week review" by the provincial solicitor general. As with many other registries, the impetus for Alberta's declaration came from a case where a young girl had been murdered. As with many such crimes, however, the person charged was a family friend, with no reported record of sexual offences. The utility of a sex offender registry was therefore somewhat unclear.

Two weeks passed with no further announcement, but the province's continuing interest in the matter was evidenced by a May 31, 2001, press release from a meeting of Western premiers:

> Premiers expressed concern about violent sexual offenders. They highlighted the importance of providing the police with the tools they need to protect our communities—and particularly our children—from high-risk sex offenders. They noted that since sexual offenders often move, there is a need to keep track of their movements. Premiers agreed that a national sex offender registry would be the most effective solution to this problem. In the absence of a federal commitment to a national registry, Premiers agreed that provinces and territories should take action on this matter.

As of the fall of 2002, Alberta had not created a sex offender registry, but had instead created a "high-risk offender Web page." Offenders who have completed their sentence but are considered to pose a risk of significant harm to the public may have their photograph and personal information posted on the site by Solicitor General Alberta. The offender is not afforded any hearing or other opportunity to contest the notification. The information may remain on the Web site indefinitely, although offenders may apply after one year to have it removed, if they are able to demonstrate they are no longer a threat to the community.

In addition to Ontario and the western provinces, Nova Scotia also signaled its interest in creating a registry. By the time federal, provincial, and territorial Justice ministers met in September 2001 at their annual meeting, there was even more consensus among the provinces and territories that a national registry was needed, even though there was less than complete agreement on the precise details.

OTHER JURISDICTIONS

Similar pressure had peaked a few years earlier in the United States. As Travis notes, there were only eight states with registration schemes in the mid-1980s, but by 1998 all states had sex offender registry legislation (2002:22). The *Jacob Wetterling Crimes Against Children and Sexually Violent Offender Registration Program* (*Wetterling Act*) established the minimum national standards for registration and community notification, with states free to tailor particular requirements. But it is important to examine the details of this apparent unanimous support across the country. Travis explains: "the 1994 *Crime Act* required each state to enact a sex offender registration law within three years or lose 10 percent of its federal funding for criminal justice programs." (2002:24.) Consequently, it is difficult to know how many states adopted registry legislation because of a firm belief in its effectiveness or because of the loss of funding upon failure to do so.

The United Kingdom also enacted sex offender registration in 1997. Persons convicted of specified sex offences are required to register for periods of time linked to sentence length. While the registry is not proactively available for public access, police have the authority to use the information from the registry to issue public warnings that a particular sex offender is living in a particular neighbourhood. Within a year of the legislation coming into force, 94.7 percent of those required to register had done so (Plotnikoff and Woolfson, 2000). By the time of the first evaluation in 2000, this already high rate was even higher, with only 4 percent of the 8,600 individuals required to register being in noncompliance.

NATIONAL CANADIAN SEX OFFENDER REGISTRY

In the fall of 2002, the federal government announced its intention to create a national sex offender registry, based in CPIC and administered and enforced locally by police. At the time of tabling the necessary legislation in Parliament, on December 11, 2002, the registry was designed to be accessible by police only, to provide a rapid tool to investigate sex offences by identifying possible suspects known to reside near the offence occurrence. Like sex offender registries elsewhere, it was designed as an offence-based system, with no assessment of individual risk. Sex offences that may trigger a registration order are listed in law. After conviction for one of the specified offences, the Crown attorney can apply to the court for a registration order; the test for countering the application is "gross disproportionality" relative to the protection of society and the administration of justice.

The length of the registration is tied to the maximum penalty available for the offence, with up to lifetime registration where the offence carries a maximum of life or the offender has a prior sex offence. Offenders must reregister annually while the order is in force or whenever they change address. Offenders are able to apply for a judicial review at set times during the order, if they wish to argue that it should be lifted. It is an offence to fail to register after an order has been issued. It is also an offence for anyone to disclose information from the registry for any purpose other than a police investigation.

Research on Effectiveness

In drawing conclusions from the experiences of the various registries, it is important to know that they vary in terms of their scope and purpose. These differences include who is registered, the process for registration, and enforcement mechanisms. The purposes of different registries also vary and include crime prevention through increased tracking of offenders in the community, including using the registration information as a basis for community notification of offenders' whereabouts; more efficient criminal investigation when a crime has occurred; and the alleged deterrent effect that ostensibly arises from knowing that registration will be one of the consequences of committing certain crimes.

To date, the research has shown a fairly high rate of initial compliance in registering when a program has been created. However, the evidence also reveals that there is little systematic follow-up to verify addresses and other particulars, and that enforcement is almost entirely reactive. There is limited and only anecdotal evidence of crime prevention or investigation benefits. The costs of sex offender registries have generally not been tracked, as registries have usually been implemented within existing resources. This is often cited as a reason for failure to implement adequate verification, monitoring, or enforcement measures (Plotnikoff and Woolfson, 2000). In light of this, high rates of initial compliance with registration requirements are not informative as to program effectiveness.

Legal and Operational Challenges

Sex offender registries face a number of operational and legal challenges. Operationally, police resources are required in order to confirm registration information and monitor its continuing accuracy. It may be difficult to take much comfort from a statement from Ontario about its registry: "It will keep [offenders] in close contact with police. At least once a year, the police will see them." The highest risk offenders may be least likely to comply with registration orders and/or will adopt evasive techniques such as "commuting" to commit their crimes at a sufficient distance from their residence. Most registries also make no effort to distinguish high- from low-risk offenders, as is the case with an offence-based approach. And registries provide only a control function, unless they are paired with some form of ongoing treatment.

With respect to legal challenges, Canadian sex offender registries are likely to find themselves subject to ongoing *Charter* scrutiny. Examples of questions that might be raised are:

- s. 6 (mobility): Does a requirement to register or reregister infringe an offender's mobility rights?
- s. 7 (life, liberty, and security): Are there due process issues raised by the nature of the registration hearing or hearings relating to alleged failure to register?
- s. 9 (arrest/detention): Is a requirement to register at a police station a form of detention that may be open to challenge?

- s. 11(h) (double jeopardy): Is the imposition of a registration order a form of double punishment, if the offender has already been sentenced for the offence?
- s. 12 (cruel and unusual punishment): Is registration cruel and unusual if the registry process does not distinguish on the basis of individual risk and the offender is an extremely low risk to reoffend?
- s. 15 (equality): Because Aboriginal Canadians are overrepresented in the criminal justice system, are they more likely to be affected by registration requirements, thus breaching s. 15 equality rights?

In assessing these questions, courts may be guided in part by arguments as to whether registries are a form of punishment or, as they are generally framed, legitimate tools of crime investigation and prevention. Courts will also examine recidivism rates of sex offenders. For example, if a court were to find that a registry breached a *Charter* right, it could nonetheless be found to be valid under s. 1 of the *Charter* (demonstrable justification) if it were shown, amongst other things, that sex offenders have a high rate of reoffending and thus pose a substantial danger to the community.

Given the longer history of registries in the United States, litigation has been extensive there. The matter was finally put before the U.S. Supreme Court in November 2002, in the case of *Connecticut Department of Public Safety et al. v. John Doe et al.* The Connecticut sex offender registry required that the offender register following conviction, with no court hearing on the matter. In addition, the legislation required that the registry be placed on a publicly accessible Web site. Information on the Web site included name, address, photograph, and description. The public can search the Web site by entering a town or zip code. The argument advanced by John Doe was that the Connecticut scheme stigmatized him as a danger to public safety without providing notice and an opportunity to be heard as to whether he does in fact pose such a danger. While the Court of Appeal accepted his argument, the Supreme Court reversed the decision and upheld the legislation. In a companion case, *Smith et al. v. Doe et al.*, the Court also upheld similar Alaskan legislation that had been challenged on the basis of its retroactive application.

While the outcomes of these cases will be instructive for Canadian authorities, there are significant differences between them and the Ontario and Canadian schemes, in terms of the availability of a hearing, the test used at the hearing, and public access to the registry.

CONCLUSION

Sex offender registries are the latest in a series of recent initiatives aimed at controlling or preventing the behaviour of certain categories of offenders. While popular with many groups, their effectiveness is not yet clear from

252 PART FIVE • CURRENT ISSUES IN CRIMINAL JUSTICE

evaluations done to date, nor is their legal viability fully assessed by the courts. In determining effectiveness, it is important to bear in mind distinct differences among the various registry models and the purposes behind them. Some are narrowly cast, with access only by police and only for the purpose of quickly investigating a suspected crime. Others, particularly those that are disclosed to the public, are ostensibly oriented toward crime prevention. And considerations of effectiveness might also take into account whether treatment is provided to the registrant or whether only surveillance is provided.

Questions of fairness and legal rights are also raised in the different models, as some operate automatically upon conviction for specified sex offences while others provide a court hearing. These issues are important on their own, but also because they are linked to the question of risk in individual cases: few registries allow for an assessment of the current dangerousness of the individual offender, but rather presume a level of risk based on the offence that was committed.

Finally, sex offender registries should be evaluated as one element in a continuum of responses that could be made to the problem of sex offenders. The effectiveness and legality of registries should ultimately be assessed not only on their own merits but also in comparison to other actions that could be taken to prevent and respond to sex offending. Comprehensive, research-based strategies may provide the best means of responding to public concerns about these offenders.

DISCUSSION QUESTIONS

1. *In your opinion, are sex offender registries a good idea or not? Do you think they are a reasonable response to the problem of sex offenders?*
2. *Some American states permit members of the public to access information about someone's criminal record from the criminal record database. What problems can you see arising from this expanded access to the database?*
3. *Do you think that there should be a limit on the amount of time that an individual has to register in these sex offender registries, or should they carry lifetime reporting requirements?*

FURTHER READINGS

Coflin, J. 2001. *Sex Offender Registration Programs—A Status Report*. Ottawa: Solicitor General Canada.

Jenkins, P. 1998. *Moral Panic: Changing Concepts of the Child Molester in Modern America*. New Haven, CT: Yale University Press.

Petrunik, M. 2003. The hare and the tortoise: Dangerousness and sex offender policy in the United States and Canada. *Canadian Journal of Criminology and Criminal Justice*, in press.

Petrunik, M. 2002. Managing unacceptable risk: Sex offenders, community response, and social policy in the United States and Canada. *International Journal of Offender Therapy and Comparative Criminology*, 46:483–512.

REFERENCES

Statutes

An Act in Memory of Christopher Stephenson, to Establish and Maintain a Registry of Sex Offenders to Protect Children and Communities ("Christopher's Law") S.O., ch. 1, 2000.
Jacob Wetterling Crimes Against Children and Sexually Violent Offender Registration Program (Wetterling Act) 42 U.S.C. 14071 (1994 & Supp. V 1999).
Sex Offenders Act 1997 (U.K.), 1997, c. 51.

Cases

Connecticut Department of Public Safety et al. v. John Doe et al., 538 U.S. ___ (2003).
Smith et al. v. John Doe et al., 538 U.S. ___ (2003).

Texts

Travis, J. 2002. Invisible punishment: An instrument of social exclusion. In M. Mauer and M. Chesney-Lind (Eds.), *Invisible Punishment: The Collateral Consequences of Mass Imprisonment*. New York: The New Press.
Plotnikoff, J. and Woolfson, R. 2000. *Where Are They Now? An Evaluation of Sex Offender Registration in England and Wales*, Police Research Series, Paper 126. London: Home Office.

CHAPTER 21
Responding to Intimate Partner Violence

INTRODUCTION

Violence against intimate partners has become one of the most important problems that the criminal justice system attempts to address. It is only in recent years, with the creation of victimization surveys, such as the 1993 Violence Against Women Survey and the 1999 General Social Survey on Victimization conducted by Statistics Canada, that Canadians have come to appreciate the full scope of the problem. In this chapter, two experts in the field of law and sociology review the principal criminal law responses to this problem.

Criminal Law Responses to Intimate Partner Violence

Gillian Blackell, Department of Justice Canada, and
Holly Johnson, Canadian Centre for Justice Statistics[i]

Intimate partner violence affects a substantial number of victims each year in Canada and commands the attention and resources of the criminal justice, health, and social service systems. For the purposes of this article, intimate partner relationships include marital or common-law spousal as well as dating relationships, including same-sex relationships.

In 1999, Statistics Canada estimated, through results of a national telephone survey, that 220,000 women and 177,000 men had been victims of spousal violence in that year alone (spousal violence does not include violence in dating relationships) (Pottie Bunge and Locke, 2000). Approximately 690,000 women and 550,000 men reported violence by a spouse (both common-law and marital partners) in the preceding five-year period. During the decade 1991–2000, 846 women and 210 men were murdered by intimate partners. Police noted a history of family violence in over half of all spousal homicide cases during this time period (Pottie Bunge, 2002).

Although women and men report similar prevalence rates of spousal violence committed against them, the impacts and consequences differ sharply for female and male victims (Johnson and Pottie Bunge, 2001). At least 80 percent of victims who require medical attention, are hospitalized, suffer lost productivity, or fear their lives are endangered by a violent spouse are women (see Figure 21.1). Women also outnumber men by a ratio of 4 to 1 as victims of intimate partner homicide.

Public awareness of intimate partner violence is relatively recent, dating back to the early 1980s. Domestic violence and sexual assaults in intimate relationships have historically been viewed as "private matters" that did not necessarily warrant intervention from the criminal justice system. Over the past two decades, however, a wide range of interventions including legislation, policies, and support services have been implemented by federal, provincial, and

Figure 21.1 *Victims of Serious Spousal Violence*

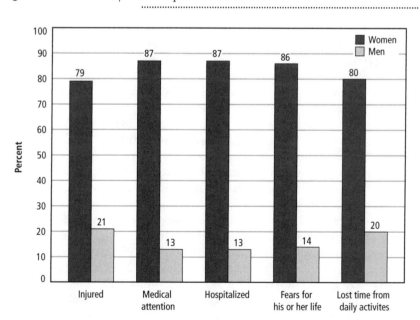

Source: *1999 General Social Survey,* Statistics Canada.

municipal governments as well as community organizations in Canada to respond to the problem of intimate partner violence.

These include shelters and other supports for victims, treatment for abusive partners, interagency collaboration at the community level, prevention and public awareness campaigns, specialized court processes, changes to both the criminal and civil law, and zero-tolerance or mandatory charging or prosecution policies for police and Crown prosecutors. Without exploring the full range of interventions to address intimate partner violence, this article provides a brief summary of some of the means by which the criminal and civil law have been utilized to improve the legal response to this problem.

One of the primary tools in responding to intimate partner violence involves changes to criminal law policies and procedures. While the *Criminal Code* does not contain any specific offence of domestic or intimate partner violence, a wide range of criminal offences cover violence within relationships. These include assault, sexual assault, homicide (murder, manslaughter), criminal negligence, forcible confinement, uttering threats, and criminal harassment (commonly known as stalking). The *Criminal Code* also provides procedural protections, preventative measures, and sentencing principles that are relevant. The following subsections briefly examine some of the more significant responses of the criminal law to intimate partner violence.

CRIMINAL HARASSMENT

The offence of criminal harassment was enacted in 1993 following several heinous incidents of estranged male partners harassing and stalking female victims, eventually leading to their death. Laws prohibiting loitering or uttering threats had been in place for some time, but these did not address the types of harassing behaviours that were likely to be used by stalkers. Police were able to lay charges only for minor offences and only after perpetrators made overt threats or assaults on victims.

The criminal harassment offence under section 264 of the *Criminal Code* enables police to intervene if the behaviour is repetitive or threatening and causes victims to reasonably fear for their safety or that of someone known to them, even in response to seemingly innocuous acts such as watching someone's place of residence or leaving unwanted gifts on their doorstep. This offence, modeled on similar offences in the United States, is particularly relevant in circumstances of intimate partner abuse, where the risk of violence or the escalation of violence is often heightened during or immediately following separation. For example, according to the 1999 General Social Survey (GSS) on Victimization, 40 percent of women and 32 percent of men in violent relationships indicated that the violence continued after separation. In 24 percent of cases where violence existed after separation, the violence became more serious, and in 39 percent of cases, the violence commenced after separation. Moreover, women have a heightened risk of spousal homicide after marital separation; ex-marital partners are responsible for 28 percent of all spousal homicides perpetrated against women, but only 10 percent of homicides perpetrated against men (Hotton, 2001).

A 1996 amendment to the *Criminal Code* included a prohibition of firearms upon a conviction for criminal harassment. A 1997 amendment states that a conviction for criminal harassment while under a restraining order is a confounding factor that should be reflected in sentencing (s. 264(5)), and homicide committed while committing an offence of criminal harassment is deemed to be first-degree murder irrespective of whether the murder was planned and deliberate (s. 231(6)). The maximum penalty for criminal harassment upon indictment was recently increased from five to ten years (July 2002). As a result, offenders convicted for criminal harassment offences can be subjected to dangerous-offender applications under s. 759 of the *Criminal Code*.

The number of criminal harassment incidents reported to police in a sample of 95 police departments in Canada between 1995 and 2001 shows that about three-quarters are directed at women and half of these involve intimate partners.[ii] Although estranged wives make up the largest group reporting intimate partner stalking, 7 percent of incidents involved current partners, which suggests that, in many cases, stalking begins while the couple are still living together. A strong association has been found to exist between stalking and intimate partner violence. Tjaden and Thoennes (1998) found, in a large random sample survey of American women, that 81 percent of women who reported being stalked by intimate partners were also assaulted by the same partner. One in five said the stalking occurred before the relationship had ended and one-third said it occurred both before and after separation. Studies have also found stalking to be a precursor to intimate partner homicide (McFarlane et al., 1999).

Rates of police-reported intimate partner stalking increased over the 1995–2001 period (see Figure 21.2). However, this should not be interpreted necessarily as reflecting a rise in the incidence of stalking. It is plausible that, in the early years following the implementation of a new law, awareness rises among both police and the public, and these offences are reported to police and recorded in official statistics in increasingly greater numbers.

PREVENTIVE AND PROTECTIVE MEASURES

The *Criminal Code* provides, under s. 810, for the issuance of recognizances (peace bonds or protective court orders) by a justice of the peace or a judge to protect against possible criminal offences. These require alleged offenders to adhere to conditions, such as staying away from the victim's residence or place of work and surrendering any firearms they may possess. A breach of conditions is an offence under the *Criminal Code*. Although the standard of proof is a civil standard, (on a balance of probabilities there may be future violence) the application requires a court appearance, which can be intimidating and time consuming (Bala and Ringseis, 2002:2).

Figure 21.2 *Number of Criminal Harassment Incidents Reported to Police by Intimate Partners, 1995–2001*

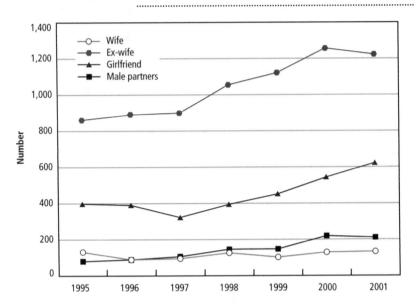

Source: Revised Uniform Crime Reporting Survey, Statistics Canada.

In 1995, these provisions were amended to facilitate obtaining peace bonds, to make them more effective, and to increase the maximum penalty for a breach from six months to two years (s. 811). In light of pro-charge and prosecution policies in domestic violence cases, peace bonds are generally not used if there are reasonable and probable grounds to arrest the abuser for a criminal offence.

In addition to peace bonds, the *Criminal Code* provides the justice or judge at a bail hearing with the power to make recognizance orders or undertakings with conditions to prevent the accused from communicating with or harassing the victim or witness, or other relevant conditions. In response to concerns regarding violent occurrences during the 24-hour period between arrest and the bail hearing in domestic violence cases, the *Code* was amended in 1999 to permit a justice of the peace who remands arrested persons into custody to order the person not to communicate with any witness or other person between the time he or she is detained and his or her first bail hearing.

Following the mass killings in Montreal on December 6, 1989, public pressure to update gun control legislation was significantly increased. In 1991, changes to the Firearms Acquisition Certificates (FACs), such as screening checks and safety courses for FAC applicants, were introduced. Then in 1995, the federal government introduced the *Firearms Act*, which provided for licensing possession of firearms, a national registration system for all firearms, and a mandatory minimum sentence of four years of prison and a lifetime prohibition against the possession of a restricted or prohibited firearm upon conviction of specific violent offences, including sexual assault with a weapon and aggravated sexual assault. The registration of firearms permits police to be alerted to the presence of firearms in scenes of family violence. Moreover, in issuing FACs, risk factors associated with incidents of family violence must be considered, and spousal consent is required.

PROCEDURAL MEASURES

In 1991, the Supreme Court of Canada struck down provisions of the sexual assault legislation that prevented a defendant from introducing evidence regarding the complainant's sexual history. In *R. v. Seaboyer* (1991), the court struck down s. 276 of the *Criminal Code* on the basis that it violated an accused's *Charter* right to a fair trial. Subsequent to this decision, new "rape shield" legislation was introduced in 1992. It provided a test to determine whether evidence of a complainant's previous sexual activity could be admitted at trial and, in addition, provided a definition of consent for the purposes of the sexual assault provisions. The amendments also clearly set out that the defence of mistaken belief in consent could not be used if the belief stemmed from the accused's drunkenness, recklessness, or wilful blindness, or if the accused did not take reasonable steps to determine whether the victim was, in fact, consenting. The new "rape shield" legislation was upheld as constitutional by the Supreme Court of Canada in *R. v. Darrach* (2000).

In 1995, the Supreme Court handed down another significant decision in relation to procedural protections for victims of sexual assault offences. In *R. v. O'Connor* (1995), the Court ruled that counseling or other personal records of sexual assault victims could be ordered to be produced for the accused's defence in criminal court proceedings. The Court outlined a two-stage process to determine admissibility of the records. In response to substantial concerns raised by the *O'Connor* case, sections 278.1 to 278.91 of the *Criminal Code* (production of records provisions) were introduced in 1997, requiring an accused who seeks the personal records of a complainant or witness to satisfy the judge that the records are "likely relevant" to an issue at trial. Once this is established, the judge would decide whether to order the records released to the accused based on a two-stage process. In each stage of examination, the judge must balance the *Charter* rights of both the accused and the victim or witness. These provisions were challenged in more than 50 cases across the country. However, the Supreme Court upheld the constitutionality of these sections in the case of *R. v. Mills* (1999).

In 1999, other changes to the *Criminal Code* included:

- expanding the scope of victim impact statements and requiring that these statements be considered by courts and review boards following a verdict of not criminally responsible on account of mental disorder

- extending to victims of sexual or violent crime up to age 18 protections that restrict personal cross-examination by self-represented accused persons
- requiring police officers and judges to consider the victim's safety in all bail decisions
- allowing victims and witnesses with a mental or physical disability to have a support person present while giving testimony, and
- making it easier for victims and witnesses to participate in trials by permitting the judge to ban the publication of their identity where it is necessary for the proper administration of justice.

In 1995, the sentencing provisions of the *Criminal Code* were amended to provide that where an offender, in committing the offence, abuses his spouse or child or a position of trust or authority, this shall be considered an aggravating factor for sentencing purposes. Amendments were also made to the restitution provisions of the *Code* to entitle a victim to seek restitution for actual and reasonable expenses for moving out of the offender's home to avoid bodily harm.

BATTERED WOMEN AND SELF-DEFENCE

Sections 34 to 37 of the *Criminal Code* govern the law on self-defence. According to these provisions, a person who is attacked is not criminally responsible for using a reasonable or proportionate amount of force against his or her attacker. A person can also use defensive force against an apprehended assault or attack because a threat to apply force constitutes an assault under the *Code*. The law also permits the use of reasonable force to defend someone else from harm or death. However, in all cases, the law does not permit the use of excessive or unreasonable force. A successful claim of self-defence results in an acquittal for the assault or homicide.

Prior to the Supreme Court of Canada's groundbreaking decision in *R. v. Lavallee* (1990), the law of self-defence in Canada was difficult to apply successfully in cases where battered women killed their abusive partners in self-defence. For instance, in *R. v. Whynot* (1983), the accused was charged with first-degree murder for the killing of her abusive partner when he was passed out in his truck. Evidence revealed that the accused had suffered brutal abuse at the hands of the deceased for five years and acted only after he had threatened to kill her son. The Nova Scotia Court of Appeal rejected the plea of defensive force because the attack against the accused's son was not "imminent." The requirement of imminence was reinforced subsequently by the Supreme Court of Canada in *Reilly v. The Queen* (1984).

However, in 1990, the Supreme Court handed down the *Lavallee* ruling, which was significant for a number of reasons: (1) in regards to the admissibility of expert evidence related to "battered women's syndrome," which in turn helped to dispel myths about why battered women remain in violent relationships; (2) the impact of this evidence on the "imminency require-ment"; and (3) the court's acceptance that the women's experiences and per-spectives in relation to self-defence may be different from those of men and must now inform the "objective" standard of the "reasonable person" (*R. v. Malott* (1998)).

Lyn Lavallee was charged with the murder of her violent common-law partner, Kevin Rust, who had regularly subjected her to physical abuse. She shot him in the back of the head as he was leaving the room after he beat her and told her that if she didn't kill him he would kill her when their guests left. Expert evidence demonstrated that the accused had been terrorized by the deceased and that, as a battered woman, her actions were based on a "reason-able" belief that she had no other option but to shoot the deceased. In order to explain the perspective of the accused, the expert referred to the "battered woman syndrome," which is based on the work of Dr. Lenore Walker (1979).

Dr. Walker identified three phases of the cycle of domestic violence. The first phase, known as the "tension building phase" is characterized by a series of minor assaults and verbal abuse. During the second phase, known as the "acute battering phase," the batterer is unable to control the rage and severely beats the woman. This is followed by the third phase, that of "kindness and contrite loving behaviour"; the batterer behaves kindly toward the woman, asking her forgiveness and promising never to repeat the violence. This phase provides the woman with positive reinforcement for staying in the relation-ship. To explain why women remain in violent relationships after the cycle has been repeated more than once, Dr. Walker argued that battered women are psychologically paralyzed because they have learned from the repeated beat-ings that they cannot control their circumstances. This is known as "learned helplessness."

Based on the "battered woman syndrome," the expert testified that Ms Lavallee's actions constituted the final desperate act of someone who sincerely believed that she would be killed that night. The jury in the lower court acquitted Ms Lavallee. The decision was appealed all the way to the Supreme Court of Canada, which decided unanimously to acquit her of the charge of murder. The Court ruled that expert testimony is admissible to assist in com-prehending the experiences and perspectives of the battered woman. The evi-dence helps dispel myths that battered women are not really beaten as badly as they claim, otherwise they would have left the relationship, or that women enjoy being beaten, that they have a masochistic strain in them. The court also held that expert testimony assists the fact-finder in assessing the ability of an accused to perceive danger from her partner, which speaks to the deter-mination of the reasonableness of the victim's fear and her mental state at the time she committed the lethal act of violence.

Although the requirement of "imminent danger" was not technically before the Supreme Court of Canada in this case, the majority noted that requiring "a battered woman to wait until the physical attack is 'underway' before her apprehensions can be validated by law would ... be tantamount to sentencing her to 'murder by installment'" (p.883). Moreover, the practical application of the expert evidence in the *Lavallee* case resulted in a dismissal of the imminency requirement.

While the *Lavallee* decision was lauded by those who work with abused women, some feminist scholars expressed concern that it might lead to the "syndromization" of women's experiences as had been the case in the United States (Boyle, 1990; Grant, 1991; Comack, 1993; Noonan, 1993; Shaffer, 1997; Sheehy, 2001). The concerns regarding the battered women syndrome included the risk that this would portray battered women as dysfunctional, deviant, and even pathological. Likewise, concerns were also expressed regarding the creation of a new stereotype of the "authentic" battered woman, thereby restricting the applicability of the syndrome evidence to women who fought back or did not otherwise fit the passive victim profile. While some authors indicate that cases subsequent to *Lavallee* have fallen prey to the "syndromization" of battered women (Shaffer, 1997; Sheehy, 2001), the Supreme Court was careful in both *Lavallee* and in *Malott* to indicate that the battered women's syndrome is not a defence in itself but rather a tool to understanding the "reasonableness" of a battered woman's actions.

Following *Lavallee*, in October 1995 the minister of Justice and the solicitor general of Canada established the Self Defence Review (SDR) to discover whether any women who had been convicted prior to or after *Lavallee* should have benefited from a self-defence claim. The SDR, under the lead of Judge Ratushny, reviewed the cases of women convicted of murdering their intimate partners. The SDR Final Report, released in July 1997, recommended relief in seven of these cases and included recommendations for reforming the self-defence provision in the *Criminal Code*. In the end, redress was granted in just five of the cases examined, and no woman was actually released from jail as a result of the SDR (Trotter, 2001).

Numerous commentators have indicated that, despite the promise of the *Lavallee* decision, few battered women have subsequently been acquitted for killing their abusers in self-defence (Sampson, 2001; Shaffer, 1997; Sheehy, 2001). This is attributed to the mandatory minimum sentence for murder, which encourages battered women to plead guilty to manslaughter (which has no minimum) rather than gamble on an acquittal and risk a minimum of imprisonment for life (s. 235 of the *Criminal Code*) with a minimum of 10 years imprisonment before eligibility for parole (s. 745) (Noonan, 1993; Sampson, 2001, Shaffer, 1997; Sheehy, 2001). Despite this barrier, *Lavallee* has contributed significantly to raising awareness of the realities of battered women among the judiciary and other criminal justice personnel and is regularly cited in cases. Moreover, the courts have used *Lavallee* and the sentencing principles in s. 718.2 of the *Code* to consider the spousal abuse suffered by battered women who kill their abusers in issuing relatively minimal sentences in manslaughter cases (see *R. v. Gladue* (1999)).

DOMESTIC VIOLENCE POLICIES AND COURTS

One cornerstone of the criminal justice response to intimate partner violence has been the implementation by 1986 of some directives or guidelines to police and crown prosecutors with respect to spousal violence cases. These are referred to as pro- or mandatory charging and prosecution policies. They generally require police to lay charges in cases of spousal violence where there are legal grounds to do so. Some policies require Crown prosecutors to prosecute spousal violence cases regardless of the victim's desire to proceed with prosecution. The aims of these directives or policies are to ensure that spousal assaults are treated as a "criminal," rather than a "private," matter and to remove the responsibility and blame for pressing charges from the victims, thereby reducing the potential for retaliation. In addition, the policies send a message to abusers that spousal violence is a crime, and they help ensure that victims are supported and offenders are treated seriously by the criminal justice system. In April 2003, a federal–provincial–territorial working group released a report reviewing these policies, the first comprehensive review since their inception. The report recommends the retention of these policies as well as the enhancement of supporting services.

Domestic Violence courts have been created in many jurisdictions, also with the aim of improving the justice system response to partner violence. In 1990, the first specialized Family Violence Court in Canada opened in Winnipeg. Components of this court include a zero-tolerance charging policy, a specialized unit of 11 Crown attorneys assigned exclusively to prosecute family violence cases, a Woman's Advocacy Program and a Child Abuse Witness Program, and court time dedicated to hearing family violence cases. Following the implementation of this court, there has been a steady increase in cases and dramatic changes in sentencing patterns. In response to a sharp increase in the number of court-mandated treatment orders, Manitoba Corrections department created a special probation unit to deliver treatment programs to batterers (Ursel, 1998).[iii]

Over the past few years, other jurisdictions have implemented either specialized courts or court processes to respond to cases of partner violence, including Ontario in 1997, Calgary in 2000, Yukon in 2000, and Edmonton in 2002. The primary goals of these courts are to expedite court processing, increase victim cooperation, improve conviction rates, provide better support to victims throughout the criminal justice process, and provide appropriate sentencing, such as treatment for abusers. It appears that the Winnipeg Court has had some success achieving these goals. The number of spousal violence cases coming before the court more than doubled between 1990 and 1998 (Ursel, 2000). The most common sentence is supervised probation and treatment for abusers. All provincial correctional institutions also operate batterer's treatment groups for incarcerated offenders.

In Ontario, two models have been implemented in 16 cities throughout the province: (1) an early intervention component with a focus on early access to treatment for abusers with no prior conviction for domestic violence, and where no weapon was used during the offence, and where no significant harm was inflicted on the victim; and (2) a coordinated prosecution component that emphasizes the collection of corroborative evidence through a variety of sources in order to improve the prosecution of partner violence cases. As of February 2000, approximately 4,500 cases had been processed through these specialized courts, one-quarter in locations with an Early Intervention focus, and three-quarters in courts with a focus on coordinated prosecution (McCallum, 2000).

Calgary established the Domestic Violence Courtroom in 2000 as part of a four-year pilot project called HomeFront. The goal of this initiative is to reduce domestic violence by linking the victim and offender more quickly and effectively with specialized services in the community. Domestic Violence Courtroom caseworkers contact victims immediately following arrest to offer ongoing support and referral to other services. In the first two years of operation, there was a substantial increase in the number of charges laid, probation orders, and court-mandated treatment for offenders. In January 2002, Edmonton also introduced a Domestic Violence Courtroom, modeled after the HomeFront project in Calgary.

In 2000, the Domestic Violence Treatment Option of the Territorial Court was established in Yukon. Following the laying of a charge for a domestic violence offence, an accused person who accepts responsibility for his or her actions can make an application to participate in the Spousal Assault Program. If accepted, the accused enters a guilty plea and the court orders him or her to enter the treatment program, which may include alcohol/substance abuse treatment. If ineligible, the accused returns to the formal court system. During the treatment period, the offender is brought before the court on a monthly basis to report progress. Following completion of the program, the sentencing judge imposes a sentence that reflects both progress made by the offender and remaining needs for counseling and safety issues. Support is also provided to victims in the form of safety planning, counseling for themselves or their children, updates on the offender's progress, court accompaniment, and assistance with the preparation of victim impact statements.

Feminist scholars have raised important questions about the potential for mandatory charging and prosecution policies to disempower victims by removing control of the situation from them once a report is made to police (Currie, 1990; Snider, 1998). The primary need of victims when calling the police is to receive protection and to stop the violence from continuing. For many reasons, including financial, emotional, or child-related, the victim may be reluctant to see the abuser arrested and incarcerated. But calling the police puts in motion the weight of the entire criminal justice process, regardless of the victim's wishes. In recognition of this difficulty, the Winnipeg Family Violence Court has undergone a recent change of culture, the aim of which is to ensure that the process does not revictimize victims and to give them some decision-making power over the outcome of cases (Ursel, 2002).

An important shift has occurred away from equating success with conviction. Rather than defining success on this single event, prosecutors in the Winnipeg Family Violence Court have begun to put greater emphasis on the process and on providing a service to victims. Victims are encouraged and supported to testify against an abusive spouse, but prosecution does not proceed without victim cooperation, except in cases where there is a serious risk to the victim or the community. Victims are encouraged to consider testifying at another time. According to Ursel (2002), "It is important that the Crown leave the message with the victim that she will not be harassed with warrants for failing to appear and she will not be treated as a hostile victim if she recants."

Ursel (2002:58) argues that the high rate of stays of proceedings in Family Violence Courts is the result of the "single-incident framework" of the criminal justice system. Some spousal violence cases can appear several times as stays in court statistics, but one conviction can be based on an accumulation of charges over time. She argues that it is important that the victim knows that the system is there to help her and that she will be taken seriously and treated with respect if she reports to the police and charges are laid in future. This follows more closely the philosophy of shelters for battered women, where the focus is on providing support and where efforts are not considered to fail when these women return to an abusive partner.

Responding to Intimate Partner Violence through Civil Law

In addition to the criminal sanctions that apply across Canada, seven provinces and territories have introduced civil legislation to better protect victims in situations of domestic violence—Saskatchewan (enacted in 1995), Prince Edward Island (in 1996), Yukon (in 1999), Manitoba (in 1999), Alberta (in 1999), Ontario (passed in 2000 but not yet proclaimed), and Nova Scotia (passed in 2001 but not yet proclaimed). These civil recourses include emergency protection orders, orders providing temporary exclusive possession of the family home, civil restraining orders, and other provisions necessary for the protection of victims and their children. These measures are intended to complement the criminal law process, and jurisdictions are encouraged to proceed with criminal charges where applicable. The prime value of civil domestic violence legislation is seen to be the immediacy of protection and practical intervention it offers by way of remedies to victims and their children.

SUMMARY

Over the past 20 years we have witnessed a form of dialogue between feminists and community organizations, the courts, researchers, and governments concerning the harms of intimate partner violence. Effectively addressing intimate partner violence requires multiple interventions from health, social, community, and justice service providers. As indicated in this chapter, intimate partner violence continues to be a persistent and pervasive problem in Canada, and the responses of the criminal and civil law continue to evolve, adapting to the growing body of social science research, case law, and data on this important social problem.

DISCUSSION QUESTIONS

1. *Do you think that the reforms to the law described in this chapter are likely to increase the level of confidence that victims have in the criminal justice system?*
2. *Can you think of any other steps that the justice system can take to more effectively respond to the problem of violence between intimate partners?*
3. *Before reading this chapter, were you aware of the incidence of intimate partner violence in Canada?*

FURTHER READINGS

Johnson, H. 1996. *Dangerous Domains: Violence Against Women in Canada.* Toronto: Nelson Canada.

Bonnycastle, K. and G. Rigakos. 1998. *Unsettling Truths: Battered Women, Policy, Politics and Contemporary Research in Canada.* Vancouver: Collective Press.

McKenna, K., and J. Larkin. 2002. *Violence Against Women: New Canadian Perspectives.* Toronto: Inanna Publications.

REFERENCES

Bala, N., and E. Ringseis. 2002. Review of Yukon's *Family Violence Prevention Act.* Under contract with the Canadian Research Institute for Law and the Family for the Victim Services Office of the Department of Justice, Yukon Territory.

Boyle, C. 1990. The "Battered Wife Syndrome" and Self-Defence: *Lavallee v. R. Canadian Journal of Family Law* 9:171–179.

Comack, E. 1993. Feminist engagement with the law: The legal recognition of Battered Woman Syndrome. *The CRIAW Papers.* Ottawa: Canadian Research Institute for the Advancement of Women.

Currie, D. 1990. Battered women and the state: From the failure of theory to a theory of failure. *Journal of Human Justice,* 1(2):77–96.

Feder, L. and L. Dugan. 2002. A test of the efficacy of court-mandated counseling for domestic violence offenders: The Broward experiment. *Justice Quarterly,* 19(2):343–375.

Grant, I. 1991. The "'syndromization'" of women's experience. *U.B.C. Law Review,* 25:51–59.

Hackett, K. 2000. Criminal harassment. *Juristat.* Vol. 20(11). Catalogue No. 85-002-XIE. Ottawa: Canadian Centre for Justice Statistics, Statistics Canada.

Hotton, T. 2001. Spousal violence after separation. *Juristat.* Vol. 21(7). Catalogue No. 85-002-XPE. Ottawa: Canadian Centre for Justice Statistics, Statistics Canada.

Johnson, H., and V. Pottie Bunge. 2001. Prevalence and consequences of spousal assault in Canada. *Canadian Journal of Criminology,* 43(1):27–45.

McCallum, T. 2000. Ontario Domestic Violence Courts initiative. In V. Pottie Bunge and D. Locke (Eds.), *Family Violence in Canada: A Statistical Profile, 2000.* Catalogue No. 85-224-XPE. Ottawa: Canadian Centre for Justice Statistics, Statistics Canada.

McFarlane, J., Campbell, J., Wilt, S., Sachs, C., Ulrick Y., and Xu X. 1999. Stalking and intimate partner femicide. *Homicide Studies,* 3:300–316.

Noonan, S. 1993. Strategies of survival: Moving beyond the Battered Woman Syndrome. In E. Adelberg and C. Currie (Eds.), *In Conflict with the Law: Women and the Canadian Justice System* (pp. 247–270). Vancouver: Press Gang Publishers.

Pottie Bunge, V. 2002. National trends in partner homicides, 1974–2000. *Juristat.* Vol. 22(5) Catalogue No. 85-002-XIE. Ottawa: Canadian Centre for Justice Statistics, Statistics Canada.

Pottie Bunge, V., and Locke, D. (eds.). 2000. *Family Violence in Canada: A Statistical Profile, 2000.* Catalogue no. 85-224-XPE. Ottawa: Canadian Centre for Justice Statistics, Statistics Canada.

R. v. Darrach, [2000] 2 S.C.R. 443.

R. v. Gladue, [1999] 1 S.C.R. 688.

R. v. Lavallee (1990), 1 S.C.R. 852-9000.

R. v. Lavallee, [1990] 1 S.C.R. 854.

R. v. Malott, [1988] 1 S.C.R. 123.

R. v. Mills, [1999] 3 S.C.R. 668.

R. v. O'Connor, [1995] 4 S.C.R. 411.

R. v. Seaboyer, [1991] 2 S.C.R. 577.

R. v. Whynot (1983), 9 C.C.C. (3d) 449.

Reilly v. The Queen, [1984] 2 S.C.R. 396.

Sampson, F. 2001. Mandatory minimum sentences and women with disabilities. *Osgoode Hall Law Journal,* 39:589–609.

Shaffer, M. 1997. The Battered Women Syndrome revisited: Some complicating thoughts five years after *R. v. Lavallee. University of Toronto Law Journal,* 47:1–33.

Sheehy, E. 2001. Battered women and mandatory minimum sentences, *Osgoode Hall Law Journal,* 39:529–555.

Snider, L. 1998. Struggles for social justice: Criminalization and alternatives. In K. Bonnycastle and G. Rigakos (Eds.), *Unsettling Truths: Battered Women, Policy, Politics and Contemporary Research in Canada.* Vancouver: Collective Press, 145–154.

Tjaden, P., and Thoennes, N. 1998. *Stalking in America: Findings from the National Violence against Women Survey.* U.S. Department of Justice.

Trotter, G.T. 2001. Justice, politics and the royal perogative of mercy: Examining the self-defence review. *Queen's Law Journal,* 26:339–395.

Ursel, J. 1998. Mandatory charging: The Manitoba model. In K. Bonnycastle and G. Rigakos (Eds.), *Unsettling Truths: Battered Women, Policy, Politics and Contemporary Research in Canada*. Vancouver: Collective Press, 73–81.

Ursel, J. 2000. Winnipeg Family Violence Court report. In V. Pottie Bunge and D. Locke (Eds.), *Family Violence in Canada: A Statistical Profile, 2000*. Catalogue no. 85-224-XPE. Ottawa: Canadian Centre for Justice Statistics, Statistics Canada, 45–47.

Ursel, J. 2002. His sentence is my freedom: Processing domestic violence cases in the Winnipeg Family Violence Court. In L. Tutty and C. Goard (Eds.), *Reclaiming Self: Issues and Resources for Women Abused by Intimate Partners*. Halifax, NS: Fernwood, 43–63.

Walker, L. 1979. *The Battered Woman*. New York: Harper Perennial.

ENDNOTES

[i] The views expressed in this chapter represent those of the authors and do not necessarily reflect the views of Justice Canada or Statistics Canada.

[ii] These data are from Statistics Canada's *Revised Uniform Crime Reporting Survey*, which includes 95 police agencies that have reported to this survey continuously since 1995. These police agencies accounted for 42 percent of the national volume of crime in 2001.

[iii] The rise in pro-charging policies and Domestic Violence courts has brought about a rise in court-mandated treatment for batterers even though the evidence concerning the effectiveness of treatment programs is mixed (Feder and Dugan, 2002).

CHAPTER 22

The Overrepresentation of Aboriginal Offenders in Canadian Prisons

INTRODUCTION

No problem has been discussed as much, or attracted as much attention, as the high number of Aboriginal Canadians in Canada's prisons. The problem has provoked a number of commissions of inquiry as well as a wealth of scholarship. In this chapter, Carol La Prairie, one of the leading scholars in the field over the past 20 years, discusses the seemingly intractable problem.

Aboriginal Overrepresentation: No Single Problem, No Simple Solution

Dr. Carol La Prairie, Principal Researcher, Department of Justice Canada

Contrary to conventional wisdom, the greatest challenge in the area of Aboriginal justice is that there is not a single justice problem or set of problems that will be solved with a single solution or a move to Aboriginal governance over criminal justice matters. This is a bold statement and one that belies much of the Aboriginal and non-Aboriginal political and community rhetoric about self-government and its capacity for redressing justice problems. For two decades now the assumption has been made that if Aboriginal people have control over their own justice system, the problem of Aboriginal overrepresentation in the criminal justice and correctional systems will be solved.

This assumption may not be well founded. In this chapter I explore and discuss some of the relevant data pertaining to the problem of high rates of Aboriginal admissions to custody.

It is essential to begin the discussion where most of the attention has been and continues to be centred—on the issue of Aboriginal overrepresentation in the criminal justice system, what it means, and some of the problems with calculation. From there, the discussion will turn to a discussion of Aboriginal crime and victimization, the characteristics of prison populations and the role that cities, being a Registered Indian,[i] and living on a reserve play in contributing to the overrepresentation problem.

THE MEANING OF OVERREPRESENTATION

For the past 20 years, overrepresentation has been the dominant Aboriginal criminal justice issue in Canada. It has provoked royal commissions in Alberta, Saskatchewan, Manitoba, and in Nova Scotia, with the inquiry into the wrongful conviction of Donald Marshall. Simply put, overrepresentation means that in relation to their numbers in the population (where they account for approximately 2 to 3 percent), in 2000–2001, Aboriginal people accounted for 17 percent of federal and about 19 percent of provincial admissions to custody (Hendrick and Farmer, 2002). The issue of overrepresentation has also played a central role in criminal justice agendas in other countries with indigenous populations, namely New Zealand and Australia (Doone, 2000; Crime Research Centre, 2002:2).

However, understanding Aboriginal overrepresentation is not as straightforward as it appears at first glance. For one thing, Aboriginal admissions to custody have always been calculated as a percentage of the total number of sentenced admissions, when total sentenced admissions have generally been declining. This makes Aboriginal percentages look more extreme. Second, comparing percentages of Aboriginal sentenced admissions and the percentage of Aboriginal people in the population of the various jurisdictions is also problematic because Aboriginal people are generally undercounted in the Census surveys. This also tends to overestimate the degree of Aboriginal representation in prison admissions or prison populations. Third, we have known for a decade or more that there is considerable regional variation in overrepresentation in provincial and territorial institutions in Canada, yet this is rarely acknowledged. However, despite these problems, Aboriginal overincarceration percentages and rates calculated on unclear data have been widely used—in commissions of inquiry, criminal justice legislation, and government department policies and programs.

For the purposes of the argument put forward in this chapter, let us take the commonly used overrepresentation data at face value. While there may be problems in the calculations of overrepresentation, there clearly has been and continues to be a problem of Aboriginal involvement in the criminal justice and correctional systems. If this problem is to be resolved and prevented in future generations, we need to have a better understanding of the elements that contribute to it. That is the focus of this chapter.

Table 22.1 reveals that Aboriginal admissions as a percentage of total admissions are much higher in the Prairie provinces of Alberta, Saskatchewan, and Manitoba, and lower in Quebec and the Maritimes. For example, in the Maritimes and Quebec, overrepresentation is about 1.5 times what would be expected given the information available on the size of the Aboriginal population in those provinces, but in Manitoba, Saskatchewan and Alberta, it is about 9 times. This is a significant difference, the cause of which has not been adequately explained or even explored. One reason for the lack of attention is the endurance of the most widely used and most common explanation for overrepresentation, i.e., that the criminal justice system unfairly apprehends and processes Aboriginal people in relation to how it treats non-Aboriginal people. Common usage states that the criminal justice system "fails" Aboriginal people.

Table 22.1 *Aboriginal Population, Aboriginal Admissions to Provincial/Territorial Institutions, and Percentage Overrepresentation, 1999/2000*

Jurisdiction	Aboriginal percent in Adult Population	Aboriginal % of Total Correctional Admissions*	% Overrepresentation of Aboriginals
Newfoundland	2%	7%	3.5%
Prince Edward Island	1	0	0
Nova Scotia	1.5	6	5.0
New Brunswick	1.5	6	5.0
Quebec	2	2	0
Ontario	2	9	4.5
Manitoba	9	57	6.3
Saskatchewan	8	75	9.3
Alberta	4	39	9.7
British Columbia	3	19	6.3
Yukon	18	66	3.6
Federal	2	17	8.5

* These data reflect the number of Aboriginal sentenced admissions as a percentage of total admissions.
Sources: Statistics Canada (1996, 1997, 2001c) and CCJS (2001c).

That explanation is by itself too limiting for developing a fuller and more comprehensive understanding of the nature of the problem and/or for devising more long-term and lasting solutions. One important demographic factor in any comprehensive explanation for overrepresentation is the size of the Aboriginal and non-Aboriginal age groups between 15 and 24. This is the age group most vulnerable to involvement in the criminal justice system. In the general Aboriginal population, 18 percent of the population occupies the 15–24 age group compared to 13.4 percent of the non-Aboriginal population. This means that there is a larger Aboriginal "pool" of people in the most crime-prone age group. When one looks at the 24 and under Aboriginal population in Canada in 1996, it is 53.1 percent as compared to 33.4 percent in the non-Aboriginal population. There are also dramatic Aboriginal regional variations in the under-24 age groups. For example, in the Atlantic provinces, the under-24 group comprises 51 percent of the Aboriginal population; in Quebec it is 48 percent; in Ontario 49 percent; in Manitoba it is 56 percent; in Saskatchewan it is 60 percent; in Alberta it is 55 percent; but in B.C. it goes back down to 49 percent—a level similar to Ontario (Statistics Canada, 1997).

In the Prairie provinces, Aboriginal overrepresentation is probably even greater than the official figures suggest because the proportions of Aboriginal adults are lower in those provinces than in the other provinces or in the Yukon. For example, in Saskatchewan, only 58 percent of the Aboriginal population are 15 and over, whereas in Quebec, Ontario, and the Maritimes it is about 68 percent. If the operation of the criminal justice system were the main reason for overrepresentation, there would be a larger pool of adults for the criminal justice system to process in Quebec, Ontario, and the Maritimes, so the overrepresentation figures would be much higher than they are.

While discriminatory practices of the criminal justice system may be one explanation for Aboriginal overrepresentation (and the one most frequently invoked in Canada), there is growing evidence that the same factors that explain the presence of some non-Aboriginal people in the criminal justice system also explain the involvement of Aboriginal people. American criminologist Michael Tonry, an expert on the issue of race and crime, has argued that explanations involving class and socioeconomic disparity grounded in historical processes may be more powerful explanations for minority overrepresentation in the criminal justice system in western countries than those based exclusively on discrimination. He stated that "a consensus is emerging among researchers in most countries that the disparities result primarily from racial differences in offending patterns" (Tonry, 1994:158).

But Tonry also argues that these are the consequence of historical experiences and contemporary social and economic circumstances. There are two fundamental questions emanating from this explanation that have relevance to the Canadian situation. First, what do we know about Aboriginal offending patterns and socioeconomic conditions? Second, how do class and socioeconomic disparity explain both Aboriginal and non-Aboriginal patterns of incarceration?

ABORIGINAL CRIME AND VICTIMIZATION

Although the controversy over causality continues, there is now a solid body of research that documents several facts about Aboriginal crime regardless of location. Research reveals a consistent pattern of elevated levels of Aboriginal offending and victimization and also that Aboriginal people are overrepresented as offenders and as victims of interpersonal violence. When compared in aggregate terms (i.e., Aboriginal vs. non-Aboriginal offence data), some important and distinctive characteristics of Aboriginal offence patterns can be found. Aboriginal crime is quantitatively disproportionate to the amount of crime in the non-Aboriginal population (Canadian Centre for Justice Statistics (CCJS, 2000a; La Prairie, 1996; Trevethan, 1991; Roberts and Doob, 1994). In other words, the rates of Aboriginal crime (i.e., crimes committed by Aboriginal offenders per 100,000 members of the Aboriginal population) are considerably higher than rates of non-Aboriginal crime. There are also significant qualitative differences between Aboriginal and non-Aboriginal crime. More Aboriginal than non-Aboriginal crime is violent (Moyer 1992; Silverman and Kennedy, 1993; Griffiths et al., 1995), and many of the Aboriginal crime problems dealt with by police and courts are of an interpersonal nature.

In the Aboriginal criminal justice-related literature, the incidence of crime and victimization varies widely across communities, and Aboriginal and non-Aboriginal crime differs in degree and kind (Roberts and Doob, 1994). For example, in one study in Saskatchewan, the Aboriginal crime rate was found to be 11 times higher than the non-Aboriginal rate. In Saskatchewan, the on-reserve crime rate was five times higher than in urban or rural areas, and in Regina and Prince Albert, 42 percent of victims were Aboriginal although Aboriginal people comprised only 2 percent of the population. In these same sites, victimization was also predominately intraracial (CCJS, 2000b).

It is also well known that Aboriginal inmates in Canada are more likely to be incarcerated for crimes against the person and, disproportionately, for offences against spouses and ex-spouses. Available research on Aboriginal victimization in Canada presents a disturbing picture of disproportionate levels of violent victimization often involving Aboriginal females. In 1999, the General Social Survey (GSS) on victimization collected data on race and cultural status, including Aboriginal status. An analysis of the data found that approximately 35 percent of the Aboriginal population reported having been the victim of at least one crime in the 12 months preceding the survey compared to 26 percent of the non-Aboriginal population. Aboriginal people were also more likely to be victimized more than once and to be victims of violent crime. While the rates of theft of personal property were similar for both Aboriginal and non-Aboriginal people, Aboriginal people experienced violent crime at a rate that was nearly three times greater than for non-Aboriginal people. (For visible minorities, the rates were similar to those of the general population; for the immigrant group, the rates were lower than for the general population.) Aboriginal people, and particularly

Aboriginal women, were found to be at much greater risk for spousal violence (CCJS, 2001a).

This brief overview illustrates that there are characteristics particular to Aboriginal crime and victimization, such as the disproportionate levels of crime, the involvement of alcohol in the commission of crime, and the intraracial nature of crime.

CHARACTERISTICS OF ABORIGINAL AND NON-ABORIGINAL PRISON POPULATIONS IN CANADA

If class and socioeconomic disparity explain victimization and the involvement in the criminal justice system of minority groups, they should also explain involvement of the non-Aboriginal population.

When gender, age, employment, and education characteristics are examined for all inmates in correctional institutions in Canada, one finds that (a) males are vastly overrepresented in prison populations (i.e., males comprise 98 percent of the prison population but only 49 percent of the Canadian population); (b) young people are overrepresented in prison populations, (i.e., the mean age of inmates is 33, but the mean age of the general Canadian population is 41); (c) 49 percent of inmates were unemployed at admission to correctional institutions as compared to an unemployment level of 10 percent in the Canadian population; and (d) the prison population is much less well-educated than the general population, (i.e., 37 percent of prison inmates had Grade 9 or less compared to only 12 percent of adults in Canada) (see Table 22.2). This tells us that the young, the poor, the uneducated, and males are all seriously overrepresented in general prison populations. It should be remembered when looking at the characteristics of the prison populations that the majority of correctional institution inmates are non-Aboriginal.

Perhaps the most critical question regarding the overrepresentation of Aboriginal people in inmate populations is how the general Aboriginal population compares to the general non-Aboriginal one in Canada. The variables most

Table 22.2 *Characteristics of Canadian Prison and Non-Prison Populations, 1996*

Characteristics	Prison Population %*	General Canadian Population %
Male gender	98%	49%
Mean age	33 years	41 years
Unemployed	49% (at time of admission)	10%
Less than Grade 9 education	37%	12%

*combined for provincial and federal inmates

Source: Finn et al. (1999).

relevant for comparison purposes are gender, age, employment, and education because it is these factors that appear to best characterize the general prison population, as can be seen in Table 22.2. However, because the gender ratio is similar for the Canadian and the Aboriginal populations—49 percent male to 51 percent female, the comparison factors that are most relevant to this discussion are age, employment, education, and "being a child of single parents" (because of its oft-cited relationship to problems experienced by children). The age, education, unemployment, and "child of single parents" status data for the Aboriginal and non-Aboriginal populations are presented in Table 22.3.

Table 22.2 reveals that the general prison population is disadvantaged in relation to the general nonprison population, and that younger age, poor employment, and lower education levels characterize the inmate group. Table 22.3, on the other hand, reveals that on these same factors known to characterize prison inmates, the Aboriginal population is generally more disadvantaged than the non-Aboriginal one. It follows, then, that if the factors that characterize prison populations are also more similar to the general Aboriginal population than they are to the general non-Aboriginal one, we should not be surprised by Aboriginal overrepresentation in the correctional system in Canada. Aboriginal inmates are disadvantaged even within the inmate population itself because existing research reveals that Aboriginal inmates are younger, have less education, and are more likely to be unemployed when compared to their non-Aboriginal counterparts. They are considered higher risk to reoffend (more prior offences) and have higher needs (personal/emotional, marital/family and employment, and substance abuse problems) (CCJS, 2000a).

The demographic differences between Aboriginal and non-Aboriginal populations in Canada would suggest that there might be more useful and accurate ways to define and understand overrepresentation. While overrepresentation has generally been described in racial terms such as "Aboriginal" overrepresentation, it might be described more accurately as the overrepresentation of the "poor," the "unemployed," and the "uneducated." Members of these groups are disproportionately found in the Aboriginal population.

Table 22.3 *Select Canadian and Aboriginal Population Demographics*

Demographics	Canadian %	Aboriginal %
Ages 0–24	34%	53%
Ages 45+	33%	16%
Children living with single parents	15%	29%
Unemployed	10%	24%
Less than Grade 9	12%	20%

Sources: Statistics Canada (1996, 1997)

Table 22.4 reveals that by using the characteristics that appear to best describe who goes to prison and who does not, i.e., age, employment, and education, the Aboriginal population is generally seen to be more disadvantaged than the non-Aboriginal one. Therefore, it is more a matter of this group's being young, unemployed, and poorly educated than it is of being Aboriginal. There is no reason to believe that middle-class Aboriginal people are any more vulnerable to being incarcerated than are middle-class non-Aboriginal people. Aboriginal population and incarceration data from provinces with the largest proportion of adults in their Aboriginal populations support this assertion. While the Maritimes and Eastern Canada have higher proportions of Aboriginal people 15 years of age and over, they also have among the lowest incarceration levels. If being Aboriginal were the cause of overrepresentation, this would be reflected in higher incarceration figures for Aboriginal adults in those provinces. By contrast, however, the provinces with the largest and youngest Aboriginal populations (the Prairie provinces) also have the highest levels of Aboriginal youth involved in the criminal justice system.

But how do we explain the variation in levels of Aboriginal incarceration across the country? One explanation is that Aboriginal populations exhibit regional variation in the sociodemographic factors that characterize involvement in the correctional system, which explains the variation in incarceration levels. This variation may be explained by paying particular attention to the role that cities (particularly those in the Prairie provinces) play in contributing to levels of overrepresentation. Previous research suggests Aboriginal inmates primarily commit the offences for which they are incarcerated in urban areas (McCaskill, 1976).

Table 22.4 *Select Canadian, Aboriginal, and Inmate Demographics*

Demographics	Canadian Population %	General Provincial/ Federal Inmate Population %	Aboriginal Population %	Aboriginal Provincial/ Federal Inmate Population %*
Male gender	49%	98%	49%	91%
Mean age	41 years	34 years	41 years	30 years
Unemployed**	10%	49%	24%	70%
Less than Grade 9	12%	20%	37%	52%

* It is important to remember that the majority of Aboriginal inmates are Registered Indians.
** Those not employed and seeking work. Does not include those who have stopped searching for work.
Sources: CCJS (2001b) and Finn et al. (1999).

DISCUSSION

The body of research that suggests the causality of overrepresentation may be grounded in socioeconomic and other factors indicates that overrepresentation cannot be explained by discriminatory practices that are embedded in differential criminal justice system charging and processing of Aboriginal suspects, accused persons, and offenders. Therefore, calls for separate Aboriginal justice systems to solve the problem of Aboriginal overrepresentation in the criminal justice and correctional systems are inappropriate.

A response to the problem that depends solely on criminal justice is likely to fail. While responses such as separate Aboriginal justice systems are likely to fulfill self-governance aspirations (and may well have other benefits for Aboriginal communities), they are much less likely to solve criminal justice problems because the same problems that plague the mainstream system will continue to plague Aboriginal-controlled ones. The socioeconomic differences between Registered Indians living on reserve and other Aboriginal groups (and in some cases Registered Indians living off-reserve, which are increasingly documented [see Maxim, 2002; La Prairie, 2002]) raise more questions about the nature of reserve life than about being Aboriginal.

Understanding and responding to overrepresentation involves better understanding the meaning of rates and levels; the role of cities and reserves as contributing factors in overrepresentation; the relationship between social and economic factors and involvement in the criminal justice system; criminal justice system policies and practices; and the impact of growing social stratification among Aboriginal people. Until these critical issues have been addressed, it is unlikely that appropriate long-term solutions to the problem of Aboriginal overrepresentation in the criminal justice and correctional systems can be devised.

In the same way, marginalized and disadvantaged people are vastly overrepresented in our system of justice. Until issues of social and economic disparity are also addressed more widely, it is unlikely that the overrepresentation of Aboriginal and of disadvantaged and marginalized non-Aboriginal Canadians in the criminal justice and correctional systems will be resolved. If criminal justice reforms are to be considered, they must be considered for all offenders—not only one group.

DISCUSSION QUESTIONS

1. *The* Criminal Code *contains a provision (s. 718.2(e)) that directs judges at sentencing to consider alternative sanctions for all offenders, but in particular Aboriginal offenders. Do you think this might be an effective remedy to the problem of Aboriginal overincarceration that the author discusses in this chapter?*
2. *La Prairie does not discuss in detail the kinds of reforms that might remedy the problem of high rates of incarceration among Aboriginal Canadians.*

What, in your view, can the federal or provincial/territorial governments do about this problem?

3. *In this chapter, La Prairie makes the point that young, uneducated males are overrepresented in prison populations. If reforms are required for all offenders and particularly for those who are disadvantaged, what do you think those reforms might look like?*

FURTHER READINGS

La Prairie, C. 2002. Aboriginal over-representation in the criminal justice system: A tale of nine cities. *Canadian Journal of Criminology,* April:181–202.

Stenning P. and J.V. Roberts. 2001. Empty promises: Parliament, the Supreme Court and the sentencing of Aboriginal offenders. *Saskatchewan Law Review,* 64(1):137–168.

Trevethan, S. 2000. *The Over-Representation of Aboriginal People in the Justice System.* Prepared for the Evaluation Unit, Department of Justice, Ottawa: Statistics Canada, Canadian Centre for Justice Statistics.

REFERENCES

Canadian Centre for Justice Statistics. 2000a. *The Over-Representation of Aboriginal People in the Justice System.* Prepared for the Evaluation Unit, Department of Justice, Ottawa: Statistics Canada.

Canadian Centre for Justice Statistics. *2000b.* Police-Reported Aboriginal Crime in Saskatchewan. *Ottawa: Statistics Canada.*

Canadian Centre for Justice Statistics. *2001a.* A Profile of Criminal Victimization: Results of the 1999 General Social Survey, Ottawa: Statistics Canada.

Canadian Centre for Justice Statistics. 2001b. *Aboriginal Peoples in Canada,* Ottawa: Statistics Canada.

Canadian Centre for Justice Statistics. 2001c. *Adult Correctional Survey, 1999/2000.* Ottawa: Statistics Canada.

Crime Research Centre. 2002. Executive summary. Crime and Justice Statistics for WA: 2000. Perth: University of Western Australia.

Doone, P. 2002. *Report on Combating and Preventing Maori Crime,* HEI WHAKARURUTANGA MO TE AO, Ministry of Justice, Crime Prevention Unit, Wellington: Department of the Prime Minister and Cabinet.

Finn, A., S. Trevethan, G. Carriere, and M. Kowalski. 1999. Female inmates, Aboriginal inmates, and inmates serving life sentences: A one day snapshot. *Juristat* Vol 19, No. 5, Ottawa: Statistics Canada, Canadian Centre for Justice Statistics.

Griffiths, C.T., E. Zellerer, D.S. Wood and G. Saville. 1995. *Crime, Law and Justice Among the Inuit in the Baffin Region, N.W.T. Canada.* Burnaby: Criminology Research Centre, Simon Fraser University.

Hendrick, D. and L. Farmer. 2002. Adult correctional services in Canada, 2000/01. *Juristat*, Volume 22, Number 10.

La Prairie, C. 1996. *Examining Aboriginal Corrections in Canada*, Aboriginal Corrections Policy Unit. Ottawa: Ministry of the Solicitor General.

———. 2002. "Aboriginal Overrepresentation in the Criminal Justice System: A Tale of Nine Cities." *Canadian Journal of Criminology*, 44(2): 209–232.

Maxim, P. 2002. *A Sectoral Analysis of Aboriginal Women in the Labour Force*. London: University of Western Ontario (unpublished).

McCaskill, D. 1976. *A Study of Needs and Resources Related to Offenders of Native Origin in Manitoba: A Longitudinal Analysis*. Ottawa: Correctional Planning Branch, Ministry of the Solicitor General.

Moyer, S. 1992. *Race, Gender and Homicide: Comparisons between Aboriginals and Other Canadians*. Ottawa: Ministry of the Solicitor General.

Roberts, J.V. and A.N. Doob. 1994. Race, ethnicity and criminal justice in Canada. In M. Tonry (Ed.), *Crime and Ethnicity, Crime and Justice*. Annual Vol. 21, Chicago: Chicago University Press.

Silverman, Robert and Leslie Kennedy. 1993. Canadian Indian involvement in murder. In R. Silverman and L. Kennedy (Eds.), *Deadly Deeds: Murder in Canada*. Toronto: Nelson Canada.

Statistics Canada. 1996. Census of Population. Ottawa: Queen's Printer.

Statistics Canada. 1997. Aboriginal Peoples' Survey, Census 1996. Ottawa: Queen's Printer.

Tonry, M. 1994. Editorial: Racial disparities in courts and prisons. *Criminal Behaviour and Mental Health*, 4:58–162.

Trevethan, S. 1991. *Police-Reported Aboriginal Crime in Calgary, Regina and Saskatoon*. Ottawa: Canadian Centre for Justice Statistics.

ENDNOTES

[i] *The Constitution Act of 1982* recognizes that Aboriginal peoples include North American Indians, Métis, and Inuit. More specifically, Registered or Status Indians refers to those peoples who qualify for registration under *The Indian Act of 1985*. The "identity" concept was introduced in the 1996 Census, whereas previously there was only the "ancestry" concept.

CHAPTER 23
Community Corrections

INTRODUCTION

Correctional systems in all western nations are shifting to a community-based model. In practical terms, this means that more and more offenders are serving sentences in the community, through programs such as day parole and full parole. These programs serve to promote the rehabilitation and reintegration of the offender, goals that are much more difficult to achieve while the offender is in prison. As well, community-based correctional programs are much more economical than keeping offenders in custody, so both society and offenders benefit. In this chapter, corrections policy expert Richard Zubrycki reviews the community-based corrections in Canada and places them in the broader context of other ways in which offenders are punished in the community.

Community-Based Corrections in Canada

Richard M. Zubrycki, M.S.W., Director General, Corrections, Department of the Solicitor General Canada

Simply put, the term "community corrections" refers to correctional programs that are located in the community rather than in a custodial facility such as a jail, prison, reformatory, or penitentiary. Community correctional programs and those sentences that authorize them are often called "alternatives to incarceration" or simply "alternative measures."

In addition to sentences that are served in the community (such as probation (see Chapter 16) and conditional sentences (see Chapter 5), "conditional release" refers to forms of release during a sentence of imprisonment that may be served in the community. During this time the prisoner is subject to conditions and under the supervision of a parole officer. Conditional release is a form of community corrections and may utilize similar community resources and programs as other community corrections measures such as probation; indeed, conditional release may be almost indistinguishable from them.

PROBATION, PAROLE, AND DIVERSION

In Canada, criminal justice responsibilities are shared between federal and provincial levels of government; the federal government is assigned constitutional responsibility for "penitentiaries" whereas provincial and territorial legislatures are responsible for the maintenance of "prisons and reformatories." These terms are not defined in the *Constitution Act*. Rather, they are distinguished from one another in s. 743.1 of the *Criminal Code* of Canada, which assigns all sentences of less than two years ("two years less a day") to provincial custody and all sentences of two years or more in length to federal penitentiaries. This is commonly known as the "two year rule." Conditional release to the community under supervision (often referred to generically as "parole") can be from either level of institution under the federal *Corrections and Conditional Release Act (CCRA)* or the *Criminal Code*, with regard to life sentences. Brief releases with or without escorts, known as temporary absences, are governed by the *CCRA* for penitentiaries and by the federal *Prisons and Reformatories Act* for provincial institutions.

Whereas probation and parole are the two most common ways that community programs are authorized by the sentence of a court, diversion out of the formal criminal justice process may occur without a sentence being handed down or even without the case reaching the sentencing stage. Diversion relies on a partnership among police, crown attorneys, and the courts. Reducing the "penetration" of the offender into the formal criminal justice system limits penal stigmatization and saves resources.

One way of understanding the relationship among these various forms of community correctional mechanisms is to view them structurally, within the broader criminal justice system. Viewed along a functional continuum from investigation to the completion of a sentence, the system can be visualized as shown in Figure 23.1.

Figure 23.1

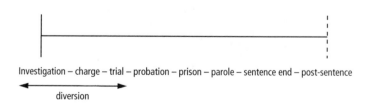

Investigation – charge – trial – probation – prison – parole – sentence end – post-sentence

diversion

Community programs may be implemented at each of these stages. The focus of this chapter will be community correctional programs, which take effect at the end of the continuum.

THE EMERGENCE OF COMMUNITY CORRECTIONS

David Rothman (1971, 1980) provides accounts of the emergence first of the American penitentiary at the beginning of the 19th century and then, 100 years later, the community correctional movement in the form of "aftercare" following release from prison. Originally focused only on offenders after leaving prison, the concept of dealing with offenders in the community instead of in prison gave rise to the introduction of probation and parole. During the past century those notions have taken hold in Canada until today 80 percent of offenders under sentence (or on remand) are being dealt with in the community, as depicted in Figure 23.2.

The arguments in favour of community corrections are simple:

1. *Community correctional programs are at least as effective as incarceration.* Considerable research over several decades supports the effectiveness of community programs when measured by reoffending. A meta-analysis conducted by Smith, Goggin, and Gendreau (2002) integrated the results of hundreds of such studies and concluded that a slight decrease in reoffending was associated with alternative measures compared to a slight increase associated with prison sentences.
2. *Community programs help maintain social integration of offenders* who will eventually return to the community in any event.

Figure 23.2 *Distribution of Sentenced Adults in Canada, 1999–2000*

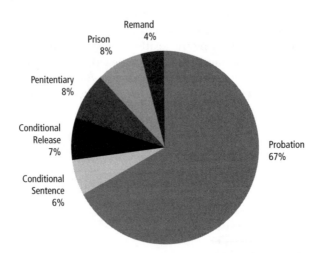

Source: Canadian Centre for Justice Statistics, 2001.

3. *Community programs help reduce the collateral social cost of incarceration* experienced by families of prisoners and other social systems from which they are withdrawn (Mauer and Chesney-Lind, 2002:1–36).
4. *Community programs are comparatively inexpensive.* In addition to saving taxpayers' money, they allow scarce correctional dollars to be focused on the highest risk offenders who require the most costly programs and services—including intensive security.

In Canada, community correctional programs have been institutionalized by enabling legislation, professional probation and parole services that incorporate them in their correctional case planning, and courts and prosecutors who recognize their legitimate place in our criminal justice system. But perhaps most important of all is a voluntary sector that creates and maintains community programs in communities across the nation. Indeed the voluntary sector was instrumental in launching and advocating first aftercare programs and later an increasing variety of community-based programs with the support of their communities. Volunteers have been the most effective innovators of new community programs during the past century and longer.

In the late 1800s, voluntary organizations, guided by their experience visiting prisoners and motivated by altruistic and religious values, invented the concept of "aftercare." They recognized that many offenders leaving prison could benefit from support, guidance, and assistance to adjust successfully to the community. Today the Canadian Criminal Justice Association, John Howard Society, and Elizabeth Fry Societies are a few examples of direct descendents of those earliest organizations. These organizations have been instrumental in the invention of probation, parole, court workers, halfway house residences, and community service orders, to name a few. While continuing to innovate and create new programs, these (and other) organizations deliver residential, counseling, and supervision programs in partnership with federal and provincial/territorial government agencies.

Community voluntary organizations often provide the ideas and are able to mobilize the human resources to bring community correctional programs into being but, as importantly, they provide a bridge to community acceptance that is essential to success. Some theorists make a distinction between community-based programs that are simply "in" the community as opposed to those that are "of" the community (Fox, 1977:1; Griffiths et al., 1994: 561; Lauen, 1990:12). Lauen discusses "community-managed" programs that are arguably the most effective because they are created and operated by the community for its members—both offenders and nonoffenders. Programs that are simply operated in the community by the official correctional system are arguably less effective because they and their clients are more likely to be seen as foreign to the community and ostracized by it.

Probation and parole officers working in the community with their voluntary sector partners—who are of the community—assist offenders to develop and implement community release plans that address their residential, education, employment, and criminogenic needs in the community. A variety of voluntary organizations operate over 190 halfway houses across Canada and are able to accommodate close to 2,000 parolees at a given time. They may offer programs related to specific needs, such as substance abuse, or simply basic room and board. In addition, over 10,000 individuals volunteer in various roles with Correctional Service Canada. They help provide pro-social role models and often continue to offer support and assistance in the community after release.

In Canada, Aboriginal people face special challenges, often having been isolated on reserves for decades with unequal access to employment, education and health care as well as many other social and economic disadvantages. Today Aboriginals represent under 3 percent of Canada's population but over 17 percent of its penitentiary inmates. In the prairie provinces, Aboriginal inmates account for over 80 percent of the prison population. On average, Canada incarcerates Aboriginal offenders at eight times the rate of non-Aboriginals. Culturally appropriate community services and programs are often lacking for Aboriginal people, making their reintegration into both Aboriginal and urban communities especially difficult.

COMMUNITY-BASED CORRECTIONAL PROGRAMS

Conditional Release

While serving a sentence of imprisonment in either a federal or provincial correctional institution, offenders may be released into the community for brief periods of time or for the remainder of the sentence under certain conditions, including supervision of a parole officer. The gradual transition back into society is thought to be the best and safest way to reintroduce offenders to community living and to monitor their ability to maintain a law-abiding lifestyle.

The National Parole Board is the paroling authority for all federal offenders, the territories, and all but three provincial jurisdictions. British Columbia, Ontario, and Quebec administer their own parole boards under authority delegated to them under the *Corrections and Conditional Release Act*.

Parole comes under attack when a prisoner on parole commits a serious crime that is widely publicized by the news media. Some people argue that the public do not support conditional release programs and would prefer a correctional system in which prisoners served their entire sentence in prison. However, systematic research has shown that even though the public tends to overestimate the proportion of prisoners who are granted parole, as well as the proportion of parolees who reoffend, people are generally very supportive of release programs. This was convincingly demonstrated in a public opinion survey in which a representative sample of the public was asked to determine whether they preferred "A system which keeps inmates in prison right to the end of the sentence and then releases them back into the community" (no parole option) or "A system which releases some inmates into the community under supervision until their sentence ends." Given this clear choice, the public favoured parole by a ratio of three to one (Roberts, Nuffield, and Hann, 2000). This finding of strong public support for parole has emerged from earlier polls on the subject (see Roberts, 1988).

Most provinces utilize temporary absences under the *Prisons and Reformatories Act*, often in succession ("back-to-back"), to provide conditional release for the vast majority of their inmates who serve sentences of less than 90 days. Most provincial offenders are still released on the date established by earned remission, during the last third of their sentences, without supervision except that which is available from voluntary-sector agencies.

The *Corrections and Conditional Release Act* provides for the types of conditional release set out in Table 23.1.

A similar philosophy underpins both conditional release and community-based sentences such as probation. Except where the risk posed by the offender is unacceptably high, the best way to promote his or her integration into social relationships and patterns of community living is to keep the person as closely related to the community as possible with appropriate supports and remedial opportunities. Ultimately, those social relationships are far more powerful regulators of behaviour than are criminal justice interventions. Simply put, giving ex-offenders an incentive to reintegrate into society is a more effective way of preventing them from returning to crime than simply threatening them with more punishment. Therefore, to make a period of community supervision most effective, correctional programs that are "of" the community are of utmost importance.

Correctional Service Canada and the National Parole Board must balance the potential risk to the community posed by offenders under their jurisdiction who are eligible for conditional release with their potential to successfully reintegrate into the community with appropriate support and controls. Beginning at admission to penitentiary, offenders are assessed to determine (1) their

Table 23.1 *Types of Conditional Release*

Type of Release	Prisoner Is Eligible after Serving
Escorted Temporary Absence	First Day of Sentence
Unescorted Temporary Absence	One-sixth or 6 months (the greater)
Work Release	One-sixth or 6 months (the greater)
Accelerated Day Parole	One-sixth or 6 months (the greater)
Day Parole (regular)	6 months before Full Parole Eligibility
Full Parole (& Accelerated F.P.)	One-third of the sentence
Judicial Determination (Full Parole)	One-half of the sentence (if ordered by a court)
Statutory Release	Two-thirds of the sentence (presumptive)

level of risk to reoffend and (2) their "criminogenic needs." Criminogenic needs are those characteristics of an offender that contribute to the risk of his or her future involvement in crime, such as, for example, substance abuse, illiteracy, or poor anger management. Criminogenic needs are risk factors that can be changed and are sometimes referred to as dynamic risk factors for that reason.

It is useful to consider the custodial and community portions of a penitentiary sentence as a continuum starting with admission to penitentiary and ending with warrant expiry at the end of the parole or statutory release period of community supervision. Beginning with the initial assessment period following admission, the assessment of risk and needs leads to the development of a correctional plan that includes research-based programs that can address the various criminogenic needs areas of the offender. Periodic assessments monitor change in risk levels and readiness for release. In preparation for release, a release plan is developed with the offender and, if approved by the National Parole Board, is followed up in the community by the Parole Service, an arm of the Correctional Service. The Parole Board considers the Correctional Service's assessment of risk and the viability of the release plan. During release, any indication of elevated risk is referred back to the Parole Board to consider whether the level of risk remains acceptable or if certain changes in the release plan will be sufficient to manage the risk; if not, the conditional release can be revoked and the offender returned to custody. This occurs in about 30 percent of releases, with well over half of those revocations resulting from a breach of a condition of release (Canada 2002: 77–82).

Correctional Service Canada operates halfway houses in most large cities; these Community Correctional Centres bring offenders closer to the communities they will be returning to when their sentences end. But they cannot replace the diversity and uniqueness of those Community Residential Centres that emerge from the mobilization of community resources to facilitate the return to a law-abiding lifestyle of community members who have been convicted of criminal offences. Many specializations exist among community organizations and the residences and programs they operate. Some may be oriented to substance abusers, others to those with mental health needs, still others to sex offenders or those sentenced to life terms. Moreover, they reflect the diverse cultural mix of values and norms that may vary among regions of the country. Working in partnership with parole officers to assist, support, and monitor offenders in the community, halfway houses have helped to achieve encouraging improvement in the success rate of conditional release.

COMMUNITY PROGRAMS AFTER SENTENCE COMPLETION

Support of the voluntary sector also extends beyond the end of the sentence and beyond the mandate of the formal correctional system. Established voluntary organizations founded in the traditions of aftercare have never regarded the boundaries of a sentence to confine their activities where there was a need. Recently, this philosophy has led to the creation of a new program model called Circles of Support and Accountability. Groups of community members (usually faith groups) provide ongoing friendship and practical supports as well as set limits and monitor accountability targets for high-risk offenders. In some instances the Circles of Support collaborate with police and local social agencies that are also targeting or have as clients the same high-risk offenders. These support networks are very promising, especially with serious sex offenders for whom community ostracism may be the biggest hurdle.

CONCLUSION

Community-based correctional programs comprise a broad spectrum of program models and exist in virtually all large communities across Canada. Some version of community-based correctional programs is available at virtually every stage of the criminal justice process, from during investigation to after a sentence of imprisonment has ended. Eighty percent of offenders under sentence today are in the community. Arguably, the most effective programs are those that are "of" the community where community resources are mobilized and a sense of ownership exists. Partnerships with the formal criminal justice system—from police to parole—provide opportunities to maintain or restore community ties that encourage law-abiding behaviour. While not without their critics, particularly with regard to effectiveness and net-widening, community-based correctional programs are today an essential (and growing) part of the Canadian correctional system.

DISCUSSION QUESTIONS

1. *Why have community-based correctional programs become so prevalent during the last 50 years?*
2. *In what ways are community-based correctional programs superior to custodial programs?*
3. *What are some of the limitations and potential drawbacks of community-based correctional programs?*

FURTHER READING

Griffiths, C. and Hatch Cunningham, A. 2003. Release and re-entry. Chapter 8 in *Canadian Criminal Justice. A Primer*. Toronto: Thomson.

Hendrick, D. and Farmer, L. 2002. Adult correctional services in Canada, 2000/01. *Juristat*, Volume 22, Number 10.

Winterdyk, J. 2001. Community corrections and the future of corrections. Part 5 of *Corrections in Canada*. Toronto: Pearson Education Canada.

REFERENCES

Bonta, James. 1997. *Offender Rehabilitation: From Research to Practice*. Ottawa: Solicitor General Canada (www.sgc.gc.ca).

Canada. 2002. *Corrections and Conditional Release Statistical Overview*. Ottawa: Solicitor General Canada (www.sgc.gc.ca).

Canadian Centre for Justice Statistics. 2001. *Adult Correctional Survey, 1999/2000*. Ottawa: Statistics Canada.

Fox, Vernon. 1977. *Community-based Corrections*. New Jersey: Prentice-Hall.

Lauen, Roger J. 1990. *Community-Managed Corrections: and Other Solutions to America's Prison Crisis* (2nd ed.). Washington D.C.: American Correctional Association.

Mauer, Marc and Meda Chesney-Lind, eds. 2002. *Invisible Punishment: The Collateral Consequences of Mass Imprisonment*. New York: The New Press.

Roberts, J.V. 1988. Early release from prison: what do the Canadian public really think? *Canadian Journal of Criminology*, 30:231–239.

Roberts, J.V., J. Nuffield, and R. Hann. 2000. Parole and the public: Attitudinal and behavioural responses. *Empirical and Applied Criminal Justice Research*, 1:1–29.

Rothman, David J. 1980. *Conscience and Convenience: The Asylum and its Alternatives in Progressive America*. Boston: Little Brown.

Rothman, David J. 1971. *The Discovery of the Asylum: Social Order and Disorder in the New Republic*. Boston: Little Brown.

Smith, Paula, Claire Goggin, and Paul Gendreau. 2002. *The Effects of Prison Sentences and Intermediate Sanctions on Recidivism: General Effects and Individual Differences*. A report to the Research and Development Division of the Corrections Directorate, Solicitor General Canada. Ottawa: Solicitor General Canada (also at www.sgc.gc.ca).

CHAPTER 24
Restorative Justice

INTRODUCTION

In Chapter 1 we described two models of justice, the crime control and due process models. Another dichotomy has recently emerged. The traditional model of criminal justice is retributive in nature, meaning that the system punishes offenders in direct proportion to the seriousness of their crimes. However, an alternative model, restorative justice, has emerged in many countries. In this chapter, Liz Elliott, a restorative justice expert from Simon Fraser University, discusses the origins and nature of restorative justice.

From Scales to Circles: Restorative Justice as Peacemaking and Social Justice
Liz Elliott, Simon Fraser University

> As a critical criminologist, I find it more difficult to witness crime or to think about crime. Instead, I envision a world without crime, and that vision comes from imagining a world that would not produce crime. To be critical, to be a critical criminologist, is to imagine what might be possible in this human existence. —Richard Quinney, 2000

Restorative justice is a concept that is understood in various ways. A common perspective is that restorative justice is a program, and usually a program that diverts young, nonviolent, first-time lawbreakers from jail to community-based measures. This view is the understanding of most governments in Canada, which are attracted to the perceived cost savings of these alternatives to jail. The fate of restorative justice in this rendition is that it begins with the same assumptions of the familiar retributive system and is inevitably deployed as an "add-on" program to that system.

Practitioners who begin with this understanding of restorative justice may eventually develop a new appreciation for the more inclusive and egalitarian processes of these programs. But without a shift in our framework of understanding crime itself, the opportunity to develop new ways of understanding problems and developing solutions is lost. Howard Zehr, one of the grandfathers of late 20th-century restorative justice thought, suggested that "the lens we look through determines how we frame both the problem and the "solution" (Zehr, 1990:178).

Without this change of lens, the appreciation for valuable aspects of restorative processes remains limited to the realm of conventional criminal justice systems. In this chapter, I try to make the case for a vision of restorative justice that emerges when a paradigm shift is made and different questions are asked. To this end, restorative justice is described through the lenses of peacemaking and social justice, followed by an overview of restorative process models found in current practice.

RESTORATIVE JUSTICE AS PEACEMAKING

Through the retributive lens, the focus of justice is on rule or law-breaking, identifying culpable perpetrators and punishing them according to the seriousness of the crimes that they have committed. The "justice as scales" metaphor conveys the idea of balancing, equalizing, measuring. From this perspective, the equality in the relationship between the parties to the crime is generally sought through punishment (Llewellyn and Howse, 1999:30–31). Punishment "intends inflicting pain, suffering or loss" (Haan, 1990); its purpose in inflicting harm on the offender is to "equalize" the harm suffered by the victim. Justice is a destination that is definable in the conclusion of each case, through the finding of guilt as well as the declaration of a proportionate sentence and its subsequent implementation.

The processes of justice familiar to us at the beginning of this century are quickly recognizable in images of police, courtrooms and lawyers, jails and prisons, and parole officers. Processes are governed by rules of evidence and procedure that aim to ensure a fair contest between the offender and the state. Justice is the domain of professionals and institutions acting on behalf of the people actually involved in the conflict, criminal or otherwise. This institutionalization of justice appears to have increased the dependency of citizens on criminal justice and other professionals to solve conflicts, decreasing citizen and community capacity to handle their own personal and local problems.

When we view justice through a restorative lens, the image of the scales of retributive justice may be replaced by the image of a circle. In the restorative lens, justice begins with a focus on harms suffered by real people, attends meaningfully to the needs of all the affected parties that require attention, and aims to restore and/or build relationships among the parties themselves, their families/friends, and the community at large. There is no definable "end" or destination in a circle, just as there is no definable beginning. The image is a continuous line, representing a series of human relationships. The emphasis on this interconnection is found in the perception of crime as a problem of the community as well as the individuals involved. Justice is an ongoing process of righting relationships damaged by the harm; it is the pursuit of peaceful relations.

The implications of "peace as practice" are significant in restorative justice. The idea that "process is product"[i] means that restorative justice practices need to emulate peaceful ways of resolving conflict. Consequently, seasoned practitioners of restorative justice speak of "values-based processes," where the means used to address conflicts embody the guiding values of the community at large. Examples of typical community values are respect, equality, inclusion, caring, honesty; practitioners in a community upholding these values would then aspire to develop processes for handling conflicts that are respectful of every participant, treat each equally, are inclusive of all relevant interests, care for everyone, and make it possible for the honest expression of each participant's truth and their needs.

The idea of criminal justice as peacemaking reflects, but is not restricted to, traditional Aboriginal ways of dispute resolution. Many Aboriginal communities have embarked on healing journeys inspired by the gradual reclaiming of their traditional ways and teachings. This is a challenging process for individuals and communities that have been silenced to varying degrees by residential schools and land claims disputes—not to mention the general, pervasive effects of colonial culture and governance on Aboriginal traditions.[ii] Circle processes and an attention to harm-doing that invites the full participation of offender, victim, and community are evident in the examples of Hollow Water, Manitoba,[iii] and Carcross, Yukon Territory.

Restorative justice proponents who operate from a peacemaking perspective often find themselves in a similar position to Aboriginal people whose traditional ways conflict with the structures of a formal legal system. Our familiarity with the conventional criminal justice system and the tendency of many restorative justice programs to operate within that system make the task of developing values-based restorative processes a challenging one. Yet the challenge is necessary in order that restorative justice be afforded a full expression and to avoid the fate of the many alternatives to incarceration developed in the 1980s that helped to widen the net of formal criminal justice. Restorative justice approaches can still operate within the formal system, as long as the integrity of the processes is not compromised by conventional expectations.

RESTORATIVE JUSTICE AS SOCIAL JUSTICE

Criminological theory and research from the beginning of the 1900s has attempted to delineate various factors involved in harm-producing behaviours. The factors affecting the offender's actions have been considered historically by theorists such as Becker (1963) and Hirshi (1969), who spoke of the influence of social learning, labeling, and the primacy of basic social arrangements such as the family. More recently, we have seen the utility of crime prevention through the reduction of opportunities[iv] and social development.[v] The primacy of prevention is recognized as a universal best interest of the individual, the community, and the larger society.

The capacity of the criminal justice system for crime prevention, however, seems limited. A classical school premise is that people will be deterred from committing crimes in the anticipation of punishment.[vi] This punishment, however, must be swift and certain, an ideal situation that is compromised by the reality that not all crimes are detected and therefore punished or that trial delays are common. And apart from the general problem of enumerating how many people are, in fact, deterred from crimes they might be tempted to commit, there is also the difficulty in demonstrating exactly what deters people from committing crimes—the fear of punishment or their own values. The only certain crime prevention utility of the criminal justice system lies in the incapacitation of detected offenders for the time they are incarcerated, and even this notion is mitigated by the argument that the prison experience itself often exacerbates criminal behaviour.

Positivist[vii] theories encourage us to consider factors that increase individual conditions favourable to crime in seeking its prevention. While our legal system begins with classical school assumptions, it also incorporates positivist thought in determining mitigating/exacerbating factors in sentencing, factors that are later revisited by the corrections system in treatment programs. However, the amount of prevention offered by a justice system that is mandated to intervene only after the commission of crimes is not likely to account for much of the total preventable crimes. And since most of the crime prevention through social development is likely to occur outside of the purview of criminal justice, it is not often targeted for criminal justice funding. The connections between criminal justice, public schools, the family, and social welfare are often obscured by discrete departmental mandates that inhibit holistic collaboration of agencies toward crime prevention. Particularly troubling is the focus on the needs of the offender only, with minimal attention to the needs of the victim and the crime prevention opportunities associated with victim healing.

In restorative justice processes, the needs of both the offender and the victim are given full attention. The active involvement of community members—as supporters of both victims and offenders, as professionals, or as interested parties—extends the knowledge of these needs, case after case, into the community itself. The community has its own needs as well, primarily the need for a restored sense of safety (Sharpe, 1998:46). As an important source of informal social controls, the community also plays a key role in crime prevention (Clear and Karp, 1999:37–57). Restorative processes afford a clearer picture of what is not working in the community, creating opportunities for its members to remedy specific deficits and to continue supporting certain community assets.

By focusing on needs, restorative justice opens the possibilities for increased community awareness of its more generic social problems. These problems—which typically include variables such as substance abuse, family violence, sexual abuse, and the neglect and abandonment of children—require remedies that are implemented in the fabric of the community itself. While individual attention to such problems is obviously required on a case-by-case basis, it is also important to consider the cases on an aggregate basis. If a community begins to recognize the human face of child neglect, for example, the next step is to determine the extent of the problem in that community and to develop resources and strategies of service that respond to it in a meaningful way. Governments will be a necessary part of that process, but it takes the community, neighbour by neighbour, to attend to the needs of neglected children.

The presenting social problems revealed by criminal justice processes are generally interpreted as the problem of the individual. Restorative justice processes, while useful in helping individuals explore their own behaviours as part of crime prevention (Haley, 1996), also have the potential to explore aggregate problems as symptoms of larger social injustices such as poverty, racism, and sexism. The greater the community involvement in responding to conflict and harm, the greater the awareness of social justice issues present within the community itself. Crime prevention, then, is not merely about erecting more streetlights and reporting suspicious behaviour, but also about attending to deeper social inequities that are reflected in individual acts of harm. Youth gang violence, for example, might be viewed as a symptom of a larger problem of racism in the high schools. Individual community members involved in restorative processes with such cases may be personally motivated to develop strategies in local schools to address the roots of racism.

A common criticism of restorative justice is the emphasis placed on the notion of the community, which is seen as idealistic rather than realistic, particularly in larger urban centres. In restorative justice, the community is not seen as a simple geographic entity (although it could be), but as defined by interests. As such, we likely belong to several different communities of interest (McCold and Wachtel, 1998) based on work, school, recreation, neighbourhoods, families, and friends. Since crime is a product of some kind of dysfunction in a community, it is reasonable to conclude that the community must be part of the solution. Weak communities can be strengthened by the involvement of members in conflict resolution processes that give them an active role to play (Crawford and Clear, 2001). Indeed, our inattention to social injustices may be significantly related to the current "arms-length" position of the community in handling its own conflicts. The idea that conflicts are the property primarily of those most affected by them has been compromised by the professionalization of criminal justice (Christie, 1977). Communities need to be involved in their own conflicts and problems, so that issues of social justice remain personal and real as opposed to general and abstract. Crime prevention through social justice affords a human and ethical approach to harm reduction in communities.

FROM PHILOSOPHY TO PRACTICE

Establishing the peacemaking and social justice tenets of restorative justice is important for developing processes that transform conflicts into opportunities for individual and community healing. The significance of values-based processes is underscored by the peacemaking goal of conflict responses and the inclusion of community by the goal of greater social justice. The question of how to respond to harms generally and crimes specifically, then, must attend to these concerns at all stages of the process. As will be seen, this is a prominent challenge for restorative justice practices.

Restorative justice cannot be limited to the domain of criminal justice any more than can retributive justice. Evidence of retributive justice is found not only in courts and criminal sentences, but also in child-rearing and school disciplinary practices. Based on the pleasure/pain principles articulated by Bentham in 1789,[viii] conformity to social and legal codes of conduct is sought by retributive justice through the articulation of rewards and punishments, in the family, the schools, the workplace, and the courts. An understanding of restorative justice, then, requires a similar appreciation for its broader application. Restorative justice begins with each individual and moves outward from there to the ways we raise our children, to school disciplinary practices, and ultimately to criminal justice. Further, restorative justice is applied in different ways, from community to community and even case by case. Flexibility is a benchmark of restorative processes.

The diversity of restorative approaches makes it difficult to create any meaningful classification of practices. In the schools, for example, are a variety of restorative programs that are both preventive[ix] and responsive. The diversity of restorative processes is evident in criminal justice itself, where restorative options may take the form of police diversions,[x] crown-approved alternative measures,[xi] collaborative justice (see Chapter 25 of this volume), sentencing circles,[xii] and post-sentence victim-offender mediation in violent offence cases.[xiii] Some agencies will work only with youth in conflict with the law, while others work with both youth and adults. Similarly, some agencies will work only with criminal justice cases, while others further offer restorative processes to the schools and the community itself.

EXAMPLES OF RESTORATIVE JUSTICE PRACTICES

These caveats taken into consideration, there are three basic models of restorative justice practice: victim–offender meetings, family group conferences, and circle peacemaking (Zehr, 2002:44–52). All of these models offer an encounter, at least between the victim and the offender, often with key participant supporters and other community members. The processes are led by volunteer or professional facilitators trained to organize and run the encounters in a way that balances the concerns of everyone involved. These models generally include three components: a discussion of the facts, how the parties felt as a result of the harm/conflict/crime, and what possible resolutions might be pursued in order to meet the obligations created by the harm. Agreements are created by the parties involved and are expected to respect the healing mandate of restorative justice.

Victim-Offender Reconciliation Programs

Victim–offender meetings were first developed in Canada in Kitchener-Waterloo, Ontario, with the Victim–Offender Reconciliation Program (VORP).[xiv] This model involves a face-to-face meeting between a victim and an offender that is mediated by a trained community volunteer (Gilman and Bowler, 1995). VORP is a pioneer restorative program, which eventually provoked more formalized thought around restorative justice theory. Traditionally used for property crimes, the VORP concept was extended in British Columbia to include victims and offenders of serious personal crimes. Under the title of Victim Offender Mediation Program (VOMP), this restorative process began in 1991 as a pilot project conducted through the Correctional Service of Canada for federal offenders and their victims.[xv]

Victim–offender encounters are used for the purposes of healing and reconciliation. The process usually begins with the mediator receiving a referral and approaching the victims and offenders to hear their stories. If the victim and offender agree to meet, an encounter is arranged, but only when the mediator senses that an encounter will be helpful to both parties. The amount of time in pre-meeting counseling will vary according to the needs of the parties; and the needs of victims and offenders in serious cases are usually greater. A meeting between the victim of a car theft and the teenage boy who stole it might require a few weeks of preparation; to prepare a victim of serious sexual assault and her assailant for a meeting may take several months or years. This can pose a problem for cases that are constrained by court schedules, but most violent offence mediations occur post-sentence.

Family Group Conferencing

Family group conferencing originated in New Zealand, with the reform of the *Children and Young Persons Act* in the 1980s. The development of the replacement *Children, Young Persons and Their Families Act* (1989) resulted in the creation of family group conferences. These conferences deal with both child protection cases and youth justice cases and include the youth in question, as well as family members and community professionals (Hassall, 1996). Family group conferencing is based on restorative justice values such as respect, sensitivity, and sharing of power, with a particular criminal justice emphasis on victim inclusion and offender accountability. Adaptations of family group conferences were made in Australia and initially developed by the police, using a scripted model of facilitation and paying particular attention to the dynamics of shame (Zehr, 2002:48).

This model has been adopted and practised in Canada by the RCMP since 1995, when RCMP and crown counsel implemented a process in Sparwood, B.C., that became known as community justice forums (Shaw and Jané, 1999). Also called "conferencing," this model brings the victim, the offender, their supporters, and other community stakeholders together to talk about the harm and possible solutions to it. The offenders are often young, and the outcomes generally involve some kind of material restitution and an agreement to attend to certain presenting problems like substance abuse or truancy. Conferencing has even been used in cases of domestic violence, in pilot projects in Newfoundland and Labrador (Shaw and Jané, 1999), where the problem is brought to greater community awareness. Similar processes take place in school conflict conferences in response to harmful acts in the educational context, generally in place of conventional disciplinary penalties such as detentions and suspensions.

CIRCLES

Circle peacemaking is strongly rooted in Indigenous cultures, and was brought to broader North American societies from the Canadian north. Participants sit in a circle and pass a talking piece around, ensuring that each person has an opportunity to speak. There is a strong emphasis in circle peacemaking on values—such as respect, integrity, and truth telling—which are emphasized during the process (Pranis et al., 2003). The circle includes the victim, offender, their supporters, and also other community members. Circles are used for sentencing and are practised as well for a number of other purposes, such as healing and general community dialogue. Most criminal cases handled by a circle process involve preparatory circles and follow-up circles in addition to that of the main encounter.

Circles were adapted to the demands of the formal court system in Canada's north, when judges recognized the limited impact of the conventional criminal justice response to crime in Aboriginal communities. In circle sentencing, the community and the victim are given active roles in the offender's hearing, with an emphasis on building connections to and within communities and expanding the scope of issues considered (Stuart, 1996b). In cases where the victim's safety is compromised by the offender's liberty, imprisonment may be a sentencing outcome. This process, when carefully deployed, may be useful in cases of domestic violence where stringent measures are taken to ensure that power imbalances in intimate relationships are attended to. Circle sentencing is used for all kinds of offences, generally in cases where the offender pleads guilty.

Whatever the model used in restorative justice, there are several principles that need to be respected. These are summarized in Mika and Zehr's "Signposts of Restorative Justice" (see Figure 24.1). The overriding principle might be to "do no harm" in whatever restorative endeavours are undertaken—whether in criminal justice or the schools, in minor disputes or major crimes. At a minimum, this requires a constant reflection of intentions and practices, and a willingness to learn from mistakes made in restorative innovations.

CONCLUSION

Can restorative justice ever replace the existing criminal justice system? The question is probably premature. Current efforts in the area of restorative justice are more concerned with preventing it from being co-opted within an overriding retributive system that often threatens to extinguish the peacemaking and social justice potential of restorative programs in favour of punitive justice. Perhaps there might come a time when restorative justice is used as the first option for criminal justice interventions, with the retributive

---

Figure 24.1 *Signposts of Restorative Justice*

1. Focus on the harms of crime rather than the rules that have been broken.

2. Show equal concern and commitment to victims and offenders, involving both in the process of justice.

3. Work toward the restoration of victims, empowering them and responding to their needs as they see them.

4. Support offenders, while encouraging them to understand, accept, and carry out their obligations.

5. Recognize that while obligations may be difficult for offenders, those obligations should not be intended as harms, and they must be achievable.

6. Provide opportunities for dialogue, direct or indirect, between victim and offender as appropriate.

7. Find meaningful ways to involve the community and to respond to the community bases of crime.

8. Encourage collaboration and reintegration of both victims and offenders, rather than coercion and isolation.

9. Give attention to the unintended consequences of your actions and program.

10. Show respect to all parties—victims, offenders, justice colleagues.

Source: Mika and Zehr, 1998.

system playing a backup role. A more likely scenario is that restorative justice processes will establish themselves alongside retributive justice systems, as an option for offenders who want to take responsibility for their actions and victims who want a restorative encounter as part of their own healing. The limited evaluations of the effectiveness of restorative justice programs to date have been promising (e.g., Flaten, 1996; Latimer et al., 2001; Umbreit, 1994.)

Restorative justice challenges us to consider what we want from justice and the kind of world we want to live in. If the purpose of justice is peace, then we need to consider the tools we use to get there. This will require deeper thought on concepts and practices that have enjoyed unchallenged primacy in responses to crime, such as punishment and formal criminal justice institutions. Perhaps the simple availability of other response options to harm-doing afforded by restorative justice will help to broaden this understanding; if the only tool we have is a hammer, every problem looks like a nail. We might also consider Quinney's thoughts on imagining a world without crime, a challenge for criminologists who have traditionally begun their inquiry with crime, criminals, and criminal justice.

DISCUSSION QUESTIONS

1. *In your view, what is the most important advantage of restorative responses to offending?*
2. *Critics of the restorative justice movement have identified a number of problems associated with this new paradigm. Do you see any difficulties with the restorative response?*
3. *How do you think the public is likely to react to this alternative form of justice?*

FURTHER READINGS

Braithwaite, J. 1999. Restorative justice: Pessimistic and optimistic accounts. In M. Tonry (Ed.), *Crime and Justice: A Review of Research*. Chicago: University of Chicago Press.

Roberts, J.V. and Roach, R. 2003. Restorative justice in Canada: From sentencing circles to sentencing principles. In A. von Hirsch, J.V. Roberts, A. Bottoms, and K. Roach (Eds.), *Restorative Justice and Criminal Justice*. Oxford: Hart Publishing.

Roach, K. 2000. Changing punishment at the turn of the century: Restorative justice on the rise. *Canadian Journal of Criminology*, Vol. 42:249–280.

REFERENCES

Beccaria, Cesare. (1985, orig. 1764). *On Crimes and Punishments*. Translated, with an introduction by Henry Paolucci. New York: Macmillan Publishing Company.

Becker, Howard S. 1963. *Outsiders: Studies in the Sociology of Deviance*. New York: Free Press.

Bentham, Jeremy. (1948, orig. 1789). *An Introduction to the Principles of Morals and Legislation.* Introduction by Laurence J. Lafleur. New York: Hafner Press.

Brandt, Clare C. 1990. Native ethics and rules of behaviour. *Canadian Journal of Psychiatry,* Vol. 35, August:534–539.

Brantingham, Patricia and Paul Brantingham. 1990. Situational Crime Prevention in Practice. *Canadian Journal of Criminology,* Vol. 32, Number 1: 17–40.

Christie, Nils. 1977. Conflicts as property. *British Journal of Criminology,* Vol. 17, Number 1:1–14.

Clear, Todd R. and David R. Karp. 1999. *The Community Justice Ideal: Preventing Crime and Achieving Justice.* Boulder, Col.: Westview Press.

Crawford, Adam and Todd Clear. 2001. Community justice: Transforming communities through restorative justice? In Gordon Bazemore and Mara Schiff (Eds.), *Restorative Community Justice: Repairing Harm and Transforming Communities.* Cincinnati, Ohio: Anderson Publishing Company, (pp. 127–149).

Felson, Marcus. 1994. *Crime and Everyday Life.* Newbury Park, CA: Pine Forge Press.

Flaten, Caren L. 1996. Victim-offender mediation: Application with serious offences committed by juveniles. In B. Galaway and J. Hudson (Eds.), *Restorative Justice: International Perspectives,* (pp. 387–401). Monsey, N.Y.: Criminal Justice Press.

Gilman, Eric and Christie Bowler. 1995. *Victim Offender Mediation Training Program, Revised Edition, Training and Resource Manual.* Langley, B.C.: Fraser Region Community Justice Initiatives Association.

Haan, Willem de. 1990. *The Politics of Redress: Crime, Punishment and Penal Abolition.* Boston: Unwin Hyman.

Haley, John O. 1996. Crime prevention through restorative justice: Lessons from Japan. In B. Galaway and J. Hudson (Eds.), *Restorative Justice: International Perspectives,* (pp. 349–371). N.Y.: Criminal Justice Press.

Hassall, Ian. 1996. Origin and development of family group conferences. In J. Hudson, A. Morris, G. Maxwell and B. Galaway (Eds.), *Family Group Conferences: Perspectives on Policy and Practice.* Monsey, N.Y.: Criminal Justice Press.

Hirschi, Travis. 1969. *Causes of Delinquency.* Berkeley: University of California Press.

Latimer, Jeff, Craig Dowden and Danielle Muise. 2001. *The Effectiveness of Restorative Justice Practices: A Meta-Analysis.* Ottawa: Department of Justice Canada, Research and Statistics Division.

Linker, Maureen. 1999. Sentencing circles and the dilemma of difference. *The Criminal Law Quarterly,* Vol. 42, Number 1, May:116–128.

Llewellyn, Jennifer and Robert Howse. 1999. *Restorative Justice—A Conceptual Framework.* Ottawa: The Law Commission of Canada. Also at www.lcc.gc.ca.

McCold, Paul and Benjamin Wachtel. 1998. Community is not a place: A new look at community justice initiatives. *Contemporary Justice Review*, Vol. 1, Number 1:71–85.

Mika, Harry and Howard Zehr. 1998. Fundamental principles of restorative justice. *The Contemporary Justice Review*, Vol. 1, Number 1:47–55.

Pranis, Kay, Barry Stuart and Mark Wedge. 2003. *Using Peacemaking Circles in the Justice System*. St. Paul, Minnesota: Living Justice Press.

Quinney, Richard. 2000. Socialist humanism and the problem of crime: Thinking about Eric Fromm in the development of critical/peacemaking criminology. In K. Anderson and R. Quinney (Eds.), *Eric Fromm and Critical Criminology: Beyond the Punitive Society*. Chicago: University of Illinois Press.

Roberts, Tim. 1995. *Evaluation of the Victim Offender Mediation Project, Langley, B.C.* For Solicitor General of Canada, (March) by Focus Consultants, Victoria, B.C.

Ross, Rupert. 1996. *Returning to the Teachings: Exploring Aboriginal Justice*. Toronto: Penguin Books.

Sacco, Vincent F. and Leslie W. Kennedy. 1998. *The Criminal Event*, 2nd ed. Toronto: ITP Nelson.

Sharpe, Susan. 1998. *Restorative Justice: A Vision for Healing and Change*. Edmonton: Edmonton Victim Offender Mediation Society.

Shaw, Margaret and Frederick Jané. 1999. *Family Group Conferencing with Children under Twelve: A Discussion Paper*. Ottawa: Department of Justice. At www.canada.justice.gc.ca/en/psy/yj/rp/doc/paper107.rtf

Stuart, Barry. 1996a. Circle sentencing in Canada: A partnership of the community and the criminal justice system. *International Journal of Comparative and Applied Criminal Justice*, Vol. 20, Number 2, Fall:291–309.

Stuart, Barry. 1996b. Circle sentencing: Turning swords into plowshares. In B. Galaway and J. Hudson (Eds.), *Restorative Justice: International Perspectives* (pp. 193–206). Monsey, N.Y.: Criminal Justice Press.

Umbreit, Mark. 1994. *Victim Meets Offender: The Impact of Restorative Justice and Mediation*. Monsey, N.Y.: Criminal Justice Press.

Zehr, H. 1990. *Changing Lenses*. Waterloo: Herald Press.

Zehr, Howard. 2002. *The Little Book of Restorative Justice*. Intercourse, Penn.: Good Books.

ENDNOTES

[i] This idea was raised by Judge Barry Stuart of the Yukon Territorial Court at the conference "Advancing Restorative Justice," Gatineau, Quebec, September 26–28, 2002.

[ii] For a discussion of Aboriginal ways of social conduct, see Brandt (1990).

[iii] See Rupert Ross, *Returning to the Teachings* (1996), Chapter 2.

[iv] See for example, Brantingham and Brantingham (1990) and Felson (1994).

^v This refers mainly to early intervention strategies and social welfare policies.

^{vi} The classical school sees the law-breaker as a rational person governed by pleasure and pain, who can be deterred only by the threat of sanction (Sacco & and Kennedy, 1998:410). For a full explication of the classical school of criminology, see Beccaria (orig. 1764).

^{vii} The term "positivism" refers to the "philosophical position, developed by Auguste Comte, that scientific knowledge can come only from direct observation, experimentation, and provision of quantitative data" (Sacco and Kennedy, 1998: 420). Positivist criminology sees behaviour as determined by factors beyond the individual. The causes of criminal behaviour are sought in biological, psychological, and social factors (Vold, et al., 2002:9).

^{viii} See *The Principles of Morals and Legislation* (1948, orig. 1789) in which Bentham outlines the framework for a utilitarian view of justice.

^{ix} Project Planet Peace, based in Mission, British Columbia, is an example of a preventive restorative program. The project provides a series of workshops that focus on values, education, and community building in the schools, modelling restorative values and practices throughout.

^x These programs are usually operated by agreement between community-based agencies and the police. Some programs are housed in police stations, while others maintain an "arms-length" relationship with the police. Not all diversion programs, however, are restorative.

^{xi} Alternative measures referrals from crown counsel are generally made to community-based agencies, which oversee the implementation of agreements such as community service orders. Not all alternative measures, however, are restorative.

^{xii} For more information on sentencing circles, see Stuart (1996a) and Linker (1999).

^{xiii} This program was developed in Canada by the Fraser Region Community Justice Initiatives Association in Langley, B.C. Victims and offenders in violent cases, primarily serious sexual assaults and homicides, are counselled by mediators trained in trauma therapy and, where possible and appropriate, brought together for a mediated encounter.

^{xiv} VORP began in 1974, when two young men pleaded guilty to 22 counts of vandalizing properties in the Kitchener area. VORP was the result of a collaborative effort between the Mennonite Central Committee and the local probation department. The two offenders met with individual victims to work out restitution agreements, launching a program that continues to the present. VORP is also offered in British Columbia, Saskatchewan, and Manitoba. The history of VORP is outlined in Zehr (1990), Chapter 9.

^{xv} A more detailed explication of VOMP is found in Roberts (1995), in his evaluation of the project that found unanimous support from both victims and offenders captured by the study.

CHAPTER 25
Mediation

INTRODUCTION

In recent years, there has been a growing interest in alternatives to the criminal justice system. This interest reflects disenchantment with the conventional response to crime: namely, the prosecution and punishment of offenders. The search for more constructive alternatives has led to solutions that lie outside the criminal process, including mediation. This is an alternative way of responding to crime that does not stress punishment; instead, it is a response that advances the interests of the victim and society without sacrificing those of the offender. Mediated disputes, it is argued, result in a more lasting solution to the problems that gave rise to the offending in the first place. Recidivism statistics show that responding to crime with severity is not the most effective way to prevent reoffending. In this chapter, the author explores some of the mediation programs in existence and discusses the role that mediation can play instead of, or alongside, the traditional criminal justice response to crime.

Mediation and Criminal Justice

Shereen H. Benzvy Miller, Director General, Rights, Redress and Resolution, Correctional Service Canada

Protecting the rights of individual members of our society is at the centre of our constitutional and legal frameworks. What this entails and how it is done is questioned and challenged daily in the media, classrooms, and courts. Such is democracy. Our legal system has developed an intricate web of procedural safeguards to protect the lone accused individual from the vastly uneven and intimidating power of the state during criminal prosecution. However, offenders and victims may resolve their disputes through mediation and similar mechanisms instead of taking them to court, or those parallel processes may be employed before or after the formal criminal justice system has run its course. This alternative process of mediating a dispute seems to be adding to the quality of justice available in Canada and elsewhere. It is another tool to aid in the quest for fairness and justice—mercurial concepts we continually strive for in the justice system.

Canada's criminal justice system evolved as a civilized way of resolving disputes between individuals. Rather than allowing the victim of a crime to avenge it, we have developed a societal response to crime that is intended to be both systematic and just. Central to our system is the fact that the state takes over from the victim with respect to responding to the offender. This explains why criminal cases are always entitled *R. v. the Defendant* ("*R*" represents *Rex* or *Regina,* depending on the gender of our monarch). Punishment is imposed, not for the exclusive benefit of the victim, but because the crime is viewed as a violation of the social contract and is therefore an act against the state. That is why the police—in the name of the state—are responsible for the investigation of the offence and the laying of the criminal charge. The prosecutor, also a representative of the state (not of the victim), is then responsible for prosecuting the case and attempting to establish the guilt of the offender beyond a reasonable doubt.

While this approach lightens the victim's burden by putting the state's vast resources to work at righting the wrong, it also distances the victim from the process. The result is that victims often feel alienated. Victims have become quite vocal recently about their needs and the shortcomings of a system that gives them little voice and is not aimed at helping them to heal. It is further argued that by exacerbating the victim's pain, the criminal justice system restores neither the victim to the life she or he enjoyed before the crime was committed nor the community to harmony. This failure has heightened recognition of the value of the "restorative justice" movement. Within the framework of restorative justice, the focus is on repairing the damage done to the victim rather than simply punishing the offender, although the concepts are not mutually exclusive.

Restorative justice principles have, in recent years, gained legitimacy within mainstream criminal justice thinking (see Chapter 24). In fact, s. 718 of the *Criminal Code* Part XXIII, R.S.C. 1985, c. C-46 outlines the sentencing objectives that the court must take into account. Three of these are derived from restorative principles. The section reads as follows:

> 718. The fundamental purpose of sentencing is to contribute, along with crime prevention initiatives, to respect for the law and the maintenance of a just, peaceful and safe society by imposing just sanctions that have one or more of the following objectives:
> (a) to denounce unlawful conduct;

(b) to deter the offender and other persons from committing offences;

(c) to separate offenders from society, where necessary;

(d) *to assist in rehabilitating offenders;*

(e) *to provide reparations for harm done to victims or to the community; and*

(f) *to promote a sense of responsibility in offenders, and acknowledgement of the harm done to victims and to the community* [emphasis added]

In *R. v. Gladue* (1999 1 S.C.R. 688), the Supreme Court examined these sentencing objectives and determined that the last three are new and reflect the restorative goals of repairing harms suffered by individual victims and by the community as a whole, "promoting a sense of responsibility and an acknowledgment of the harm caused on the part of the offender ... The concept of restorative justice ... involves some form of restitution and reintegration into the community" (paragraph 43).

Mediation is but one tool in the restorative justice tool kit. The idea behind mediation is that ordinary people are involved in conflicts (which include criminal acts, since these are a violation of one person by another, not just an affront to the state), and these people can, with some assistance from a trained third party, solve their own problems together without coercive state intervention, speaking directly to the last three principles outlined above. Mediation can remove the case from the courts; or, at the very least, take place outside the court setting. It takes the parties away from the formal rules, record-keeping, and penalty structure (Stead, 1986). By making the victim an active and important participant in the process, mediation allows the parties to focus on what can be done in the future to resolve the problems, if they can be resolved, rather than focusing exclusively on punishing the offender for his or her past conduct.

WHAT IS MEDIATION?

Mediation is just one kind of dispute resolution mechanism. Descriptions of mediation can be found in textbooks, along with "negotiation," "arbitration," "adjudication," and "conciliation." Mediation can be used in the context of a broad range of disputes: family, international, environmental, intergovernmental, and intrainstitutional (Goldberg, Green, and Sander, 1985). Mediation was first used in the courts in the context of the civil law to help litigants reach agreements without the expense of a drawn-out court process. Research in the civil law domain shows that mediation provides a form of alternative dispute resolution that generally results in a greater sense of satisfaction for the parties than would result from protracted litigation. The application of mediation to the criminal law context is more recent and is still evolving. Since damages are less likely to be easily quantifiable in some criminal cases, the challenge to find solutions to these conflicts is greater.

Mediation is a voluntary, informal process in which two or more parties agree to attempt to settle their disagreement by meeting with a neutral third party to follow a mutually agreed-upon framework for the meeting. The neutral third party (the mediator) has no decision-making authority. The ground rules for all mediations are the same:

- participation must be voluntary;
- there must be at least one specific and common issue at the basis of the perceived conflict;
- the issues discussed in the mediation will be kept confidential;
- the mediator cannot be called upon by either party to testify in future litigation;
- in the event that an agreement is reached, it will be honoured by both parties. In the context of the criminal justice system, the two primary parties are the victim and the (alleged or confirmed) offender, but their families and various other members of the community may be involved as well.

While mediation services in criminal justice go under different names (e.g., Victim–Offender Reconciliation Program (VORP) or Dispute Resolution Service), there are many commonalities (Zehr, 1990). During all victim–offender mediations, the parties have a chance to talk—either to each other or with the mediator—to discuss the crime and its impact and to voice fears and concerns.

WHEN IS MEDIATION USEFUL?

At first, mediation programs were restricted to cases where the offence involved nonviolent property crimes. This was done for obvious reasons: it is easier to compensate the victim for property loss or damage than for physical or emotional suffering. The range of criminal conflict for which mediation might be used is limited only by the imagination of the mediators, prosecutors, police, and judges and the willingness of victims to participate.

But mediation can be useful at any stage in the accused/offender's involvement in the criminal justice system. For young offenders or first-time offenders, mediation might be used as a complete "diversion" from prosecution. This allows these offenders to avoid acquiring a criminal record, which may have a stigmatizing effect. In these cases, criminal charges might be dismissed if an agreement is reached with the victim and if the terms of the agreement are met. In cases where an offender has been convicted, a judge might use mediation as a term of probation or as an alternative sentence, thereby avoiding incarceration. Victim–offender mediations have been conducted in prisons or after an offender's release from prison. Sometimes, the offender's impending release from prison might provide the victim with the motivation for seeking mediation.

Since the 1970s, victim–offender mediation programs have flourished in North America and Europe. More recently, they have caught on in Australia and New Zealand. Canada started to use such programs to deal with young offenders, and this is now also done extensively throughout the United States and parts of Europe. These programs have increased dramatically in popularity, and after 20 years they are just now moving from the fringes to the mainstream of the criminal justice system. During the 1970s, there were only a handful of mediation and reconciliation programs. By 1996, programs were operating in at least 13 countries, including 175 programs in North America alone (Bronstein and Gainsborough, 1996). By the early 1990s, more than 150 of the victim–offender mediation programs in the United States operated in the juvenile justice system at both diversion and postadjudication levels.

Referrals to a victim–offender mediation can be made through the police departments at the charging stage and can result in charges being withheld pending the outcome of mediation. Referrals can also be made by prosecutors, who are in a good position to identify a large pool of cases that are likely to benefit from mediation. Other options include court referrals or postsentencing referrals by probation authorities or other organizations. However it is offered, a majority of victims choose to avail themselves of the programs; victim participation rates range between 60 and 70 percent in many programs.

Regardless of when mediation is attempted, it always involves certain stages. At the "intake phase," the parties to the conflict are contacted separately and interviewed. Often the mediator will meet with the victim and the offender separately prior to the joint mediation session. The purpose of these initial contacts is to build trust with each party and to begin to understand the issues each will need to deal with in the mediation. This stage can take months. The next stage is the actual mediation. Two schools of thought govern mediation. The first advocates effecting direct contact between the victim and the offender facilitated by the mediator. The second involves no face-to-face meetings between the victim and the offender, but rather a series of discussions between the mediator and each party separately. This is also referred to as "shuttle mediation" or "indirect mediation." The form of mediation used is determined by the needs of the parties and can be very fluid; as their needs change, so can the format of the mediation. The follow-up phase of mediation has to do with monitoring restitution or other undertakings made in the mediation agreement.

For the sake of illustration, let us examine two Canadian examples of programs that provide an alternative to the traditional legal framework for effective resolution of disputes in the field of criminal law.

THE DISPUTE RESOLUTION CENTRE OF OTTAWA-CARLETON (1989–2000)

Created in 1989, the Dispute Resolution Centre of Ottawa-Carleton was typical of mediation projects in other jurisdictions. Because mediation is not yet part of the standard criminal justice institutions, funding for these projects is usually shaky. This program was cut due to fiscal conservatism, not because it didn't contribute immensely to the community. The Centre, a postcharge, pretrial mediation program, accepted referrals from police, assistant crown attorneys, defence counsel, accused (both adult and youth), complainants, and outside agencies. The program's goal was to improve the quality of justice for complainants and the accused; to expedite the processing of minor criminal cases with concomitant cost savings; and to establish a model for the introduction of similar programs in other jurisdictions within the provincial and federal justice systems. Typical criminal charges included common assault (47 percent), uttering threats (14 percent), assault causing bodily harm (12 percent), and mischief under $1,000 (10 percent).

In determining whether a case was suitable for mediation, the executive director would make an assessment as to the likelihood that an accused would honour an agreement based on the parties' common understanding. Unlike many other mediation programs, it was not a prerequisite that an accused admit responsibility for the commission of the offence that led to the laying of the charge. Once a case was deemed suitable for mediation, the victim (complainant) would be contacted by a representative of the centre and offered the opportunity to pursue mediation. If the victim elected to participate in mediation, the defence counsel would be notified of the tentative mediation date. Once an accused had agreed to the option (only 1 percent refused the offer of mediation), the date would be set.

At the mediation, the parties agreed to attempt to settle their disagreement knowing that the final decision on disposition of the case would still rest with the crown attorney. More often than not, an agreement based on common understanding and communication resulted from the session. A copy of the agreement would be given to the crown attorney for consideration in the handling of the case. All information disclosed during the mediation session remained confidential. Legal counsel were not permitted to attend the mediation sessions.

Some interesting trends emerged from the experience in Ottawa-Carleton. First, mediation agreements were reached in 92 percent of all mediated cases (regardless of whether the accused was a young offender or an adult). Second, 83 percent of charges in mediated cases were withdrawn from the criminal justice system with no further involvement of the system. An additional 9 percent resulted in the withdrawal of charges and the imposition of a peace bond. Only 2.3 percent of mediated cases resulted in a trial. Finally, 60 percent of matters mediated by the centre involved alleged physical assaults (although charges resulting from abusive spousal relationships were excluded from the program).

THE COLLABORATIVE JUSTICE PROJECT

The Collaborative Justice Project was established as a pilot project in 1998 in the Ottawa provincial courthouse. It was intended as a restorative justice initiative that would go beyond the narrowly defined legal issues to address the full range of needs that arise for people when their lives are affected by crime. The project was established to test the concept that a restorative approach could be used in cases involving more serious offences. The project utilizes and integrates a network of human, justice, and social services (e.g., legal, medical, counseling, conflict resolution) and takes a multidisciplinary approach that respects the impact that a crime has on the whole person. This approach springs from the fundamental belief that the criminal justice process ought to encourage constructive reparation over punitive and custodial measures. The project has taken an average of 40 cases per year and has employed an average of three paid staff and a host of community volunteers. The following is a case completed by the Collaborative Justice Project using a combination of shuttle mediation and face-to-face mediation.

Collaborative Justice Project: A Case Summary

Impaired Driving Causing Death

The Facts: The accused, Yves, was driving the wrong way on a multilane divided highway. After traveling 2 km in the wrong direction, narrowly missing several vehicles, he collided with the victim's car, killing a 60-year-old man and injuring his wife. Yves had close to three times the legal limit of alcohol in his blood and was charged with impaired driving causing death and criminal negligence causing death.

Collaborative Justice Project: The caseworker met with Yves to assess his interest in and appropriateness for the project. Yves was 50 years old and had a steady and responsible job, but had been using alcohol for years to relieve stress. Yves almost died in the collision and had to spend months in the hospital recovering after the accident. It was not clear that Yves would ever walk again. Yves was very emotional, but was willing to take responsibility for the offence and work toward reparation. He was prepared to meet with the victim's family if that would help them.

Satisfied that Yves met the project's criteria, the caseworker met with Scott, the adult son of the dead victim and Scott's mother, Claire, who had been injured. Scott wanted some good to come out of the tragedy and felt that Yves might be able to speak to people about the dangers of drinking and driving. However, Scott felt certain that Yves would not want to speak publicly, so he didn't expect his hope to be realized. Scott wanted to meet Yves to assess if he was likely to drink and drive again. Claire did not want to meet him but needed more information from the police in order to move on in her grieving process.

The caseworker obtained the information and forwarded it to Claire and met with Yves regularly over the next six months to discuss his life situation, his alcohol problem, whom he had harmed, and what might be done to assist in the healing process. Yves received ongoing psychological and addiction counseling. The caseworker also met regularly with Scott to support him and his family, to explore what he needed in the process, and to prepare for a possible face-to-face meeting. The caseworker conveyed information to Yves and

Scott so that each had a better understanding of the other's situation and needs. Six months later Yves and Scott met in a mediation. They talked to each other in a supportive manner about the impact of the incident and about what they would like to see happen. While Yves had previously indicated that he was unable to speak publicly about what had happened, after meeting Scott he agreed to join him in addressing a high school class. The students were deeply moved.

Sentence and follow-up: Yves received a sentence of two years in prison. The crown attorney initially sought three to five years, but the work done by the accused and the victim in the mediation and their interest in continuing to work together had mitigated the sentence.

WHAT ARE THE BENEFITS OF MEDIATION?

Mediation has not yet proven to be effective at relieving the pressure on an overtaxed court system when used to divert cases from the more formal judicial process. Perhaps this is because most of the mediation projects in place deal with only minor matters. Mediation does, however, have the benefit of being substantially less costly than a trial, and participants seem more satisfied with the process at the end of the day. But the true benefits of mediation may lie elsewhere, beyond the question of costs. Alternative dispute resolution mechanisms may be a better solution for people who have become disillusioned with punishment-based systems of justice. Consider this: If punishment and imprisonment were the best crime prevention strategy, then the United States—where billions of dollars have been pumped into building big prisons and increasingly sophisticated police forces—should be the safest country in the world. Over the past quarter century, the United States has increased its prison population by 700 percent. Its incarceration rate continues to climb, and yet people remain fearful.

Mark Umbreit's two-year study of four program sites in Canada (Calgary, Alberta; Langley, B.C.; Ottawa, Ontario [the Ottawa-Carleton Dispute Resolution Centre]; Winnipeg, Manitoba) produced a large amount of qualitative and quantitative data: 610 interviews with complainants/victims and accused/offenders, 45 interviews with criminal justice system officials, 24 observations of actual mediations, interviews with program staff, and reviews of program records were conducted (Umbreit, 1995). While the findings of the study cannot be generalized to all offender mediation programs or criminal mediation programs, they do provide insight into the possible benefits of mediation programs. Some of the findings include the following:

- Successfully negotiated agreements that were accepted by both parties were reached in 92 percent of the cases that were mediated.
- Client satisfaction with the manner in which the justice system responded to their case was significantly more likely to be found among

complainants/victims (78 percent) and accused/offenders (74 percent) who participated in mediation than among similar complainants/victims (48 percent) and accused/offenders (53 percent) who were referred to, but did not participate in, mediation.

- Satisfaction with the outcome of the mediation session they participated in was found in the vast majority of complainants/victims (89 percent) and accused/offenders (91 percent), and an even higher percentage said they would participate in mediation again (complainants/victims 91 percent, and accused/offenders, 93 percent).
- The mediated agreement was viewed as fair to the complainant/victim by 92 percent of complainants/victims and fair to the accused/offender by 93 percent of accused/offenders (Umbreit, 1995).

Studies have shown that the victim's motivation for participating in mediation relates to the victim's need for answers to questions about the crime and the need to confront the source of much anger and confusion—namely, the offender. Some of the most common questions by victims are the following: "Why did you do this to me? Was this my fault? Could I have prevented this?" Obtaining closure to the incident is therefore a strong motivator for participation of victims in mediation and a source of satisfaction after completion of the process.

Sometimes offenders are motivated by self-interest and the hope of mitigating the punishment that may be imposed by the court. But for offenders at the postsentencing stage, the need to express remorse and the desire to make amends take on greater importance. Regardless of the timing or motivation for entering mediation, offenders often take meaningful responsibility for their actions in mediation. They can do this by negotiating a restitution agreement with the victim to restore the victim's losses. Restitution may be monetary or it may involve working for the victim, performing services in the community, or anything else that gives the parties a sense of justice and fairness.

Studies also find higher restitution completion rates in mediation programs (Umbreit, 1994). It seems that offenders rarely view court-ordered restitution as a moral obligation. Perhaps it is the emotional distance of dealing with an agent of the state (the prosecutor) during the court process that makes offenders believe that it is just another state-imposed fine rather than a personal obligation.

It has become clear that victim-offender mediation humanizes an otherwise alienating experience for victims and offenders. It also allows for more active involvement of victims and community members (as volunteer mediators) in the justice process. Not surprisingly, studies indicate that mediation also reduces fear among victims and reduces future criminal behaviour (Umbreit, 1994).

CONCLUSION

There is clearly widespread dissatisfaction with the criminal justice system as it is currently constituted. While it is based primarily on denunciation of the crime, deterrence, and punishment of the offender through the adversarial process, mediation and other restorative measures shift the focus to reparation of the harm done to victims, community involvement, and the accountability of the offender. And though this is a positive step, there is a need to move with caution when circumventing the criminal justice system. We must be diligent in maintaining the standards of fairness, impartiality, and justice that our rules of evidence and criminal procedure were drafted to protect.

Mediation is one of several options that will allow us to improve the criminal justice system and the quality of life in our communities. Mediation has the potential to enhance the quality of justice experienced by victims and offenders. It can provide a powerful medium through which offenders may take meaningful responsibility for their actions and victims can become actively involved in the process of holding the offender accountable. The use of mediation in a wide range of criminal conflicts is gaining support in public policy. It may well provide some relief for the battle-weary criminal justice professionals and a ray of hope for victims and their advocates.

DISCUSSION QUESTIONS

1. *If your car were stolen, would you want to participate in a mediation with the offender? If you had been assaulted, would your views be different?*
2. *What are the pros and cons of mediation for the victim? For the offender? For the community? For the criminal justice system?*
3. *The judicial process is a complicated one. In order for justice to be served, it must single-mindedly focus on protecting the offender from the potentially oppressive power of the state. It can be said that the complexity of the demands placed on the system are such that it cannot serve two masters: victims and offenders. How can these conflicting interests be reconciled?*

FURTHER READING

Macfarlane, J. (ed.). 1997. *Rethinking Disputes: The Mediation Alternative.* Toronto: Emond Montgomery Publications.

Umbreit, M. 1994. *Victim Meets Offender: The Impact of Restorative Justice and Mediation.* Monsey, NY: Criminal Justice Press.

Zehr, H. 1990. *Changing Lenses.* Scottsdale, PA: Herald Press.

REFERENCES

Bronstein, A., and Gainsborough, J. 1996. Prison litigation: past, present, and future. *Overcrowded Times* 7(3):1–20.

Consedine, J. 1995. *Restorative Justice: Healing the Effects of Crime.* Wellington, New Zealand: Ploughshares Publications.

Goldberg, S., Green, E. and Sander, F. 1985. *Dispute Resolution.* Boston: Little, Brown and Company.

Stead, D. 1986. *The Effectiveness of Criminal Mediation: An Alternative to Court Proceedings in a Canadian City.* Denver: Faculty of Social Sciences, University of Denver.

Umbreit, M. 1994. *Victim Meets Offender: The Impact of Restorative Justice and Mediation.* Monsey, NY: Criminal Justice Press.

———. 1995. *Mediation of Criminal Conflict: An Assessment of Programs in Four Canadian Provinces.* St. Paul, MN: Center for Restorative Justice & Mediation, School of Social Work, University of Minnesota.

Zehr, H. 1990. Mediating the Victim–Offender Conflict: The Victim Offender Reconciliation Program. Winnipeg: Mennonite Central Committee.

COPYRIGHTS AND ACKNOWLEDGMENTS